The Strength to Endure

Praise for
THE STRENGTH TO ENDURE

"Paul's memoir is a remarkable and riveting narrative by a true American hero. In clear, concise language, Paul recounts his triumphs and tragedies as a farmer, fighter pilot, loving husband and father, with amazing clarity and minimum emotion. He captures nearly eight excruciating years as a prisoner of the North Vietnamese.

When I first met "PK" at Ramstein Air Base in Germany, he was one of those whose star shown the brightest. Not only did he save several aircraft during in-flight emergencies, he also managed the all-important squadron intelligence and targeting enterprise. During his tenure at Ramstein, Paul won the multinational NATO fighter competition and was awarded Top Gun in 1963.

Paul was shot down in June 1965 as a 29-year-old Captain with an extraordinary future and probable star rank ahead. Eight years later, Paul emerged from seemingly endless days of captivity as a Major, legally blind due to maltreatment and malnutrition (he dropped from 173 pounds to 103 pounds during this period), but with unfailing integrity and a still uncommon devotion to duty and country.

Paul's story is a mesmerizing account of strength, fortitude and faith. A must-read!"

—*Maj. Gen. Michael C. Kerby, USAF (Ret.) Commander, 57th Fighter Weapons Wing, Nellis Air Force Base, Nevada Director, Air Force Legislative Liaison, U.S. Pentagon*

"Thank you for the privilege of pre-reading your book, *The Strength to Endure*, prior to its submission for publication. I must say I was moved to tears on multiple occasions. Your writing and storyline are nothing short of breathtaking. This book is a must-read for any student of American history and, in my opinion, should be made part of the curriculum for every high school American history class in the country. The way you interweave the realities of growing up and how the mental toughness you developed as a child and young man came to play a crucial role in being able to endure your POW ordeal is nothing short of brilliant.

I am an immigrant to this country and a child of two World War II refugees. I have a keen interest in firsthand accounts of history, especially of the WWII era. Your book does for the Vietnam experience what Jack Bradley's book, *Flags of our Fathers*, does for the American Pacific war experience during WWII.

Thank you again for the privilege of reading this masterpiece."

—*Christopher D. Riemann, M.D., Cincinnati Eye Institute*

"Thanks for being a man in a world of wussy-wimps, Paul!

I called my friend Paul yesterday—Independence Day—to let him know we are grateful. Paul spent eight years in the "Hanoi Hilton" prison in Hanoi, Vietnam, after he was shot down.

He was doing what his government asked him to do. He never betrayed his government. For eight years, his captors tortured him, trying to make him say things against America. He never did. He refused to be guilty of treason. But now our "wussy-wimp" politicians and media are saying those things he refused to say—and worse. Treason is what it is.

I thank God for Paul and every other American that has served in my country's military. They all deserve to be called heroes."

—*Dave Ohlerking, Founder Children's Cup*

"I've known Paul Kari since 1960. We were lieutenants, fighter pilots, and friends.

As a new fighter pilot graduates from fighter training, he gets to pick his assignment according to how he was rated by the squadron instructors, ground school exams and flying evaluations. Paul was the top student and he got the first pick. All students know (by word of mouth) which are the most desired assignments.

I was fortunate to be a member of the 417th TAC Fighter Squadron at Ramstein, Germany: the No. 1 fighter squadron location in Europe! Consequently, when a fighter training class graduated, the top new fighter pilots wanted to be assigned to the 417th.

Enter Lt. Paul Kari. Paul was top of his class, picked the 417th, and was welcomed to the squadron.

He hit the ground running. Quickly, Paul learned what was happening in the squadron, how he fit in, what his additional duties were, and what he could do to help make the squadron better. He became a great team player and an excellent pilot.

At that time, I was a full-time fighter pilot, as well as the squadron intelligence officer and VIP briefer. When I was reassigned to Cannon AFB, Paul took my place in each of those positions.

The next thing I knew about Paul was several years later, when I heard he had been shot down over North Vietnam! Which brings me to his book, *The Strength to Endure*.

I really wanted to read it, but I also knew it would be wrenching. I knew many friends who were shot down; many were killed; many were prisoners. I got in touch with Paul and we had long, healthy conversations. He provided a copy of his book.

I decided I would only read one chapter and then pause a day or two between chapters. This was a good decision. This was a person I know. This wasn't a "book character." This was my friend I was reading about. Often it was wrenching—and I shed tears. But he cleverly interlaced chapters of his earlier life and his later life which gave it balance and a peek into his whole life. There are a lot of "take away lessons" from the book.

This is a very well-written book. It's not a novel. It's a real insight into who our fighter pilots are; their dedication; and what our POWs did before, during and after the Vietnam War.

I highly recommend it."

—*Gen. John T. Chain, Jr., USAF (Ret.), Chief of Staff, Supreme Headquarters, Allied Forces, Europe, Commander and Chief, Strategic Air Command, Omaha, Nebraska, Executive Vice President, Operations, Burlington Northern Railroad, Fort Worth, Texas*

"I have known "PK" for more than five decades. I've read, and been deeply affected by, the memoirs of Lt. Col. Paul Kari. Most of us experience lives that seem to be on a pendulum that swings between choice and fate. Choice brought to PK a military career in which he demonstrated unusual excellence as an Air Force fighter pilot. Fate brought the Vietnam War where he was shot down by anti-aircraft flak on a mission over North Vietnam, followed by eight years as a Prisoner of War.

For an ex-fighter pilot, this book is a revelation about combat flying. For the novice, I am astounded at PK's ability to communicate and explain technical concepts in such a manner as to make them understandable to anyone.

This is such a great story! It is masterfully told in a fashion that keeps anyone busy turning pages. The North Vietnamese (the NVN) were able to imprison PK's body and torture him to the extent that he lost his center vision and, when repatriated, was no longer allowed to fly high-performance military fighters. What the NVN could not do was to imprison his mind! PK knew there was a cause and effect relationship between our thoughts and our circumstances. This story teaches us how he took his unfortunate circumstances and turned them into stepping stones to a future more full of life than could ever be anticipated. Among others, the major lesson for his readers is that being a POW was not his biggest heartbreak! The processes and principles he had learned in the jungle prisons were effective in successfully dealing with each obstacle and disappointment he encountered as his life moved forward. Readers can see, learn and use PK's pattern of success. He persists in pressing forward, meeting and overcoming every obstacle with positivity, planning, extremely hard work and a commitment to be Christ-like in his thoughts and behavior toward those who brought his greatest disappointments and heartbreak into his life.

If you like to be entertained, and want to be trained, this is a book you must read!"

—*Paul R. Eckel, Fighter Pilot, 417th Tactical Fighter Squadron, 50th Tactical Fighter Wing, USAF, System Chief Pilot, Continental Air Lines, Brigham Young University Alumni Association President (1983-84)*

THE Strength TO ENDURE

A Memoir

Paul Kari
with
John Gladden

ORANGE *frazer* PRESS
Wilmington, Ohio

ISBN 9781939710-161
Copyright©2015 Paul A. Kari

No part of this publication may be reproduced in any material form (including photocopying or storing in any medium by electronic means and whether or not transiently or incidentally to some other use of this publication) without the written permission of the copyright holder except in accordance with the provisions of the Copyright, Designs and Patents Act 1988.

Orange Frazer Press
P.O. Box 214
Wilmington, OH 45177
Telephone: 937.382.3196 for price and shipping information.
Website: www.orangefrazer.com

Book and cover design: Lindsey Buck and Orange Frazer Press

Library of Congress Cataloging-in-Publication Data

Kari, Paul, 1935- author.
The strength to endure : a memoir / Paul Kari with John Gladden.
pages cm
Includes index.
Summary: "Paul Kari was shot down in 1965 as a 29-year-old captain in the Air Force. He was captured by the Viet Cong and spent almost 8 years as a prisoner of war. The memoir recounts the triumphs and tragedies he endured as a farmer, then a fighter pilot, a husband and father. He emerged from prison as a Major, legally blind, due to maltreatment and malnutrition, but with unfailing integrity and a still uncommon devotion to duty and country. It's a story written with clarity and minimum emotion, as he overcomes every obstacle with positivity, planning, hard work and commitment. Great insight into the minds of fighter pilots, the hearts of POWs, and the facts of the Vietnam War"-- Provided by publisher.

ISBN 978-1-939710-16-1
1. Kari, Paul, 1935- 2. Vietnam War, 1961-1975--Prisoners and prisons, North Vietnamese. 3. Vietnam War, 1961-1975--Personal narratives, American. 4. Prisoners of war--United States--Biography. 5. Prisoners of war--Vietnam--Biography. 6. United States. Air Force--Biography. I. Gladden, John, 1966- author. II. Title.
DS559.4.K37 2014
959.704'37--dc23
[B]
2014031017

Third printing   Revised

This book is dedicated to my father, Tony Kari. He taught me honesty, integrity, self-reliance, perseverance, timeliness, neatness and about the fulfillment that comes with hard work. And lastly, he taught me to respect God's Ten Commandments.

To Shawn, Ali, Jaime, and Jackie,
To paraphrase what another Ohio farmer, Louis Bromfield, once wrote to his own children: *The Strength to Endure* was written for the four of you and for your children and grandchildren. If anyone else likes it, so much the better. With love, Dad

ACKNOWLEDGEMENTS

I want to offer a heartfelt word of thanks to Carol Jilling, Carol Strouse, Dave and Janet Aikman, Tom and Mary Driscoll, Ron and Maude Vorhees, Bill Peelle, Jack Chain, Mike Kerby, Paul Eckel, and all who urged me to write my memoirs.

John Gladden is an award-winning writer based in Seville, Ohio. I am grateful for his help in preparing this book for publication. John's column collection, *How to Elevate a Cow*, was published in 2007.

Table of CONTENTS

Foreword	xv
My Longest Day	3
Early Farm Life	11
The Bombing Run	21
Caught in a Blizzard	27
Captured	37
The Big Move to Spencer	45
Eating Snake	59
High School Years	67
Hanoi Prison	81
The Ohio State University	91
The Cruelty of the Briar Patch	101
First Flight	113
The Hanoi March	121
Primary and Basic Pilot Training	127
International War Crimes Tribunal	141
Gunnery Training	153
A Christmas Program	163
Sitting Nuclear Alert	171
Coming Home	187
A Hurry-Up Wedding	197
Meeting Family	215
TDY to Ubon, Thailand	229
The Divorce	253
My Cattle Venture	267
The Farm at Spencer	289
High Plains Farming	317
Settling in Southwest Ohio	325
The Bombshell	343
Reflections	351
About the Author	357

FOREWORD

Like many young boys of my generation, I grew up with an insatiable appetite for heroes. It started with comic books and cartoons and was fed throughout my teenage years by the movies depicting one man standing in the gap, sacrificing himself to save his friends.

It wasn't until an experience in the jungles of Asia that I would understand what it really meant for a person to be a hero. I went on a mission trip to Vietnam with a gentleman I did not know very well until we started flying halfway around the world to this place that represented an intense crucible of valor for him.

I learned it was in this country that my friend Paul Kari was shot down during his tour of duty in the Air Force. I was only born toward the end of the war in Vietnam and my American History teacher had quickly buzzed past most of the details of this conflict, leaving me, like most Americans, with little understanding of what happened. It was through the life of Paul that I came to understand many of the details of this war, but more importantly, the characteristics of a true American hero.

As long as I live, I will never forget the moment we were riding through the streets of Hanoi, Vietnam, when my new friend Paul tensed up and said, "I remember this road." It was on this road that his captors sought to humiliate and punish Paul and the accompanying POWs. I watched as an enormous amount of emotion came over my friend, Mr. Paul.

Then something almost unbelievable happened. Our Vietnamese guide said, "Mr. Paul, I have to tell you. I was in that crowd."

Wow! I couldn't believe what I was hearing. I didn't know what would happen next as I watched my friend Paul start to almost boil over with rage. But then suddenly, a transformation of great peace swept over him as he issued words that still ring in my ears. "I forgive you."

After all the stories of what his captors did to him, how could anyone forgive? It was the most incredible object lesson in the power of forgiveness that I have ever personally experienced. The story of Lt. Col. Paul Kari is one about which movies are made. The difference is his story is true! His love for God, his dedication to his country, and his compassion for people will encourage, empower and inspire you—just as his friendship has done for me.

—*Ben Rodgers, Executive Director, Children's Cup*

The Strength to Endure

My Longest Day

CHAPTER 1

It was a day I never should have flown.

Growing up on a farm in Spencer, Ohio, I'd seen a lot of storms roll in across the fields on hot summer days, but nothing like this. It was monsoon season in North Vietnam and the weather this day was foreboding.

Flying into the storm at 25,000 to 30,000 feet, I looked up at the clouds and I couldn't see the tops of them. Here, the thunderclouds were sometimes 100,000 feet tall. They rose up like haystacks above my airplane, way, way out of sight.

At daybreak, our flight of F-4C Phantom II's had taken off from Ubon Air Base in Thailand, where we were stationed as part of the Air Force's 45th Tactical Fighter Squadron. We were bound for a mission deep in a mountainous area of northwest Vietnam. It was Sunday, June 20, 1965—Father's Day.

Our primary job was to MiG cap for a group of F-105 Thunderchiefs out of Korat and Takhli Royal Thai Air Force bases. We would fly overhead and watch for enemy MiG fighters while the F-105s made their bombing runs—although we almost never engaged any MiGs. Or, I should say, the MiGs rarely engaged us. They were no match for the speed of our F-4s and the North Vietnamese knew it. Once the F-105s had dropped their bombs, we'd swoop in, drop ours, and MiG cap again on the way out.

By this point in the war, I had flown 69 combat missions in 70 days. Most were four to seven hours long. Sometimes it would be two shorter missions in one day, anywhere from 2 ½ to four hours each. The pace was grueling, but at age 29,

I was thriving. Years of training had prepared me for this work. I was flying a lot. It felt good.

Most of my fellow fighter pilots had already been to Bangkok for some rest and relaxation, but I had little desire to take time off.

Finally, the squadron commander said: "Kari, I'm forcing you to go to Bangkok for three days."

I never would have asked to go, but once it became an order, I began to look forward to it. It was only a short jaunt by courier plane from Ubon. My friends who'd already been there told me they had a fun time.

"OK," I said. "I'll go."

The first R&R of my 90-day deployment was scheduled to begin June 20. But, the night before, my squadron commander, Caspar Sharpless Bierman, came to see me. Like his name, which we often ribbed him about, Cass was larger than life—and an outstanding pilot.

Another pilot had turned conscientious objector, Cass said, and refused to fly the next day's mission. In our four-aircraft formation, Cass flew the No. 1 position and I was always his No. 2. The conscientious objector was supposed to take my spot while I was away, but now Cass was in a bind.

"Do you mind taking it, PK?" he asked. Almost everyone called me by my initials.

"Of course not," I replied. "They want me to go on R&R, but I'd rather fly."

We got up Sunday morning, knowing it was going to be a long day. We asked the base cook to make us up a few fried egg sandwiches. He wrapped them in wax paper and we stuck them in the bottom pockets of our G-suits for a quick lunch in the sky.

The F-4 was a two-man aircraft, with a pilot up front and a back-seater who acted primarily as a radar operator and navigator. It was a set-up no one was entirely happy with. Navigators, who were trained as pilots, naturally wanted to be at the controls of their own fighters. As a pilot, I can tell you we took immense pride in our ability to do the whole job—fly, navigate and hit a target—all by ourselves. That said, however, the addition of the navigator is part of what made the F-4 such an effective weapon. And my navigator, Curt Briggs, was one of the best back-seaters in the squadron.

Curt told me years later he had a premonition that something was going to happen that day. During our pre-flight briefing, he mused about getting shot down. If it ever happened, Curt said, he was sure he wouldn't be rescued. For some reason, it was clearly weighing on his mind. I made a mental note of it.

During the briefing, we were given the weather report. It called for thunderstorms. That was not a good thing.

We walked into a little building that housed our personal equipment, where I strapped into the harness for my parachute. Front-seaters were issued two-way radios, which a downed pilot could use to communicate with rescuers in the air. The radios were lined up one after the other inside a charging booth. Back-seaters carried a Search and Rescue and Homing Beacon, SARAH for short. The beacons were hanging on racks nearby. They didn't require charging.

Curt was right behind me. I knew he was still feeling uneasy about the mission.

"Here," I said. "I'll take yours and you take mine."

I gave Curt the two-way radio and I took his SARAH beacon. I hoped that would help take his mind off his worries. We headed for the tarmac and our four-plane flight took off with Cass in the lead.

We'd flown a mission in the very same area just two days before, escorting a pair of RF-101 Voodoos, which were taking reconnaissance photographs over the Western Vietnam Military Training Area in Son La Province. Intelligence had told us there was no anti-aircraft artillery in the vicinity. As we made the high-speed pass over Son La, I looked down at the mountains and heavily forested terrain below. I said to Curt, "If you had to get shot down, this would probably be a good place. Better than those flat rice patties. At least you'd have someplace to hide."

I've often thought about those words, "If you had to get shot down, this would be a good place." At Creation, God spoke the world into existence. I learned never to speak things into existence myself ever again.

On our Father's Day mission, I was flying No. 2, as usual. I'd always asked Cass if I could fly No. 3. Someday, you'll get shot down, I told him. In that event, No. 3 would take over as flight lead and I needed the experience.

"No," Cass said. "Our primary mission is to MiG cap and I don't trust anyone else to protect me."

Once you get into a hassle with the enemy, air-to-air combat becomes incredibly violent. The job of No. 2 is to protect No. 1, so you have to be able to anticipate his moves. I took pride in always being in position and Cass knew it. Although it was a position of honor, it was also the most dangerous position. If a ground-to-air gunner missed hitting No. 1, he almost always corrected his aim in time to hit No. 2.

It was a long flight to our target, requiring us to refuel in the air. The F-105s we were escorting had to refuel, too. Visibility was terrible due to the storm.

The F-105s were single-seaters, meaning the pilots had to both fly and navigate. They were chattering about the weather with the tanker crews on the refueling frequency on the radio, saying they were having a hard time picking them up on their radar.

The refueling tankers were "in the soup," which is what we called heavy cloud cover. The trick was to lock on the tankers with your radar and slow your airspeed until you could make visual contact within a couple thousand feet. The F-105s were struggling to find the tankers in the bad weather.

Cass radioed Saigon and asked permission for us to fuel-up on the tankers first, then drop our bombs before the F-105s, instead of after. Saigon said: Under the circumstances, go ahead and do it. Because of our navigators, the F-4s were able to hook up to the tankers, get a full load of fuel, and head north to the target. Cass and I had the two best navigators in the squadron and it really paid dividends in situations like this. The F-105s eventually got on the tankers some time later.

When you're flying over foreign territory, and there are few railroads and no interstates for landmarks, it's very hard to locate a small target in a jungle. So, in those days before GPS devices and other guidance systems, we'd pick out some prominent point on the map while we were still back at the base and call that the "Initial Point" or IP. In this case we selected a big bend in a river, which may have been the Red River, I'm not sure now. Then we calculated how long it would take at a given speed to reach the target area from that Initial Point. We carried the map on a clip board—careful never to mark our point of origin, in case we were shot down and the enemy recovered the map. Often the clipboard stayed with the pilot when he ejected. I estimated we would reach the target in three minutes and 26 seconds after passing the IP.

We began to let down through the clouds, which seemed to be getting lower and lower themselves. Normally, on a dive bomb run like this, we rolled in at 10,000 feet above the terrain. Here, the mountains rose a couple of thousand feet above the ground. Our altimeter said we were already well below 10,000 feet. We were only 6,000 or 7,000 feet, maybe 8,000 feet maximum, above the ground. The cumulus clouds kept dropping.

I was flying right in trail with Cass. About 30 seconds before the time elapsed that we should have seen the target, I veered off just a little to the right, so I'd come in at a 15- to 20-degree angle different from him. If we encountered fire, they'd have to shift their guns to hit me.

"I can't see the target," Cass said over the radio.

It surprised me to hear him say that. In the course of his 70-plus missions, Cass had almost never missed a target. By then, we were down to 7,000 feet above ground level, or only about 5,000 above the mountains. Far too low. I said to myself, *we should not be doing this. The conditions are too bad.*

"Cass, it's right under you," I said.

"I've got it," he said.

Back when we first arrived at Ubon, the experienced F-105 pilots gave us a briefing. All the bombing charts say you can be more accurate on a 30-degree dive angle than on a 45-degree angle. However, they told us far more aircraft got shot down on 30-degree dives than on 45 dives. They recommended against going in at 30 degrees.

Cass started into a 270-degree turn toward the target. Now, we were full of fuel and heavy—each plane carrying 11 500-pound bombs, as well as small missiles. We were cruising at 360 knots, which was customary, because it's simpler to calculate your position at 10 seconds per mile. The clouds continued to close in. I followed Cass, trying to stay a little outside of him, yet keep him in sight.

All aircraft have a warning light as well as a pedal-shaker when you approach a stall. The shakers on the rudder pedals do just what it sounds like they do. They vibrate, giving the pilot a physical signal that the plane is in danger of losing its lift.

Trying to keep Cass and the target both in sight, I probably was pulling 2 ½, maybe 3 Gs. The pedal-shaker was going the whole time. I looked at my airspeed and I was down to 250 knots. In the turn, I told Curt to take the stick for just a second so I could look up the sight settings for a 30-degree dive angle, remembering the advice of the F-105 pilots. I had made my own charts, which were under the map on my clipboard.

The bombing sights on the F-4 could be raised or lowered to allow for different angles and speeds. Right in the center of the sights was a dot we called a "pipper." How they ever came up with that name, I don't know. When the pipper was on the target, we hit a button called the "pickle" button to release the bombs. Within a few seconds, I had the new setting and took the controls back from Curt. We were just short of a stall. The airplane was shuddering terribly. We were getting really low.

Our flight had the reputation of never missing a target. I think that's the reason Cass went in that day. It was probably a point of pride that we weren't going to go back to the base and say, "Oh well. We couldn't drop our bombs today. The conditions were too bad." It wasn't the right decision, but Cass was a boisterous, go-ahead, we'll-get-it-done, kind of guy.

By now, I wasn't more than a couple thousand feet above the terrain. We were supposed to be at 10,000 feet. I kicked the F-4 into afterburner, because I knew I had to get up to 450 knots to make my bombing run. The afterburner pours fuel into the back of the engine where it ignites and generates additional power. I rolled out and started to climb. You can't just "hump over" when you accelerate like that. If you pull negative Gs, everything comes up off the floor. So I pulled the nose up and rolled over, still gaining airspeed.

We were approaching 350-375 knots. The afterburner was still in. I began to "walk" the pipper up to the target. Just before I got there, I saw Cass drop his bombs. They were off the mark.

"Cass, you missed!" I said.

I knew I couldn't reach 450 knots and I'd probably have to drop at 400. To compensate, I decided instead of hitting the pickle button as my pipper came up to the target, I'd let the pipper go a little beyond the target to allow for the slower airspeed.

Just about the time I got the pipper to the target, I heard a little "thud." The fire warning light for the left engine blinked on. I put the pipper just a little beyond the target, hit the pickle button and dropped my bombs. They made a direct hit.

I had one hand on the dual throttles—one for the left engine, one for the right. I tried to pull back the throttle for the left engine to shut it off. It wouldn't budge. The afterburner was still on.

There's a button we called, appropriately, the "panic" button. When you hit it, all the bombs and missiles attached to the underside of the wings, as well as the pylons that hold them in place, release and fall away, making the airplane lighter. The saying we have in the Air Force is, "We're going to trade airspeed for altitude and ideas." I brought the nose up and hit the panic button to clean off the wings.

Since I couldn't pull the left throttle back, I hit the left engine-off switch. About that time, the other fire warning light came on. The cockpit started to fill with smoke.

We had gained altitude all right—now we were back up in the clouds. I had no idea exactly how high up we were. The smoke was so thick I couldn't see the instrument panel in front of my face. I told Curt to blow the canopy off the airplane so I could see the gauges. When you eject, there are two explosions—one that blows the canopy off and another that sends you clear of the airplane. We both had separate switches that would blow just the canopy. Curt hit the switch and the canopy was gone.

Without the protection of the canopy, the force of the wind rushing by was tremendous but at least I could see the airplane's controls. Thankfully, I had already put down the visor on my helmet, which we are instructed to do in combat, to reduce the chance of losing your eyesight if the plane is hit. One look at the controls told me what my instincts already knew.

Every pilot in the world, whether commercial or military, when you get into a situation like that, you say two words.

"Oh, sh--," I said.

I always boasted I'd never get shot down. "If the enemy was ever going to get me, they'd need a silver bullet," I said.

Well, that day, somebody had the silver bullet.

CHAPTER 2

Early Farm Life

The skies over the North Vietnam jungle were a long way from the skies over my mom and dad's Northeast Ohio farm. And yet, it was the toughness and resiliency I learned there as a boy that would help me survive what lay ahead.

As the only boy in a family of four children, I learned the meaning of hard, physical labor at an early age. That work ethic came from my parents, Tony and Mary Kari, and it is hard wired into my DNA.

My father was born in Somogyszil, Hungary, in 1905, the second of two illegitimate children. His mother was a strikingly beautiful woman—and apparently the princes and nobles found her quite attractive, too. It was through one of them that she became pregnant with my father.

I remember she loved Chihuahuas and she practically worshipped them. She even had little grave markers with the names of the ones that died. Grandmother was never mean to us, but as a child I was afraid even to go into her house. Perhaps it was the sound of the Old Country in her voice that scared me.

My father's family had emigrated from Germany to Hungary. Believing German farmers were more industrious than her own people, the queen of Hungary thought she could make her country's cropland more productive by importing Germans to work the soil. Instead of integrating into the population, the Germans remained in their own little enclaves around the country, maintaining their own language and customs.

My grandmother brought Dad to America in 1921 when he was 16 years old. He was working in Akron, Ohio, when Dad heard American author Horace Greeley's classic call: "Go West, young man, go West …" And that's just what he did.

Dad worked for a Mexican foreman at a ranch near Del Rio, Texas. Since the foreman spoke only Spanish, Dad quickly picked up enough of the language to get by.

As was common in those days, one night they were sleeping under the stars after a day of chasing cattle for round-up. Dad was awakened by the sensation of something crawling on his chest. He opened his eyes to discover a big old rattlesnake curled up right there on his belly, drawn by the warmth of his body.

DAD, MOM, RUTH AND ME CIRCA 1940

Fortunately, Dad had been warned if that ever happened, just to let the snake go away on its own. Don't panic and above all, don't try to grab it. He managed to keep still and eventually the rattlesnake slithered away.

That was enough of Texas for him! Dad decided he'd rather be a farmer. When he returned to Akron, he developed a chronic cough. He was told it could be a symptom of tuberculosis—a potentially deadly infectious disease, which had claimed the life of his younger brother.

Dad entered a sanatorium in Akron where the dreaded diagnosis of TB was confirmed. It was here that he met Mom, who was working as an LPN. Her parents, Jacob and Mary Pamer, immigrated from Gyorkony, Hungary, to Akron in 1913. Mom was born there a year later.

My older sister Ruth was born in 1934. I was born in Akron on November 25, 1935. Karen came along in 1942 and Carol in 1945. Today, my sisters all live in Colorado.

My parents said I never spoke a word until I was 3 years old. Of course, they didn't have the money to send me to a speech therapist. One day I went with Dad to the Cleveland stockyards. As we left the stockyards, I saw several dead sheep lying on the ground.

"One sheep died," I said.

Those were the first words I ever said. Dad was both shocked and elated. He just about drove off the road.

"What?" He exclaimed. "You said something!"

Years later, I asked Mom if it had worried her that I didn't say anything in all that time. She replied that, yes, they were concerned. However, she added, I quickly made up for lost time because after that I never shut up!

I can recall wanting to do a man's work beginning when I was only 4 or 5 years old. At that time, we lived on a farm south of Akron. We were visiting my dad's mother, who had a house nearby. My sister, Ruth, who was a year-and-a-half older, had a sickle. I told her to give it to me because I wanted to cut weeds along a fence.

Ruth refused to turn over the sickle, so I attempted to wrestle it away from her. In the process of trying to pull it out of her hands, I sliced off the end of her finger. It was hanging off to the side, with only the skin holding it on to the rest of the finger.

Dad, who was a master molder at an Akron foundry, was at work. Mom didn't know what to do. She had no car to take Ruth to the hospital. Remembering how people in the Bible were anointed with oil, she put the end of the finger back in place, wrapped it up and put olive oil on it.

"God, you've got to take care of this," she prayed, "because I don't have any way to get to a doctor."

Mom saved me from a whipping that night when Dad got home and found out what had happened. "No," she told him, "I think he feels bad enough already." And she was right.

My father's fondest wish for Ruth was for her to become a piano player and in his mind, my wresting away the sickle and cutting off her finger had dashed that dream. That's what made him so upset.

Amazingly, Ruth's finger healed perfectly and she did go on to become a beautiful piano player. Evidently, I cut the finger right at one of the joints, because you can't even see a scar. Mom said later the only problem was she left the bandage on too long!

In 1941, my parents bought a farm in Medina County, just west of Akron. Located along Columbia Road in Lafayette Township, it was 111.89 acres—mostly yellow clay soil, which wasn't ideal for farming. They purchased it from the Federal Land Bank for $6,000. Evidently it had been in foreclosure.

Dad kept his job at the foundry in Akron. We had a small dairy of maybe a dozen cows and shipped milk to Elm Farm Dairy in Medina.

ME RIDING MY PONY

Because Dad worked at the foundry and I was still relatively small, Mom became our family's representative during threshing time. This was back when it was customary for farm families to go together and share the cost and labor of threshing grain at harvest time. Different communities had different threshing groups. Ours consisted of up to a dozen families. We would go to each farm in turn and thresh the grain.

Every farm had to furnish a wagon, along with a horse or tractor, plus one or two farm representatives—one person to drive, another to throw the bundles on the wagon. Mom was born in 1914, so she would have been only in her late 20s and early 30s. I remember her on the wagon, stacking shocks of wheat. She might have been the only woman working on the threshing crew and worked as hard as any man.

We'd start at the Carlton's, and then go to the Albright's, to the Mann's, and then across the road to Holdridge's. There were two more farms by the B&O railroad tracks. After that, it was up to the Walker's, the Boles', the Wideman's and the Yuha's—an old Hungarian family. On up the road was Mr. Yeager's farm. He worked in Cleveland and had a big 12-cylinder Lincoln automobile, which I used to drool over. Economically, Mr. Yeager was a cut above the rest of us.

Mom took Ruth and me along at threshing time. When we were very young, we'd play near where they were loading shocks of wheat. I had three toys during my entire childhood: a little tractor, a cast metal team of horses pulling an earth mover, and an army truck, which I have to this day.

Other than those three store-bought toys, I made my own playthings. At Lafayette School, someone taught me how to take a spool of thread, put a matchstick through it, and wind it up with a rubber band so that it would spin across a table. I liked the speed with which it moved.

One of the best parts of being in a threshing group was the food. The farms with the best cooks were our favorite places to go. Mrs. Bole made the best cherry pie—except she never took the pits out! You had to be careful not to swallow them.

As busy as Dad was—working full time and farming on evenings and weekends—he was generous with his time when neighbors needed help.

One of our milk haulers was John Drotloff. He'd say to my dad, "Tony, will you come plant my corn for me?" Dad had a two-row planter on a Farmall H. Dad was soft-hearted and he'd always do it. Neighbors often helped each other that way. Even though I eventually learned to do every job on the farm, I never planted corn until I had my own place. That's something Dad always did.

Our home in Lafayette was a typical farmhouse of the day. There was no electricity in the house and no indoor plumbing. Our bathroom was an outhouse.

It was customary among Europeans for unmarried children to give any money they earned to their parents. That's what both my mom and dad did. Mom began working at age 16 and my father didn't get married until he was 27 years old!

My mom's father, Grandpa Jack Pamer, felt sorry for the conditions she was living in at the farm, so he returned to her all the money she had earned after she got out of school. He had saved every penny and gave it all back to her. Mom and Dad used it to have electricity installed in the house, barn, and milk house. That was a pretty big deal in those days.

There was no creek nearby—and of course we didn't have a swimming pool. For entertainment, we kids hauled water from the pitcher pump in the kitchen to a wash tub in the yard and let the sun warm it up all day. We could hardly wait until the afternoon to jump into that little thing! It was barely big enough to sit in, but to us, that was our summer swimming pool.

As I got older, my parents let me walk to the local swimming hole, located in a creek a mile or two away. I had to cross U.S. Route 42 to get there. Looking back, it's hard to believe they let me do that. I'd meet my friends at a place in the creek deep enough that you could climb a nearby tree and dive into the water. To us, it was like Lake Erie. When we came home, we'd be covered in leeches.

Early on, I learned it was better to get work done immediately instead of procrastinating. The farmhouse had a big yard, as well as a U-shaped driveway with grass and a big maple tree growing in the middle. Starting when I was maybe about 7 years old, it was my job to cut the grass with an old-fashioned reel mower—no motor, just me. One day, when I didn't feel like doing it, I decided that if I just let the grass grow, it would get too tall for me to push the mower through and I'd get out of it. There's no way my parents could expect a little kid to work that hard, right?

Wrong. They still made me do it. The grass was probably six inches tall. I'd push that mower as hard as I could and it would travel about a foot before it would plug up. I'd have to pull it back, unclog it, and shove it forward again.

I decided then and there I would never, ever procrastinate again for the rest of my life.

When I was 8 or 9, we visited Bowers Dairy—another farm in Lafayette Township located on State Route 162. I remember being very impressed because the dairy seemed so neat and modern. The places where the cattle stood were nice and clean.

I came home and I told myself we should do the same thing on our farm. While Dad was at work in Akron, I took an ice pick and chipped away at the inch or so of compacted manure on the floor of the barn where the cows stood. I scraped it all away, right down to the concrete, then washed it out with water. I worked all day.

When Dad came home, I said to him, "Hey, look at that. That's just like Bowers. Don't you like that?"

"That's great," he said.

From my dad, it was high praise.

Even though I was expected to work from a young age and had very few toys, I do recall two things my father did for me that made me very happy. He bought me a half-dozen animal traps, which I used to earn my own spending money.

Dad also bought me a pony, which is something I had always wanted. It was a beautiful, brown Shetland. There's a wonderful picture of me sitting on its back—and I'm almost as brown-skinned as the pony was. I never wore a shirt or shoes around the farm all summer long.

As a boy, I was always interested in trapping and hunting. I kept talking about trapping muskrats, mink and all the rest. Dad didn't have a lot of money, but one day I came home from school and there were six brand-new traps sitting inside the back porch. I thought I hit a million-dollar jackpot! I couldn't wait for trapping season.

I have so many vivid memories of growing up on the farm—especially one that no boy could ever forget.

We owned some ground diagonal from the house. One day Dad asked me to go back to those woods and pick up the cows. That is, to lead them up to the barn for milking.

I knew there was an electric fence, but Dad had never really told me anything about it. As I walked and called to the cows, I had to go to the bathroom. For no good reason, I decided to pee right on the electric fence. You can imagine the shock I got—in more ways than one! It knocked me right back on my heels. As I said, it's something no boy would ever forget.

I was pretty naïve about things. Mom and Dad once told me if I wanted to catch a rabbit, all I had to do was take a salt shaker to the pasture and sprinkle some on its tail. So, I took a salt shaker out to one of the fields in hopes of sneaking up on a rabbit and catching it. Of course, every rabbit took off like a shot as soon as I got close.

Returning to the house in exasperation, I told my parents, "That didn't work! They all ran away!" My mom and dad laughed and laughed.

Another day, I got off the school bus and walked up to the back porch. Mom confronted me at the door.

"What did you do?" she asked sternly. "The truant officer is in the living room!"

I started shaking.

"What do you mean the truant officer?" I stammered. "I didn't do anything!"

"Well, you're in trouble," Mom said.

I walked into the house and there were my aunt and uncle from Akron. I thought that was a pretty dirty trick! I was so scared I almost wet my pants.

During World War II, everyone was encouraged to buy war bonds. Mom gave Ruth and me a dime or quarter each week to tuck into a little coin folder we received at Lafayette School. We were so excited to fill it up with enough money to buy a bond. I've always wondered whatever happened to all of those bonds.

Children also gathered milkweed pods for the war effort. The pods contained a downy, white fluff that was used to fill life preservers for sailors and flyers. We may have received a quarter or so per gunnysack that we filled.

The church was everything to my parents. It started when Dad was in the sanatorium with tuberculosis. There was a preacher making the rounds visiting patients. I don't know how much English Dad could even speak then, but the preacher stuck his nose into the room and introduced himself. Before the preacher left, he said, "I understand you've got TB. Do you mind if I pray before I leave that God will heal you?" Dad, who was Catholic, said yes, go ahead.

According to Dad, he felt something happening while the man prayed. He didn't know what. He just knew he was OK. The next day, he went down to the front desk and asked to be released.

"You just got here," they told him. "You've got TB!"

"God healed me," Dad said.

"We'll see," they said.

Well, with tuberculosis, even if they arrest it, the scars remain in your lungs. They X-rayed Dad's chest. There were no scars.

That's why he was a devout Christian his whole life. He read the Bible every day and never worked on Sundays. Period. Even if it meant we would lose a whole crop of hay.

My parents found a German-speaking church, which happened to be an Assembly of God church in Akron. We drove into the city every Sunday in the same old four-door Chevy Dad drove back and forth to work. It was missing one of its rear fenders, which we weren't able to get replaced until after the war.

Boy, did they preach hellfire and brimstone at that church. I didn't understand a thing they said. Now I realize how Catholics must have felt when their services were conducted only in Latin.

Our beat-up old car had an AM radio and on the way home from church, Dad always listened to a political roundtable discussion out of Chicago. One of the speakers was Hans Morgenthau. My father thought he was the coolest guy and always would speak out in agreement with him. I had no idea what they were talking about on the radio, either.

Because we didn't understand German, church was boring for us kids. I remember once I got antsy—I'm still fidgety that way. I can't sit still very long. I started acting up in church and my father yanked me outside and gave me a spanking. My aunts and uncles who were there told me later they could hear the whipping he gave me over the voice of the preacher! The bottom line is, I never made another peep.

After church, we came home and had a big dinner. Mom always had something really good. Roast chicken, mashed potatoes, a couple of vegetables, pie and cake.

Our church had a monthly magazine called *The Evangel* and Dad became friends with one of its writers, Brother Steinberg, who was from Kansas. He'd come out to our farm and watch Dad load manure—relaxing and meditating on his next article, I guess.

Dad still used a horse-drawn manure spreader. In the spring, he'd go out to the manure pile on the south side of the barn, shovel it into the spreader, and haul it out to fertilize the fields as Brother Steinberg watched.

I liked to listen to Brother Steinberg talk. He told us about life in Kansas, where the wheat fields were so big, a farmer could start at daylight and be able to make only one round of the field before noon. That sowed a seed in me. It made me want to travel out West to see any field so big you could only make two rounds a day.

Growing up, we were quite poor and enjoyed few of the comforts most average families have today. Every morning when the weather was cold, Dad would go into the basement to cut wood for kindling and start up our old coal furnace. Once, a train car filled with big lumps of coal spilled its load along the tracks that bordered our farm. The railroad said we could have it. So we loaded up the coal and took it home on a hay wagon. It gave us enough coal for the entire season.

Our water came from a pitcher pump next to the kitchen sink, which we used to fill a bucket. When we were thirsty, we'd dip a ladle into the bucket for a drink. Some winter mornings, it was so cold in that farmhouse, there was ice on top of the water.

When Dad went outside to do chores, he wrapped his feet in rags before he put them inside his rubber boots. I can still picture that. He made sure us kids had clothes to wear, to the point he couldn't afford to buy socks for himself.

That was my dad.

On that farm, life was idyllic in many ways. In others, it could just about break your back—and your spirit. But, I'm grateful for the seeds of discipline it sowed in me. It certainly would come in handy.

CHAPTER 3

The Bombing Run

With the fighter's canopy blown clear of the plane, the smoke instantly dissipated. I could see by the instruments that the F-4 was losing power. Fast.

I had a rear-view mirror, just like a car. In it, I could see Curt's helmet slumped down behind me. Immediately I thought he must have been hit or injured.

"Curt!" I shouted through the intercom. "You better eject!"

The airplane wanted to roll to the left. I had to back-stick and use the right aileron, feeding in the right rudder, to keep it steady. We were really slowing down.

"Curt, you better go out!" I repeated. "You better jump out!"

No reply.

The wind was screaming through the cockpit. If Curt ejected, I wouldn't even have heard the charges go off. The airplane was in the soup. The clouds were so thick I had no visual contact with my flight commander, Cass, or any of the other planes. I had lost all radio contact as well. Maybe the intercom was down, too, and Curt couldn't even hear me. We were losing altitude quickly and I knew I was rapidly approaching the point I would have to eject.

"Curt, I've got to go!" I said. "I don't know if you can go or not, but I have to go!"

No answer. There was nothing more I could do. I had to eject.

Normally, when you let go of a plane's control stick, it goes back to neutral. Except this time, it didn't. The stick was frozen over my right leg.

I said to myself, *oh, my*.

All the later models of fighters had leg restraints, which you attached when you strapped into the plane. They're connected to a reel in the lower part of the seat so that when you eject, your legs are instantly pulled back from the rudder pedals. If you were to eject with your feet forward on the pedals, the force of the blast could cause you to lose your legs on the instrument panel.

Now the air around me was becoming smoky again. I could just hear the plane beginning to come unglued. I reached down and undid the right leg restrainer and lifted my leg over the frozen stick.

The F-4 had a Martin-Baker seat, which was made in England. It had four stages of rockets, which were supposed to fire relatively slowly at first and then really shoot you out. Despite this design, it was none too gentle. Virtually everybody who's been shot out of an F-4 has had back problems—even in peace time, let alone under combat conditions.

In training, they tell you to be sure to eject with your spine straight up. Otherwise, because the seat shoots you out at such tremendous force, it can snap your back.

At this point, things were happening so fast. Sitting sideways now in the pilot's seat, I reached up for the little half-moon-shaped ejection lever. It was on a piece of canvas designed to drop down and protect your eyes if you were to eject at supersonic speed. I pulled the lever.

Nothing happened.

"Oh, my," I said.

The good news was all my training came back to me in a millisecond. I remembered that our instructors had said sometimes you may not pull the ejection lever hard enough. I yanked with all my strength. I pulled so hard, it came out in my hand—the lever, the cable, plus a little piece of canvas.

And still, nothing happened.

I said, "Oh, my."

Next I tried to find the back-up ejection lever. It was a little T-handle far enough down between your legs that you had to bend over to get hold of it. In the F-4, you sat on a seat cushion with your parachute underneath. The lever was down below that, just above the floor.

The secondary ejection lever was installed largely for the benefit of pilots who were flying low-level missions to deliver nuclear weapons. When you're flying at the treetops at 500 knots, it's quicker to reach down for the lever between your legs than to reach up for the one above your head. At that speed, in the few extra seconds it would take to reach the primary handle, you'd crash into the ground before you ever ejected.

I began to get a little frantic, sitting sideways, leaning forward, and trying to find the release lever. Finally, I had it in my hand and pulled.

That's the last thing I remember. The seat exploded out of the plane.

In those anxious seconds before ejecting, I didn't have the presence of mind to straighten my body back up. I was pretty well bent over. In fact, if I had straightened my spine, I don't know that I would have been able to reach the secondary lever. As a result, the force of the ejection crushed several disks in my spine.

I blacked out. Whether I completely lost consciousness, I don't know. When you pull a certain number of Gs, you get tunnel vision, then lose sight all together. Your brain still may be functioning, but you can't see. That may have been the situation because I remember a huge fireball exploding upwards, right in front of me. It didn't really register in my mind what it was. It was almost as if my eyes were closed, but I could sense it was there.

The blackout lasted only a few seconds. The next thing I knew, I came to, and I was floating in a parachute. I shook my head and looked around. The realization slowly came over me that I was still alive.

About 45 degrees to my right, I could see another parachute, far away. However, I seemed to be coming down a lot faster than it was. It looked as if the parachute was empty.

Oh my gosh, I thought to myself. *What happened to Curt?*

I probably wasn't thinking rationally, but I assumed Curt somehow became disconnected from his parachute. Something must have cut him off when he ejected. Curt was married and had children.

"Oh, God. What happened to him?" I said.

Meanwhile, I was coming down fast. Looking up, I could see a couple of panels were missing from my parachute. I could hear rifle shots on the ground below.

I had never jumped from a plane or hung in a parachute. Yet, once again, everything my instructors said during survival training came back to me. They had told us how to steer the parachute to avoid landing in a tree, where it was easy to get hurt or get stuck.

The ground seemed to be flying toward me. A tree appeared, seemingly from nowhere. There was a rice paddy right next to it. Where did that come from? I thought.

Reaching up, I grabbed the lines of the parachute and tried to steer away from the tree. And it worked. You *can* steer these things, I thought to myself, almost smiling. They were right. But the wind was still blowing me right toward the tree.

I hit the tree about halfway between the trunk and the edge of the branches. It had a canopy about 30-40 feet wide and was maybe 40 feet tall. I put my legs together and crashed down through the tree. I could still hear rifle shots in the distance.

Extending my legs, I made a tiptoe landing. The tree eased my descent and I gently touched the ground. I entirely give God the credit for placing that tree there and guiding me down. I was too distracted and too filled with adrenalin to realize my back had been broken by the ejection. But God knew my back was a mess. If I had made an ordinary landing, the impact could have severed my spine and I might not be here today. My parachute got hung up in that tree just enough to slow me down.

Quickly looking around, I didn't see anyone, but I could hear yelling, followed by more shooting. Immediately, I reached for the rescue beacon on my flight suit and pulled the lanyard that activated it.

The rice paddy I had seen on my descent was about three or four acres in size. Great, I thought. Ironically, I remembered what I'd said to Curt just two days earlier. "This would be a good place to get shot down because it was a jungle," I had told him. "At least you could find some cover. You can't hide in a rice paddy." Now, here I was, staring at a rice paddy.

I pulled my parachute down, tearing it from the limbs of the tree. The parachute was orange and white—which makes it nice and visible! I wanted to get it down as fast as I could. I gathered up the parachute and disconnected it from my harness. Scratching up some brush and leaves, I wadded it up and covered it as best I could under the tree.

It was between 9 and 9:30 in the morning, but already the weather was terribly hot and sticky. The air was filled with the sound of birds.

I knew from the shouting and gunfire there must be North Vietnamese close by. My survival instincts began to kick in. They told me to run. I had to get away from there. But which way to go?

On one side was the rice paddy. I knew I didn't want to go there. In the other direction was a ridge. I ran that way and found a path, about 15 inches wide that led up the hill. In survival training, they tell you to stay off paths, but I followed it, running until at last I was out of breath.

I was not conscious of my broken back at all. In a situation like that, your survival mode is stronger than your immediate health needs—which our instructors had told us would happen. If you get hurt, you'll forget about your pain, they said. Your No. 1 instinct is survival. We'd sit in class, looking at each other, and thinking, gee, that's easy for you to say. It kind of went in one ear and out the other. But I found out it was true. I didn't feel any pain at all.

Since I never thought I'd get shot down, I'd left my captain's rank on, which was shiny silver. Also very visible. In addition, I wore a big red squadron nametag that said "Capt. Paul A. Kari." My flight suit was olive green and blended in with the foliage, but I was afraid the red and silver would stand out.

I pulled out a small survival kit, which contained a knife, gold coins, and a few other things. Taking out the knife, I cut off my rank and my name tag.

As I buried them in the jungle floor, I thought of my 2-year-old son, Shawn. He will never know what happened to his dad, I told myself. My brand-new daughter, Ali, was only a 5-month-old baby. We never got the chance to know one another at all. I knew in my heart I was going to be shot and killed.

A couple of days earlier, one of the crew chiefs had stopped me as I was headed to my plane.

"Capt. Kari," he said. "Look at this article in *Time* magazine."

It was a story about a pilot who had been captured and beheaded by the Vietcong.

The voices were coming closer. I was sure that dead pilot soon would be me.

There was about 12 hours' difference between Ohio and Vietnam. Half a world away, my parents had just returned from Sunday evening services at church and crawled into bed, when they heard a little noise in the dining room. They were used to the rumble of the trains on the nearby tracks, but this was a different sound. My dad got up to see what it was.

Hanging on the wall were photographs of each of us four kids. Somehow, my high school graduation picture had slipped from its frame and fallen to the floor.

Mom and Dad told me later they knew something terrible had happened to me. With their deep faith in God, they immediately picked up the phone to place my name in our church's prayer circle. My parents had no way of knowing the circumstances—only that I needed all the prayer power I could get.

And they were right.

CHAPTER 4

Caught in a Blizzard

God blesses each person with unique abilities. And at an early age, I discovered mine was an aptitude for operating machines. I imagine that's why flying came so easy for me. Whether I was running a tractor, driving a truck or flying a plane, it was like second nature.

I learned to drive a tractor when I was either 8 or 9. We had two Farmall H tractors and I thought they were the cat's meow. I was so proud that Dad allowed me to pull a hay wagon all by myself with that Farmall H. However, I still had a few things to learn. Once, I turned too sharply into the driveway and the wagon hit a fence post. I felt terrible, but Dad said, "Oh, don't worry about it."

Farming was, and still is, a very dangerous and difficult profession. One of my childhood friends, David Walker, had an awful accident. He was refueling an old John Deere tractor and inadvertently spilled fuel on the hot engine. It caught fire and burned him terribly. I always felt so badly for him after that.

His family's farm on U.S. Route 42 was where I learned to ride a bicycle. I was always on the small side and the bike really was too big for me. But I'd push it up to the slope of the bank barn and ride it down, over and over. I don't know how many times I crashed before I figured it out, but eventually I learned to ride it pretty well. I also played with David's brother, Russell, and with Larry Mushay, who lived just north of us on Columbia Road.

Farming is a labor-intensive enterprise—and that was especially true in the 1940s when I was growing up. Although I never shied away from work, I was always interested in making things more efficient.

Dad had a corn binder that would tie a string around the bundles of corn and dump them on the ground. There was a conveyer that would move the bundles out of the way so that when the tractor came around the next time, it wouldn't run over them. But you had to come back and pick those bundles up.

Dad bought his equipment from Wallace Implement, which was in the county seat, Medina, right on Public Square. He soon bought an elevator that attached to the binder. You could drive alongside with a second tractor and a hay wagon. That way the elevator would bring the bundles right up to the wagon. You still had to have a person on the wagon to stack the bundles, but it was easier than picking them up off the ground.

The only problem was that it took three workers—one stacker and two drivers. So Dad talked Mom into driving the corn binder tractor and let me drive the tractor with the wagon. He was the strongest, so he stood on the wagon to catch the bundles.

The trick to pulling the wagon was not to go too fast or too slow, or make sudden stops and starts. I had to keep perfectly in sync with my mom as she drove the corn binder. In essence, I was 9 or 10 years old and learning to fly formation with two Farmall H tractors instead of two aircraft! I was proud of myself that I got a load of corn in without making Dad fall off the wagon. I can still picture it in my mind. Although that field on our old farm is filled with houses today, I still look at it and remember these experiences every time I drive by.

After we harvested the corn, which we would use for silage, Dad sent me back up to the field to disk the stalks so he could plant wheat. It began to get dark, so Mom and Dad sent my sister Ruth up to ride on the fender of the tractor and keep me company. They must have thought I would get scared when it got dark—and they were probably right. Ruth brought me a drink and something to eat.

Needless to say, I had no experience in disking. The tractor had headlights, but you could only see what was in front of you, not the entire field. There are two parts to a field—the headlands, which go across the top and bottom, and the lands, which go the length of the field at right angles to the headlands. Well, no one had told me I needed to lay all that out in the daylight when I could see! Because it was dark, my lines weren't straight and I had to go back and disk a bunch of triangles I'd missed. Mind you, I was only 10!

This particular field ran right alongside the AC& Y railroad tracks. It was dark, the tractor was running, and I was concentrating on what I was doing. Suffice to say, I didn't notice there was a train coming up behind me while I was disking close to the tracks. I'm sure the fellows running the engine, not knowing it was two kids on the tractor, said to themselves, "Hey! Let's give them a little surprise!"

They got right up behind us and blew out steam on us. The noise and heat scared us to death. I'm sure that didn't help me keep my disking lines straight. I probably was just short of wetting my pants. I didn't swear in front of my sister, but I told Ruth that was about the dirtiest trick anyone could pull. I don't know if we got the field finished that night, but we got back home in one piece.

We did not have a silo, but I would go down and drive a tractor for our neighbors, the Holdridges, when they filled their silo. Harold Holdridge, their youngest son, was in high school. He and another boy, Ellet Mann, were my heroes. They seemed to me as big and strong as grown men and could run fast. I remember Ellet and another one of their buddies decided they were going to catch Harold and put lipstick on him. I was rooting for them as they tried to catch him between bringing in loads of corn for silage.

One farm chore I never liked was taking care of chickens. I liked to eat them well enough, but tending them always annoyed me. It was my job to go to the chicken house to feed the chickens and collect eggs. There was a rooster that always waited for me as soon as I came through the gate. He'd run after me and frighten the heck out of me. Every time, I told Mom I was never going in there again, but of course, I always had to.

One day, I told myself I was going to get this rooster. I took an ear of dried corn and shucked the kernels from half the cob, making a nice handle on one end. I decided if that rooster bothered me, I was going to lob it at him like it was a hand grenade.

Sure enough, he came after me like always. I threw that ear of corn from probably 12-15 feet away and hit him right in the head! It was a lucky shot. He ran around in circles for a while and suddenly it dawned on me how much trouble I'd be in with Mom if I killed her rooster. I don't know what happened to him, but he never bothered me again.

Sometimes I could be naïve about the simplest things. Once Mom sent me to the garden to pick tomatoes. In among the tomato plants, I could see a bee flitting from flower to flower. No one had ever told me a bee can sting. I looked at it a while and said gee, that's interesting and went to grab it. Man, did he ever put a barb in my thumb. I came running into the house to find Mom.

"Well, you shouldn't have done that," she said.

"Nobody told me!" I replied.

I learned a lot of things the hard way.

Beyond church, we really didn't know much of the world. We never got a newspaper, although I do remember a salesman coming by and selling Mom subscriptions to *Look* and *Life* magazines. I thought we'd hit the big time!

Growing up, I read many books about hunting and fishing. I also liked to read a lot of Westerns in high school. The fact is I read too many and should have been better about studying.

Later I subscribed to *Outdoor Life* and *Field & Stream*. In the back of one of those magazines, I saw an ad for a florescent tie. When you turned out the lights, it would glow with the words, "Kiss Me in the Dark, Baby."

The ad said, "Send no money!" It was "C.O.D." I had no idea what that stood for, but I thought, "Hey. No money. That's a pretty good deal!" So I sent my order form off in the mail.

Some time afterward, I came home from school to find my mother irate.

"What did you do?" she said. "I thought I raised a son who had more sense!"

"What are you talking about?" I asked.

She pulled out the tie.

"Look at this!" Mom said. "'Kiss Me in the Dark, Baby!' And I had to pay for this!"

I don't remember how much it was, but in those days, it was quite a bit. Probably all my parents' spending money for the week.

"But it said not to send any money," I stammered. "It's C.O.D."

"Yeah," she said. "That's 'Cash on Delivery!'"

Oh my gosh, I was humiliated. My dad never said anything. He didn't have to.

"Kiss Me in the Dark, Baby." I have no idea what became of that fluorescent tie! I never wore it, I know that. Mom probably burned it.

One cold winter day, Dad and I went to Bowman's in Medina to buy feed and also coal for the furnace. We put the hay wagon on one of the Farmalls and headed for town, about three miles away.

The snow began to fall hard. The wind was blowing fiercely from the west, making drifts from three to five feet tall in the road. Dad was driving and eventually we got stuck. He tried to get the Farmall out of the drift, but to no avail.

"Dad," I said, "let me give it a try."

He looked at me as if to say, "What do you know that I don't know?"

But, he let me try. My dad always let me do things probably the average dad would not.

The Farmall had separate brakes on each rear wheel. I had gotten stuck once in mud and I remembered if you pressed the brake on the left side, the right wheel would go, or vice-versa. I thought maybe I could inch my way out of the drift. And by golly, it worked. Dad sort of looked at me and we drove on home.

Since I hadn't dressed for the bitter cold weather—and neither had Dad, for that matter—I became very sick. As I lay in bed, I think they were afraid I was going to die from pneumonia. It was the only time I ever saw a doctor between the day I was born and when I had to take a physical to play high school sports. I must have been pretty badly off for my parents to call a doctor to the house, but I made it through.

Dad rented land on what was known as the Lehman Farm a few miles away from our place and planted his first crop of soybeans. I helped him shovel eight tons of lime, which Dad spread with a team of horses. Mom packed me a lunch of bread, sausage links and pickles, along with a jug of water. She always packed my lunch in a bread wrapper.

Some time after Dad planted the soybeans, we drove down to the field to take a look at them. From a distance, the field looked green and beautiful. We were excited that the soybeans were doing so well. However, when we got closer, we could see it was nothing but weeds. I don't know if the seeds were bad or what the problem was. It's all part of farming, but I felt so bad for my dad.

I attended Lafayette School through fifth grade. You could say I was a little bit ornery.

The school had a stairway going right up the center. And on all three floors, there was a drinking fountain near the steps. It was an open staircase so you could look down when you were on the top floor and see the next floor, clear down to the basement. There was a girl down there standing and talking.

"Watch this girl," I said to my friends. "I'm going to see if I can hit her on the head with a mouthful of water."

I took a big gulp, lined up the shot, and let her go.

Little did I know, the principal, Mrs. Rieger, was standing right behind me.

"Son, you come with me," she said.

Mrs. Rieger took me to her office. I mean to tell you, she bent me over and gave me a paddling I can still remember.

By the way, it was a perfect shot. I hit that girl square on the head.

On the playground, we played all the old childhood games, like Pom-Pom Pull-Away. One winter, I put my tongue on the railing of the outdoor steps—and of course my tongue froze right to the metal. The only toilets we had at the Lafayette School were outdoors. There was one for the boys and one for the girls.

Lafayette was a small crossroads community, consisting of the school, a church, a gas station, a store, an auto repair shop and the old-fashioned general store. It was right across the highway from the school and was called Harrington's Grocery. They sold candy, but we weren't allowed to go there during school because crossing U.S. 42 could be dangerous.

One day, I was feeling brave. On a bet, I went up along side of the school, crossed a little creek where there was a bunch of brush, and crawled across a yard. I ran across the highway and bought a candy bar. I went back the same way and showed the candy bar to my friends.

"I did it!" I said.

Maybe that was the start of my military survival training. My parents never found out—and Ruth didn't tell on me. But my sister wasn't always so good about keeping my escapades quiet.

One day, it was time to walk down the driveway and wait for the school bus. We were running late and Mom warned us we'd better get moving.

"I expect you to be out there at the road waiting for the bus. Don't make everyone wait for you to walk from the house to the road," she said. "I won't tell you a second time."

Well, we missed the school bus. Ruth and I both.

"I guess you're going to have to walk to school," Mom said.

Now that's a couple miles. I was probably 8 and Ruth was 10 or so. Today, a parent wouldn't think of saying that.

"And don't you hitchhike," admonished Mom.

We assured her we wouldn't.

After hoofing it half a mile down the county road and out of sight, we came to the highway—U.S. Route 42.

I looked down the road and here came a milk truck, headed toward Lafayette. It just so happened I knew the driver. I stuck out my thumb. He stopped and we got in.

"You know we're not supposed to do this," Ruth whispered.

That was true, but it didn't stop her from getting into the truck, too!

Now, what's the first thing Ruth did when we got home from school that afternoon? She told Mom.

"Paul hitchhiked and we got a ride to school!" she said.

Mom tanned my fanny really good.

I said to her: "But Ruth rode with me! That's not fair. You didn't whip her. She got the benefit of what I did!"

That was about the only time I actually got into trouble. I learned to respect my mom and dad because if I stepped out of line, I knew I would be punished. Dad really got after me only once. It was Mom who put the fear of God in me. It's much different today. Kids don't have a healthy fear of their parents like that and they do things they shouldn't do.

I had a very close relationship with my dad. Yet, my dad and mom never, ever told me they loved me. They never told me they were proud of me. They never told me I did a good job at something. Some Germans just never talked that way, it seems.

I knew my dad felt those things. He didn't have to tell me. I knew it by the way he gave me all those opportunities on the farm. I'd go to school, tell my friends what my dad let me do at home, and they wouldn't believe me.

"Don't tell us you're driving a tractor. Plowing at age 10?" they'd exclaim. "You're crazy!"

They ridiculed me, but it was all true. I even started drinking coffee when I was 6 or 7 years old.

My dad had brown hair and an infectious smile. He was not large in stature, but he was as strong as steel. Anyone who knew Tony Kari loved him. He was the kind of person who never met a stranger. Dad had a difficult time writing English and spoke it with an accent, but he could write and speak German and Hungarian fluently.

My mom, whose maiden name was Mary Julia Pamer, was strict in her parenting style. I think it's because her own German mother was the same way. Grandma ran the house by striking terror into those around her. All Grandpa could do was say, "Yes ma'am, no ma'am, when and how high would you like me to jump?"

Dad didn't have a middle name, but it could have been the word "generosity." He often loaned immigrants the funds they needed to travel to America from Hungary. And they always paid him right back. He routinely gave money to help others—but refused payback or charged no interest. Instead, he'd tell them, "Just help someone else."

The Bible says to help others and my father lived those instructions to a "T."

To him, the farm in Lafayette—though primitive with no electricity and no plumbing—was the fulfillment of the dream shared by so many of his fellow immigrants. Mom, however, was rarely satisfied. It was a tough life at the Lafayette farm—an outhouse for a bathroom and her working on threshing crews while Dad worked at the foundry. She pressured him to move to California—where his mother now lived—and buy an orange grove. They could buy a 10- to 20-acre orchard and it would make a lot more money than this clay soil farm, she said. Mom thought that would be a better life for us. Finally, she convinced him and Dad put the farm up for sale.

Our neighbor, Harold Holdridge, bought it in 1946 for $16,000. The Holdridges operated a dairy just down the road. Dad had an auction and they bought quite a few pieces of our equipment, as well.

Before Dad had decided to sell the farm, he traded an old John Deere B for a new Farmall H. The John Deere didn't have an electric starter. Mom had almost lost her insides trying to start that thing by hand.

It was a snowy day when Wallace Implement delivered the new Farmall. We arranged to keep it in a neighbor's barn. I went in there and just sat on it. It was so shiny and red. The next thing I knew, Dad had sold the farm. I was extremely upset I didn't get to drive that brand-new tractor.

During the equipment sale, I watched as the men stood around, smoking cigarettes and flipping the butts onto the ground. Back then, it seemed like everyone smoked. To a 10-year-old farm boy, it looked pretty cool.

After everyone had gone, I collected some of the cigarette butts and put them into a corncob pipe I had made. Sneaking one of Mom's kitchen matches, I lit it up. I just about croaked! It made me so sick.

As it turned out, Dad got cold feet about moving to California—and I don't blame him. Although he still had difficulty with English, Dad finally was feeling comfortable in America. To him, moving to the West Coast was like moving to an entirely new country. And perhaps his previous experience with the rattlesnake in the Wild West also gave him reason to pause.

Dad began looking around the area for a better farm. He stopped at the bank in Spencer, a small town about 10 miles west of Lafayette, to ask if there were any local farms for sale. The bank consisted of a single room in the back of the hardware store.

CHAPTER 4

Yes, they told him—the Billman place on River Corners Road in Spencer Township. It was 110 acres and had a huge barn. Dad bought it.

I was reluctant to move. I had been young enough that I didn't really remember moving to the Lafayette farm. Now I had friends and I didn't like the idea of leaving them. But, I spent the rest of my fifth grade year at Lafayette School and in the summer of '46 we moved to Spencer.

Starting over. It would be a feeling I'd come to know well.

CAPTURED

After I cut the name tag and rank from my flight suit and buried them in the jungle floor, I decided my best chance for survival was to keep moving. I scrambled back to my feet and continued running up the ridge. It wasn't long before I could hear North Vietnamese voices ahead of me on the path.

I also recognized the distant sound of a four-engine propeller aircraft orbiting overhead. It was our rescue coordinator—and the plane was tantalizingly close. I hoped the next thing I'd hear would be a U.S. helicopter swooping in to pick me up. I'd given my pilot's two-way radio to my back-seater, Curt, in exchange for his SAR-AH beacon. So there was no way I could communicate with the rescue team—only trust they were homing in on the "beep-beep-beep" of the rescue beacon. All I had to do was stay alive long enough for them to find me. Needless to say, Curt's premonition that this was the day we'd get shot down turned out to be right on the money.

The North Vietnamese voices drew closer. Peering through the jungle growth, I could see them—guerilla fighters in civilian clothes, carrying battered rifles that looked like hand-me-downs from the 1700s. I couldn't tell how many of them there were. They were about 20 yards away. One of them pointed in my direction.

Then I heard it, the sound of a rescue helicopter. It was headed my way.

Back in training, our instructors told us if ever we were to be shot down, avoid getting into a fire fight—unless there was one man between you and being rescued. It was a matter of mathematics: There were 17 million of the enemy and only one of you. A downed pilot was almost always going to be outmanned and outgunned. Nevertheless, I expected to see the helicopter overhead any minute. I needed to buy some time.

I drew my .45 automatic and fired a couple of shots up the path in hopes of at least slowing them down. I put the pistol back in its holster and headed into the tall brown grass along the path. Called "tiger grass," it was 10 feet tall and thick as hair on a dog. I turned my body slightly sideways, trying to push through it.

Making my way 30 or 40 yards through the grass, I came to a massive rock. It was at least 25 feet long and six feet high. Beside it was a smaller rock. Things seemed to be happening so fast. I got down on the ground and backed into the space between the two rocks as far as I could trying desperately to disappear.

I could hear the voices chattering as they pushed through the grass in my direction, likely following the path I had made through the tall stalks. Peering from my hiding place, I could see there were five or six men, a couple of them wearing old uniforms. They had a dog, which led them right to my hiding spot.

I crawled out with my hands up. Immediately, they took my pistol and unsnapped the SARAH beacon from my G-suit. I could tell they were interested in the beacon.

They took everything I had on me—including my watch, wedding ring, the custom boots I was wearing, and a beautiful Puma hunting knife I'd gotten at a rod and gun club in Germany while I was stationed at Ramstein Air Base. I don't know why I flew with it, but I really loved that knife.

All that was left was my flight suit and G-suit, which they began to examine to see how to take it off—probably to make sure I wasn't hiding any more weapons. The flight suit had a covered zipper down one side, which evidently they didn't see. All I had on underneath were briefs and a pair of socks.

After talking a while about how to get me out of my G-suit, one of the men produced a machete. It was what POWs would later refer to as "the camp tool" because the North Vietnamese used its sharp blade for everything. They began to hack the flight suit off at my right hip with the machete.

The suit was made from a tough nylon and was very tight-fitting. The man wielding the machete tried to pinch the fabric and pull it away from my skin, but there simply wasn't much slack for him to grab. I thought, I have got to say something or else he's going to chop my hip apart. I lowered my hand, as if to say, "Can I show you there's a zipper there?"

However, as my hand came down, apparently they thought I was going for another weapon. One of the soldiers hit me hard with the butt of his gun, directly on my right ear. It would be the first of three times one of my ear drums would be shattered. It hurt terribly and immediately I put my hands back up in the air.

They chewed and chewed at my flight suit with that machete—never finding the zipper until after they had it off. Despite all the hacking, I didn't suffer a single cut. How they managed that, I don't know.

38

As they tied my arms tightly behind my back at the wrists and elbows, I could still hear helicopters in the distance. Stripped down to my socks and underwear, the guerillas marched me back to the path, with a couple of them leading the way and two or three more following behind with their rifles. I had no idea where they were taking me. They probably just wanted to get me out of the immediate area and hand me off to someone with higher authority.

The "wap-wap-wap" of the choppers drew closer until one came in low, right on the treetops. The rescue beacon probably was still beeping because the North Vietnamese hadn't yet figured out how to turn it off. I knew the helicopter crew was looking for me, but at this point, with my arms tied behind my back and being marched at gunpoint, my gut reaction was anger that they had not arrived sooner.

I turned my face to the sky. "It's too late now!" I screamed at the helicopter.

My captors probably thought I was trying to communicate with the helicopter and give the crew information they could use to kill the guerillas. The North Vietnamese got very angry and shoved me off the trail, trying to hide me from the helicopter. Unable to use my arms for balance, I stumbled and fell, landing right on an anthill.

It was three feet across, 18 inches tall, and crawling with ants. They didn't bite, but still, it was a hot, sticky day, and it was a terrible sensation to feel them crawling all over my skin. If I got up, I was sure the guerillas would shoot me, thinking I was trying to signal the aircraft. Slowly, I tried to ease myself off the anthill. That was when I first felt the twinge of pain in my back, signaling that something was very wrong.

The force of the ejection, combined with the fact I was bent over in my search for the back-up ejection, had broken my back. The rush of adrenalin, and the fast pace of events, had masked the pain until now. The helicopter circled a time or two, the guerillas blasting away at it with their ancient guns. Then the chopper disappeared.

Remember, at that time, the U.S. government did not want to call the fighting in Vietnam a "war," so it would not let Air Force or Navy helicopters rescue downed pilots. It was bizarre reasoning. The U.S. paid two contractors—Air America and Bird & Son—$10,000 for every pilot they picked up. I don't know which company's helicopter flew over that morning, but although I could still hear helicopters in the distance for much of the day, it never came back.

Later, a fellow prisoner would tell me the guerillas had managed to kill the pilot of the rescue helicopter. The copilot managed to pull the pilot's slumped body off the controls and set the helicopter down in a nearby clearing. After moving the pilot to the back of the craft, they flew home and didn't look for me any more that day. At some point a rescue helicopter returned, but I had already been moved some distance down the road. Somewhere far above, my flight commander, Cass, was orbiting, too, refusing to give up looking for me.

As we marched along, I assumed I was being taken to the headquarters of the Western Vietnam Military Training Area, which had been the target of our bombing. It was like Fort Campbell or Fort Knox in the United States, filled with GIs in training.

My back hurt worse with every step. Finally, I couldn't walk any more and sat down in the road. Probably thinking I was faking it, my captors became angry.

They made me kneel in front of a hole that had been dug in the ground. One of the guerillas had his rifle pointed right at my back. My hands were still tied behind me. I immediately assumed this was my grave. Not thinking clearly, I didn't realize it probably was a foxhole used by North Vietnamese soldiers in their training.

Why they made me kneel down, I don't know. Maybe it was to scare me. But in my mind, this was the end.

Minutes passed, each more agonizing than the last. My back hurt. They say when your body is in shock, your system uses up all the available moisture in your tissue. My tongue was so dry you could have struck a match on it. My muscles were tense. I said to myself, *Any second now. Any second, I am going to die.* I prayed, saying, "Oh, God, I haven't been the best boy in the world, but I do love you."

This may sound morbid to some, but I wondered which way I would fall when they shot me. Would I fall backward? Or would I roll forward, neatly into the hole, just like in the old movie Westerns? The more I waited, the more fidgety I became. I began to itch all over. I couldn't stand it. What is going on, I wondered?

If I turned around fast, I knew the guy with the gun would shoot me. So I began to turn around ever so slightly, in super-slow motion. It probably took me a minute to move 45 degrees. I made eye contact with him and he came unglued. He motioned for me to turn back around, which I did.

Pretty soon, they hauled me up and we were on the march once again. I found out later they were trying to locate an interrogator who could speak French. Vietnam was a former French colony, so it was not uncommon to find someone who still could speak the language. I knew only a few words of French.

We arrived at an acre-sized pond with a little island in it. A crowd of about a dozen North Vietnamese people gathered around to stare at me, as if to say, "Hey, look! An American! They got one!" They were talking excitedly with one another.

A man came up to me and started speaking French. I didn't know much, but I didn't want to let them in on how much I knew. That way, I thought maybe they would speak candidly to one another in front of me, not realizing I could understand what they were saying. I threw out a few words in Spanish, thinking it might fool them.

The man produced a card, something guerilla leaders were issued in the event they captured an American. "We cannot guarantee your safety," he read in stilted English.

They took me to the little island in the pond. Again, I thought, *this is where they will kill me, away from the crowd of people, where there's no one to hold them accountable.*

As before, we waited. Thirty minutes passed. Maybe an hour. It felt like an eternity. I began to lose track of time. Everything had happened so quickly.

But, again, they soon had me back on the road, which was nothing more than a jeep trail. My back was killing me. The weather was hot and humid. I was thirsty, but I didn't ask for water. I no longer heard the sound of rescue aircraft. There was nothing to hang my hopes on now.

In each village we marched through, I became the center of an impromptu pep rally. Most villages were no more than a small collection of huts. The people were very poor, probably earning their living by growing rice or cutting timber. My captors tried to incite the crowds that gathered around me, pointing to me, as if to say, "Here's one! Here's one of the Americans who have been killing our women and children!"

In one of the villages we paused in, I fell to my knees in exhaustion. By this time, I couldn't care less if they shot me. A crowd of 30 or 40 people gathered around.

Among them were a man and a woman, standing right beside me. I don't know if they were brother and sister, or husband and wife, or what their relationship was. As the crowd pressed in and bent forward to get a good look at me, I looked up and couldn't help but notice this woman was wearing a loose-fitting top with nothing underneath. In fact, her top barely covered her at all. Even with the desperate condition I was in, from my place down on the ground, it was quite a nice view.

I thought to myself, *well, if I'm going to die, I'm at least going to enjoy the beauty God has made!*

I tell this story to show that when things are at their worst in life—and things were only going to get worse for me—there often are moments of levity to ease the burden.

Well, the man she was with saw exactly what I was looking at as I gazed upward. He grabbed the woman and pulled her away. He pointed his finger at me. I thought, *oh, man. I'm in trouble now.*

But, shortly after, they had me back on the road. I could hardly walk because of the pain in my back. Finally, I laid down right in the road. They screamed at me, telling me to get up. I had no idea what they were thinking, but I simply could not go on.

My hands still were tied behind me at both my wrists and elbows. Now they attached a rope to my arms, just above my elbows. Why are they doing that, I wondered?

Soon, a jeep came along, which the North Vietnamese immediately commandeered. They turned me around, hooked me to the back of the jeep and proceeded to drag me down the road.

I thought, *oh, Lord. If they're not going to shoot me, I guess this is how I'm going to die.* I realize that thought occurred to me many times that day. Every moment seemed like it could be my last.

All I was wearing were the briefs I had on under my flight suit. They didn't drag me more than a couple hundred yards before the rough surface of the road had worn away the entire backside of my shorts. The fabric was mostly shredded. They unhooked me and I struggled to my feet. For the rest of the day, it was like I was wearing little more than a loincloth. By this point, my socks were pretty well worn through, too.

The jeep went on and so did the forced march that continued from village to village. I don't know how far it was from the point I had bailed out—I'm guessing three or four miles. If it was around 9:30 a.m. when I got shot down, it was now almost dark as we approached a military complex. It looked different on the ground than it does from the air, but my guess was that it was the military headquarters at Son La we had bombed that morning.

North Vietnamese camps were quite a bit different from our military camps. There was no gate. As we walked in, I could see all types of low huts, with women and children coming out to see the captured, all but naked American.

I thought, *oh, God, if they only knew what they were going to come up against tomorrow.* We—meaning the U.S. military—would be coming back to finish what we had started. These civilians weren't supposed to be here. It's a military complex. I really felt compassion for these women and children—whom I found out later would shoot me just as quickly as a man would. But still my heart went out to them.

Now it was dark. They took me to an empty soccer stadium with concrete stands, where a guard held me until another man came. He read in disjointed English from a little pamphlet.

"Who are you?" he asked.

"I'm Paul Kari," I said.

"What's your unit?"

"I can't answer that," I replied.

He evidently knew just enough English to understand if I was answering his questions or not. His finger would go down to a different spot in the pamphlet, as if the instructions in English said, "If he doesn't answer that, then you say this."

The man continued.

"We cannot guarantee your safety if you no cooperate," he said, before repeating his question, "What unit?"

"I can't tell you."

He asked again, a little more forcefully. I repeated my answer.

"You are in Vietnam," the man said. "We can't guarantee your safety."

After about five minutes of this, the guard took me to a Russian half-track truck, similar to an armored personnel carrier. He threw me in the back, which was filled with all kinds of junk, and shut the tailgate. There must have been 15 or 20 GI backpacks inside.

Like the time earlier with the woman and the loose-fitting top, this was another occasion when, as bleak as my situation was, and with as much pain as I was in from my broken back, a little bit of humor briefly lifted my spirits.

This half-track had windshield wipers that pivoted from the top. The problem was they had no wiper blades on them. The one on the left side was wrapped with a piece of rag that cleared a little spot in the window, just enough for the driver to see.

I remember thinking, *if this is what we're up against, it's going to be a long war!* Americans would ground a vehicle that didn't have a windshield wiper.

Oh my goodness, I was so thirsty. I started fumbling around and found a canteen. My hands were still bound behind my back, so I have no idea how I got it to my mouth. But I drank the whole thing. The water was warm, and it had a little taste of tea to it. I wouldn't have cared if the water was spoiled. I hadn't had a drop of liquid all day.

Later that night, a guy came in, looking for his canteen, and of course it was his I had drank up. Boy was he mad. He started screaming and hollering and swearing, even though all he had to do was walk a few steps and fill it up.

In training, we were told the earlier you try to escape, the better. I decided it was now or never. I worked at the ropes binding my wrists and elbows. I loosened them just enough to get my hands on the latch inside the back door.

The tailgate flopped down—which of course made a loud "clunk." I jumped out and started to run, but soldiers appeared from everywhere. They caught me right away and threw me back into the truck, and posted a guard for the rest of the night.

It had been an eventful day. I tried with little success to quiet my racing mind and find a comfortable position for my battered body. I had been shot down, broken my back, been captured, stripped, beaten, dragged behind a jeep, and paraded at gunpoint almost naked through villages, where I was gawked at and derided.

It was day one as a prisoner of war in North Vietnam. I had 2,794 days to go.

The BIG MOVE to SPENCER

I've always had the ability to crunch numbers quickly in my head. As a child, I think this sometimes led me to worry as much about our farm's finances as my parents did.

In 1946, when I was 10 years old, we moved two townships west to a farm in Spencer Township. It had a huge bank barn and I think that's one of the things that attracted Dad the most. You could drive a tractor and wagon into it, unload, make a 180-degree turn, and drive out. The farm was set up for dairy cows, so that's what Dad bought.

Working alongside Dad so often, I always sensed the urgency that came with farm life. So much of your livelihood depends on the weather and the farmer's ability to hustle and get work done when the conditions are right. Dad worked all day at the foundry, gobbled his dinner when he got home, and worked on the farm all evening. Farming can be a beautiful way of life, but it can also be very stressful.

I knew Dad sold the farm in Lafayette for $16,000 and paid the same price for the new farm in Spencer. This made me so happy. In my 10-year-old mind, it meant we would have no debt and Dad's life would be a little easier. When I mentioned this to him, he pointed out that he still had to buy dairy cows and machinery. He would have to borrow money from the bank and work to repay it.

Because he was still working at the foundry in Akron, Dad hired Mom's youngest brother, Bob, to help on the farm. He was 16 years old and had his driver's license. To a boy with a houseful of sisters, he became like a brother. We enjoyed quite a few adventures together.

Spencer Farm

Dad bought an old steel-wheel, two-cylinder, general-purpose John Deere tractor. Uncle Bob was working with it one day in the field and came in to refuel. It had an old-fashioned hand clutch and Bob could not get the tractor out of gear. He was headed for the farm yard in third gear, running wide-open—which for this old machine wasn't much faster than I could run. Bob was headed straight at the barn and he was in a panic.

"I can't stop! I can't stop!" he yelled.

All he could do was turn the steering wheel and go around in circles in the backyard. I practically fell on the ground laughing. He eventually did get the thing out of gear.

Later, Uncle Bob saved my life when I was foolishly playing in floodwaters by the road. There was a long, low-lying area that always filled with deep water after a hard rain. I didn't know how to swim and one day I got in farther than I should have. I would have drowned if Bob hadn't dived in to save me.

He was old enough to know about the birds and bees and I was just old enough to wonder about them. So I rode on the fender of that old John Deere while he was plowing and asked him every question I could think of. If my mother knew everything her brother told me, she would have killed him!

Bob stayed with us all that summer. I remember we'd go into the small village at the center of the township—also called Spencer—where there was a store just a block away from the school. It had a 12-gauge Winchester pump shotgun on display for $50. Evidently Bob was inclined to hunting. Dad paid him $50 per month, plus his room and board. And at the end of the summer, Uncle Bob bought that gun. Dad, who wasn't a hunter, was incredulous.

"I can't believe you spent $50 for a shotgun," Dad said. "You worked a whole month for a shotgun!"

Dad never let him live it down, but to this day, Bob still has that shotgun. His sons and his grandsons have won numerous trapshooting events with it. Now a classic, it's probably worth 20 times more than he paid for it, maybe 50 times. Turned out to be a good investment of Bob's $50.

Trying to save money, Dad bought well-worn tractors for the farm and probably not the best dairy cows. He also brought home an old Chevy truck. We didn't have a hammer mill back then to grind feed for the cows, so Bob and I shoveled ear corn into the truck from the farm's corn crib and set off for Medina. We took it to Bowman's feed mill, where they would grind it up, put it in bags, and we'd haul it home.

Uncle Bob always treated me well. Across from Bowman's was a little restaurant.

He'd say, "How about a piece of cherry pie a la mode?"

To me, that slice of pie was well worth the labor of loading and unloading that old truck.

I also had a taste for chocolate milk. During those first years at Spencer, a driver named John Drotloff hauled our milk to Elm Farm Dairy for processing. He knew I loved chocolate milk and would bring me a pint every day when he stopped at our farm. If I wasn't there, he'd just leave it in the milk cooler for me.

About a year after we moved to Spencer, we became acquainted with some of the neighbors. One of them, Mr. Aukerman, who lived a mile down the road, told us his grandson was coming out from Cleveland. Mom took me down to their place so the two of us boys could play while she visited with Mrs. Aukerman. I didn't know what we were going to do, but I did know it was the first chance I ever had to get away from work and have fun.

Aukermans had just gotten a new refrigerator and it arrived in a cardboard container. Their grandson, whose name unfortunately I don't recall, suggested we lay it on its side and camp inside that night. I thought that sounded great.

After some begging on my part, Mom let me go back down to the Aukermans' house that evening after chores. To me, it seemed like a vacation to be able to camp in that refrigerator box and play some more the next day.

Well, the next morning, about half an hour after daylight, we were still lying in the cardboard box when I heard a car pull into the driveway.

"Paul!" my mother's voice called.

I stuck my head out of the box.

"Dad wants you to come home and help him shock oats because it's going to rain," she said.

Grudgingly, I said goodbye to my new friend and climbed into the car. I thought to myself, *man, the only chance I have ever had to get away and it's cut short.* I went home to shock oats, none too happily. Most days, I enjoyed farm work. But I rarely got to enjoy being a kid.

Our farmhouse, built in 1900, had old wood siding. A company from Akron came out peddling asbestos shingle siding. Today, that's hard to believe with what we know about the potential effect of asbestos on human health, but it's true.

They gave Dad a price—somewhere between $800 and $1,000. I thought, *oh, man, that's astronomical!* He'll never be able to afford that. But he did it and it made the house look really good. Of course, he found out later that maybe the asbestos wasn't the best choice. We finally got indoor toilets, as well. I thought we were really uptown then.

We always had a huge garden—as most farmers did, especially those with lots of kids to feed. There were four children in our family and tending the garden was our responsibility. Mom would plant and it was our job to cultivate. It was near the railroad tracks on what seemed like the poorest part of the farm. It was tough ground to hoe.

(L-R) CAROL, RUTH, KAREN, AND ME

One day, Mom told my sister Carol to go pick tomatoes. She ran right into a weed and it made an indentation in the middle of her eye, causing her to lose part of her vision. I don't even know if they took her to the doctor.

I remember I was teaching her to shoot a .22 rifle and she wouldn't hold the gun the right way as she looked through the sights. When I asked her why, she said she couldn't see out of her one eye. I really, really felt bad for her. Carol and I are extremely close and always have been.

We often ate our meals in a combination summer kitchen and garage behind the house. The summer kitchen is where Mom canned everything out of the garden. All winter long, she would send one of us kids down into the cellar to get the vegetables she canned and froze.

We'd travel to Grandma's house in Barberton to pick cherries—a chore I absolutely hated. Everyone else got to pick the low-hanging fruit. I had to climb all the way to the top of the tree—almost 30 feet—and pick the cherries up there. Many years later, I went back and found the farm, but that old cherry tree was long gone.

Christmas was a relatively simple affair. We always had a tree cut from Steele Nursery in nearby Chatham. Most gifts were practical things: pants, shirts, sweaters, gloves or underwear. Sometimes there would be tools: a silage fork or wheelbarrow. We always opened our gifts on Christmas Eve.

My first year at Spencer School was sixth grade and my teacher was Mrs. Bertha Rowe. In the small world of Spencer, she grew up on the farm I bought many years later from a classmate, David Reisinger.

As "the new kid," I was generally accepted by my fellow students—all except for one—Lloyd Gott. He was a pretty big guy. Lloyd confronted me at recess I suppose to assert his role as the playground champion when it came to using his large fists.

"Hey, new guy. You wanna fight?" he asked.

"No," I replied. "I didn't come here to fight. What do you want to fight for? We don't have an argument."

"Well, we just ought to fight," he said.

Anyway, I talked him out of it and later we became friends.

There was another guy in my class named Joe Giar. He was the smartest kid and the most talented in sports. Just a great guy. I didn't follow college or professional sports and I didn't listen to the radio very much. But Joe had some sports heroes back then—football star Johnny Lujack and others. He admired them so much he'd write their names at the top of the school papers he handed in. Since I admired Joe, I did the same thing, even though I didn't really know who the athletes were.

Eventually, Mrs. Rowe looked at us and said, "Is this really necessary?" So I stopped and I think Joe did, too.

Math, science and shop class all came naturally for me—but I didn't like English. I stared out the window and wished I was farming instead.

There were 21 kids in our seventh-grade class. We were laid out in five rows, four desks deep, with one left over. I sat in the middle row, with my friend Dave Reisinger right behind me.

One day, I had a terrible case of gas. I held it and held it and held it and held it, until I couldn't hold it any longer. It came out in a loud burst everyone could hear. The entire class turned around to look at me.

And I turned around and looked at Dave! So did everyone else!

Later, he said to me, "Paul, I'll kill you! That was the dirtiest trick!"

It was a dirty trick, I have to admit, but it was one of the few times I ever thought fast enough to pull a good joke. Dave and I still talk about it.

When our family lived in Lafayette, I never felt as if we were poorer than other families because most everyone we knew seemed to be in the same boat. That changed a little when we moved to Spencer. Joe, whose dad was a contractor in the nearby city of Elyria, had Levi jeans, while I had to wear Lee jeans. Every Thursday was sloppy joe day on the school lunch menu. I loved sloppy joes, but they cost 25 cents, which I didn't have. Joe always had money and loaned me the quarter.

That's when I realized there were financial differences between our family and some of my classmates. Yet, there was no one in our class who thought he or she was better than anyone else. Perhaps that's one of the reasons we remain such a close-knit group.

Though our family lived hand-to-mouth, we never lacked for anything to eat. As far as clothing, I had two pairs of jeans—one for work and one for school. Whichever pair was clean was the pair I wore to church. It was the same for shoes—one pair of work shoes and one pair of dress shoes. Up until then, I guess I thought everyone's wardrobe was like that.

Because of my parents' strict religious beliefs, I wasn't allowed to go to dances. I wasn't allowed to go to movies. I couldn't do a lot of things. But nobody ever brought it up and teased me. My classmates were so considerate.

At school alumni banquets today, our graduating class is always the most well-represented. Without exception. In addition to the school reunions, we still gather for class parties at one another's homes.

I've been very blessed by having classmates like that. My class in pilot training was Class 60-B. It had so many good people in it. Former instructors who attend our reunions say it was the best class they ever taught. It had nothing to do with me. I've just been lucky to be a part of such good groups in school and in military training.

When I was in seventh grade and old enough to drive our Farmall H and the wagon, Dad hired some high school kids to be our farm representatives for threshing so Mom didn't have to go. When the crew came to our place to thresh, he hired even more to help bag up the wheat. Two of the kids I remember well. They were Frank Varney and Jack Allison—two of our school's basketball stars who had helped Spencer win the county championship. We had no football team, so basketball meant everything. To me, it was a wonder to see these two school heroes working at our farm.

We had a neighbor down the road and across the tracks whose name was Roy Brouse. He was another one of my heroes the whole time I was growing up. He never had children and seemed to love me more than my own parents did. When he was boiling sap during maple syrup season, Roy paid me to come down and stoke the fire in the evaporator while he milked his cows.

Every night he'd have a huge bowl of ice cream. Every night! Later on he died of a heart attack, so that probably didn't do his health any favors. He would buy the latest Mercury car every year. He had two little Ford tractors and every year he'd trade the older one in on a new one. I thought for a small farm, this was the way to go. To me, he was a real cool guy.

Like many farm kids, I was involved in 4-H. The first animals I raised and showed at the Medina County Fair were a pair of male lambs. When I didn't win anything, another neighbor offered to trade one of his females for one of my males so that I could start my own herd. I thought that was great. He came over to the farm and made the swap while I was at school—leaving me the scrawniest sheep you ever saw. To top it off, she wouldn't breed. What a way to treat a kid! Not everyone was as nice as Roy.

After my experience with sheep, I switched to raising steers. The 4-H committee traveled down to Wooster to buy 50 steers or however many were needed. They'd put numbered stickers on their hind ends and you drew a number out of a hat to get your steer. You weren't allowed to go buy your own animal, like 4-H'ers do today.

Roy had a hired man named Bruce. He was the son of Vivah Walters who owned the store in Spencer. He worked for Roy every summer and that's where Bruce kept his steers. Well, Roy, God love him, was such a kind person. He chose the rations, did all the feeding—and turned out the best steers in 4-H every year! So I never did have a grand champion. I had reserve champion several times, but I never could beat him. However, I did win showmanship more than once. After all, Roy could help Bruce with everything except showing the animal in the ring.

HERE I AM WITH MY 4-H SHOW STEER.

I tried everything to beat Roy's steers. I scraped together enough money to buy something called a barley cooker, which the agriculture department at Ohio State was said to use in feeding all its show cattle. My dad was dubious.

"Why would you spend your money on that?" he asked. "Why would they like to eat that more than dry food?"

I had no idea. But, I cooked up barley, mixed it with molasses, fed the concoction to my steers, and sat back, waiting to see them grow like magic. In the end, I think my dad was right.

Like any farm, we had sick animals now and then. It wasn't cheap to call a veterinarian, but when we did, we called Dr. Barth from neighboring Litchfield Township. He'd drive up in a big old Ford car, the trunk filled with medicines and vet equipment. Dr. Barth made a lasting impression on me, making me think that someday I'd like to be a veterinarian, too.

When he visited the sick animal's pen, the first thing he'd look at was the manure. When I asked why, he told me he could learn more from that than almost anything else. Usually he'd check the animal's temperature, administer a shot, and be on his way.

My parents began attending a small Assembly of God church in Litchfield, with a congregation of 50-70 people. It was very legalistic, which I don't appreciate now and didn't then. Girls were supposed to show the least amount of skin possible—to the point I can't remember my sisters ever being allowed to go swimming or wear shorts in the summertime. We couldn't go to dances, to the movies, or anything like that. At least the church service was in English, which to us kids was a major improvement over the German-language church we had attended up until then in Akron.

I had the opportunity to attend church camp one summer down in Big Prairie, Ohio. With no farm chores to do, that was the best two weeks of my young life.

In the center of the camp was a little gazebo, where campers could buy a soda or Popsicle for a nickel each. My parents gave me $1 for spending money—and I spent it all the first week! I wrote a letter home, saying: "Please send more money!" By the time Mom and Dad got the letter, it was almost time for camp to be over. So I spent that second week watching all my fellow campers enjoy their treats, while I had none. It sure taught me one thing: How to budget my money!

It was at this camp that I gave my heart to the Lord. One night at evening service, they asked anyone who wanted to dedicate his or her heart to the Lord to come forward and I did. I've not put him as first priority sometimes in my life, but he's been my Lord and Savior ever since.

My friend Carol Buckingham and her mom and dad went to the Litchfield church, too. I was 14 by then and she was 12. They lived in the nearby city of Brunswick at the time. Carol could play the piano and the accordion very well. I remember I thought she was pretty cool, so I would offer to carry her accordion from the church out to their car.

Much later in life, Carol and I would reconnect after she saw a story about me in a local newspaper. She told me she still had the diary she kept in those days. Following our meeting at church, Carol wrote in her journal, "I really like him!" When I was a little bit older and began driving our farm's truck, Carol said when she saw me drive by, she always hoped I would pull that big red truck into the driveway and stop to visit.

After two years of milking cows at Spencer, Dad had a heart attack and sold the dairy. A neighbor convinced him to get into the sheep business. A man from the nearby town of Nova came to the farm to shear them, which I loved to watch. I've always been curious and wanted to see if I could learn how to do it.

He let me give it a try and I did pretty well. In fact, when his son suffered an accident, the man asked if I would fill in. I was 14 years old by then. Remarkably, my dad let me go around with him to different farms and help shear sheep.

The shears themselves were connected to a central motor via cables, so they were very powerful. There was a definite art to being able to work around the folds in the animal's skin and take off the wool without cutting the sheep. The hardest part was working around the sheep's hind end, where the wool could be sort of messy, to put it delicately. The work also is very tough on your back because you're bending over so much of the time.

After about two years of raising sheep, Dad decided he didn't care for it anymore and I didn't, either. They were susceptible to many diseases, demanding a farmer who really knew what he was doing. Dad knew cattle much better, so he elected to go into steers.

Instead of traveling down south to buy feeder cattle, Dad always preferred to go west. He'd buy the cattle and arrange to have them shipped home by train. We had a '51 two-door Mercury. It was blue and gray, and boy, did that thing run.

"Paul," Dad would say, "we're going out to the Kansas City stockyards and we're going to buy us a train car load of cattle."

I always loved to go with him. We'd get up early—maybe 2 or 3 a.m.—and get to Kansas City before dark. And that was on two-lane roads. We used to kid one other that the only car that ever passed us was a DeSoto. I suppose it was only a coincidence. After the Mercury, we had a couple of Oldsmobiles. I liked riding across Missouri. The roads were good and the scenery interesting enough to keep you from falling asleep.

One year, Dad had met this cattleman named Mr. McDonald, who was from Pagosa Springs, Colorado, which is now all ski resorts. He leased a lot of federal lands. They became friends and wrote back and forth about when the cattle would be ready to ship. When the time was right, we drove out to Kansas City to meet him.

We arrived and began looking for a hotel in downtown Kansas City. While we were driving around, Dad spotted Mr. McDonald walking into a bar. What are the odds of that? We parked the car and followed him inside.

MY DAD AND ME WITH OUR NEW COLT.

Mr. McDonald decided he was going to wine and dine us—mostly dine us. We went to a really fancy restaurant—well, fancy to me. I had never had lobster, in part because I knew Dad could never afford to buy it. Probably back then it was a whole $5 or $8. Since it was on Mr. McDonald's tab, I ordered lobster—and I got sick. It was so rich.

The more I ate, the worse I felt. I almost wanted to go throw up, but I was embarrassed because I didn't want to insult Mr. McDonald. Finally, I leaned over to my father.

"Dad, can you eat this?" I asked.

He traded plates with me and I was able to finish his dinner. It was a terrible experience, yet later in life, I learned to love lobster.

Another year, Dad bought cattle in Kansas, stopping to visit the family of Brother Steinberg, the writer who liked to watch my dad load manure at the Lafayette farm. On that trip, Dad also bought a cutting horse named Flossie. They built a special pen to separate her from the cattle at the end of the railroad car for the trip to Ohio. I was so happy to get a horse.

Flossie had a colt in her and it was a Palomino. As the colt got to be full grown, I told Dad the colt ought to be broken. He disagreed, saying you don't want to break a horse too young.

Finally, in 1953 when I graduated from high school, Dad decided it was time. Well, the first time I got on that horse, it bucked and threw me off. I landed and I broke two bones in my wrist. It hurt like sin. Mom drove me to the hospital in the nearby town of Lodi, where they put me out while the doctor set it.

The next day, the doctor called, saying he wanted to see me again—but at his office in Spencer, not at the hospital. This story is hard to believe, but it's the gospel truth.

Mom sat in the waiting room as the doctor ushered me into the back. He said he had the feeling he had not set the broken bones correctly and wanted to make sure. The doctor took off the cast, put my wrist over the edge of the table, and pushed down on it hard, popping the bones into place.

I screamed in agony and Mom came running into the room. It's the only time in my life I can remember her really getting angry with someone on my behalf. I thought, *well, I guess Mom does love me, even if she would never say it out loud.*

My wrist did heal, but I disliked that doctor ever after. I spent the whole summer working on the farm with only one hand. Of course, as a typical kid, it wasn't the first or the last time I met with bodily injury.

Dad had bought a Farmall H and a couple of years later, a Farmall M. Those were pretty good-size tractors in those days. He got a set of two-row cultivators for each—back then we planted at 42-inch rows. In addition to our place, Dad rented land a couple miles away. All told, he was probably farming about 250 acres, which was a lot for that time period.

He and I each drove a tractor to the rented farms to cultivate corn. We didn't use spray back then, so we cultivated until the corn got so tall that we'd start to knock it down when we drove over top of it with the tractor. Dad and I were a team. We'd cultivate in the morning while the dew was on, then we'd fly home on the tractors to cut hay. We'd take the cultivators off, put the sickle bar mower on one tractor and a hay rake on the other. Usually I'd mow and Dad would rake.

We were the second farm in the county to get a new International 50-T twine-tie automatic baler. Man, oh man, was that something. Before that, we were making it the hard way—loose. It was dusty work throwing that loose hay up into the mows.

The baler had a Continental engine, which was hard to start. I remember we were just opening up a field back by the woods. I was driving the tractor and came up to a big wad of hay that plugged the baler. We shut it down, cleared out the blockage, and then went to restart it using the hand-crank starter.

My back was right up against a fence. I was trying to start that thing when the engine kicked and the hand crank came around and hit me in the head. It was hard enough to knock me over backwards, but I don't think I lost consciousness. Dad was right there. He picked me up and asked if I was OK. I shook my head said yeah. It sure hurt. I was seeing stars.

Another time, a friend from church, Milton Johnson, promised to teach me how to make money raising rabbits. I told him I was all for making money—I hadn't made any yet!

We built rabbit hutches at our farm, then Milton took me over to his house in his Model B Ford to get the rabbits.

CHAPTER 6

We were heading down a dirt road filled with potholes. There were woods on the right, a field on the left. Milton wasn't speeding—I'm guessing he was going only 35 or 40 mph. He wasn't cutting up or doing anything he shouldn't have been, but he swerved to miss a pothole and over-corrected. We ended up in the ditch upside down—and that's the last thing I remember. I was knocked unconscious. The car caught fire and I have no recollection of getting out. Milton told me later he pushed me through the open window. The next thing I knew, I was standing outside watching the car burn.

When I finally got home, my mom said that was enough of making money with rabbits!

EATING SNAKE

After a short, fitful night locked in the back of the truck, the North Vietnamese pulled me out and moved me to a cave. In those cramped quarters, my body had stiffened overnight and my broken back felt like a knife had been jabbed into my spine. I also had a gash on my head that was of great interest to my captors.

The night before I got shot down, some of us had been drinking in our makeshift officers club in one of the hooches at Ubon Royal Thai Air Base. Let's just say that most of us weren't feeling any pain—at least for the moment.

We were throwing darts in the O Club—which was about the only recreation we had on that base. Cass, my flight commander, was big, blustery—and this night, a inebriated. Not surprisingly, he found himself in the middle of an argument over who knows what. When you've got a bunch of fiercely competitive fighter pilots drinking and battling it out over a game of darts, anything could happen. And it did.

Cass and some of the other guys were riding one another about who could hit the target and who couldn't. In his characteristic braggadocio style, Cass said, "I bet I could throw Kari and hit the bull's eye!"

In those days, I weighed about 173 pounds—a little too much on my 5-foot, 9-inch frame—but Cass was as strong as an ox. In a blink, he grabbed hold of me, picked me up and threw me head-first at the board like a human dart!

Unbeknownst to any of us, there was a spike sticking out of the wall to the right of the dart board. It was like a big nail, about four inches long. Why it was there, I don't know. My head collided with the head of the nail and put a long gash in my scalp. I hit the floor, bleeding like a stuck pig.

Cass felt terrible. He picked me up as easily as you'd pick up a baby and carried me to the flight surgeon.

The whole way there, Cass repeated, "I'm sorry! I'm sorry! I'm sorry!"

"I am, too!" I said.

The flight surgeon asked what happened.

"I screwed up!" was all Cass said. "Just fix him up. He's got to fly tomorrow!"

The flight surgeon said, "Cass Bierman, you are crazy."

And that was the truth. Cass certainly was a wild and crazy guy.

So for the first few days after I was captured, my North Vietnamese keepers would point to the gash in my head and make gun sounds like, "pow-pow-pow." They wanted to know if one of them had grazed me with a bullet. It clearly would be a source of pride for them to know a North Vietnamese's shot had hit an American in the head. I could only shake my poor head and say, "No, no."

Thankfully, the morning march on my second day as a POW only lasted about 30 minutes. They took me from the camp to a cave. It was as if the commander didn't want me inside the camp, lest I somehow learn their secrets and escape.

The cave overlooked a small pond, maybe 120 feet across. In the center was a walled well, reached by a walkway, like a long pier. Evidently, this was where people who lived in the surrounding area came to get their water.

I still hadn't eaten, but my captors did give me a drink of water. As I stood looking at the pond, wondering what would happen next, I realized my tongue hurt. My hands were tied behind my back, so I ran my tongue around the inside of my mouth to try to figure out what was wrong. I discovered my tongue had almost been severed, about an inch from the tip. The end of my tongue literally was flopping around inside my mouth, barely attached. In addition to breaking my back when I ejected from my plane, apparently the force of the explosion had also caused me to bite down on my tongue. I remember wondering if it would ever be able to heal.

The remarkable thing was the fact I hadn't noticed it until that moment. It gives you an idea of how your senses temporarily rewire themselves when your body is focused 100 percent on survival. I was so preoccupied with trying to live from one minute to the next I didn't even notice my tongue was almost bitten off.

Two uniformed North Vietnamese soldiers appeared at the walkway to the well and I could see they had something in their hands. It was my SARAH beacon. With their guns slung back over their shoulders, they were looking at it and talking intently. In the distance, I could see fighter jets. They were no more than a mile-and-a-half away. I was convinced my back-seater, Curt, was dead because I had seen what looked like his empty parachute floating down after we ejected. But I knew as long as that beacon was sending out its signal, rescue crews would be trying to find us.

The two North Vietnamese GIs fiddled with the beacon, placed it near the walled well, then disappeared into the jungle. In a few minutes they'd return, play with the beacon some more, and put it back down. It was as if they were checking on it, making sure it was sending out its signal. The beacon was green and about the size of a Lean Cuisine frozen dinner. It didn't emit any light or sound, only a silent radio signal.

Instantly, I knew what those dirty rats on the pier were up to. They intended to sucker in U.S. planes or helicopters using the signal from the survivor beacon. As soon as the aircraft were in range, they'd open fire on them. All through my restless night in the back of the half-track, I had heard trucks traveling in and out of the camp, busily hauling in anti-aircraft artillery.

Several days earlier, when we had escorted the two RF-101s on the reconnaissance mission over this very area, the intelligence said there was no antiaircraft artillery. Well, the North Vietnamese weren't dumb. They began to bring it in. I'm guessing my plane was hit with something relatively small, a 37 mm or 50 mm antiaircraft gun. Now, they were bringing in more powerful weapons and hoping to draw U.S. fighters and rescue craft into their trap.

I said to myself, *I don't know how I'm going to do it, but somehow, I've got to get that beacon.*

In the time since I had been shot down, I had not gone to the restroom—I hadn't needed to and I still didn't have to go. Nevertheless, I hollered to the uniformed soldiers by the pond and one of them came up the hill to see what I wanted.

I motioned to him that I had to use the restroom. He went down to confer with his commander and returned minutes later. The GI motioned for me to follow him.

The North Vietnamese are a very proud people. They did not like to lose face in any way. From their perspective, me going to the bathroom in their presence would have been more embarrassing for them than for me.

They escorted me down the hill to a little thicket not far from the pier that led to the well. It was like a patch of saplings. The few leaves the trees had were up high. There wasn't much privacy, but it must have been just enough cover that they wouldn't feel insulted by having to watch the American use the bathroom. That said, they weren't so gracious as to offer me toilet paper.

My elbows remained tied together, but they removed the rope from around my wrists so that I could somewhat move my hands. I went behind the brush and squatted down, keeping one eye on the guards, who were about 120 feet away. The beacon was perhaps 60 feet away on the pier.

As soon as the GIs were looking the other way, I made a mad dash for the beacon. I still didn't know what I was going to do when I got there. What I did know was it would be a footrace. At the first sound of me making a break from behind the brush, the North Vietnamese whirled around and sprinted after me.

Again, in these moments, you are operating more on instinct than on logic. All I knew was I had to put that beacon out of commission and keep them from luring in our aircraft and blowing them out of the sky.

I thought if I could jump on the beacon, maybe I could smash it. Not stopping to realize, of course, that it was made out of metal and designed not to be easily smashed. I came down on it full force with my right knee. It's a wonder I didn't crush my kneecap. It seemed to do no harm to the beacon.

The North Vietnamese soldiers were at a full run and getting closer. With my arms still tied behind my back at the elbows, I turned around, grabbed the beacon with my hands, and hit it as hard as I could against the top of the walled well, trying to smash it. As the guards reached me, I dropped it into the well, where it sank to the bottom.

The GIs were crazed with anger. I'm sure they thought their commander would kill them for allowing this to happen. They came absolutely unhinged. One of them took his rifle and smashed the butt into the side of my head—shattering my left eardrum just as the right one had been broken the day before. I don't know if they are trained to go for the eardrums or if it just happened that way, but on top of being excruciatingly painful, now I could hardly hear at all.

They took me back up the hill and threw me into the cave, tying my arms so tight, I thought I was going to lose all feeling in my hands. As the sun rose higher in the sky, the sound of the American aircraft in the distance faded away. I assumed they must have stopped looking for Curt and me.

As I discovered later, I was wrong. In fact, Curt had been rescued that day, having survived the ejection from our plane and eluded captors overnight in the jungle.

It never entered my mind that by destroying the beacon, I was eliminating virtually any chance I had of being located by rescuers. All I thought about was preventing those aircraft from flying into a trap and giving them a chance to find Curt, if he was alive. My only concern was to protect them. For these actions at the well, I was later awarded one of my two Silver Stars.

Air Force Gen. Robbie Risner, a fellow POW and a good, good man, also nominated me for the Medal of Honor, the nation's highest military award. It was denied, he told me, only because Congress decided it had already given out as many medals as it intended to award during that particular legislative session. Robbie had been too upset to tell me until 10 years after our release.

I didn't do what I did that day to earn a medal. My only intent in destroying the beacon was to protect Curt and the aircraft crews looking for him. It would have been one thing if the award nomination had been rejected for good reason. But to have it denied without a fair hearing, after all I had suffered, I'd be lying if I said it didn't hurt me as much as it did Robbie.

After I dropped the beacon in the well, they kept me in the cave in the side of the hill, where I would spend the next three nights. From my survival training, I knew my best opportunities for escape probably had passed. The realization began to settle over me that I was going to be in this situation for the long haul. And if I did somehow manage to escape, I figured my chances of being bitten by a king cobra in the jungle were at least as good as being shot!

One of the guards came up to the cave entrance. Speaking in gestures, he put his hands together and laid them alongside his face, as if to indicate "sleep." I don't think it was a threat of death or violence. I took it to mean I was headed to prison, where I would have nothing to do but sleep.

He marched me into the dense foliage of the jungle. To my surprise, there was a man standing there with my flight suit and helmet. Oh, gosh, I thought. What's this? They untied my arms and told me to put on my gear. As I did, a film crew arrived carrying a pair of movie cameras—the kind with big old-fashioned reels on top. They were there to re-enact my capture for a propaganda film.

Along with the three or four people in the camera crew, there were several guerillas—grisly looking old men with beards and ancient rifles. They set up a scene along a little pathway and instructed me to walk with my hands held up in surrender. They made me do at least a couple of takes.

I thought to myself, *someone in America is going to see this eventually*. To show them the scene was fake, while my hands were raised above my head, I made a "V for victory" sign with one hand and gave the North Vietnamese my middle finger with the other! I did this in every propaganda film thereafter and my captors never caught on. I know in my heart that film must still exist in some forgotten archive. I would dearly love to have that picture of me in my flight suit giving the enemy the one-fingered salute more than any other photograph from the war.

After the filmmakers were satisfied, they took my flight suit away and gave me a pair of pajamas. It was the first time I had anything to wear besides the briefs that had been shredded when I was dragged behind the jeep.

I hadn't eaten since before I had been shot down. And by the second day in the cave, I was getting hungry. I kept running my nearly severed tongue around my mouth, wondering if I would even be able to eat. My back and my neck were in constant pain.

Late that afternoon, I saw my guards had used long poles to capture a snake down around the pond. I watched as they skinned it and thought *they eat this stuff?*

In early evening, they came up the hill bearing an enameled tin plate with a metal spoon like you'd get in a Chinese restaurant. On the plate, there was some rice and a thick cross-section of that snake. Before they even got close to me, I could smell the pungent odor of the meat. I thought, *good Lord, I'm not going to eat that thing.*

They gave it to me, along with some water. I gladly ate the rice and warily looked at the snake. The guards were pointing to the meat, as if it was Kobe Beef, indicating they wanted me to taste it. I kept eating the rice and looking at the snake. Finally, I told them I couldn't eat it. They got very angry. They were talking to one another and almost grinding their teeth, as if to say, "we'd love to have that food and instead we sacrificed it for you."

So, I took the spoon and broke off the smallest bite of snake meat I could. It was like a very stringy piece of chicken. I took a sliver about the size of three toothpicks laid side by side. I put it in my mouth. Oh my gosh, it was gamey. I spit it out. But they were happy that I tried it. They didn't harass me anymore. I ate the rest of the rice and handed them back the snake meat on the plate.

As I sat in the cave, my thoughts turned to the possibility of torture. If they forced me to talk, I had a lot of information to spill. I knew every unilateral and multilateral war plan in Europe. From all my training in how to deliver nuclear weapons, I practically knew how to build one myself—I don't know why they ever gave us that level of detail, but they did. And here I was with all that stored in my head.

I realized if I ever was to be tortured to the point I could no longer take it, that would be a lot of valuable intelligence for the enemy to pick up. I decided I had to try to change the story of my life and rehearse it over and over until I believed it myself.

I would tell them my parents were alive and that I was married with two children. But when the questions turned to military matters, that's where the truth would end and the fiction would begin.

Drawing on my agricultural background, I decided I would tell them I had been stationed at Hereford Air Force Base, Angus Air Force Base, Shorthorn Air Force Base—all names of different breeds of cattle—and invented locations for them back in the States. For my commanding officers, I used the names of farm tractors. I would tell interrogators I was under Colonels J.I. Case, John Deere, Allis Chalmers, Massey Harris and all the rest. I chose things I could remember under duress, yet would sound plausible to my captors.

Of course, this went completely against what we were taught in survival training. Our instructors warned us that an interrogator will write down everything you

CHAPTER 7

CAPTURED

say. If you're inventing stories under pressure, there will be inconsistencies and the enemy eventually will use those to trip you up. At Ramstein Air Base, we met with Jim Low, a former POW in the Korean War, who warned us, *they know more about you than you think they do.*

Still, just in case, I created these fictional people and places. Sitting in that cave, I went over and over them for two days until I was confident I had them down pat.

My captors had been trying to commandeer a jeep to take me to Hanoi. The third night in the cave, I heard one drive in. With my arms tied behind me, as always, they blindfolded me for what would be the first of many times, and put me in the jeep.

Son La, where I was shot down, was about 100 miles west of Hanoi. We drove all night, into the next morning. The roads were awful. There was a pothole every six feet. Each bounce was a painful jolt to my injured back.

Gradually, we came out of the mountains into a delta. Stopping for a few minutes, the guards gave me a bottle of pop, but nothing to eat. I got so I could see little bit out from under my blindfold. It was raining and the roads were slippery. I saw a six-by-six truck, apparently hauling supplies, hanging off a cliff. Guys were screaming, trying to pull it to safety. I sometimes dozed off for 10 minutes at a time. When I began to hear the sounds of car horns and traffic, I knew we were in Hanoi.

We arrived at Hoa Loa Prison, which had been built by the French during the colonial era. I felt a familiar anxiety rise in my chest. I still couldn't shake the memory of the *Time* story about the pilot who had been beheaded. Again, I thought to myself, *maybe deep inside these walls, out of the sight of the world, is where it was going to happen at last.* Back home, my family had been informed I was Missing in Action. I expected I would never see them again.

The jeep stopped just short of the prison entrance. As I sat there, my mind racing, unable to see, a familiar sound somehow made its way into my broken ear drums. It was whistling. Someone inside the prison walls was whistling "Yankee Doodle."

I said to myself, *there's another American here!*

In my heart, for the first time in days, I felt a spark of hope.

High School Years

My father Tony was the hardest-working man I've ever known. He would milk the cows in the morning before work. After pulling an eight-hour shift at the foundry in Akron—driving an hour each way—he came home, milked again, then labored in the fields until dark. Dad was working himself to death.

The long hours and the stress of farming caught up with him in 1947 when he had a slight heart attack at age 42. In keeping with my parents' frugality, he didn't go to the hospital that I remember. One day I found out he was selling off the dairy cows. When I asked Mom why, she told me he'd had a heart attack and needed to cut back.

That monthly dairy check was a major part of our family's income and something had to take its place. So, we went into the egg business. We put 1,000 laying hens in the barn and stored the eggs in our cellar, which had a dirt floor and was cool and damp. Buyers from Wooster drove up to get the eggs. And that's what we lived on to buy our clothes and groceries. We traded a milk check for a weekly egg check.

Even as a young kid, I always knew how much things cost because Dad would tell me. He'd say how much we got for eggs that week, whether the prices were up or down, and how much we paid for feed.

Mom raised the baby chicks, but it was my job to water and feed them, morning, noon and night. I also collected the eggs every day—even on Sunday after church, otherwise the chickens might start to break them. Let me just say I liked to eat chicken, but I despised taking care of them!

For a short time, Dad was able to farm full-time, leaving his job in the foundry. In the early 1950s, he went into beef cattle and bought more than 100 steers. He borrowed all the money, which is customary, and paid it back when he sold the cattle at market. Well, beef prices fell and he lost quite a bit of money. So, it was back to the factory—this time Kasper Foundry in Elyria. Dad worked nine-hour days and I did as much of the farming as I could after school and in the summer. But, I couldn't bale hay and load it at the same time. When Dad got home from work, we'd bale 200, 300, 400 bales and unload them in the barn.

My father was a gifted master moldsman. At Kasper, he built molds that turned out cast-iron parts for huge printing presses. It would take him two days to make a mold from sand and fire-treat it before it was ready to receive the molten metal. I didn't know very much about it until years later when Dad got me a summer job there. I saw he was one of the two best moldsmen in the foundry and I was very impressed. In Hungary, Dad entered the workforce after sixth grade as an apprentice carpenter. Hard work was all he ever knew.

I've had a bad habit my whole life of eating too fast, which isn't good for your body. It's a trait I must have gotten from him. Dad would come into the house from work, eat dinner quickly, then look at me and say, "Let's go."

When Dad was growing up in Europe, people of Jewish descent weren't allowed to own land. Most were business entrepreneurs and had to work extremely hard to make up for the prohibition against owning property. They demanded the same from anyone who worked for them.

Dad was a journeyman for a master carpenter. When it was time for lunch, Dad had to clean up the shop and lay out the patterns and tools for the next job so everything would be ready when the carpenter returned from his break. As a result, Dad said he only had five to eight minutes to eat his own lunch. He maintained that habit all through his working life and passed it along to me. Every ounce of my work ethic came from my dad.

We were the second farm in the county to get an automatic twine-tie hay baler. It was an International with a Continental engine. If you shut off that engine when it was hot, it was almost impossible to restart. If we were baling anywhere near the house, we'd just leave it running, sprint into the kitchen for something to eat, and run back outside to bale more hay. That's how we lived.

I was still only a kid and some days I'd had enough of work. If it was raining, I'd try to talk Dad into running an errand in town—dropping off a part to be fixed or picking up a new battery for a tractor. I could usually talk Dad into buying me a bottle of pop along the way. I just wanted to get away from the farm for a while.

Sometimes I was successful in talking him into taking a break, but as often as not, Dad would find work for us to do in the barn if it was too wet to get into the fields. One of those jobs was cleaning out the granary. It was a small room inside the barn, with a walkway down the middle and three or four bins on either side. We stored oats there and when the granary was almost empty, we'd go in and bag up the last bin or two of grain. Dad always liked a neatly swept barn, with no junk or anything else lying around. I grew up to be the same way—another characteristic I inherited.

I learned from a young age how to take a burlap bag and fold back the top so it would hold itself open as we poured in the oats. When the bag was full, I tied it shut with a miller's knot. I got so I could do it pretty fast—and I still can.

Although Dad didn't have a very good school education, he liked math and he'd quiz me while we worked. Subjects like algebra, geometry and trigonometry were a challenge for me, but I became very good at adding, subtracting, multiplying and dividing in my head. I couldn't very well stop and pull out a pencil as I was opening and tying bags of oats, so thanks to Dad's prodding, I learned to do it in my mind. Though I still wished I was in town drinking a bottle of pop!

One summer during my junior or senior year in high school, our relatives in Akron sent my cousin, Donnie Prack, out to the farm "to learn to work like Paulie." I didn't like it when they put the "ie" at the end of my name, but that seemed to be part of the German tradition. Another boy came along as well—Fred Autz, whose father was a friend of Dad's. Fred turned out to be a good worker, but we joked that Donnie spent the summer catching butterflies! He later went on a deep-sea dive off the coast of Mexico and died after suffering from the bends.

Once during that summer, we had the seven-foot sickle-bar mower on the back of an H Farmall. Why I didn't have the shield on the power take-off, I don't know. Fred was riding back there and the spinning shaft caught the leg of his pants. I was driving the tractor and facing forward, so I didn't see it happen, but I heard him say something and reflexively put in the clutch, which disengaged the PTO from the engine. It was a good thing, because if it had made one more revolution, it might have broken Fred's leg.

As it was, I had to cut his pants leg off to free him from the shaft. Later, when Mom was doing laundry, she held up the mangled pants and asked Fred what happened. I don't know what he told her, but I know it wasn't the truth. If he had told her exactly what happened, I would have gotten a beating!

My parents had no real knowledge of the opportunities the world had to offer, so they never expressed any hopes or dreams for their children—save one.

My father loved and respected music. As a child in Hungary, he played violin and accordion in the town square on Saturday nights to earn money. To him, the violin was the most beautiful instrument in the world. Dad wanted each of us to learn an instrument.

There was a musician in our church orchestra who played trumpet, so I decided that's what I wanted to play. But, my parents said they couldn't afford to buy me an instrument. Instead, they gave me an old guitar that was up in the attic and I took lessons for two years—hating every minute of it. My sisters, however, all became excellent musicians and play three or four instruments each. I think Dad was disappointed I didn't follow in their footsteps. He wanted each of his children to be musically inclined, yet he made it clear that as the only boy in the family, farm chores were my priority.

When she got to high school, my older sister Ruth brought home books every night and studied long into the evening. Naturally, I thought that's what you were supposed to do. So when I got to high school, I vividly remember bringing a stack of books home, too.

"What are those?" Dad asked.

"Those are my books," I said.

"Don't they give you time to study in school?" he asked. Dad didn't know the term "study hall," but that's what he meant.

"Yes," I replied.

"Well, you study there," he said. "You've got work to do when you come home."

I never brought another book home for the next four years, yet I was able to graduate third in my class of 21 students.

A devout, committed Christian, Dad read the Bible every day, but he didn't know enough English to write it. When I asked him why he never learned English, all he said was that he hadn't gotten around to it. If I went with him to the Creston Auction or anywhere else he needed to write a check, I always wrote it out for him.

Our house was the first stop on the school bus route, so I got up about 6 a.m., put on my work jeans and did chores, which took about 45 minutes. Then I'd put my good jeans on for school and catch the bus. After-school chores took an hour or more.

Because I didn't get an allowance, I had to figure out a way to earn money if I wanted a class ring or a school jacket. Usually I would run a trap line, which meant getting up at 4:30 or 5 a.m. to walk the mile or so to Pawnee Creek, where I set my traps. Then I'd hustle home and do my chores before school. I mostly caught muskrats, which I sold to Frank Kostecki, who ran a local trading post. The pelts weren't worth that much, so it took a while to earn the money for the things I wanted, but I did it. I remember I had a pair of hip boots for walking the creek, which I'd wear folded down, the way I saw all the bigger boys wear them. It was the cool thing to do.

My only social life was going to school and to church. We went to church four times per week: Sunday morning, Sunday night, the Tuesday night young people's meeting, and Friday prayer meeting.

I never dated at all in high school. Our parents forbade us to go to the movies or to dances—though as many teenagers do, I did a little sneaking. Our school had an annual Junior-Senior Banquet. It was held at the Pine Tree Inn in Medina one year and at the Oberlin Inn the next. Afterward, we went to a theater in Cleveland to watch a movie. I had never been to a theater before and was sure God would strike me dead for setting foot in one. But it didn't happen.

Spencer had a boy's basketball team. I remember the first game I attended was in Homerville, where the court was so small, shots would sometimes hit the exposed plumbing that ran across the ceiling. I loved basketball and installed a backboard in the barn where I could shoot during the winter when farm work slacked off. I really enjoyed that.

I was small, but quick. When I got into high school, I told Dad I wanted to play basketball. No way, he said. Practice every night after school? Impossible. There was too much work to do at home, he said. By the time I was a senior, I told him if he didn't let me play, I'd run away. I don't know if I would have followed through on that threat, but Dad said OK. Of course, I spent most of the year sitting on the bench, since most of the other players had five or six years of experience. But the coach did play me now and then and I had a great time.

My parents never went to a single game. They didn't have time for that. It was either church or work. That was their whole life. They attended three events during my 12 years of school: My junior and senior class plays, and graduation.

Our basketball games were on Tuesdays and Fridays. I remember asking our pastor, "Why not have young people's meeting and prayer meeting on Wednesday night? That way there wouldn't be a conflict with basketball games." Well, he wouldn't change it, but guess what? Now the whole world has weekday services on Wednesday nights!

There was a similar attitude toward television. When it first came out, the pastor told members of our church we shouldn't have one. TV was of the devil, he said. I don't know how old I was at the time, but I bet the pastor he'd own two televisions before the day he died. And he did.

I wasn't even allowed to join the Boy Scouts. One of my cousins from Akron was a member. He was athletic and tried out for the Olympics in swimming and diving, though he didn't qualify. Because I loved the outdoors and looked up to him, I asked Mom if I could join the Boy Scouts, too.

"Oh, no," she warned. "Whenever a war breaks out, the boys who were in Scouts are the first ones they come for in the draft."

That's not true, of course. I don't know if she actually believed it or if she simply didn't want to have to drive me to Boy Scout meetings. Either way, it seemed unfair.

Still, for every opportunity my parents denied, I received another. Just like I learned to drive a tractor at an early age, necessity also taught me how to drive a truck when I was 14. I may not have been allowed to do all the things my friends were doing, but I certainly got to do things they were never allowed to do.

In 1950, Dad ordered a red 2 ½-ton, single-axle International stake truck. It arrived at Sommer's—a GM dealership in the village of Lodi, eight miles south of our farm.

We took the car to pick it up. Dad looked at me and asked, "So, which vehicle do you want to drive home? The truck or the car?" Needless to say, I didn't have a driver's license.

Given the choice, naturally I opted for the new truck. We were headed home on state Route 83 north of Lodi when a cat or a rabbit darted across the road. This truck didn't have air brakes, but it did have vacuum-boost brakes, which were a major improvement over what I was used to on the tractor. I slammed on the brakes and lurched so hard, I banged my head on the steering wheel. Dad about rammed into me from behind in the car. I said, "Man, those are good brakes!"

Dad wanted to build a wooden bed on the truck big enough to haul a load of hay or straw three bales across. He had the idea he was going to sell it to the Amish and to the paper mills.

Our preacher, who was a good carpenter and came over to help, laughed and said, "Tony, that's completely illegal! You can't go down the road with a bed that wide!"

We had a supply of oak lumber, which was hard as steel. I remember our poor pastor cutting all those four-by-four posts to length. Dad also ordered a bunch of green oak to make cattle racks. They were so big and heavy we could hardly lift them! No wonder my back is in such bad shape!

He found out the mill up in Sandusky would buy straw to make paper. There was also a paper mill down in Coshocton.

Dad would go around and buy straw from farmers after they combined—either on shares or for cash. I don't know how many fields of straw I mowed, but it was a lot. Then we'd rake it, bale it, and store it in our huge barn. In the winter we'd drive it to the paper mills. It was just a way of making extra money.

Dad hauled hay down to the Amish in Holmes County. I remember thinking their way of life was cool. I wanted to be Amish! It seemed totally different than Spencer, with all these beautiful farms, buggies and neat horses. Every time we unloaded the hay, they'd invite us into the house, where they'd be roasting cashews on a cookie sheet. They'd buy the nuts in 50- or 100-pound bags from a feed company in Wooster.

I drove the truck on a regular basis between the farm and Lodi Equity, the elevator where we had our corn ground into feed. Dad showed me how to get there on the back roads, but I still sweated it when I hit the village limits, afraid I might be spotted by a State Highway Patrol trooper.

It was all I could do to drive that truck. It had no power steering. I was so small I could barely reach the pedals. Even though I had the seat all the way up, I still had to sit on a cushion to see out. Sometimes I drove by looking through the steering wheel! To this day, people still talk about seeing me driving that International truck. A 2 ½-ton truck isn't big now, but back then, it was the biggest truck any farmer had. And Dad let me drive it all over. Nowadays, they'd have thrown the book at him for letting a kid do that. But we didn't think of those things back then. The work needed done and I just did it.

Walter Bowen—who much later would become my father-in-law—operated a road grader for the county. Every time I saw him, the grader was parked by the side of the road. I drove that truck a lot, all over the county. The whole time I was growing up, every time I passed him, I'd see the road grader stopped. I said to myself, *they ought to fire that guy. He never does any work. He's always parked.* I often mentioned it to others.

Years later, his daughter Kathleen Susann and I were married. I went up to him and said, "Mr. Bowen, I have a confession. I told many people you ought to be fired. How come every time I saw you in your road grader, you were parked?"

He looked at me.

Mowing hay at 12 years old.

"I'd see that red truck coming with you behind the wheel and I'd pull over because I was afraid you were going to run into me!" he said.

So, as Paul Harvey would say, now I knew the rest of the story!

When we needed to grind feed, we'd shovel the truck full of ear corn at the farm, shovel it off at the elevator, then load the bags of ground corn back on the truck for the trip home. One thing I fault Dad for was not buying a hoist for the truck that would have made loading and unloading a lot easier. It would have been a good investment, but I guess he figured he had cheap labor in me!

The workers at Lodi Equity felt sorry for me, I suppose, and always helped me load and unload. They didn't even know my name. Instead, they called me "Little Tony," after my dad. They'd say: "He'll never get that done. He'll be here two or three hours. We'd better help Little Tony." And they'd pitch in and help.

Ironically, when I finally did get my driver's license, my parents never would let me borrow the car, saying they couldn't afford the insurance. However, they would let me drive the truck up to Cleveland to pick up a load of fertilizer—although Mom had to go with me. I'm sure they didn't have insurance on me for that big truck. It didn't go down well that I could drive for farm work, but couldn't drive to go on a date or to a basketball game.

One time Mom was riding with me in the International and we came across black ice on the highway. There was an S-turn and I slid off the road. A road sign went right between the dual tires on one of the rear wheels. Mom was sitting there with her crocheting in her lap and I remember it flew all the way up to the roof of the cab.

She said, "I told you to go slow around that corner!"

All the guys up at the fertilizer plant would say, "Here comes Little Tony. Man, would you look at that guy drive that truck!"

There were 60 acres around the fertilizer company with tall orchard grass growing in it. They gave it to my dad to make into hay. How are we going to get all of our equipment up there, I asked? Somehow we did.

My little sister Karen came up to help when she was only 12 or 13 years old. She was driving that old H Farmall and pulling the baler. The guys at the fertilizer plant would point to her and rib one another. They'd say, "Look at that little girl! She knows more than you do! All you know how to do is work here all day and get drunk at night!"

Karen was indeed a tomboy. In fact, when I went into the service, she took all my traps and ran a trap line herself. She was also kind of stubborn. We'd be baling hay—she was driving and I was on the wagon—and I'd tell her to go faster. "I want to go the speed I want to go!" she replied.

Finally, one day I took a little snake that came up in a bale and I threw it at her. We laugh about that to this day. She had it in for me after that!

One fall, we took the truck up to Sandusky to buy lime. The federal government was offering a program where it footed most of the bill. The lime was practically free for the hauling. I don't remember exactly how much Dad got, but it was between 50 and 100 tons. We hauled it home and shoveled it off, making two or three trips per day.

We were on our way home with a full load and both of us were exhausted. Dad was driving and he was so tired. He could hardly keep his eyes open.

"Do you want to drive home?" he asked.

"Sure," I said.

I was about 15 years old and still didn't have my driver's license. But, I pulled out my trusty cushion and waited until we could switch places.

We stopped in a line of cars at an intersection and hopped out of the truck. I ran around to the driver's side and Dad ran around to the passenger side. As I jumped in the truck, I could see two cars behind us was a State Highway Patrol cruiser.

"Dad!" I said. "There's a state patrolman behind us!"

By this time, the traffic had started to move again. The International had a five-speed transmission with a two-speed axle. I was up to second or third gear when Dad and I decided we had better switch back. One of us slid over and one of us slid under as we switched places on the fly!

"Is he still behind us?" I asked.

"No, he turned off," Dad said.

Oh my, was that a close call.

I guess Dad had a lot of confidence in me. I couldn't imagine a child doing that sort of thing now. Maybe it was because Dad started farming with a team of horses and was making the switch to tractors about the time I came along. We both learned about tractors at the same time. I was mechanically inclined enough that I could keep up with him, even though I was younger. To be able to handle that tractor and truck felt awesome. I was proud of that.

Somehow, Dad just seemed to have no fears when it came to me. We had a 50-foot silo at the farm and he'd have me climb to the top through the chute, carrying a rope to thread through a pulley up there. The pulley was 10 feet away from the chute and I had to straddle the 2½ foot slab wall of the silo to reach it!

I must have been 16 or 17 years old and I was scared to death. I've never liked heights. Finally, after doing it twice, I told him I couldn't do it again and we built a walkway along the inside. I can't imagine doing that now—let alone asking a kid to do it!

We had a huge three-compartment chest freezer. We were probably one of the first in the township to have one. When we were still driving to church in Akron every Sunday, we stopped to buy 10 or 12 quarts of ice cream at Lawson's Dairy for 21 cents per quart. Dad loved ice cream. They'd put it on dry ice to get it home.

We always had so much ice cream that we'd invite the neighbors over to share it. Pretty soon they wanted to buy some, too. There were times we'd come home from Akron with 40 quarts of ice cream packed in dry ice.

One time, when Donnie and Fred were visiting, we spent the whole day baling hay. It was probably about 4 p.m. when Dad suggested we take a break and get some ice cream.

Mom wasn't home. She was kind of like the ice cream Gestapo. But we'd been working for hours in the hot sun and ice cream sounded like the perfect thing for our parched throats.

Well, just as we each walked out of the house with a pint of ice cream and a spoon, Mom pulled into the driveway.

"What are you doing?" she demanded. "It's almost supper time!"

We all just stood there, not sure what to say.

"I'll fix you," she said, and marched into the house.

Mom emerged with four more pints of ice cream and parceled them out so each of us now had a full quart.

"You want to eat ice cream just before supper?" she asked. "I'll teach you a lesson. Go ahead! Eat up. Every bite."

She stood over us like a drill sergeant and watched as each of us doggedly ate our way through a quart of ice cream apiece.

God love Dad. He ate his whole quart. I couldn't get mine down, so he even ate the rest of mine!

That was the last time we ever sneaked ice cream.

I know my parents had arguments like most couples, but they were always out of earshot of us kids. Only once did I see them quarrel. And it was over me.

It was time for Mom to drive me to my weekly guitar lesson in Elyria. It was 5 p.m. and I had been working out in the field all day long. I dragged myself to the house to take a quick shower or at least to wash my face. We were running late and Mom stood there, hands on her hips, glaring at me for making her wait. I was about 14 years old.

"Mom," I said. "I really don't want to go today. I am so tired."

"No!" she said. "I've been waiting for you. You're going!"

It was one of the rare times Dad stepped in.

"He's been working like a hired man all day," he said. "Could you give the kid a break?"

She was furious.

"That's it," Mom said. "I've had it with him!"

She turned around, marched into the house, and never treated me the same again.

I enjoyed farming, although it was hard work. I liked to watch things grow—both the cattle and the crops in the field. It was just something I inherited from my dad, I think.

Later, when I was a captain in the Air Force stationed in Germany, my wife Kathy would find me alone in the kitchen at 10 or 11 o'clock at night, doodling on napkins.

I was drawing diagrams of cattle feeding operations, trying to design ones that maximized efficiency. I have always been like that when it came to farming—perpetually trying to think of ways to do things bigger and better.

When I was a kid, nearby Franchester Farms were the first to use a system that instead of baling hay in the field, processed it into pellets for the cattle. That was in the days before silo technology offered better ways of making and storing feed. That's the kind of modern operation I wanted to have at my own farm someday.

Yet, I was always conscious of the fragile bottom line at our family's farm. Dad was always in deep debt from buying the land, animals and equipment he needed to earn a living. I don't know how his stomach took all the stress that comes with owing a lot of money. As a kid, I was always aware of how much everything cost, from buying cattle to paying our fuel bill.

High School Graduation Picture.

I graduated from Spencer High School in 1953 and it was understood that I would take over the entire operation. Dad would keep on working at the foundry and maybe we'd buy another farm.

After my senior year, Dad and I struck a deal. I bought 10 head of beef cattle. If I worked on the farm, Dad wouldn't charge me anything for their feed. The cattle would grow and whatever profit they generated when they were sold at the end of the season would be my wages for the year. It may seem unusual now, but it was the sort of deal a lot of farm families made in those days.

So, one afternoon in August of 1954, I took the cattle to the Cleveland stockyards to sell them. The market was so poor, I received less for the cattle than I had paid for them in the first place. I lost money. I worked all that summer and had nothing to show for it.

I'd always planned to go into farming when I graduated from high school. They didn't really have college preparatory classes in Spencer, anyway. The idea of continuing my education never really entered into my thoughts.

I once overheard Mom and Dad say when they passed away, all four kids would get equal shares of the farm and everything our parents owned. I thought to myself: Something doesn't add up here. More than likely, my sisters would go off to college and get married. I'll still be here on the farm, sweating my butt off for a 25 percent share. Nothing against my sisters, but that return on my investment of labor just didn't make sense to me.

It was 5:30 p.m. by the time I got back from my disappointing trip to the Cleveland stockyards. I knew I'd soon hear the sound of Dad's car coming down the road as he returned home from work at the foundry. What was I going to tell him?

There was a large silver maple tree in the front yard between the house and the road. I sat down to wait for Dad and to contemplate my future. I had lost my shirt on those cattle. Is that what my future was going to be? A lifetime of borrowing and stress and back-breaking labor? A slave to factors that were outside my control? I wasn't sure I could work another whole season not knowing if I'd have anything to show for it.

I lay down on the grass in the shade of the tree, looking up through the leaves into the blue August sky.

What was I going to do?

HANOI PRISON

Still blindfolded, I heard the sound of the jeep starting up again, followed by the creaking of the big doors of Hoa Loa Prison, which opened and shut behind us as we drove inside.

Although I couldn't see my surroundings at the time, I can picture them because in 1995, I had the opportunity to visit Vietnam and retrace my path that day. I have a clear image of the infamous complex that would later be known as the Hanoi Hilton to go with the sounds that are imbedded in my memories.

I could tell we were between two sets of doors in some sort of walled area. It felt as if I was being taken somewhere underground. It brought to mind the Bible story of the imprisonment of the Apostle Paul. I prayed. *God, I don't know if I can take this*. Being a farm boy and a flyer, I had grown accustomed to the freedom of wide-open spaces. I was afraid of what claustrophobia might do to me.

I heard the second set of doors open and I was taken to a small building, known to POWs as the Heartbreak Hotel. It had a central hallway with five rooms down one side and five rooms down the other. It's where new prisoners spent their first days in solitary confinement prior to their initial interrogation. My room at the Heartbreak was the first one on the right.

After removing my blindfold, the North Vietnamese handed me a pair of striped pajamas and shut the cell door. As soon as the footsteps of the guards faded, a voice called out. It was the first American voice I'd heard since being shot down.

"Hey, new guy!" the voice said.

The roster of U.S. POWs was still a short one at this early stage of the Vietnam War. Navy pilot Everett Alvarez was the first to be shot down and captured in August of 1964. Bob Shumaker followed in February of the next year and Hayden Lockhart in March. Now it was the 23rd of June, 1965. I was the 12th man captured. All of us were Air Force or Navy pilots.

"Hey, new guy," the voice called again. "Who are you?"

"Paul Kari," I said.

"Do you know the tap code?"

"What code?" I asked.

"The tap code," the POW repeated.

"No," I said.

"Well, you better learn it," he said and quickly taught me.

When I went through survival training in 1959, no one ever said anything about a tap code. It was surprisingly simple. Take the letter "K" out of the alphabet, leaving 25 letters. Place the letters in five rows of five. When needed, the letter "K" was represented by the letter "C." It forms a grid, which looks like this:

ABCDE

FGHIJ

LMNOP

QRSTU

VWXYZ

As an example, to communicate my first name to a fellow POW in an adjoining cell, I'd tap three times, showing the letter I wanted was in line three of the grid. Then I'd tap five times, indicating the fifth letter in that line, which is "P." The "A" would be a single tap, followed by another single tap, signifying the first letter in the first line. The letter "U" would be four taps followed by five taps. The letter "L" was three taps followed by one tap.

To someone who hasn't experienced being a POW, the tap code may seem slow and cumbersome. But to us, it was our lifeblood. Prisoners were not supposed to talk, so we only dared use our voices when we thought the guards were out of earshot. But since we couldn't see them, it wasn't always easy to tell where the guards were. By tapping through the walls, or on a fellow prisoner's leg when we were jammed into a truck to be moved to a new camp, we were able to share information, relay orders from ranking officers, and offer messages of support to help us keep our chins up during times of torture and deprivation.

It was a good thing I knew the code, because our North Vietnamese captors wasted no time in questioning the new American prisoner. The guards pulled me out of my cell and immediately took me to interrogation.

My questioner was different than the North Vietnamese guards and GIs. He was much more neatly dressed—almost spiffy looking. By his demeanor and the rank on his collar, I could clearly tell he was an officer.

"We need to know your name and your unit," he said, smoking a cigarette. His English was very good.

In accordance with my training, I told him only my name, rank, serial number and date of birth.

"That's all I'm supposed to give you and that's all I'm going to give you," I said.

"Would you like a cigarette?" he asked.

I declined.

"We cannot guarantee your safety," he said. "You are not a prisoner of war. Just as in the Korean Conflict—which we, the Communists, won—war has not been declared."

"You did not win in Korea," I said.

"Yes, we did," he replied.

Our exchange lasted half an hour. It was the first of four interrogations I had that day. When I returned to my cell, my first meal was waiting on my bed.

It was a typical North Vietnamese lunch box, comprised of four small dishes made of porcelain over tin. They stacked neatly one on top of the other and could be carried together, like a pail. Customarily there would be rice in the bottom dish, soup in the next, then meat, then bread.

My lunch consisted of a piece of French bread, a little piece of meat, and some kind of vegetable. It was a lot better than I expected and I ate it all up.

As I finished the meal, I sat on the bed and looked around my cell. Of course, "bed" is a term I use loosely. It was nothing more than a concrete slab, three inches thick. There were two beds in the room. The cell itself was about seven feet wide and nine feet long. It was lit by a single 25-watt light bulb in the ceiling, about 12 feet up. To this day, if I'm ever in a room with a low-watt bulb, I feel like shooting it out. There is something about dim light that is harder on your eyes than total darkness.

A small, barred window high in the wall gave me a little glimpse of sky. There was a peephole in the door for guards to look in and iron stocks for fastening a prisoner's legs.

I could take exactly three paces across my cell—which is what I did, all day long between interrogations. I just walked, back and forth.

VISITING HANOI HILTON IN 1995.

We were issued rubber flip-flops cut from the sidewalls of old tires. There were two slits on either side to accommodate straps made of old inner tubes, which held them on your feet. The flip-flops were curved, just like the side of a tire, and not at all contoured to fit a human foot. They were uncomfortable.

On the floor, there was a little channel that ran through the middle of the room between the bunks and a small hole where it went through the wall into an open sewer. I'm sure the idea was to make it convenient to hose out the cells, but they never washed anything the whole time I was there. Instead, the opening in the wall served as a doorway for rats that crawled into our cells during the night.

For a toilet, we were given a two-gallon tin "honey pot." Usually it was old and rusty. If you were lucky, it had a handle for you to pick up the bucket when it was time to empty it. The cell across from mine had been converted into a shower, where we were taken once or twice a week. If you were a "disobedient" prisoner, they might only let you shower every two weeks. For the most part, you got a shower whenever the guards felt like taking you. They were lazy.

The one humane thing our captors did at the Heartbreak was to give each of us a mosquito net—which I didn't have earlier when I was held in the jungle. However, there was no easy way to hang the net in my cell. The builders had thrown little trowelfuls of concrete against the walls, making them very knobby. It was difficult, but we managed to tie our mosquito nets over our beds by attaching them to these little chunks of concrete protruding from the walls.

For the first couple of days, it was four interrogations per day. POWs referred to them as "quizzes," probably because the word was easier to tap. Often we abbreviated it using just the letter "Q." I was required to sit on a concrete stool in the interrogation room, which was just a little bigger than my cell, about 10- by 12-feet. The uncomfortable seat exacerbated the pain in my back. Meanwhile, my questioner sat behind a desk in a comfortable chair, smoking cigarettes one after the other. Every session, he would tell me he could not guarantee my safety. He continued his effort to indoctrinate me, trying to convince me the North Vietnamese would prevail over America in this conflict.

A few days after I arrived, they brought in a new prisoner and put him in the last cell. Scotty Morgan, another pilot, was opposite him. Scotty kept trying to get the new POW to tell him his name, but he wouldn't respond. It aroused suspicion, because we were on guard against any spies the North Vietnamese might try to plant among us.

We could hear the guards take the new POW to his quizzes in the interrogation room, but still he refused to identify himself to us. This went on for the better part of a week. Scotty tried everything he could to goad him into a response.

"Hey, new guy," Scotty said one day. "What are you? A f-----g jar head?"

"Jar head" was a somewhat derogatory name used for members of the Marine Corps. For some reason, that got his attention. They mystery POW hoisted himself up to the transom above his door.

"Who said that?" he shouted.

Scotty found out who he was and taught him the tap code.

Learning that code, which dated back to 1800s Russian prison camps, was our morale booster. Our cells were made from laid-up block spattered with that rough coating of concrete, but you could hear the taps clearly through the walls. The sound was pretty subdued, but usually you got it.

Eventually, our captors discovered POWs were communicating by tap code, which led to more questioning and torture of prisoners than any of their efforts to learn military intelligence from us. We also were frequently punished for failing to bow, which we were supposed to do every time we saw a North Vietnamese person.

As a consequence of rapping on the concrete walls, we got calluses on our knuckles. An interrogator noticed this on one POW's hands during a quiz and tortured him until he broke down. Our captors were never smart enough to figure it out on their own. They had to torture somebody and get him to tell them what we were doing. After that, we began tapping with the ends of our fingers. It was more difficult, but it made any calluses less noticeable.

We weren't allowed to have anything in our rooms that would make sound. If a guard was bringing you back from interrogation and you saw a nail on the ground, you'd try to pick it up, but you almost never got away with it. If they caught you, they'd torture you and take it away. So you just had to use your hands and tap as best you could. Sometimes you could hear the tapping better if you put a cup against the wall.

At my first interrogation, I was told we'd get three meals a day, but I only ever received two. One came mid-morning, the other mid-afternoon. Finally, during a subsequent quiz, I asked why.

"Well, don't you save part of your French bread for the next morning?" the interrogator asked.

Oh, I said to myself, so that's how it works. About the first week or 10 days we had French bread—and it was pretty good—but after that, they gave us rice instead.

One night, as instructed, I saved a piece of bread—keeping it with me inside my mosquito netting as I slept. I awoke in the middle of the night to find a humongous rat had chewed its way through the netting and was trying to get my piece of bread. I snatched the bread away just in time.

At one of the early interrogations, the questioner asked, "What do you know about Vietnam?"

Well, the week I got shot down, there was an article in one of the news magazines about a rat epidemic in Vietnam.

I replied, "Well, I know you've got a lot of rats up here!"

Apparently, that was the wrong thing to say.

"That's all you Americans know?" he asked. "That we got rats? You calling us rats?"

The interrogations now lasted about an hour. We were always one-on-one with our questioner, who never wore a weapon. The guard brought us in, sat us on the concrete stool, and then left the room—but he was never far away.

Sitting for long periods on that stool put excruciating pressure on the broken discs in my back. The pain became so unbearable, I'd have to stand up. Sometimes I just fell to the floor. Even after I explained about the pain in my back, the interrogator demanded I return to the stool.

"You can't do that!" he admonished. "You're a criminal!" That's what he called me over and over, a criminal.

If I failed to get back on the stool, the interrogator would call the guard in to beat me around. He'd hit me in the back with his gun butt or slap me around until I sat back down on the stool. It was either force myself to sit down or be beaten to death, I thought. I forced myself to return to my seat, as painful as it was.

Such beatings were not unusual, but it was unusual for it to happen in front of the interrogator. Usually he'd tell the guard to take you back to your cell and the guard would work you over in there, out of sight.

By now, they were starting to bend me around pretty good. The guards bound me so tightly in ropes and wrist irons that I'd lose the feeling in my hands. I didn't know how much worse it was going to get, so I decided to make up a story—even though in training they tell us not to—in case I needed to make the torture stop.

My airplane, the F-4, was the latest in fighter technology and my squadron was the first to fly them in Vietnam. I assumed the objective of my interrogation and torture was to learn more about the F-4.

Our captors' torture strategy was to do everything they could do to get you to talk, but without leaving a mark on your body. The North Vietnamese could push you to the point that you would spill your guts and do anything to make it stop, but no one would ever see a scar on your body. The only real marks most POWs had were from the rubber straps guards used to tie us up when they ran out of rope. The rubber had a way of eating into your skin. Usually the torture was more subtle—and more painful.

For example, they once tore my shoulder out of its socket, like you'd tear a chicken wing. But to look at my shoulder today, you would never know. They'd make you sit on one of those concrete stools for hours and sometimes days, until the blood pools in your legs, making them swell up so painfully that all you can do is scream.

Finally, as the torture the North Vietnamese were inflicting on me was becoming greater and greater, I said to the interrogator, "You can either kill me or you can keep me alive, but you never know which one is more advantageous to you."

That got his attention.

Now, I want to be clear: Never once did I divulge what sort of plane I was flying or give up any legitimate information. But I did say, "I think you might be interested in knowing how we're going to shoot your MiGs down."

Oh my gosh, now he was really interested. He let me leave the interrogation session early. I had no idea what would happen next.

The next day, the guard came to get me for my quiz. In addition to the interrogator, there was a man so distinguished looking that he could have been the chief of North Vietnam's Air Force. Clearly, he was very high up in their chain of command. He was clean-shaven and sharp-looking. His uniform was pressed. The interrogator introduced him to me, but I can't recall his name—it may have been a fake name, anyway, as a precaution. He did not speak English, so the interrogator acted as a translator.

"So, you have news for us about MiGs?" he asked.

"Yes," I said. I told him my made-up story. If anyone from the U.S. Air Force had been there, they would have laughed out loud. But to him, I made it sound plausible.

"You know," I told him, "we have very fast aircraft. You no have fast aircraft."

He nodded his head as if to say, yes, that's true—which was amusing to me even then, that he would basically admit their aircraft could not compete with ours.

"Here's what we're going to do," I said. "We're going to knock all of your airplanes out of the sky." I proceeded to give him a 100 percent fictional battle plan of how our fighters would maneuver this way and that to take down a MiG, if they ever were to engage one. I made every word of it up.

"But," I concluded, as if to say everything I had just told him didn't really matter, "you never come up to fight us."

The North Vietnamese Air Force official shook his head and smiled. He had been chain-smoking cigarettes the whole time. He pushed the pack across the table to me. Even though we're told never to take them, I accepted one and took it back to my cell.

That's when the reality of what I'd done began to sink in. I thought, *the North Vietnamese are going to find out what I told them was a lie! Then what? They're going to kill me—or worse*. I was scared.

In the meantime, they eased up on my torture. They had every POW on a different program, which we knew by communicating through the tap code. My interrogations went from four times per day, down to three, then two. By late August, it was once per day. Finally they were coming and getting me only every other day. My food ration was the same. The only difference was they weren't interrogating me as much.

Then, one night, the guards came and yanked me out of my cell. It was about midnight and a total surprise. Normally they only came for us in the daytime.

All along, I had told myself that someday they were going to find out I had lied to them. Asians do not like to lose face. It's their trump card.

They took me out, tied me up with ropes and wrist irons, and proceeded to beat the hell out of me. They hit me with broken fan belts and anything else they could get their hands on. When they were finished, they threw me back in my cell.

All the other POWs knew immediately that something was up, since the timing was so unusual. Soon, I received a message through the tap code, asking me what happened. I told them what I had done and that I assumed I had been found out.

Sometime later, a new POW arrived at the Heartbreak and filled in a few more details. We were always anxious for information on how the war was going. Through the tap code, he told Scotty the U.S. recently had shot down its first three MiGs. It was strange, the new prisoner said, because the MiGs had employed the strangest tactics. They came up to engage us in such a way that they were like sitting ducks. We just wiped them out, the POW said. It was almost laughable.

Well, it didn't take long for us to put together that the MiGs had acted on the fake strategy I had given to the North Vietnamese Air Force official that day in the interrogation room! But, strangely enough, my interrogator never brought it up. He never confronted me for lying.

"You are the worst criminal," he would say. "You are the blackest criminal. You will never see your family again." And the torture resumed.

During this time, the British philosopher Bertrand Russell convened an international war crimes tribunal to investigate the U.S. role in Vietnam. Our interrogators tortured POWs in an attempt to make us write letters or make confessions that Russell could use in his inquiry.

Finally, after the incident of my fictional war strategy, I told the North Vietnamese, "What good is it to torture me? You never know if I'm telling you the truth or not."

While I was stationed at Ramstein Air Base, former Korean POW Jim Low had given us a piece of advice. If you can draw a hard line early on in your interrogations, he said, the enemy likely will respect you and leave you alone. It's the POW who vacillates that they will really hone in on and convince to talk. I took Jim's words to heart.

It was probably due to my lack of cooperation that the North Vietnamese never allowed me to receive letters or packages from home or to write to my wife and family for five years. I have no way of knowing, of course, but that had to be the reason.

When you are imprisoned week after week, year after year, and you could only speculate what was really going on in the war, it was difficult to keep up your morale. You begin to wonder, *Am I ever going to go home?* Several POWs attempted suicide.

The North Vietnamese had a propaganda newspaper called the *Daily Ninh Zanh*, which they read over speakers they had installed in our cells. They wouldn't give us enough food to eat, but they had the resources to put speakers in everyone's cell! And they would read from that newspaper in English. You could almost tell how the conflict was going by believing the opposite of the "news" they were reading.

I will say in those days I didn't have very much respect for President Lyndon B. Johnson. So one of the hardest things I ever had to do in an interrogation was to answer the question, "What do you think of your leader, President Johnson?"

"Oh," I would say. "He's a great man."

In truth, I disliked him a lot. Not because I became a POW on his watch, but because I had read a book before I was shot down that raised some pretty compelling questions about his political career. The bottom line is, when you don't like someone, and you have to say he's a great leader when you believe he's not, it's difficult.

That's one of the great things about America. We're free to disagree with our leaders. But, if I would have told the North Vietnamese I didn't agree with my president's politics, they would have used that to the hilt in their propaganda and indoctrination efforts and forced me to sign letters saying as much. So it could have been worse.

Every human being has his or her own mental and physical breaking point. Expert interrogators, like our captors in North Vietnam, knew exactly how to push each prisoner closer and closer to that line. For now, despite the pain being inflicted on me, I was holding my ground.

For now.

The Ohio State University

My father pulled into the driveway in the late afternoon, returning home to start the farm work following his regular shift at the foundry. I had been lying under the maple tree in the front yard agonizing over the money I lost on the cattle I'd spent all year raising, and contemplating my future.

I walked over to Dad as he was getting out of the car and told him what had happened at the stockyards, how I'd worked for most of the year and not earned a cent.

I didn't know what he was going to say, but I knew what I was going to say. I'd made up my mind.

"Dad, I think I'm going to go to Ohio State and be a veterinarian," I told him. "I'm sorry I'm going to leave you with all the work to do on the farm."

His reaction took me by surprise.

"Well, four years will go by in a hurry," he said. And that was it.

I expected him to be upset, to say: "What? You can't leave me holding the bag like this!" To me, it was the nicest thing he could have said. I don't recall Mom saying anything at all about my decision to go to college.

As much as I had always looked up to our veterinarian Dr. Barth and wanted to become a vet myself, I truly felt terrible about leaving my dad. Even though we never spoke aloud about our bond, he was both my father and a friend.

Yet, looking back, losing money on that cattle was the best thing that could have happened to me. It changed the course of my life and propelled me toward a career in which I would excel. I still loved farm life, but at the moment, I felt trapped in a cycle I wasn't sure I'd otherwise escape.

I craved love and adoration, even a simple thank-you from my parents. I worked my fanny off for my father. Everybody who knew me said I worked like an adult man from a young age. After I performed a complex task or worked hard all day, I just wanted Mom or Dad to say, "Good job!" or "You know, it was really nice of you to do that." It would have meant the world to me. But they never said it.

Once when I was little, Dad met me when I got off the school bus and said he had to see one of our neighbors, Charles Lons, who lived around the corner on Smith Road. As always, I was glad to ride along.

We arrived just before the Lons children—Nancy and Charles Jr.—got off their school bus. Dad and I were in the house talking to Mr. and Mrs. Lons. As soon as the bus pulled up to the end of the driveway, it was like a switch went off. The mom stopped talking. The dad stopped talking. Both of them greeted the kids with big hugs and immediately started asking them about their day at school.

I could almost feel my eyes filling with tears. Why can't my parents do that, I wondered? It's what I wanted from them most of all. They never expressed affection for us kids—or for one another, at least when we were around. Sometimes, I thought it must be a European trait, until I saw the Lonses, who were from Poland. No, it must just be something with my parents, I concluded.

Fast-forwarding many years into the future, to when I had a daughter of my own named Jackie, I never missed an opportunity to say, "Jack, I love you."

Finally, one day she said, "Dad, I'm so sick and tired of hearing you say that! Please don't say it again."

"The reason I say that is because I never heard those words from my mom and dad," I said. "I want you to know I love you."

"OK," Jackie said. "You can tell me you love me as much as you want!"

So, when I announced my decision to go to Ohio State, for my dad simply to say, "Well, four years will go by in a hurry," was to me a welcome sign of approval. Looking back, that moment was one of the great turning points in my life.

The only problem was I had never even considered going to college. And here it was August! It was getting late in the year and I had no idea where to begin the process of getting into Ohio State.

So, I began with a call to Mr. John Florence, my principal at Spencer High School. His son Dwight, a classmate of mine, was already in college studying aeronautical engineering. I told Mr. Florence what I wanted to do.

"I'll help you," he said.

Somehow, he managed to wrangle all the paper work I needed and got me in. His son even gave me a ride to Columbus.

By this point, there weren't too many rooming houses left. I was able to find one just off the south side of the OSU campus. It was a single room on the third floor—which is a nice way of saying I lived alone in the attic.

Mom and Dad never paid one cent of the cost of my college education. I worked and saved and paid my own way. Of course, it wasn't as expensive in 1954 as it is today. The entire bill—for books, tuition, room and board—was about $1,000 per year. It wasn't until the last quarter of my senior year that I needed to borrow $500 from my dad, which I paid back shortly after finishing school.

On the first day, I was to report to the Oval—a large, park-like space in the heart of the campus. Students were grouped according to their areas of study. I found the line for the agriculture department and signed in.

I'd never been to Ohio State University and to me it was absolutely overwhelming—which is saying something, because back then it wasn't as crowded as it is today. I had never even seen a college campus before, so I had no way of picturing what one would look like. All I knew was if I wanted to be a veterinarian, that's where I had to go. Just a few weeks earlier, college was nowhere in my plans. Suddenly, here I was. Almost immediately, I felt apprehensive, wondering if I had made the right decision.

For a naïve kid from the country, everything was a learning experience. My house mates on the lower floor—they all seemed to be from New Jersey—were playing poker one night and invited me to sit in. I had never played cards in my life.

"That's OK," they said. "We'll teach you!"

Well, I thought to myself, maybe I can learn something here. Boy did I. They cleaned my clock! I lost every bit of my spending money for that quarter. It was the first and last time I ever played cards. I have nothing against card games. I just never picked up on how to play.

I took all the pre-veterinary medicine courses. They were all pretty heavy in chemistry, which was not my strong point. While I struggled for C's in classes like English and chemistry, I scored straight A's in all my agricultural courses, which I really liked.

Anything I chose to take, I did well in. Courses I was required to take were more of a challenge. There were a couple of exceptions—geology, for one. My class was taught by the chairman of the department, who was an outstanding professor. That's one class I really enjoyed. Another of my favorite classes was in heredity and genetics. Again, it was taught by the chairman of the department and I just ate it up. To this day, I remember some of the things I learned about heredity, which has a lot of application to farming.

One particular instructor at Ohio State really left a lasting impression on me. It was Dr. William J. Tyznik, who was professor of feeds and feeding. He was extremely sharp—earning his doctorate by age 23 or 24 and developing his own feed line called Tizwhiz. Dr. Tyznik was very highly regarded across the campus.

First-year students were required to take some sports. I took basketball, as well as swimming and diving, which I was anxious to learn more about. During a heated basketball game, I remember a guy shoved down on my head—I was just 5-foot-9—and I crumpled to the floor. I hurt my back, which was to be the first of many problems there.

I was pretty disciplined in my studies—and I had to be. I was way behind a lot of kids who had taken college prep courses or attended private schools. So I had a lot of digging to do. Mom and Dad never pushed us kids in school. You would never hear them tell us to go and study, though I think my sisters and I all were pretty conscientious about getting our schoolwork done. We certainly couldn't go to our parents with homework questions. Dad attended school only through sixth grade. Mom went at most through tenth grade.

In the spring quarter of my freshman year, I joined an agricultural fraternity, Alpha Gamma Sigma. It was one of those fraternities that truly was about building camaraderie, not about parties and alcohol. I was prompted to join by two cattle buyers I had met from Producers Livestock in Cleveland, John Bricker and Glenn Cope. They were cool guys and very good buyers. When they found out I was headed to Ohio State, they encouraged me to join AGS, which they had been members of, too. If that fraternity turns out products as good as these two, I thought, that's where I wanted to go. And it was a great experience for me.

I probably learned as much from the fraternity as I did from my college studies. I was very backwards socially because of the way I was raised. I couldn't dance. I didn't know the names of any of the actors in the movies of the day. I didn't know any of the popular songs. Friends have pointed out that I really didn't have much of a chance to grow up and enjoy being a kid, which is true. I basically went from the crib to the workforce, which in many ways was unfortunate.

AGS allowed me to develop some of the social skills I had missed out on. I began to go to movies and even to dances—not that I ever became a very good dancer.

Still, I didn't date any girls at Ohio State. I think the main reason was my trip home every weekend to help Dad on the farm.

My childhood friend from church Carol Buckingham told me recently that when we were growing up, there were plenty of girls who would have accepted if I had asked them out on a date. In fact, they couldn't understand why I never asked any of them. The truth was, I was so shy, I never thought I was good enough.

CHAPTER 10

During my entire childhood, any time someone gave me a compliment, my mom would put me down. Without exception. Even if he never said so out loud, I knew Dad was proud of my abilities because he let me do so many things. I think it created something of an inferiority complex that held its grip on me for a long time.

For example, my aunts and uncles would come out from Akron and see me work. They'd say to my parents, "Oh, you're so lucky to have a son like that. He's such a good boy."

My mom would only sniff.

"Now don't give him a big head," she'd reply. "I've got to live with him."

That would just crush me. The kindness of my aunts and uncles was exactly the sort of affirmation I was looking for from my own parents, but never received.

I once kept a diary when I was young, but it didn't even last a month. I quit when I realized all I was doing was filling it up with negative feelings about my parents' inability to express gratitude or affection.

I never developed self-confidence around other people until I went to college. I played intramural basketball and my quickness allowed me to achieve some degree of success. I said to myself I may not be the best, but I'm not as bad as I thought I was, either. It was a small thing, but it was important to my self-esteem.

My fraternity brothers helped me believe in myself. The rule at AGS was to accept anyone who was honorable. The fraternity wouldn't pledge anyone who was a braggart or a drunkard. It made me feel good to be part of a group like that. Everyone was so kind to me. I learned more about people by observing them and interacting with them than I ever learned at home.

I'm not sure why Mom treated me the way she did—whether it was just her personality or if she thought she was doing me a favor by toughening me up. Even late in life, when she was in her 80s and 90s, I'd call her just to visit. As soon as I said hello, her response was, "What do you want?"

"What do you mean, 'What do I want?'" I'd ask her. "I just want to talk to you!" That's just the way Mom was.

We've often talked about that, my sisters and I. They seem to think it was because I had come to know more than our parents in areas like math and farming technology. I was always saying to Dad, "Why don't we try doing it this way? It's easier." My siblings think it was Mom's way of throttling me back and keeping me under control.

I moved into the fraternity house as a sophomore and stayed there the next three years. I cleaned the whole house in return for my room and washed dishes and served tables to earn my board.

I also worked at the meats laboratory, starting at 35 cents an hour, with a nickel per hour raise every quarter I stayed on. We supplied meat to virtually the entire campus, including the dorms.

My job was boning out meat and slicing bacon. The beef quarters hung in a big cooler on rails. I weighed 130 pounds and some of the quarters were 150 to 175 pounds each. Fortunately, I was pretty strong and didn't have much trouble lifting them off the hook and carrying them out to be cut.

One day, however, I lifted one off, turned around to walk out of the cooler, and a guy let the door slam on me. The floor was sawdust, so I didn't want to drop the side of beef. I hung on, though it almost bent me double. I pushed the cooler door back open and managed to put the meat down on the table.

My back was never the same after that day. I went to the health clinic and it turned out I had crushed a couple of disks. I wish I knew then what I know now and I would have gotten additional medical attention.

When Mershon Auditorium opened at Ohio State, the first play performed there was "South Pacific." I went and I really liked it. However, my studies—especially with the three jobs I was working—didn't leave me much time for things like that. Every weekend, I drove home to Spencer to help Dad. Every weekend. I still felt guilty that I'd left him with all the farm work.

My first car was a 1950, two-door Chevy hardtop, which I bought in late 1953 after graduating from high school. In my junior year of college, I managed to buy a brand-new, 1956 2-door Oldsmobile hardtop. Every Friday, I'd return home to help with chores, bringing my dirty laundry for Mom to wash. My parents gave me a full tank of gas, which pretty much lasted me the week.

I wasn't treated all that differently when I came home. Still, my parents were so legalistic in their religion, I'm sure they worried about the fact I wasn't attending a Bible school and probably thought my faith was going down the tubes. My sisters all went to Bible schools, but in those days, many were not accredited. I didn't want to work for four years to receive a certificate instead of a degree. To me, that seemed ridiculous. I always said those schools should be accredited and today most of them are.

Only two people in my high school class went to college—the principal's son and me. Yet, as I've said before, no one in my class has ever treated anyone differently because of his or her station in life. My best friend was Dave Reisinger and to him it wouldn't have mattered if I was a ditch digger, a junk dealer, or a college student. We were friends and that was what was important. Still, I felt very lucky to be going to school.

I would make suggestions to Dad about the farm based on what I was learning in school. I saw the way they would feed out the cattle at Ohio State and thought we should do the same. I had decided I wanted to be a dairy farmer instead of a beef farmer and kept trying to talk Dad into switching back. Milking parlors were just coming into use then. I knew dairying was harder work—seven days a week—but I liked the idea of a neat and clean set-up. With dairy, you can keep records of every cow's production then breed the best cows to continuously improve the herd. When you buy steers to feed out, you're more at the mercy of the person selling them to you. You don't always know what you're getting. With beef cattle, sometimes all you have in the end is manure!

But, Dad only shook his head.

"You don't know what dairy is like," he said.

Looking back now, considering his heart problems, I can understand why Dad didn't want to return to the dairy business.

I tried out for the meat-judging team at Ohio State and made it the fall quarter of my junior year. Up to 20 or 30 people tried out and only five or six were selected. I made both the livestock and meat-judging teams, which to me was quite an honor.

We were on the road a lot, traveling to competitions in Kansas City, Chicago and Springfield, Mass. Today, the college pays the team's travel costs, but in those days, most of it came out of our own pockets.

THE OSU LIVESTOCK JUDGING TEAM.

Judges would be presented with four choices in each of 12 different classes. It may be four pork loins, four hogs, four steers, etc., which we ranked in quality. In at least eight of the 12 classes, you had to articulate the reasons for your selections. We were awarded 50 points for a perfect placing and 50 points for a perfect set of reasons for our placings.

I learned that in judging meat and livestock, when in doubt, it's almost always best to go with your first impression. I think there's a lot of truth in that when it comes to figuring out people, too. I also learned that if I couldn't articulate a reason for my placings, I shouldn't try to make one up. In other words, don't try to fudge your way through things. Say what you know. And when you don't know, keep your mouth shut.

On one trip to Kansas City, I was one of three drivers heading to the competition. I had a whole load of kids in my new '56 Olds. We hadn't even left Columbus when I hit a patch of black ice. It was a minor crash and no one was hurt, but it did a lot of damage to my new car. The repair shop did a pretty good job of fixing it, but it was never the same. To this day, my college friends still talk about that car.

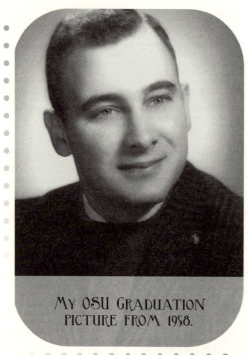

My OSU graduation picture from 1958.

During my first two years at Ohio State, participation in the Reserve Officers Training Corps was mandatory. Students did have the freedom to choose which branch of the service. I didn't want to go into the Army and didn't know anything about the Navy. So, I picked the Air Force and I'm glad I did. Two of my ROTC instructors were former pilots—one flew a bomber and the other a fighter. I instantly gravitated toward the fighter pilot, who was vivacious and funny, with plenty of good stories to tell.

In some of the more intensive courses required for veterinary school, we'd watch films showing various surgical techniques. Watching those operations always made me feel lightheaded, which was strange. Growing up, I learned to castrate hogs and vaccinate animals and it never bothered me at all. I felt terribly embarrassed and never told my parents or anyone at school that the movies impacted me that way. I just told myself that if I stuck with it, I would be able to get over my apprehension and everything would be fine.

So I made the decision to apply for advanced ROTC. My plan was to fulfill the required three-year commitment in the Air Force and then go to veterinary school on the G.I. Bill. I hoped that being older and a little more mature would help me overcome my aversion to the surgical films.

CHAPTER 10

As part of the application process, I had to take a Stanine test, which was one of the most difficult tests I've ever taken. It lasted a full day. When it was all over, I was sure I hadn't passed. But, to my amazement, I made it.

During my senior year of college, the Air Force bumped the service requirement up to five years, which I accepted. Much later, during many a long night in a prison cell in North Vietnam, I had plenty of time to wonder if maybe I should have toughed it out and gone on to veterinary school instead. My path in life might have been much different.

But the real transformative event during my college years at Ohio State happened when a fraternity brother asked me a simple question.

"Hey, would you like to go up in an airplane?"

The Cruelty of the Briar Patch

As the American presence in Vietnam increased, so did the number of POWs being captured. I was only at the Heartbreak Hotel in Hanoi for about a month before they began dispersing us to prison camps throughout North Vietnam.

I was among a group that was moved to an old French movie studio christened the Zoo. Again drawing some comfort from my farm background, I gave names to the buildings in the compound; the Barn, the Stables, the Pig Sty, the Garage, and the Office.

It was at the Zoo that I met an American hero—U.S. Air Force Lt. Col. James Robinson "Robbie" Risner, who was shot down Sept. 16, 1965, and placed in the cell next to mine. Even though I had never crossed paths with the Korean War ace, I knew who he was because he had been on the cover of *Time* magazine on April 23, just a few months earlier.

When Robbie first arrived, I was able to talk to him through a gap under my door and taught him the tap code. By then, I'd been a prisoner of the North Vietnamese for nearly four months.

"How is the war going?" I asked him.

"It's going well," Robbie said. "We'll probably be out of here by the end of the year."

Then he paused.

"I'm just trying to give you guys hope," he added. "I don't know."

That fall of '65, our captors had eased off the interrogations or "quizzes" a little bit. They frequently moved us from room to room. I was later in a cell next to Spike

Nasmyth, an avowed atheist. Ironically, they gave him a Bible. That was just like the North Vietnamese to give the guy who was the atheist a copy of the Bible! I asked him why he had accepted it.

"Well," he said, "I just wanted to read what I was against!"

Years later, when several of us were moved to another camp, I saw Spike again. One night, as the POWs were trying to decide what to do to entertain ourselves, he offered to tell us the story of the Bible. And he did. The entire thing. He told it in a narrative form that made more sense to me than anything I ever learned in Sunday school.

Soon, the Zoo began to fill up, too. Eventually I would be brought back, but for now, the North Vietnamese transferred about a dozen of us to another prison camp Scotty Morgan dubbed the Briar Patch.

Moving from camp to camp became a familiar exercise—although repetition never made us feel any less apprehensive. We never knew if the place we were headed would be better or worse than where we had been. I was moved 26 times during my captivity and the prison conditions rarely changed for the better.

When it was time to shuffle POWs off to someplace new, the guards, who spoke no English, would come up to us and make a chopping motion at our wrists. This meant we were to put on our long pajamas—which was all we had. They always blindfolded us and always moved us at night.

Packing never took very long. We each had a mosquito net, a bamboo sleeping mat no more than a quarter of an inch thick, one blanket, and one spare set of pajamas we used for a pillow. Each pair of pajamas had either long stripes or a number on them, which never seemed to correspond to anything. If the North Vietnamese had assigned me a prisoner number, I never learned what it was.

Our dinnerware consisted of two dishes, a bowl, a soup spoon like you'd get in a Chinese restaurant, a cup and a one-quart water pot.

The North Vietnamese also issued us a toothbrush and a tube of toothpaste. The handle on the toothbrush never lasted long—the quality of their plastic was much worse than American-made plastic. The handle almost always broke about an inch down from the bristles, which made it hard to brush your teeth. When we asked the guard for a new toothbrush, he'd laugh and get out his cigarette lighter. He taught us how to melt both ends of the broken handle until the plastic was runny, then jam the pieces back together. Sometimes it held and sometimes it didn't. The mosquito net and the toothpaste and brush were the only humane things they did for us.

The Briar Patch was out in the boonies—hidden in the jungle about 30 or 40 miles from Hanoi. Like other prisons, it was built by France to house Vietnamese prisoners when the country was a French colony. The complex consisted of about nine structures surrounded by a wall.

Most of the POW buildings were about 16-feet square and contained four cells, each about eight feet square, with doors that faced outside instead of an interior hallway. The rooms contained two wooden bunks and a single window with bars across it. At the beginning, I was thrown into solitary confinement behind a heavy, two-inch-thick mahogany door.

Because we were in the jungle, the mosquitoes were terrible. Like the Heartbreak Hotel, the cell walls were spattered with mortar, making them rough and knobby. If you were lucky, you could steal some thread out of your pajamas to help suspend your mosquito net from the bits of mortar sticking out of the wall. It was not easy. Sometimes you could only partly hang the netting over your bunk.

Outside each cell, there was a little concrete catch basin, about 15 inches square, where they would bring us water to wash ourselves and our dishes. The first morning, they opened up my door and I got a closer look at the basin. It contained six or eight inches of water, covered in green scum like you'd find on a frog pond. I said to myself, *if I make it out of here without dying from sickness, I'll be really lucky.*

The water at the Briar Patch was fetched from an unwalled well. One day, a guard got me and took me down to draw water. It was on the other side of the camp, about 100 yards away from my cell.

Being a graduate of Ohio State University's animal science program, I had noticed there weren't any animals around and wondered if they even had any around the complex. As I got closer to the well, I saw a Vietnamese potbelly pig. I'd never seen one before. Now our hogs back home have an arch to their backs, with not too much fat on them. By contrast, this pig looked like a camel. It had a swayback and its belly was almost dragging on the ground. It was black, maybe 30 inches long, and fat, fat, fat. Just the opposite of the way we breed pigs in the United States.

I burst out laughing. I think I may have even said out loud, "Oh, if only my Ohio State professors could see this pig. They would laugh, too." Of course, the guard didn't know what I was laughing at. He goosed me along a little with his bayonet and told me to get down to business and draw the water. So I drew four or five five-gallon buckets of water and he took me back to my cell.

By then, the Americans had started to bomb pretty close to where we were being held. The North Vietnamese took us out and held us in a filthy building while peasants dug holes about two feet deep in the concrete floors of our cells. That's where we were supposed to hide if the camp was bombed.

The blasts got so close to the Briar Patch, the force of one bomb cracked the transom over my cell door. It was terribly nerve-wracking, tying my stomach up in knots so that I could hardly eat. I said, "Lord, if I'm going to die, just make it quick."

The bombing was sporadic, which made it difficult to figure out what the target was. I tapped to another POW, wondering if they were bombing dikes that held the water for rice production.

After a couple of weeks in solitary, I was moved to the building nearest the front of the camp and placed in a cell with my first roommate at the Briar Patch, Robert Purcell. Percy was an F-105 pilot who had been shot down about three weeks after I was. He was just a peach of a guy and became one of my best friends. We stayed there together maybe a week, when they moved him out and moved in Bill Tschudy. He was an A-6 navigator for Capt. Jeremiah Denton—a POW who later became a U.S. Senator from Alabama. Bill and I were held together about a week, when they moved me back into solitary and put me in the third building.

The fact I was moved from the first to the third building became critical because it meant that during our entire first winter at the Briar Patch, I was the last POW to receive his meal. The guards carried our food in on a pole, with a basket of rice on one end and a pot of watery soup on the other. The soup was made from whatever weeds they could find out in the jungle to boil. We usually got a chunk of what they called "meat," but was actually a piece of pork fat. If you were lucky, it might still have a tiny sliver of meat on it.

The guards would bring the food to the first building, serve those four cells, then do the same in the second building. When they came to the third building, because of the cell I was in, I was last. I got what was left—and in most cases, it wasn't more than half a bowl.

I tapped to the other POWs and asked how much food they were getting. Everyone seemed to be receiving a full ration but me. Finally, I complained and motioned to the guard dishing out my food to put more into the bowl. But there was no more to put in. The North Vietnamese prepared the minimum amount of food for us and the guards weren't about to take the time to see each POW got an equal share. They were lazy and wanted to get the work of feeding us over as fast as possible.

If that wasn't enough, during the winter, the guards deliberately allowed our food to sit outside until it got cold. We were in a hilly area and the temperatures regularly dipped into the low 40s and high 30s. That cold rice and cold soup didn't feel very good in your belly when you were already shivering from the weather. During my entire captivity, I was never held in a building that had any type of heater. That went on for the winter of '65-'66.

Later I got another roommate, J.B. McKamey, who was a Navy A-4 pilot. In the Air Force, we called those planes "Tinkertoys." They were small, used primarily for close air support, and couldn't carry many bombs. The plane had long struts that made it sit high up, so it looked like a Tinkertoy.

The camp commander's interrogation room was outside the walled area of the camp in a separate building. For some reason, he zeroed in on J.B. and me. I don't know if they were interrogating anyone before or after us. Every night, after dark, they'd take one of us to interrogation. First they'd take me. Then the next night, they'd take J.B. The night after that, it was my turn again. They alternated between the two of us like that all winter.

Up to this time, I had not told my interrogators where I was from, what aircraft I was flying or anything that would be of potential use to them. The objective of these quizzes was to convince us that in this conflict, the North Vietnamese were in the right and we Americans were in the wrong. They'd bring up the American Revolution against the British as an example. They'd say in that war, the Americans were right and the British were wrong. In this conflict, however, the North Vietnamese are right and the Americans are wrong.

The interrogators kept tempting me with the possibility of an early release if I cooperated. Absolutely not, I told them. Our code of conduct does not allow that. I won't be tempted.

The next evening, it would be J.B.'s turn and they'd say the same thing to him. There was no torture, so to speak, that whole winter, except that we suffered from the cold, with too few clothes and blankets to keep us warm. As a consequence of the meager rations, I lost a lot of weight.

Our showers consisted of cold water—naturally—and lye soap. In addition to not giving us enough to eat, the North Vietnamese only gave us the minimum amount of water we needed to survive. Each POW had a quart-size pitcher, which the guards were supposed to fill twice a day. But again, that required work on the part of our captors. And they were not about to expend one extra ounce of time or energy on U.S. prisoners.

The water sources were unsanitary, so the guards had to boil our drinking water. That meant cutting wood and building a fire. "Boil" is probably a generous word. I'm sure they took the water off the fire as soon as they saw the first bubble.

To avoid all this exertion, the guards only poured about a pint of water into our quart pitchers, twice a day. The POWs would point and say, "Fill it up," but the guards only looked back at us coldly, as if to say, "We'll do what we want."

That's one thing I will hold against the North Vietnamese forever. They never gave us enough water to drink. For a long time after my release, I don't think I ever, ever passed a water fountain without taking a sip or two.

Once, a POW came back from taking his shower and said, "Man, I was so thirsty, I turned on that shower and I just started drinking away!"

All of us let out a collective groan. The water was like sewer water until it was boiled.

"Oh, no!" we told him. "Don't do that! You could get diarrhea, cholera, or who knows what!"

He survived, but we finally convinced him not to risk it again.

Our bathroom facilities consisted of a rusty, two-gallon can in each cell. Sometimes they had handles on them, sometimes they didn't. We weren't allowed to empty them every day, so often the contents would begin to run through the rust holes. Finally, you'd convince a guard to let you take it out and dump it.

For toilet paper, we were issued a sheet of paper the color of a brown grocery bag and about the size of a place mat. This was supposed to last us one week, which was impossible—especially since POWs often suffered from diarrhea due to the poor sanitary conditions. We economized as best we could—carefully tearing off a two-inch-square piece each time until it was gone—but we almost always ran out of toilet paper. Walking back to our cells from interrogation, if we saw a banana peel or empty cigarette pack on the ground, we'd tried to pick it up and use that. But if the guard saw you, he'd make you throw it back down. We weren't supposed to take anything into our cells.

In the wintertime, the guards might not let us shower for weeks at a time. Even though the weather was cold, you still began to feel grimy. As precious as my drinking water was, I found that if I took just a handful and washed my feet, I felt better all over.

For a POW, even everyday tasks turn into torture. The North Vietnamese forced us to shave because to them, a beard on an American was a sign of protest, a means of defiance. Every few weeks, they'd come around with clippers and cut our hair—none too well, of course.

The water basins outside our cells didn't freeze solid in the winter, but when the weather got cold, there would be a layer of ice on top. On average, they made us shave about three times a month. Sometimes it was once a week, sometimes every two weeks, depending on how lazy the guards were. We shaved with plastic, double-edged razors. Like our toothbrushes, the handles were often broken.

Without exception, the blades—which came from Communist countries like Czechoslovakia, Romania and China—were rusty. They were hand-me-downs from the guards. When they were too dull for the guards to tolerate, they were set aside for the POWs. You'd look at the guard who brought you out to the basin to shave, look at the rusty blade, then back to the guard and shake your head no way. The guard pointed his gun at you, letting you know you didn't have a choice.

Never was there warm water, only cold. We used a bar of lye soap for lather. Sometimes they handed us a broken piece of mirror, like part of a handheld mirror a woman might keep in her purse. Other times, all we had for a mirror was a shiny beer bottle cap, which of course was useless.

It was coming up to Christmas. The camp commander told us, "You shave for you holy day." Not "holiday," but "holy day." The weather was cold, probably 35-40 degrees. The concrete walls of our cells were about 15 inches thick and once they got cold, they didn't warm up, even if the sun came out during the day. We were shivering and they took us outside to shave. I was first.

I dipped cold water out of one of the vats and started shaving with whatever rusty razor and mirror they gave me. Shaving really isn't the word for it. It felt like each whisker was being pulled out. It hurt so badly. I scraped away and scraped away, my face beginning to bleed. Whenever I stopped, the guard motioned for me to keep going. I did one side and then the other. I had tears in my eyes, it hurt so much. I've got soft skin and a tough beard, but I chopped and chopped. I looked awfully scraggly, but it was good enough for the guard. He took me back in and it was my roommate J.B.'s turn.

I could see through a peephole in the door the tears streaming down J.B.'s face as he struggled to shave. It hurt so much. Finally, he put down the razor and the mirror and stopped.

"I'm not going to do it," he told the guard, and walked back to the cell door, waiting to be let back in.

The guard grabbed him by the back of the neck and took him back out to shave. This must have happened three times. J.B. did a kind of half job at it and I can only assume the guard got tired of dealing with him.

The camp commander came out just as J.B. was finishing and said, "We want you to enjoy Christmas!"

"We'd enjoy Christmas if you just would let us not shave!" J.B. said.

But it was important to the camp commander that we were clean-shaven for Christmas, and we soon found out why.

A couple of days later, on Christmas Day, we heard a commotion outside our cells. We'd stolen a nail somewhere and had used it to work a hole through the door—not easy to do on mahogany two inches thick.

The North Vietnamese were putting on for us what they euphemistically called "a banquet." Our normal diet of rice, weed soup, and pork fat was put aside.

Instead, they brought out a card table, which they moved from one cell door to another. On it, they'd place a turkey drumstick, a bowl of rice and a vegetable. Sometimes there would even be a treat like a rice cake for dessert. Beside the food was a partial bottle of beer—the guards always drank half of it first.

We could see five or six big, old-fashioned movie cameras—like the ones they used to re-enact my capture—positioned to film U.S. POWs enjoying a "typical" meal. The movies would be used as propaganda, showing the world how graciously the North Vietnamese were treating the American "criminals."

I turned to J.B.

"They're not going to photograph me picking up any of that stuff," I said.

"Me, either," said J.B.

When the card table and film crews were set up outside our cell, the guard opened our door. I walked out in my prison pajamas—my face still scraggly, but somewhat healed from the shaving ordeal two days before. I took three paces outside the cell, looked at the "banquet" with the cameras rolling, turned around, and walked right back in.

J.B. did the same. That really, really made them angry. It wasn't long before we were pulled up the hill to the camp commander's office for interrogation. Or more accurately, a tongue lashing.

"Why are you so unthankful?" he asked. "You are a criminal, you know. You didn't come to our country with a passport. War has not been declared. The Vietnamese people have sacrificed to provide you with this meal and you criminals don't eat it!"

"If you take the cameras away, I'll eat it," I replied.

"You don't appreciate what we're doing for you," he continued. "All I have asked of you is to write something to say we, the Vietnamese are right, the Americans are wrong, and you refuse. You will never go home!"

The reading of the national newspaper over the camp's public address system became a daily ritual. The guards came around and made us put on our long pajamas, even if it was a hot summer day. We would be forced to sit on our beds and listen attentively to the speakers in our cells as the commander sat in front of a microphone in his office on the hill and read to us in stilted English.

Every day he'd begin by saying, "Today, I read you the 'new.'" Never the 'news.' It was always the 'new.' We'd sit there and laugh and fiddle around. The guards would walk by and look into the cells to make sure we were listening respectfully. Whenever a guard passed a cell, the POW inside would whack the wall with his fist. It was the signal to the next cell to sit up straight and pretend to be listening. Sometimes, if you were lying on your bunk, you could see the guard's shadow approaching. I don't think they ever figured out that we knew when they were coming.

After the camp commander was done reading the whole newspaper—which may take half an hour—he would say, "What I am going to do is read the new one more time!" Oh, we'd get to laughing.

Most of the stories were so far-fetched, you couldn't help but laugh. They would say something like, "Using an antique rifle, Grandma So-and-So from So-and-So Province, shot down three F-105s while she was out plowing behind a water buffalo and increasing her rice production."

As I mentioned before when we were in Hanoi, the more exaggerated the 'news' was, the worse the North Vietnamese seemed to be doing in the war.

Eventually, the camp commander ordered one of the POWs to read the daily newspaper to us. They pestered him in interrogation for a month or so, but he wouldn't do it. Eventually they tortured him because by refusing, he was being "belligerent." I'm sure the point of forcing him to do this was to show the rest of us that there were some Americans who would "cooperate" with the North Vietnamese.

Finally, after being tortured, the POW relented. But, he stipulated, if he was going to read the newspaper, he needed to take it into his cell to practice it. The camp commander agreed and gave it to him.

The next day, our fellow POW sat down at the microphone and started to "read" the newspaper. I was soon overcome by laughter and by fear for this man's life at the same time. I said to myself, *if they ever figure out what this guy is saying, they're going to kill him!*

"OK," he said over the PA system, mocking the camp commander, "this is the new!"

Now, the North Vietnamese had the utmost reverence for their leader, Ho Chi Minh, as well for the leader of Cambodia, Prince Norodom Sihanouk.

The POW began to relay an article and every time he came to the name "Ho Chi Minh," he called him "Horse S—t Minh." Instead of saying Norodom Sihanouk, he said, "No Good Schnook."

The more he went on, the more we practically cried with laughter! We couldn't control ourselves. We laughed out loud and banged the walls of our cells in delight. The guards looked in on us and we immediately tried to sober up so they wouldn't suspect what was going on.

It was so funny, yet I was terrified the camp commander would discover the joke and take his anger out on this POW who was making fun of the North Vietnamese leader instead of reading the 'new.'

"Oh, God," I prayed. "Don't ever let them find out!"

We were laughing our insides out. On top of it all, the camp commander recorded the whole thing and played it over and over through the speakers in our cells. Suffice to say, he never figured it out and there were never any repercussions. It was a courageous act on the part of our fellow prisoner and a much-needed boost for our morale.

It's difficult to describe a POW's emotional ups and downs as the days turn to weeks, the weeks to months, and the months to years.

Naturally, your first thought once you get shot down and captured is, *how do I escape?* Once you find out that's almost impossible, your mind begins to wonder what you can do to stop from spilling your guts under torture and telling the enemy more than a soldier should—name, rank, serial number, date of birth. Then, how do you outfox them if they do manage to get you in a corner? How do you answer their questions without getting yourself in deeper trouble?

That's the process your thoughts go through. I think it's typical for most people who are captured. After you go through the stages of thinking about escape, survival, and how to take care of yourself and your fellow prisoners, your thoughts turn toward your family.

You begin to ask yourself, *if I get out of here, what will I do differently?*

Family is more important than money, of course, so you decide you need to spend more time with them. Lying on your thin bamboo mat on a hard wooden bunk in a cell in the jungle, you plan the vacations you will take together. You go over them in your mind again and again.

When you exhaust that thread, you've got to start thinking of something that keeps your mind busy. After a year and a half as a prisoner, the possibility that I may never fly again began to settle in. So I started thinking about what I could do to earn a living. I spent a lot of time building the ideal farming operation in my mind.

Some of the POWs who weren't from agricultural backgrounds built houses in their minds—coming up with architectural plans and labor-saving designs. A couple of guys said when they got out, they wanted to open bars—that was about the last thing I'd want to own—but they'd spend their time inventing new drinks and planning all the different entertainment they would offer. The important thing was finding a way to exercise your creativity during those long hours we spent in our cells.

Once, while I was stationed in Germany, I returned home to the Spencer farm for a visit. I remember seeing Dad had plastic bags of fertilizer sitting at the end of the field. When I was younger, they had been made out of paper. The problem was that if the rain got to the paper bags, they would virtually melt and the fertilizer would be ruined. Some entrepreneur decided it would be better to make them out of plastic and he or she was right.

As a POW, I thought, you know, I'm going to come up with the same thing, except for trash bags. I'll invent plastic trash bags that you can just toss into the garage until you're ready to get rid of them. Of course, by the time I got released, they were already on the market!

Things like that may sound silly now, but I can tell you this. The POWs who tried to keep their minds busy were the ones who did the best job of maintaining their sanity under difficult conditions.

Sometimes, guys would tap through the wall and say they prayed to God, asking that they not be taken to interrogation and tortured again. I said, "You know what? That's not a realistic prayer." I told them, "Here's my prayer; God, I know they're going to interrogate me again and they're going try to get this or that out of me. Please give me the strength, like the apostles in the Bible, to withstand whatever they throw at me and come out the other side with my body and spirit intact."

MY SON SHAWN.

Every day, I woke up and said, "Thank you God for giving me the ability to live one more day." You try to remember all the Vacation Bible School verses you memorized and all the Sunday school lessons you ever learned. They say there are no atheists in foxholes and I tend to believe it. You just thank God for the strength to go on.

I had a ritual I went through in my mind every time I was taken out for interrogation. It was my way of telling myself to stick to my guns, not to break down, not to take the easy way and say things I shouldn't say.

The guard would open the door of my cell, wave me out with his gun, and walk me to the camp commander's office. When we arrived there, the guard first would make a report to the interrogator, then disappear. It was always the same routine.

As I waited to go in, never knowing what sort of mental or physical torment lay ahead, I would think of my little boy, Shawn, back home. He was just 2 years old when I left for my deployment. Unless I was in so much pain that I couldn't bring him or anything else to mind, I spoke to him in my thoughts.

Almost without exception, I said, "OK, Shawn, here goes your dad. Boy, I am going to give it my best shot. I hope when they release me you'll be proud of the way I acted and that I didn't tell them anything."

First Flight

Like most farm families, we never lacked for food while I was growing up, but we never had much cash. That remained true when I graduated from high school and finally was able to save enough to buy my first car.

I had very little by way of spending money when I was home from college, so for free entertainment, sometimes my friends and I would drive up to Cleveland Hopkins International Airport. We'd spend hours sitting at the end of the runway, watching the planes land and take off. I don't know if you can even do that kind of thing in today's era of heightened airport security. Since I had no interest in drinking and carousing, and neither did most of my friends, it was a fun diversion and the only cost was gasoline, which in those days was very inexpensive.

When you're sitting on a tractor in the middle of a farm field, plowing ground or baling hay, you're all alone between the earth and the sky—almost like flying. I always had a fascination with airplanes, but I never gave it much thought in terms of my future. I was going to be a farmer and farmers flew tractors, not airplanes.

Right?

Wrong.

The Lord often has a way of turning our expectations around like that.

One of my fraternity brothers at Ohio State, Don Davis, happened to be president of the university's chapter of the Flying Farmers. It's a national organization that promotes aviation and agriculture, and develops bonds between the two.

FIRST FLIGHT

In the spring quarter of my freshman year, Don invited me to go up with him for a ride. The plane was a Cessna 120—a little single-engine, two-seater produced in the years following World War II.

It was the first time I ever flew in my life and I fell in love with it. We took off from the OSU airport, Don Scott Field, and flew a short pattern over Columbus.

Don, who would become a close friend, told me later that all I did was giggle from the moment the wheels left the ground until we landed. I didn't even realize I was laughing and smiling the whole time. It was an experience that left me filled with awe, joy and excitement.

I couldn't know at the time that Don had opened the door for me to an unexpected and meaningful career. I will always be deeply grateful to him for doing that. Many years later, Don's life ended too soon following a battle with cancer. We hadn't seen one another for some time and I didn't even know about his illness until after he had passed away. His brother told me Don had kept a picture of me in his hospital room. He often would point to it and say, "If Paul can make it through Hanoi, I can beat this." That meant a great deal to me, although I was sorry I didn't have the opportunity to visit with Don one last time.

After that first flight with him, I was hooked. Even though I never liked heights my whole life, flying seemed totally different. It's difficult to explain, but in a plane, there's something under you, supporting you—unlike when you're standing on a cliff or climbing a silo. I never felt any twinge of that old fear in an airplane.

The fall quarter of my sophomore year, I signed up for flying lessons at Don Scott Field. It was across the Olentangy River and a good eight or 10 miles from campus by bus. We had flight instruction at the airport during daylight hours and ground school on campus in the evenings. Because it was a 15- to 20-minute trip, sometimes we really had to hustle to get to class on time.

I got my pilot's license in a Cessna 140 when I was 19 years old. I had 40 hours in that plane and I just thought it was the cat's meow. It was a "tail-dragger," which means it had a little wheel on the end of its tail, instead of the tricycle-style landing gear that was just coming into use.

My favorite part of learning to fly was "slipping" an airplane. It's a way to decrease altitude quickly without gaining airspeed. Say you're approaching a field but you're coming in too fast or too high and you're unable to circle or come in another way. You just put the left wing down, give it right rudder, and effectively slide in at an angle. I always thought that was fun. Learning how to get out of a spin was initially pretty intimidating, but even that I came to enjoy. We also were schooled on emergency landing procedures. The instructor would reach over, switch off the plane's engine and say, "Now, where are you going to land?" We had to learn to make quick decisions based on altitude, airspeed and the terrain below.

Even though aviation was new to me, I had been operating farm equipment since I was a boy. I tell people that flying an airplane is just like driving a John Deere tractor in three dimensions. Back on the farm, those H and M Farmall tractors of Dad's had wide draw bars on the back where we'd hitch on a seven-foot sickle bar mower. I used to love trimming along the fence rows and prided myself on how close I could get to the fence—which was made from woven wire and not something you wanted to hit with the mower blades.

I learned quickly that if you are mowing with the sickle bar along at the edge of the fence and you turned away too sharply, the mower actually would swing toward the fence and hit it. Instead, if you needed to correct your course, you turned slightly toward the fence, stopped, backed up, and started forward again.

I'd come back to the house and I'd say, "Hey, Dad! Look how neat that mowing job is. I did it all with the tractor. I never even had to use the hand sickle!"

Dad would look at me.

"OK," he said.

That was about as generous as the praise got around our house. Then it was off to the next chore.

He never asked me to mow that precisely. Even though it was Dad's farm, not mine, I always wanted to have the best-looking fields around. It was just in my instincts and why our relatives and friends brought their kids to the farm to learn to work like "Paulie." I give God the credit for it. It's a trait that he gave me and one that served me well as a pilot.

Everybody feels some degree of apprehension before his or her first solo flight. Up to that point, you always had the instructor beside you to say, "We're going to do it this way" or "We're going to do it that way" or "I've got the wheel." All of a sudden, there's nobody there! Every new pilot must wonder, "Can I do this?" even though the instructor has said you're ready. Once you get airborne, you fly a familiar pattern and some of the doubt and fear goes away—yet in the back of your mind you know the hardest part is not taking off, but landing!

One solo trip we had to make in pilot training at Ohio State was an "out-and-back." You had to fly somewhere, land, and have somebody sign a sheet to prove you didn't just circle and come back home. My out-and-back was to Grime's Field in Urbana, Ohio, which is near where my farm is today. I remember a restaurant there bragged it had the best pie in the country. The weather was snowy, so I stopped long enough to have a hot cup of coffee before flying back to Columbus.

Another wintry day, I had to make my first long round-robin flight just south of Chicago. It was another out-and-back exercise—and a little scary. The weather report called for possible snow squalls. In low temperatures, your worry is that the plane's carburetor will ice up, so you turn on the carburetor heater, which takes some of the power away from the engine. I said I didn't care how much power I lost, that carburetor wasn't about to get iced up in my plane! I probably ran the heater longer than I needed to, which didn't hurt anything.

To obtain your license, you had to be checked out by a Federal Aviation Administration instructor. That was probably the most nerve-wracking part of the process. I took off from Don Scott Field with an appointment to land at Port Columbus International Airport. I had never landed at a major airport before. It's where TWA, one of the first major airlines to serve Columbus, based many of its planes. Just landing a little Cessna at Port Columbus was scary enough, let alone taking a flight test!

Students were to pull up to a certain building with the plane's engine running, and an FAA instructor would hop in and say, "OK, we're going to go up, and we're going to do this, this and this."

Like most beginning flyers, I was pretty nervous. I kept thinking things like, *I hope I don't screw up. I hope he's not too hard on me. I hope he's not a grouch. I hope I pass!*

I flew as he instructed, and when it was all over, the examiner handed me a form with his signature on it. I flew back to Don Scott Field and received my pilot's license.

To my parents, flying in a plane was something entirely outside their realm of experience. Their reaction was the same as always—which was little reaction at all.

But I was so happy. I told everybody in the fraternity, "Hey, I got my license!" I invited everyone I saw to go for a ride.

Three guys said, "Sure, we'll go up with you!"

So we rented a Cessna 172 with tricycle landing gear. I had never been in a plane with that many people—and that much weight.

Normally, I went down the runway and lifted right off. Well, here we were, going down the runway… going down the runway… going down the runway. I looked ahead and there was the end of the runway coming up and I still wasn't up to take-off speed. I didn't think we were going to make it. My passengers all were shouting holy you-know-what!

"We're going to crash!" they cried.

Well, we made it, lifting off right at the last minute, skimming over the cornfield just past the end of the runway. I don't remember where we flew, probably just a local pattern over the campus.

The guys said, "Kari, we thought you were a better pilot than this!"

I said, "I guess I didn't expect this much weight from you guys! It took a longer run!"

While I was in college, I came home and worked at the farm every summer except the last, between my junior and senior year. Dad knew a big cement contractor in Cleveland. He owned a farm west of Wellington and I heard he paid his workers good money. I was an average farm boy, so I thought I was tough. Well, I went to work in the cement business and I lasted one day. Those guys could haul 150 pounds on their backs all day long. I tried to mimic them and I didn't get too far.

I came home to find Dad planting corn near the house. I was so tired I laid down at the end of the row by the fence and waited for him. I told him I was beat.

"I tell you what," he said. "I didn't like the idea of you going to work for those people anyway. I'll get you a job in the foundry as a helper."

We went to the Kasper Foundry in Elyria where Dad worked. Mr. Kasper was Hungarian, so he and Dad could speak together in the old language. Mr. Kasper liked my dad and I soon had a summer job.

I learned how to work with fire brick and fire clay and to line the containers where they melted iron. On big jobs, the molten iron was poured into molds from big buckets moved by overhead cranes. I helped pour the smaller jobs using a heavy ladle, which also was lined with fire clay and weighed about 80 pounds full. I worked my fanny off that summer to pay for my new car.

I became friends with some of the workers at the foundry—some of whom never missed an opportunity to give a naïve, young college kid a hard time.

They'd say, "Hey, farmer boy. How comes you don't chew?"

"Why do I have to chew?" I asked.

"Well, you don't smoke," they said. "You ought to at least chew. You've got to do something wrong!"

They bugged me and bugged me and bugged me until finally, one day I said, "OK, give me a chew."

Well, I didn't know how to chew. So I put the tobacco in my mouth, chewed and swallowed the saliva!

Oh, I got so sick. I went out behind the kiln and I just threw up. They were all laughing. They knew why I went out there. I must have turned green.

"OK, that's good enough!" they said a few minutes later after I recovered. I had tried their chew and that was what it meant to them to be a man.

Working at the foundry that summer was quite an experience. I gained a whole new appreciation for my dad. There were two moldsmen who got the biggest jobs and one of them was my dad. He might work on a mold for two days. He'd build it out of sand then paint it. You had to get everything perfect, down to the smallest, critical details.

It was hard work. Dad would come home filthy dirty. Instead of eating dinner and putting his feet up after working a full shift at the foundry, he came home to bale hay. He had a 200-acre farm, 100-head of cattle and a family to take care of. He was killing himself with work. Later, when I finally had a farm of my own, friends would say the same thing of me.

Well, Dad was right about one thing. Four years of college went by in a hurry.

With my pilot's license in hand and advanced ROTC training under my belt, my plan was to graduate with a degree in animal science, fulfill my commitment to the Air Force, then attend veterinary medicine school on the G.I. Bill. By then, I hoped the light-headedness I experienced viewing the surgical films would have passed and I'd return to my career goal of becoming a veterinarian. In the end, however, I discovered flying a fighter came just as naturally to me as driving a tractor, and my life followed a different path.

My parents never said anything good or bad about my decision to enter the Air Force. Dad never said, "Hey, we had a deal. I thought you were coming back to the farm to help?" Yet, I could sense he saw his son slipping away from him. The traditional order of things, in which I would follow in his footsteps and someday take over the work of the family farm when he retired, was beginning to fade.

In fact, some years earlier, Dad had paid $6,000 for an 80-acre farm in neighboring Chatham Township, right across from the Old Mill on the Black River. I might have been a senior in high school by this point and asked Dad if I could buy the land from him so that I could get my own start in farming. I don't know where I thought I would get the money, but he said yes and put it in my name.

It was a very poor farm—with wet and sandy soil along the river and full of sinkholes. I got the tractor stuck there so many times. But, we cleaned it up and laid drainage tile, which helped. When I decided to make my career in the Air Force, I sold the land back to Dad for what I paid him, plus the improvements.

Despite any disappointment he may have had that I wasn't going into agriculture any time soon, I think my dad recognized how difficult farming life could be. He had no health care coverage. There were few government programs back then to assist struggling farmers. It was either do or die. I don't think Dad necessarily saw the Air Force as any more or less risky than farming, but perhaps he understood the opportunities it offered.

CHAPTER 12

In keeping with tradition, graduation was scheduled to take place in Ohio State's legendary football stadium, known as the Horseshoe. The forecast called for rain, so at the last minute, graduation was moved inside to the recently constructed French Field House. My parents made the trip to Columbus from Spencer, along with my mom's mother Mary Pamer, who was living with them at the farm. The date was Friday, June 13, 1958.

My name was called and I received both my college diploma and Air Force commission that same day. After the ceremony, I sat down next to my grandmother.

"You know, Grandma," I said, "it's Friday the 13th. I wonder if this is an unlucky day?"

"Oh," she said. "Don't talk that way."

Yet, every June 13 for seven years, that same thought would come back to me in a POW's prison cell. The anniversary of the day I was commissioned. Had I made the right choice?

After graduation, I spent about a month at my parents' farm, helping Dad and running on the back roads around Spencer to get in shape for the service. Finally, it came time to pack my '56 Oldsmobile for the drive to San Antonio for my Air Force preflight medical exam and other preliminary requirements. When it was time at last for me to leave, Mom came out to the car. Dad was at work.

My parents had given me a watch as a graduation gift. As I said goodbye through the open driver's side window, Mom reached in, grabbed my left arm, and pointed to the wristwatch.

"Don't ever forget. Now is the time to serve the Lord," she said. "Remember that every time you look at this watch."

"Yeah, Mom," I replied. "I know. I've heard that my whole life."

That was my send off to the Air Force.

Her message was clear—don't stray. My parents' faith was everything to them. I knew that was what she was trying to communicate to me. Her own two brothers had been through such hell in the South Pacific during World War II they would never talk about it. I'm sure that was on her mind, too. Now, here was her only son, going off into the service and the wild, ungodly world.

Maybe there's something to be said for a mother's intuition.

The Hanoi March

The morning of July 6, 1966, brought the sound of trucks rumbling into the Briar Patch. At first we assumed preparations were being made to transfer POWs to yet another prison camp. But, they had never moved us in the daytime before. As truck after truck continued to roll in, we sensed this time, something was different.

The guards came around and instructed us to put on our long pajamas—as would be typical in a move—but did not tell us to roll up our bedrolls and gather our things.

"What do you think is happening, P.K.?" asked my roommate, J.B. McKamey, a Navy A-4 pilot.

"I don't know," I replied. "I wonder if they're taking all of us to Hanoi for a trial?"

My guess was closer than I knew. It was a trial in the court of public opinion—a hellish day that would become known as the Hanoi March.

The North Vietnamese tied our hands, blindfolded us, and herded us onto the familiar six-by-six trucks. There were about 30 of us from the Briar Patch, and another 20 or more POWs from the camp we had dubbed the Zoo.

In addition to the anxiety of not knowing where we were going, we were concerned by the sounds of U.S. bombing in the area. Military convoys are prime targets. Our pilots would have no way of knowing there were American POWs inside these trucks.

We drove for what seemed like a couple of hours as bombs fell all around us. Sitting on the floor of the truck under the watchful gaze of an armed guard, POWs used the tap code—secretly tapping on one another's arm or leg—and exchanged conjectures about what lay ahead.

When we heard the sounds of people and cars and the hustle-bustle of a sizeable city, we assumed we had reached Hanoi. The North Vietnamese took us off the trucks and removed our blindfolds. Blinking as our eyes adjusted to the light, we could see we were inside a soccer stadium. With so many of us being held in solitary confinement or with a single roommate, it was almost startling to see such a sizeable group of POWs assembled in one place.

The North Vietnamese had a sweet food we POWs simply called rice cakes. They were about two and a half inches tall, six inches square, sticky, and very tasty. They gave one to each of us, wrapped in bamboo leaves. It was a strange juxtaposition of feelings—standing there in a stadium, enjoying a good-tasting snack, but fearful of what might come next. We weren't supposed to talk, but in a bit of gallows humor, we whispered to one another, wondering if our captors were fattening up the Christians before feeding them to the lions.

They blindfolded us again and threw us back into the trucks, where they took us to downtown Hanoi. The guards ordered us out of the trucks, put the POWs in pairs, and handcuffed us together. I was cuffed to J.B., who was a tall guy—about six-foot-two. I was now about 5-foot-8, after destroying a couple of discs in my back when I ejected.

When the North Vietnamese tortured us, they used wrist irons, which they could tighten like a vice. This time, they had American-style handcuffs that went "click-click-click" as they tightened. They cuffed my left hand to J.B.'s right, not too tight, and took off our blindfolds.

The sight that greeted us was a city piazza, with as many as eight streets spinning off in all directions. And it was packed with people as far as the eye could see. Later estimates put the assembled crowd of North Vietnamese citizens at 100,000 people. It seemed to us as if the whole city had turned out for us.

Next to each POW was a guard with a fixed bayonet. Before long, they gave us the order to start walking. J.B. and I were close to the front of the line, in about the fourth or fifth row.

I whispered to J.B.

"I don't know where they're taking us, but somebody is filming this," I said. "Someday America will get a copy of the film and see this. I don't know what's going to happen to us, but I'm going to hold my head high. I want America to see that we were proud, that we weren't cow-towed into submitting to this."

When we started to march, the crowds were 40-50 feet away, but as the street began to narrow, the people pressed in, closer and closer, shouting and shaking their clenched fists at us. They began chanting something, but of course we couldn't understand what they were saying.

An interpreter walking alongside the line of POWs said, "The people want you to bow your heads!"

I looked at J.B.

"I'll be damned if I'm going to bow my head," I said.

In fact, I stiffened my back even more and I looked straight ahead.

That irritated the guards. Ironically, they were there more to protect us from the people than to prevent us from escaping. Even so, the guard beside me began hitting me in the back of the neck with the back side of his bayonet. That edge isn't sharp, but it is made out of metal, and not something you want to be beaten with. Still, I would not bend. To this day, whenever I feel a little twinge of arthritis in that part of my neck, I think about that bayonet hitting me.

The English-speaking interpreter, who happened to be from our camp, came up beside me. Instead of saying my entire last name, my North Vietnamese captors usually just called me by my last initial, which they pronounced, "Ka."

"Ka," he said. "You need to bow your head."

The guard continued to beat the back of my neck with his bayonet. Finally, just so he would ease up hitting me a little, I bent my neck ever so slightly. But I never lowered my eyes. I still stared straight ahead.

About that time, an angry North Vietnamese woman came up to J.B., pushed past the guard, and ripped out a handful of his hair. You actually could hear the roots of the hair being torn out of his scalp. It's a sound I can hear even now. J.B. yelled out in pain.

Another woman came running at J.B., this one with a high-heeled shoe in her hand. The sight would have been almost comical, if the situation hadn't been so terrible. I don't know where that shoe came from, since every Vietnamese woman we ever saw wore flat-soled shoes. She zeroed in on J.B. and clobbered him right on the head with the spike of that shoe. I know it must have hurt.

The crowd continued to press in, beating on us, hitting us with rocks, throwing anything they could get their hands on. They were right in amongst us. The guards couldn't keep them back. Since J.B. was on my left, my right side really got beat up.

We walked that brutal gauntlet for almost two miles before ending up back at the soccer stadium, where they loaded us back onto the trucks and returned us to our camps. Oh, my gosh, we were hurting. I know I was.

Back at the Briar Patch, they threw us back into our cells. Soon, I could hear cell doors opening and closing. On top of our ordeal that day, the camp commander was pulling out prisoners for interrogation.

By the time the guard opened up my door and marched me up the hill, I'd had time to reflect on what had just happened to us. A fury had built up inside me. The Geneva Conventions required prisoners to be treated humanely. But, as we were told over and over by the North Vietnamese, we were not prisoners of war because war had not been declared. According to them, we were mere criminals.

It was late when my turn with the camp commander came, about midnight.

"What do you think the Vietnamese people think of you?" he asked.

I was so angry, I didn't care whether they killed me or not.

"That was the most inhumane thing you could ever do to people who are tied up and can't defend themselves," I barked.

And I didn't stop there.

I said, "Sir, do you know what happened the last time a nation humiliated American pilots like that?"

"What are you talking about?" he asked.

"Did you hear about Hiroshima and Nagasaki?" I replied. "We dropped atom bombs on them. Your leader, Ho Chi Minh, is responsible for what you put us through today."

The camp commander went into orbit. The North Vietnamese were highly sensitive to any mention of Ho Chi Minh that seemed the least bit disrespectful.

"Are you calling our leader a criminal?" he asked.

"You can call him that if you want," I said.

He started chattering and chattering and chattering. He was off the charts, he was so angry. I don't think any of the other POWs ever said anything like that to him. The camp commander called in a guard and said something to him before we went outside.

Normally, we followed a path that led from the interrogation building to the camp gate, but this time, we veered off to the right.

Oh, boy, I thought. What's going on?

We walked through underbrush filled with bushes and saplings. By now, several more guards had joined us. Finally, we stopped. They blindfolded me and tied me to a tree. That's when I started to worry, because I knew I had said some pretty strong things. They were talking quite a bit amongst themselves.

Evidently, the camp commander told them I had insulted Ho Chi Minh—badly—and that I needed to be punished. The guards began hitting and kicking me. They beat me with their gun butts and their fists. I don't know how long it lasted, but I stood on my feet for as long as I could, until I finally slumped down and they eased up. Eventually, they stopped altogether and just left me there alone. I remember thinking *I wonder if this is just phase one?*

CHAPTER 13

There were more POWs to be interrogated that night of the Hanoi March. The guards left me tied to the tree as they went about their business. Eventually they returned, untied me and took me back to my cell.

"Where in the heck have you been?" asked my roommate, J.B.

"You would never believe it," I said and told him the whole story, relaying my anger about how we had been treated, followed by the beating in the jungle.

"Well, you learned to keep your mouth shut," J.B. concluded.

Not exactly. It wouldn't be the last time I expressed my feelings to my captors and got punished in the bargain.

I didn't sleep much that night, but when I got up the next morning, I was so sore. My right side was almost entirely black and blue from where the crowds in Hanoi had beaten me.

The Hanoi March may have been designed by the North Vietnamese to win support from the world by putting the American "criminals" on display, but in the end, it had almost the opposite effect. The film footage from that day instead showed a helpless group of handcuffed American POWs very nearly being fed to the lions, yet holding their heads high.

As I look back, it was a moment when I was so proud to be an American. The whole world could see our resolve not to give in at any price.

Until then, not very many people knew what terrible conditions American prisoners were being subjected to in the cities and jungles of North Vietnam.

Now they did.

Primary and Basic Pilot Training

I arrived in Texas to begin my Air Force training and learned two things right away. First, it's hot. Second, I don't much care for okra.

America's interstate system was still in its infancy in the summer of 1958, so it was quite a long trip on country highways from Mom and Dad's farm in Spencer, Ohio, to Lackland Air Force Base near San Antonio, Texas for my pre-flight medical exam. When I finally reached Texas, the temperatures were in the upper 90s. I stopped in an old, little roadside diner for lunch and noticed something unique called "okra" on the menu. Being from up North, I had never tasted it before.

"What's okra?" I asked the waitress.

"Oh, it's really good," she said. "You'll love it."

What the heck, I thought. I'm beginning a fresh chapter in my life. Why not experience something new.

"OK," I said. "I'll try some."

Well, I'm sure there must be some good way to prepare okra, but this was the slimiest stuff I ever put in my mouth! I didn't eat very much of it.

Soon after I arrived at Lackland, I came down with a terrible cold. I was sicker than a dog. And here I was supposed to take a physical to show I was healthy enough to begin pilot training. I was afraid my Air Force career would be over before it started. I found out, of course, they didn't care if you were sneezing and coughing. They were only interested in checking your vital signs and testing your vision. Thankfully, I passed the physical.

INITIAL OUTFITTING

The barracks at the base were not air-conditioned. It was so blasted hot, that I threw a blanket on the wooden floor and slept with my nose up close to the door to try to get some air.

I made a good friend in those first days in the Air Force—Harold Dortch. A former football player from Tennessee, he befriended me at the swimming pool. We were never stationed together, but years later Hal later became my back-up when I competed in the first NATO Gunnery Meet. He was a close friend and a good pilot.

After meeting my preflight requirements, I was assigned to Civilian Contract Primary at Bainbridge Air Base in the southwest tip of Georgia. To earn their wings, pilots must take six months of primary training, followed by six months of basic training.

I had a week to 10 days between Lackland and Bainbridge, and I did something very stupid. I drove straight through from San Antonio, Texas, back to Spencer, Ohio. I don't recall how long it took, but I was so exhausted, it took me a week to recoup. Of course when I got home, I immediately went to work helping Dad on the farm. Some evenings, I went out with a girl named Regina Breyenton. We'd go see a movie at the Montrose Drive-In and I'd fall asleep. It didn't make any sense for me to drive home like that and wear myself out.

It soon was time to leave for Bainbridge. I still knew so little about the Air Force that I stayed in a motel right outside the base gate. Later, as I checked in at the base, someone remarked they hadn't seen me in the Bachelor Officers Quarters the previous night. I had no idea that's where I was supposed to stay. In Lackland, they had herded us from place to place like animals. So, I spent $20 to sleep in a not-very-nice motel.

In the Air Force, they told us right off that we'd be graded for everything we did every step of the way, and those grades would play a vital role in determining our future. We would be graded on our military bearing—that is, how we act as officers. We'd be graded on academics. We'd be graded on our pilot skills. Those scores would carry over to the next level—basic pilot training—and those at the top of the class would get to choose what type of airplane they wanted to fly.

That was good incentive for me because I didn't want to fly bombers or helicopters or cargo planes. I wanted to be a fighter pilot. I'm sure it had something to do with the former fighter pilot who was my favorite ROTC instructor back at Ohio State.

Without exception, the top 10 percent of the class in basic pilot training opts to fly fighters. Even then the competition isn't over because the pilots with the best scores get to choose where they want to be based. And the place everyone wanted was Ramstein Air Base in Germany. I knew that's where I wanted to be assigned, too.

I was fortunate enough to be at the top of my classes during those years of pilot training. And even in those early stages, you could almost tell which students would go on to become generals and how many stars they would earn. I had hopes of following this path myself. That was my one professional regret about being shot down—I missed out on many of the advancement opportunities my classmates were able to pursue.

During my sophomore year at Ohio State, I got my private pilot's license at my own expense for $260. Today it probably costs $6,000 to $8,000. By my senior year, the Air Force was offering to cover the cost of obtaining a private license for members of the ROTC who planned to go on to pilot's training.

I didn't think that was right. While I was still in college, I asked if the Air Force would pick up the tab for an additional 40 hours of instrument training for me, since I'd already paid for my license on my own dime. At first, the ROTC said no, but I was persistent and finally they agreed.

For about the first 10 hours of instruction, I sat in a trainer with all the outside lights turned out so that all I could see was the instruments. It forces you to trust the information from the airplane's gauges and dials instead of your own senses.

Eventually, I went up in an actual plane with an instructor who would cover me with a hood so that I couldn't look out of the plane. All I could see was the instrument panel. We flew into Port Columbus and all over like that. I got so I really enjoyed flying by instruments. It was a new challenge.

I'm glad I insisted on that extra training before entering the Air Force. It put me ahead of a lot of my classmates later during primary pilot training.

There were six Air Force primary pilot training bases, each with a total of 70 pilots in training. My class at Bainbridge was 60-B. It was made up of 70 pilots, divided into two flights of 35 each. Interestingly, my particular class contained about a dozen Japanese pilots. Most of them were young, but one was a major who had flown in World War II. They could speak some English, but not a lot. My instructor was Bob Wilson, a civilian. There were three of us at his table, including one of the Japanese pilots, named Kanichi Ondo.

The training was intensive. First, you had to learn about all the different aircraft systems—the electrical systems, the hydraulic systems. You had to know every inch of those planes by heart. In ground school, we covered navigation, mathematics, and air route traffic control.

Our first flying experiences were in a Cessna T-34 tandem trainer. At Ohio State, I'd always been taught in a side-by-side trainer with the instructor sitting right beside me. In a tandem, the seats were one behind the other, with the instructor in the back seat.

Most pilots spent 20 hours in the T-34. Since I already had my license, I only spent about six or seven hours in it before they put me into a jet trainer—a side-by-side Cessna T-37. It was the latest trainer and my class was only the second or third to use it. We called the plane the "Tweety Bird" because it had a little engine that spun at such a high speed you had to wear a headset to keep the shrill noise from damaging your ears. I was able to get checked out and solo in the T-37 pretty quickly, too.

The first scary moment I had during my early training happened one day when I was flying solo back to the base. Landing a fighter is different than landing a big, heavy bomber. A bomber comes in on a straight line from way out. In a fighter, however, you come in at 1,500 feet above the runway the direction you're going to land. As soon as you get over the point you want to touch down, you bend into a racetrack pattern. You come down wind, drop gear on base, and turn onto your final approach. The rationale is that it gets you into a pattern, so that no matter what kind of runway you find yourself preparing to land on, if you get into that same racetrack pattern, you'll be OK.

On this particular day, I was making my initial approach, coming in at about 250 knots, making sure everything was set right for the landing. I looked up, and there was another airplane, coming straight at me, head-on. How he got into my path, I have no idea, but it was a major error on his part. In the excitement of the moment, it seemed like he was only a couple of hundred feet way but it was probably a little more.

The frightening part of a situation like that is you don't know whether to pull up or go down, because if you both do the same thing, you're going to collide. To

T-37 TRAINER, BAINBRIDGE, GA

this day, I don't know which way I went. I think I chose to go down, figuring his first instinct would be to pull up. Fortunately, I guessed correctly.

I was so angry. I was not quite at minimum fuel, but it was time for me to get on the ground. Even though I didn't have much left in the tank, I turned around and chased him to get his tail number. I was determined to find out who had made such a potentially deadly error and make sure the flight commander knew about it.

I followed him as long as I could, but eventually I had to turn back. My gut feeling was there must have been an instructor in that plane, too. It's one thing for a student to make a serious mistake, but if he had an instructor with him, the instructor would have been the one in real trouble. That plane high-tailed it out of there and I never did learn who was flying it.

My roommate at the time was Charles Dawes, who had been in the Air Force as a navigator. I told him what had happened. The next morning, I got up to shave. I looked in the mirror and there in the middle of my full head of brown hair was a lock of white hair. It hadn't been there before.

"Charlie, come and look at this!" I called.

I'm convinced the near-miss caused by the other pilot scared me so badly it turned a patch of my hair white. People I told about it later wouldn't believe me, but it's true.

Nevertheless, I had a great experience at Bainbridge. The base commander was a full colonel. He oversaw the day-to-day operations and made sure the civilian instructors did what the Air Force required them to do. He must have been a sportsman because he bought about a dozen new shotguns we were permitted to borrow and take duck hunting. He also bought three or four ski boats he kept out on the Flint River, only about eight miles away. We could check those out and go water skiing. We had a lot of fun.

Following my primary training, the Air Force sent me back to Texas for basic training at Laredo Air Force Base. Before I left Georgia, my instructor, Bob, said to me, "Well, I just saw all your test scores. It's been a pleasure teaching the best in the class." I was glad to be on track to become a fighter pilot. Flying was easy for me. Just easy.

With 10 days between bases, what else would I do but drive home to Ohio to help Dad? I worked on the farm for as long as I could before I had to make the drive to Laredo. When I got there, I took one look at the next tandem trainer—a T-33—and couldn't believe how much bigger it was than anything I had flown before. I remember being struck by the fact the pilot had to climb a ladder just to get into it! I wasn't sure I'd ever be able to fly it.

My flight leader was Clarence Ondes, who was Native American. A fellow named Runevera was the assistant flight commander and Don Shiflit was my instructor. Don—whom the other instructors called "Shifty"—was a swinging bachelor. He had a 98 Oldsmobile convertible, complete with air conditioning.

"Mr. Shiflit," I once asked him, "why would you have air conditioning in a convertible?"

"Well, it gets hot down here and it feels good when you have the top up," he replied.

Our briefings were not much different.

"Well, Kari," he'd say, "today we're going up north and work on chandelles." It was a type of evasive maneuver.

"I'm going to go get a coffee. I'll be right back," he said.

And that was about all the instruction I got.

I noticed at the next table there were two students with an instructor named Roy Cooper. While I waited for Shifty to come back with his coffee, I could hear Roy going over the new maneuvers in precise detail. He explained to the student pilots what a chandelle and a "lazy eight" were. He told them what to expect and how to react if this or that happened during the training flight.

It was frustrating. I wanted to be the best. I wanted to maintain my high test scores and keep advancing toward my goal—but I wasn't sure I'd get there with the instructor I had. I wished I could move to Roy's table. However, being a student, I couldn't just go up to the flight commander and say I wanted a new teacher. Besides, I was Shifty's only student!

After about a month of this, I knew I wasn't learning as much as the other pilots. I decided to approach Roy quietly about my predicament.

CHAPTER 14

T-33 TRAINER
LAREDO, TX

"Mr. Cooper," I said, "I know I could get in trouble for asking you this, but I would like to sit at your table. Would you take another student?"

"I've already got two," Roy said. "Let me see what I can do."

Well, I don't know who ended up with Shifty, but Roy took me on as his student. He was a gifted teacher and we developed an immediate rapport.

In fact, after my Air Force career, Roy was the only instructor to track me down to find out whatever happened to me. It was Christmas of 2008 and I was in Tucson visiting my kids when I received a phone call.

It was Roy's stepson. Roy had asked him to look me up and invite me to give him a call. I did just that. And about six months later, I went to visit Roy at his home in Arkansas.

Roy was tall and strapping and always had a smile. Now in his 80s, time had taken its toll, as it does on us all. Roy was a little hunched over now and in the early stages of Alzheimer's disease. I met his wife, who was very sweet and told me that of all Roy's former students, I was the only one he'd expressed a desire to reconnect with. To me, that was an honor.

"Do you remember that day we were on mobile control?" Roy asked as we sat down to reminisce.

"No, I don't, Roy," I replied.

He proceeded to recall the whole story.

On a training base, there's a little portable tower called mobile control. It sat right at the end of the runway and had an instructor stationed inside. His job was to make sure student pilots were following correct procedures during takeoffs and landings. For example, the mobile control instructor watched to make sure you had the plane's flaps and landing gear down as you approached the runway.

One instructor worked mobile control in the morning and another in the afternoon. Roy's turn came up and since I wasn't scheduled to fly, he invited me to come out and sit with him in the tower. I took some of my textbooks along and figured I could use the time to study.

In the course of Roy's shift that morning, a student pilot took off on a solo training flight. About 30 seconds in, we heard the pilot's alarmed voice on the radio. Every pilot had his own call sign. I don't remember the one in this particular case, but let's say it was "Ziggy."

"Mobile, Mobile! Ziggy One," he called. "I've got an engine flame out!"

That means the jet engine in the single-engine plane had suddenly shut down. Needless to say, this was a problem.

Without hesitation, I rattled off the emergency start procedure, just like I was reciting my own telephone number.

Roy looked at me in disbelief.

"The wing commander wants us to go by the book," he said. "Otherwise we might miss one of the procedures. They have to be done in order."

He asked for the emergency procedure book and I handed it to him.

"It's on page 179," I said. "Lower-left corner."

"Judas Priest," Roy exclaimed.

He went to page 179, read off the procedure, and it was exactly as I had said.

"OK," said the student pilot over the radio, "I've got an air-start."

Roy looked at me.

"You have got to be kidding me," he said. "How did you know that?"

Roy said I lowered my eyes and got a little sheepish.

Very matter-of-factly, in a non-bragging sort of way, I said, "I've got a photographic memory."

"Is that right?" Roy replied. "I've never met anybody like that. Tell me, if that's true, what's the procedure for hydraulic failure when you can't get the landing gear down?"

"Page 184, in the upper right," I said.

He looked it up and said, "I'll be damned."

Roy asked me another question. I got that one right, too.

"I can't believe it," he said.

Now, here we were, 50 years later in Roy's living room. It gave me goose bumps to hear him recall this story. It made a lasting memory for him, but I had forgotten it entirely.

"I've thought about that over all these years," he said.

After I told Roy the story of being shot down over Vietnam and about my experiences as a POW, I asked him to tell me about the rest of his career.

It turned out Roy joined the CIA as an air attaché and eventually was stationed in Morocco with his family. Once, he was threatened with death if he didn't leave the country in 24 hours. Of course, the people who wanted him killed had lookouts at all the seaports, airports, and border crossings. He and his family had to drive across a desert and just barely made it out.

We must have talked until 3 a.m. Roy was full of juicy stories and it was a pleasure to spend time with him again.

My skills as a pilot really took off with Roy as my teacher. In basic pilot training, you fly about 100 hours. Some 30 hours of that is instrument time. Every once in a while, you have to fly with a different instructor, who checks you out to make sure you're learning all the right things.

One day I was flying with Roy. I was in the back seat with a hood over my head to prevent me from seeing outside the plane and force me to fly using only the instruments. He was in the front seat of the trainer to make sure we cleared any other aircraft in the area.

"OK, Kari," he said, "we're going to make a penetration."

In this exercise we were to make an approach for landing. Different airports have different beacons on different frequencies, which are listed in manuals for each region. The idea is to make a teardrop-type approach, which is just a way of lining up for the final approach. You come in at about 20,000 feet at 300 knots and let down to a certain altitude. Then you go into a 30-degree bank and intercept the beacon, which helps guide you in.

The pilot has a little four-way control called the trim button. To put the plane's nose down, you trim down. To put the nose up, you trim up, and so on. I had that plane trimmed up so perfectly, I took my hands off the stick and my feet off the rudders.

"Hey, Roy," I said. "Look!"

There was a little rear-view mirror so he could watch what was going on in the back seat. I held my hands up in the air for him to see.

"You show-off!" he said. "Break it off right now. You passed."

I mentioned that story to Roy when we visited decades later. He said he didn't remember it, so I guess that made us even.

In Laredo we learned formation flying and that's where I really came into my own. It was just like when I was a kid driving the wagon alongside the corn binder back on the farm.

We weren't allowed to take off in formation. Instead, we had to join up with aircraft already in the air. Because it would take a lot of throttle to catch up with another plane, the pilot who's already airborne retracts his gear, gets safely out of the immediate airspace then begins a turn, left or right. So if you are coming to join up with him, you simply fly across the arc he's making. That way, you catch up with him in a much shorter distance than by chasing him from behind. And once you join up, you go wherever he wants to go.

I used to love to do that. I guess it was the daredevil in me. I'd go whoosh! Right up to a guy's plane. I learned to do it traveling so fast, sometimes I'd scare the other pilot. I made sure to come in low enough that if I couldn't slow down with my speed boards—which were like barn doors that stuck out into the air to slow the plane down—I'd just go right underneath him. It was showing off a bit, but I had a good feel for joining up.

I always thought Texas didn't have much water, but I discovered it has thousands of lakes. You get airborne, even down north of Laredo, and the landscape is dotted with little lakes amidst the cactus-filled desert.

Student pilots were required to spend two weeks shadowing another job in the Air Force, just to learn more about our branch of the service. We could choose anything we wanted. I had no idea what it was, but I chose Quality Control. I'm quality-conscious, I reasoned, so it sounded appealing. It turned out to be one of my more dumb decisions. I thought I would be out and about, examining things. It was strictly an office job and not very interesting at all.

One of my classmates went into the air police—a much more exciting choice. He came back and told us how they'd tracked down an airman who had been missing for six weeks. He was in a jail in Nuevo Laredo and the Mexicans never told anybody where he was. The air police finally got the guy released. All his captors gave him was a rubber tire to use for a pillow.

Roy's younger sister was visiting from Arkansas and he invited me over to his house for a barbecue. She was just 16 or 17 years old, so it was just a get-together, not a date. She was very cute. When I asked Roy about her all those years later, he said she was the luckiest girl in the world, having ended up with 30 or 40 gas wells on her property. She became pretty well-off!

Basic pilot training lasted six months and I was first in all my classes. Not that I ever saw the scores, but we knew the top student got first pick what he wanted to fly—and I got the first pick.

There was a list of all the different types of aircraft—fighters, bombers, cargo planes and helicopters—and the number of students allowed for each one. Of course, I had always wanted to fly a fighter and that's what I selected.

There was one further choice to be made. You could either go tactical—which was air-to-ground weapons and bombs—or you could go into air defense. Much like it sounds, air defense specialized in intercepting enemy aircraft over the homeland. I selected the tactical fighter, which at that time was the F-100. For the next step in our training, we'd go either to Williams Air Force Base or Luke Air Force Base, both in Arizona.

Close to 50 percent of pilots didn't make it all the way through basic pilot training. The requirements were very, very high. I don't know what the cut-off was, but if you got below a C academically, you were in trouble.

Most people had the military bearing because they had been in ROTC or attended one of the academies. In my class of 60-B—that was six bases with 70 pilots each, so 420 pilots total—50 percent were Navy or Army academy graduates. That was important in one way. They had a lot more pertinent education than I did graduating from Ohio State with an animal science degree. Many were engineers.

But, in some cases, that worked to my benefit. I believe one reason I did better than most students is they are pushed so hard at the academies. When they finally graduate, they just almost relaxed too much. I discovered this much later when I became an Air Force Academy instructor myself. After they make it through the academy, they sort of relax. They didn't seem to have the drive, most of them, to be the best.

A number of pilots fail in the flying portion of the training. Landing is difficult and some students just never master it. Others find the physical forces they're subjected to in a jet make them sick and there's nothing they can do about it.

That's the saddest thing to see happen: Someone spends four years in college, takes six or nine months of Air Force training, and then they wash out. It's devastating for them. You can see it in their faces.

My old roommate, Charles Dawes, confessed to me once he almost quit when we were at Bainbridge. During one of our training exercises, the instructors took us up and intentionally put the plane in a spin to show us how to get out of it.

It frightened him so much, Charlie said, he tossed and turned all that night, trying to decide whether he should resign from the Air Force. He was such a laid-back guy it surprised me to hear him say all this. In the end, he stayed in.

"I've never quit anything in my life," he had told himself, "and I can't force myself to do it now."

The only way I can explain my relationship to flying is to say that from a young age, I always had the ability to connect my mind to a piece of machinery. Growing up on the farm, I once had to fix a flat tire. Of course, a flat tire means stopping what you're doing to fix it, which costs time and effort. From then on, I thought of myself as that piece of machinery. When I came to a bump or obstacle that might damage a tire, I imagined my own body stumbling and falling and getting hurt. I controlled the truck or tractor the way I'd control my own arms and legs.

In the same way, when I was flying, I felt like I was the machine. I thought like the machine. If you move an airplane's stick too fast or too far, the plane goes too fast. Instead, you just ease into it. I imagine it's like a professional basketball player shooting a ball. He doesn't stop to figure out the angle of the shot. It's instinct. He and the basketball function as one. I don't know how else to explain it.

There's a feeling of exhilaration and power when you fly a jet for the very first time, like you're better than the best bird out there. They were so much faster than prop planes—and once you got airborne, so much quieter. The faster you go, the less you have to move your stick to do a complete aileron roll. In the old days, biplanes simply had cables going to the controls and it was the pilot's strength that moved them. With increased speed, however, the wind load and air speed load on the plane reaches a point where you need help. So modern craft have hydraulics, which are tuned to give you a natural feel.

I say flying was second nature to me, but I confess that early on, I had trouble landing the T-33. I could get it safely onto the ground of course, but I wasn't "greasing it on." That was the term we used in the Air Force for gently touching the wheels to the runway. When an airliner touches down and hits the runway with a bump, we call that a "Navy landing" just to poke a little fun at our Navy pilot brothers. But when the tires just kissed the ground, we called that a "grease job" and I just couldn't get it right. I'd float along, float along, trying to gently set the plane down, and pretty soon I'd be so far down the runway, I'd have to break off the landing and go around and try again.

In fact, Roy told me all those years later this was the reason he took me on as a student. When I asked to be moved to his table, he took a look at my scores and saw I'd earned scores of 100 percent on every test I'd ever taken. There was just something about that landing that wasn't clicking for me. Roy went to bat for me with the flight commander and said we've got to get this guy so he can land a plane.

A good teacher makes such a difference in a person's life, no matter if it's kindergarten, college, or the Air Force. I am forever grateful to Roy for helping me over that hurdle.

CHAPTER 14

INTERNATIONAL war crimes TRIBUNAL

CHAPTER 15

After the Hanoi March, the North Vietnamese eased up on our interrogations. The respite, however, was short-lived. Later that summer of 1966 at the Briar Patch, they began to turn up the pressure again. We knew through the tap code that POWs were being pushed to make confessions.

The British philosopher Bertrand Russell had announced his intention to form an international war crimes tribunal against the United States and put American POWs on trial. It was his way of attempting to sway world opinion and force the United States to quit the war. It would have been of little consequence to us, except for one thing. Russell evidently told the North Vietnamese that if enough POWs signed letters of confession, it would look good on the world stage. It would appear as if we finally saw the light after a year-and-a-half of captivity.

Russell may have had the world stage in mind, but his suggestion had a personal and painful impact on American prisoners in the jungles of North Vietnam.

One afternoon, a guard opened my cell door. I didn't know if I was going for another "quiz" or what was going to happen, but I was taken to a little building, probably 10 or 12 feet square. In the middle of the room was a stool, made from poured concrete. The commander told me I was to sit down and think about my crimes.

I've thought about them for a year-and-a-half," I replied. "I haven't committed any crimes."

"Yes, you have," he retorted, launching into his familiar repertoire about how I didn't come to North Vietnam with a passport, and all the rest.

I sat there. And sat there. And sat there. Hours went by. Eventually, I had to use the bathroom. I told the guard I had to go. He simply shook his head no. Pretty soon, it really started to burn. Again, I said I had to relieve myself. Again, he shook his head no.

Of course, this was all planned. I'm sure the camp commander told the guard whatever happens, you don't let him move from that spot. If I moved at all, the guard hit me. I had to sit completely still. Three or four hours had passed. Eventually, the pressure from having to use the bathroom became so painful, I resigned myself to the fact I'd just have to go in my pants. I didn't have any other choice.

Now five or six hours had elapsed. By that point, my feet were stinging. When you sit that long without moving, the blood pools in your legs. Soon my feet began to swell like footballs inside my rubber-tire shoes. I tried to release my bladder, but I couldn't. Now I was really beginning to hurt inside. It was all very carefully calculated to inflict as much pain as possible.

I was forced to remain there, on that concrete stool, day and night, for three days. No food, no water. In the middle of the day, under that red tile roof, the temperature would climb anywhere from 120 to 140 degrees.

By that point, you're in real pain. You're thirsty. Your bladder is on fire. Eventually, you just fall off the stool and the guard starts kicking you, beating you with his gun butt, until that begins to hurt worse than sitting on the stool. So you climb up to the seat until you pass out again and the cruel process repeats itself.

The North Vietnamese knew the human body couldn't last more than three days without water. At this point, they began to give me a limited amount of water. This went on for another four days. I received just enough hydration to keep me alive, but no food.

Still, I thought to myself, *these S.O.B.s are not going to break me. I may die, but I am not making any fictional confessions.*

"All we want you to do is to write something that says the Vietnamese people are right, just like the Americans were right in your Revolution," the camp commander said when he came to see me, "and then you can go back to your room."

"It's not a room!" I said. "It's a cell!"

"You the blackest criminal," the camp commander repeated. "You never go home. You insult. We give you food and you insult us."

Finally, at the end of a week of sitting on that concrete stool, they told me to get up. I stumbled my way to the same black building where I spent the first winter and was placed in solitary confinement.

"I beat them," I said to myself. "I beat those S.O.B.s!"

As it turned out, I spoke a little too soon.

Exhausted, I lay down on the bunk. It wasn't 10 minutes before the door swung open again. Most North Vietnamese were short in stature, but here were the two tallest guards I had ever seen. They were holding wrist irons.

Evidently the camp commander decided that since I had thus far refused to do what he wanted me to, it was time for him to show me who was boss.

They took my left wrist and clamped the irons on so tight, my hand immediately went numb. I was convinced my circulation had been cut off and I was going to lose my hand.

Next, the guards reached for my right hand, but I refused to give it to them. We struggled. At last they got hold of me and bent my right arm up over my right shoulder and behind my back. Then they pulled my left hand behind my back and forced it upward to meet my right hand. Try sometime to reach your hands together that way and you'll quickly discover it's not part of the human body's normal range of motion.

The wrist irons only had a one or two links of chain between them. They kept pulling my hands together, wrenching my right arm up over the top to try to marry it up with my left. Finally, the pain was so excruciating, I blacked out.

When I came to, I was still in my cell. The wrist irons were off. I don't know how long I was unconscious or if the guards were successful in getting both wrist irons on me. All I knew was my right shoulder hurt like sin.

An English-speaking interpreter appeared at my cell door.

"Are you ready to write?" he asked.

I had always said I would never write a confession. No matter what, I would never do it. But, at this point, I realized I couldn't take a repeat of what I had just been through for the last week.

"Yeah," I said.

They brought a pen to my cell and a piece of paper, about five inches square.

This is one of the many moments during my captivity that I praise God for intervening. I never thought about what I was going to write because I was determined I was never going to sign a false confession. I knew exactly what the North Vietnamese wanted me to write. They wanted me to say I was a criminal, that I had done the wrong thing in coming to their country.

I didn't believe that and didn't want to write it, but I had to write something. All I can say is that as I put pen to paper, it was God who gave me the words to say. I wish I had a copy of it. I often think it must be filed away somewhere in a North Vietnamese archive.

I'm right-handed, but my shoulder hurt so badly, I couldn't even use a pen. So I had to use my other hand—and I'm a terrible writer with my right hand, let alone my left!

I managed four lines. I can't remember it word for word, but the gist of it was this:

"I am sorry if I have committed any sin against the Vietnamese people. I know I didn't come with a passport. They are feeding me, but I am much thinner. I'm still alive, thanks to the Vietnamese people."

And I signed it.

I motioned to the interpreter that I was done and he took it to the commander.

This isn't going to be enough, I said to myself. They wanted me to call myself a criminal, to say I committed crimes against the North Vietnamese people.

I never considered what I was going to write. God put it into my head to use the word "sin." As soon as I wrote it, I thought, *you only sin against God, not against another person*. I said to myself, *the camp commander isn't stupid. This will never fly*.

Ten or 15 minutes later, the interpreter returned. He brought a guard with him.

"The camp commander don't like your confession," he said.

Oh, no, I thought to myself.

"What didn't he like?" I asked.

He never brought up the word "sin" or that I didn't use the word "crime." It was the part about being thinner they didn't like. I was relieved.

"I can change that," I said.

There's no way of knowing, but I think I must have been the only one who got away with such a "confession." And I give God the glory for putting the thought in my mind to write it that way. After I made a few corrections that amounted to nothing more than grammatical changes, they accepted it.

And that was it for the international war crimes tribunal.

In the same way that I hardly pass a water fountain without taking a drink, I rarely miss the opportunity to visit the rest room after being made to sit on that concrete stool for a week. That may sound funny, but if you learn anything as a POW, it's never ever take the most basic necessities of life for granted.

I didn't tap for a week. I was too sore, too exhausted. Among the POWs, I think I had spent the most time on the stool, but I can't be sure. Many in our camp had been tortured to the point of writing some sort of confession. When I finally could communicate, it became apparent each POW felt bad about what he had been forced to do. But no one held it against anyone else. Nobody. We all knew we had resisted to the best of our abilities.

What made the North Vietnamese so upset was that although they would torture us, instead of just rolling over and giving up, we came back to every new torture session with a vim and a vigor as if it was the first time. Our captors never could figure that out. They said to some of the pilots: We don't understand you. You never learn! That was one of the things Robbie Risner would tell us. He would say we've got to hit it again every day. We've got to keep resisting as long and as best as we can. And even Robbie had to do things he didn't want to do. I just thank God he gave me the strength and the presence of mind that he did.

Friends have told me that my upbringing on the farm—growing up with few comforts and learning the meaning of physical labor at a young age—toughened me and helped me survive the harsh conditions of my imprisonment. I think there is some truth to that. I am basically a quiet person. In the Air Force, whenever I was at the Officer's Club with my friends, I wasn't one to brag about this or that. I was never the loudmouth of the group. I was used to performing hard work and receiving no compliments for my efforts. And I'm sure that helped during my time as a POW. I saw people who had led a somewhat cushier life and just couldn't take as much. They had a harder time when it came to day-to-day survival.

In the solitude of a prison cell, your thoughts can't help but turn to your family. I wondered about Shawn and Ali. I thought about how old they would be now. Shawn must be in preschool, I figured. Would his mom have put him in a Christian preschool? Did Kathy and the kids stay in St. Petersburg or did they move back to Ohio? You thought a lot about those things. I still would speak to Shawn in my mind before going into an interrogation, hoping he'd be proud of me when I came out. Focusing on him helped me get through it. I want him to know that.

Military survival training teaches us what to do if we're captured, but even if I had never had that training, I probably still would have conducted myself the same way because of how I was raised. I had been taught right from wrong and I knew what I should and shouldn't do. What the survival school teaches you is what to expect in detail. And everything they taught us was right on target with what we experienced.

As a nation, we didn't do as well as we could have in preparing those who became POWs in the Korean War. The armed services didn't put a whole lot of effort into teaching them what to expect and so some of them did the wrong thing. That's why the United States came out with a new code of conduct—and our training was right on.

Soon, it was our second Christmas at the Briar Patch. As POWs, we never saw a calendar and the North Vietnamese never told us what day it was. They never gave us anything to read—except their propaganda newspaper. It could be difficult to keep track of time, but I was determined to maintain that little bit of mental discipline of knowing what day it was.

Shortly after I was captured, I was at the Heartbreak Hotel in Hanoi and I told another POW it was Sunday. He said no, I was off a day. It was either Saturday or Monday. He convinced me I was wrong. From that time on, I made sure I knew the date. I never lost track again.

They had American Christmas music playing through the loudspeakers and arranged the same propaganda ploy with cameras filming POWs enjoying a "typical" meal of a chicken leg, rice, vegetables and half a bottle of beer. Even though I was hungry, I still turned around and went back in my cell, refusing to eat in front of the cameras. Many other POWs did eat the meal, but I don't blame them for doing so. Everyone is different and each of us did the best we could do.

When we got home, we asked the U.S. government, "Did we do the right thing?" One rule they give you as a POW is never to refuse food. That seemed strange to me, because often there is a price to be paid for accepting it. It was a personal decision on my part not to partake. But I have to tell you, that half a bottle of beer looked pretty good!

In the same way our captors would make sure our food sat until it was ice cold in the dead of winter, they'd make sure it was served good and hot on a 120-degree day. On those searing, humid days in our cells, the hot food would make you break out in a prickly sweat to eat it. This was true at the Briar Patch and was often the case in the other camps, too. They did it all on purpose to make sure eating was almost a form of torture and not a comfort. That's one reason— one of many—my stomach is a mess today.

I was moved 26 times as a POW—sometimes just to different buildings within the same camp. Now, along with others, I was moved back to the Zoo—the camp with the buildings I had named the Stables, the Office, the Garage, etc. They moved me to the building I called the Pig Sty. It was on the outer edge of the complex, which had been built as a French film studio. I was in solitary confinement once more.

There was a POW in the next cell who was badly beaten up. He was in a cast from his chest down. He had broken his pelvis when he ejected from his plane. I tapped to him. Even though he was lying next to the wall, he wouldn't tap back. I came to the conclusion he didn't know the tap code.

Finally, I started using Morse Code, which was very difficult. After all, how do you tap a dash? All you really can do is scrape your hand along the wall. This wall wasn't knobby like most of the others. It was pretty clean. Still, I had to be careful, because eventually my hand would wear away a spot in paint on the wall and the guards might realize what I was up to. Yet, the POW next door wouldn't respond.

So I watched and waited until I thought the guard wasn't outside. I'd say, "Hey, next guy. I'm an American. I'm trying to teach you the tap code. Can you hear me?" Sometimes he would cough, sometimes he wouldn't. It took me months and months and months to teach him the tap code.

He never came out of the room, since he couldn't even walk. The guards would take things in and out for him, which they didn't like to do. They hated to touch the buckets that served as our toilets, so they made prisoners do it. The guard would open your cell door, you'd set your full bucket outside, and it would be a POW's job to take them out and empty them. Since the new POW couldn't set his bucket out, and the guards didn't want to touch it, the guards would make a prisoner walk backwards into his cell to get it and not turn around, so that we couldn't see the injured POW.

When it was my turn to empty buckets, I'd carry two at a time if they had handles. As I walked by the new POW's cell, I'd speak to him, but as I spoke, I directed my attention to the guards, who of course didn't understand English. In front of his cell door, I'd look the guard right in the eye and say, "I'm Captain Paul Kari. I'm trying to teach you the tap code."

I pretended I was asking the guard a question about what he wanted me to do with the buckets. I actually rehearsed this act in my cell, trying to become good enough so as not to arouse the guard's suspicion, but a couple of times they caught on to my ploy.

To stall for more time for me to talk in front of his cell door, I'd purposely spill one of the slop buckets and have to clean it up. I'd be stooped down, looking at the guard, explaining the tap code out loud, and all the while cleaning up this mess of human waste with my hands. It wasn't like they'd hand me a mop or a dust pan.

In this manner, I tried to explain the tap code to the new POW every chance I had. I didn't think I was getting anywhere, until one day he coughed and hit the wall when I started tapping. Finally he got it.

The North Vietnamese made POWs do the sweeping with crude brooms made from brush gathered around the camp. The guards never caught on to the fact that we'd communicate the tap code with the broom while we worked. Just like tapping on the wall, we'd make one series of strokes with the broom to indicate the row of the alphabet and then another series of strokes to indicate the letter. We'd sweep really loud so the whole camp could hear the message! It was kind of humorous.

We couldn't wait until it was time to sweep. In fact, the senior ranking officer of the POWs told the camp commander, "Americans like things clean. Why don't you let us sweep the camp?" The camp commander said, "That's a good idea!" We suckered them right into it.

It was about this time I remember reaching for my tube of toothpaste, which sat on a little ledge in my cell. The brand name was Thouc-Rang. As I was squeezing the paste onto my toothbrush, I realized I couldn't see the letter "o" in the brand name. Holy mackerel, I said to myself, "What's happening to me?"

The next time I was taken to interrogation, I told the camp commander I was losing my eyesight. He said, "What do you mean?" I said, "I can't read the middle letter on the toothpaste tube."

His reply infuriated me. I had never before heard the name he used, but I knew exactly what he meant.

"Ah," he said. "Thailand. You go with Fly by Night."

It was their name for a prostitute. Some sexually transmitted diseases can damage eyesight and that's what he was suggesting had happened to me.

"No!" I said. "I've never done that!"

He smiled.

"Ah, you American pilots," he said. "Yeah, yeah."

My captors did make a small effort to help me. It wasn't very long before they brought me a 35 mm film canister filled with peanuts. They thought my eyesight problems were the result of a Vitamin A deficiency. But that's all they ever did for my eyes. And the problem got worse and worse.

I learned later the loss of my center vision resulted from a lack of thiamine. It likely began that first winter at the Briar Patch when I was the last prisoner to be fed. I only received whatever food was left after they scraped the bottom of the pot—usually no more than half a ration.

Each of our cells in the Hanoi Hilton had a little opening at the base of the back wall that led to a concrete channel outside. It was designed so the cells could be cleaned by hosing them down and letting the water run out through the hole.

By about 1968, some of the other American prisoners began receiving packages from home that included vitamins. I tapped to other POWs that I was losing my eyesight. The prisoner in the cell next to mine sent me a message.

"I've got some vitamins," he tapped. "I'm going to try to send one to you."

When water ran through the concrete channel outside, it ran downhill from the opening in his cell wall to the opening in mine. He wrapped a vitamin on a stick—where he got the stick, I have no idea—and floated it down. Needless to say, it was difficult to reach through the opening and grab something as it went by. I missed the first couple, but finally caught one and took the vitamin. I don't think it helped, but I'm grateful to him for taking the risk of sharing it with me.

They moved me into a building at the Zoo that was right next to a swimming pool the French had built. Since this was a former film studio, it didn't have walls around the entire complex like the Hoa Loa Prison in Hanoi. Instead, they built a wall around each building. The summer of 1968 was extra hot in Vietnam. It was so hot, at night I'd lie on the floor with my nose right up to the gap at the bottom of my cell door, just hoping a little cooler breeze might come in from the outside. Even if a rain storm came in, or a wind came up, because there were walls surrounding each building, maybe 15 feet away, you couldn't feel any breeze.

Each spring, the camp commander had peasants come in and brick up the barred window in our cells so that during the warm part of the year, it would be almost unbearably hot inside. And every fall, he had the peasants come back and knock the bricks out so we'd nearly freeze to death in the wintertime. We always wondered why they didn't just put wooden doors on them that could be opened and closed!

POWs each had a pair of shorts, which we'd wear in our cells in hot weather. However, the guards always made us put on our long pajamas when they took us out. They had ties on them, not buttons, which we had to cinch up tight.

I thank God I didn't suffer too badly from heat rash. Other guys, their whole body would be red with it. As I said, the camp commander would have the food served as hot as possible in the summer. We'd try to let it cool as long as possible, but if you let the food sit too long, the guards would come in and take it away.

Through the tap code, we heard there were two Cubans in the camp conducting a new torture and interrogation program. Evidently, the Cubans had said to the North Vietnamese, "We know how to get Americans to do anything we want them to do. If it's a confession you want, we know how to get a confession. If you let us, your socialist brothers, come in, we'll teach you how to do it."

We heard rumors that made us shudder in fear. The word was the Cubans would torture you almost to the point of death. They wanted some POWs to write confessions, which they did. As for other prisoners, it was just the Cubans' pleasure to break them, and then let them go back to their cells.

Our building had six cells on either side and I was in the fourth one down. In front of my cell, there was a board where two women would place our food. They'd dish out the rice, soup and side dish then the guards would let us come out one at a time to get our meal.

One afternoon, my door opened and I went out to get my food. I had never seen the two Cubans before, but I immediately knew who they were. They were standing out there looking for a new candidate. I became so scared. I nodded my head at them, picked up my stuff, and went back in. I was so petrified, I didn't even eat. I got down on my knees and I prayed; *God, don't let them pick me. Please don't let them pick me.* And they didn't. I thank God to this day.

They had tortured one POW by the name of Ron Storz. The saddest sight I have ever seen in my life is the last time any of us ever saw Ron alive. We watched through the cracks in our doors as he walked across the courtyard. Words cannot describe the appearance of a totally broken man. Ron's head was down. His shoulders were slumped. He was walking away and that's the last we ever saw him. They killed him. Nobody knows what happened or how they did it, but Ron never came home.

One day, the camp commander decided he wanted to make the prison into a showplace. Of course, we were glad to help him by "sweeping" the camp at every opportunity and using the broom to communicate the tap code. He decided he was also going to have POWs paint rocks around the camp with whitewash.

He instructed carpenters to come in and cut little openings in the mahogany doors of our cells to make it easier for the women to give us water twice a day. Of course, they didn't give us any more water than before. They still only filled our one-quart pitchers half-full. Our captors never gave us enough water. If they hadn't given us watery soup, we wouldn't have had enough liquid. I suppose it was all carefully calculated.

Our captors had been after us to bow every time we saw a North Vietnamese person. The camp commander told us when one of the women opens the little door to give you your water, you bow to her. Well, I wouldn't bow. It went on like that for months.

Finally, Robbie Risner, who was in the camp by that time, sent me a message, which other prisoners passed along via the tap code. He said, "Tell Kari there's nothing wrong with bowing."

Robbie said, "If you don't bow, they're going to kill you."

"I'm going to hold off as long as I can," I tapped back.

At last, the camp commander confronted me at one of my interrogations.

"You never go home," he said. "You the blackest criminal. You don't do anything the others do. You are belligerent. Where did they train you?"

It wasn't a funny situation at the time, but it seems humorous now to look back on it. He was so mad at me.

"I don't understand," I said. "Who do I bow to? I only bow to God."

"We're God!" he said.

He was angry. He didn't literally mean they were God. What he meant was, we've got you and you must submit to us.

Still, I kept up the game.

"I don't understand your system of rank," I told him. "We only salute officers above us."

"We bow to everybody," he answered.

"Well, we have to know your rank," I insisted.

Of course, the North Vietnamese always refused to tell us their ranks or their positions within the army. They didn't want us to know.

We went on, sparring back and forth. It wasn't a joking matter, but I kept questioning and he kept trying to pound it into me.

Finally, I said,

"I'm confused. I don't know who to bow to."

"You bow to anything that moves," the camp commander said.

"OK," I replied.

He'd soon wish he hadn't said that.

The next time the guard came to get me out of my cell for interrogation, he marched me up to the camp commander's office, holding a gun to my back as usual.

We left my building and as we were going along, a pig walked in front of us. I stopped and I gave the pig a long, deep bow. All the guys were watching this through the cracks in their cell doors. To them, it was hilarious.

The guard, however, began screaming. He hit me in the back with the butt of his gun and hustled me along. He immediately told the camp commander what I had done. The camp commander came unglued. He threw me back in my cell and put me in irons.

There was a Navy A-6 navigator whose cell was a couple of doors down from mine. The A-6 was a side-by-side plane with a goofy looking refueling probe that stuck out just above the nose. We Air Force guys would kid him about it.

One day, the guard took me out and as he marched me by the A-6 navigator's cell, I stuck my right arm and fingers out like the refueling probe. I knew everybody was watching through the cracks in the doors, including him. He laughed and said, "You goddamn S.O.B.!" The guard had no idea what was going on, but banged the navigator's door to tell him to be quiet.

Little moments like bowing to the pig and teasing one another were so important to POWs when it came to maintaining our morale and our human dignity. No matter how harsh the conditions were, we seized every drop of humor that we could to survive, the same way we drank every drop of water and savored every wisp of fresh air that floated in through the cracks.

GUNNERY TRAINING

In basic pilot training, we learned how to fly a jet fighter. At Luke Air Force Base in Arizona, we learned how to use it as a weapon.

There, I rejoined a friend from preflight training at Lackland, Hal Dortch. My flight commander was a Marine Corps pilot named Bill Brothers. He was on exchange duty with the Air Force and really knew flying. He had five instructor pilots under him, with one or two students per instructor.

We began with air-to-ground gunnery instruction on the F-100s four 20 mm cannons. Luke had the F-100 F model, which was just a two-seater. We got one or two rides in that with an instructor to be checked out before being allowed to fly solo in the C model, which was a single-seater. They expected pilots to make that transition very quickly. If you couldn't, you probably shouldn't have been there.

The ordnance—whether rockets, missiles, or bombs—had been loaded on the plane the night before or earlier that morning. Each weapon had a red pin in it to keep it from being fired while on the ground. Just before take-off, the four planes in each flight lined up at angle—pointing away from anyone and anything in case one of the weapons accidentally went off.

When it was time to arm the weapons, pilots were required to dangle their hands outside the plane canopies where the armament people could see them. Apparently, sometime in the past, a pilot had been fiddling and accidentally fired a weapon as the pins were being pulled. Only when the leader of the armament crew gives you a thumbs-up to signal the all-clear and you give him a thumbs-up in response, is a pilot permitted to pull his hands back inside the canopy. That was the procedure we followed for every take-off.

We were dispatched to the firing range in groups of four fighters. The target was a piece of cloth, about 20-feet square. The armament crew would dip the tips of our bullets in different colors. One pilot's bullets might be blue. The other three planes might have red, yellow, and black. We'd all fire at the same target. Afterward, the range officers would go out and count the different colors to see how we did.

If I recall, they gave us 112 rounds each, which we were to fire in three short bursts. We'd come around in a pattern, fire, then repeat the exercise twice more. We were required to come in at different dive angles and speeds, which required adjusting our gun sights to fit the situation.

When it was time to tally up the scores, they might say, Cadillac 2—which was my call sign—had the red bullets and he took 32 holes. Well, that's not very good if you had 112 shots at it!

After learning how to fire our guns, we moved on to rockets, then bombs. The bombs were 25-pounders and had the same ballistics as the real thing. We practiced dive bombing and conventional skip bombing. In skip bombing, the bomb is dropped from an altitude of just 50 feet, right in front of the target.

Next, we went on to nuclear delivery, which in those days was very difficult. Technology had developed nuclear bombs that were so powerful your plane was not fast enough to escape the blast once you dropped the bomb. As fighters, we wouldn't be delivering nuclear weapons at 20,000 to 30,000 feet like a bomber. We were to fly right down on the deck to stay under the enemy's radar. When I say on the deck, I mean as close to the treetops as you had the guts to fly.

Later, for three of the four years I was stationed in Germany, I sat on nuclear alert. It was a one-way mission. My target was so far away—600 to 700 miles—I would run out of fuel shortly after I dropped the bomb. There would be enough left in the tanks to fly about 80 miles away from the target before I had to bail out. Needless to say, World War III was chilling to contemplate for any number of reasons. The bombs themselves were 1.1 megatons—110 times more powerful than the one dropped on Hiroshima.

It was only after I left Germany the Air Force developed atomic bombs outfitted with tungsten spikes. With the newer "lay-down" weapon, you'd fly toward your target almost on the deck and have to come up a couple of hundred feet to release your bomb. An aerodynamic nose cone blew off the bomb to reveal the tungsten spike and a parachute would release from the back. Remember, the fighter is traveling at 500 knots, so the parachute was critical to slow the bomb down. It was designed to hit enemy runways, because the tungsten spike would dig itself six feet into the concrete. The nuclear bomb itself operated on a timer, which gave the fighter pilot time to get away.

In my day, the best chance we had to get away from a nuclear blast was a Low-Angle Bombing System maneuver we nicknamed "over-the-shoulder." We practiced this more than any other skill.

You'd fly in at 360 knots—that's six miles per minute or 10 seconds per mile, which made it easier to figure course corrections in your head. We'd identify an initial point, maybe 10 to 15 miles from the target. Once you hit that, you knew you were on course, and you pushed the plane up to 500 knots. You're really hauling the mail at that point.

As soon as you got over the target, you'd fly sharply upward—pulling four Gs in exactly two seconds. The bombing system incorporated a gyro. Prior to flight, you'd set the gyro for a specific release point, based on the angle and the weight of the aircraft. You'd start your pull, hit the "pickle" button, and the bomb would be released automatically seconds later at the ideal point in your climb. The effect is like a slingshot. When the bomb releases, you can feel it. The plane just jumps.

You are traveling at such a sharp angle and at such a high speed the momentum actually causes the bomb to continue to travel vertically for some time, giving the pilot a little better chance to get away. Eventually, gravity takes over, the bomb turns around, and heads down toward the target. You peel off, keep the fighter's afterburner on—which gives you 50 percent more thrust—and go like heck. This technique uses a lot more fuel than the lay-down method limiting the distance the plane could travel away from the bomb to escape the blast.

The pilot has to be precise in executing an over-the-shoulder, which can be a challenge when you have four times the normal force of gravity pressing in on you. If you're off by as much as one tenth of one degree when you release that bomb, it's going to be way off target.

In a dive bomb situation, you've got, say, a 500-pound bomb, which you release based on a chart that takes into account the drag of the specific bomb, how it will fall, and its impact. Back then we used iron bombs, just like they did in World War II. They were not laser-guided liked the bombs that came along later.

One day I had a mission to simulate dropping a nuclear weapon. The dummy bomb used in the training exercise was filled with concrete. If I'm not mistaken, it weighed 2,000 pounds. Needless to say, that's a lot of weight for a fighter to lift off the ground. It was right at the limit.

Well, I was rolling down the runway and rolling and rolling and rolling, trying to get the airplane off the ground. We weren't supposed to take off if we used more than 90 percent of the runway. That was to leave us time to slow down enough to "take the barrier." At the end of the runway was a piece of netting just high enough off the ground to catch the wheels of the plane. The netting was connected to a pair of brake drums from a B-52, which brought you to a halt.

It was a hot summer day at Nellis Air Force Base in Nevada. The exhaust of jet engines taking off one after another probably made the temperature on the runway 140 to 150 degrees. We also were at a relatively high elevation, which meant the thinner air wasn't much help in lifting the plane.

That net was coming closer and closer. I didn't know if I was going to make it. When I finally got the nose of that fighter up, I lifted myself up from the pilot seat, trying to use some body English, as I barely cleared the barrier! I thought for sure the wheels were going to hit it.

The low-level mission had a turning point over a dry lake bed. The lake bed was flat as a tabletop, maybe five or six miles across. The turning point was right in the center. Well, I was flying low, right above the ground. I just kept dropping a little lower, a little lower, a little lower. I think we all did that, as confident of ourselves as we were. I was traveling at about 360 knots.

All of a sudden, the turning point appeared. I had to pull the nose up or my wing would have dipped down and touched it when I turned! That's how close to the ground I had been flying. You look back and you say: Oh man, how stupid. What things you do when you're young.

In a way, it must be more difficult to fly today's airplanes, due to the high level of electronics involved. You almost have to be a whiz at computer games to be a pilot. It's more than us old timers can comprehend. But in the early 1960s, it was about a pilot's ability to drop munitions with precision. It required a special level of skill to be able to put that bomb where it was supposed to be. It was difficult to be accurate.

There were five things a pilot had to marry up in the same instant to get a direct hit: Altitude, air speed, angle, windage and the "pipper." The pipper is what we called the bomb sight.

We tried to roll in at 10,000 feet above the terrain. There are different dive bomb angles, but the one that was the best compromise was a 45-degree angle. So you'd go look at the chart and you'd say, OK, my airplane weighs this much, my bombs weigh this, and I've got this certain type of bomb. So I will have to be at a 45-degree dive angle at a certain altitude and at a certain airspeed.

You'd roll in at 250 knots at a 55-degree angle instead of 45 degrees, because as you gain airspeed your plane begins to shallow out. So if you want to release at 450 knots at a certain point in space, you know you have to be at a certain altitude to allow you to gain the 200 knots of speed.

We didn't have precise instruments that told us we were coming in at maybe a 42- or 43-degree angle instead of a 45. All we had was our bomb sight, which we maneuvered right up to the target. You have to have the airspeed, altitude, angle and pipper all lined up at exactly the right point, or you won't get a hit.

You also have to take into account the weather. When you're target-shooting with a gun, you know the wind can blow the bullet one way or the other. A bomb or rocket or a bullet released from a fighter jet behave the same way. Weather affects everything.

When I eventually went into combat, the first bombing mission we had in Vietnam, my leader was Caspar Sharpless Bierman. He was a big, bragging, cigar-smoking guy and an excellent pilot. That day, the second lieutenant weather officer told us the wind in our target area was coming in from 045 degrees at 15 knots.

A pilot has to compensate for the fact the wind will blow a falling bomb in a certain direction. So you learn not to work your pipper right on to the target, but slightly upwind, knowing if you drop your bomb over here, the wind will blow it over there.

Well, on that first mission in Vietnam, we blew it. All four airplanes in our flight. We dropped those iron bombs according to what the weather officer had told us and all of them missed the target. The bombs ended up way off to one side.

All the way home, I'm thinking, *I know I'm a better bomber than that and I know Cass is a better bomber than that.* I'd practiced with him enough at MacDill Air Force Base in Tampa to know.

What went wrong?

In our debriefing, I told Cass the problem is this first lieutenant doesn't know any more about the weather 300 to 400 miles north of here than we do. He doesn't have somebody up there in a Shell station taking the windage.

"Cass, I've got an idea," I said.

On our next mission, we'll go in, listen to the weather officer, nod our heads, and then go out and forget what he said. When we're in the air, Cass will drop his bombs first, with his pipper right on the target. I'll be close behind him, flying in the No. 2 position. If I see his bombs go off to the left 100 feet, I'll compensate and drop my bombs a corresponding distance to the right.

That's exactly what we did. And we never missed a target again.

From Gunnery School at Luke Air Force Base, I went on to Advanced Gunnery School at Nellis Air Force Base near Las Vegas. In three months, we learned aerial refueling and how to "fire on the dart."

The dart was like a honeycomb-patterned paper airplane attached to a line and towed by an airplane. Another F-100 pilot took off and released the dart from the back of his plane. It was on a reel and he'd let the line out about 1,500 feet. With a four-man flight of student pilots behind him, he'd make a climbing turn to get out of the way and we'd fire on the dart. Just like when we practiced air-to-ground gunnery at Luke, we had live ammunition, with each pilot's bullets painted a different color so we could be scored on our accuracy.

As always, we were being graded on every aspect of our training—academics, military bearing and flying ability. Word always came back to us from pilots who had completed their training about which air bases were the best places to be stationed. The students who had the best training scores got to choose where they wanted to go.

It was 1960 and there were three primary fighter bases in Germany: Hahn, Bitburg and Spangdahlem. Hahn and Bitburg each had a squadron at Ramstein Air Base. All the old guys coming back to Nellis said Ramstein is the place to go. They've got two officers clubs and four restaurants right on the base—Hungarian, Chinese, Italian and American. To top it off, the Autobahn goes right through the base. It was the assignment everyone who had the chance would ask for. When it was my turn to choose, I picked Ramstein.

About a week before we were to end our tour at Nellis, the squadron commander asked at our morning briefing, "Who wants to be a ferry pilot for the Thunderbirds for a week?" My hand went up so fast I nearly threw it out of joint.

The Thunderbirds are the U.S. Air Force's precision flying demonstration team. There was about a month before we had to be in Germany. Most everyone else was married and looking forward to spending the time with their families. I was single, so I immediately volunteered and was fortunate enough to be chosen.

Even though Thunderbird pilots were highly skilled, it could be a dangerous job. I recall one day I walked into the Officers Club and saw two women there who were very upset. Their husbands were on a Thunderbird team and had crashed.

They were practicing at their station at Nellis Air Force Base and both augered into the ground. Incredibly, someone saw it on the news and had called one of the wives before the Air Force had notified them. What a terrible way to find out. It was so shocking to me it happened that way.

The Thunderbirds had a show in Des Moines, Iowa, and simply needed an F-100 qualified pilot to fly in their spare airplane. They wore their trademark blue flight suits and I wore my basic Air Force green, but I was excited to fly in with them.

Later that week, they were scheduled for a show at Frontier Days in Cheyenne, Wyoming. We landed at Cheyenne Airport, which was a commercial airport. I didn't know until after I landed that Cheyenne was the location of the stewardess school for United Airlines.

The six regular Thunderbird pilots flew in and landed. Parked in front of each of their planes were six Thunderbird cars, which whisked them away.

Well, here comes Paul in last place with the seventh plane. I taxied up and shut down the engine. There was no Thunderbird car waiting for me! Eventually, someone drove up to take me downtown to our hotel, which also happened to be where the flight attendants were staying.

These Thunderbird pilots had been all around the world. Now there I was, 24 years old and "Green 16" as they would say, suddenly standing in my flight suit in a hotel lobby filled with beautiful flight attendants. All the Thunderbird pilots, having arrived well before me, were already in the bar.

A couple of the women came up to me.

"Are you with the Thunderbirds?" one asked.

"Well, I'm just ferrying an aircraft," I said. "I'm not on the team."

"Wow!" they said. "Say, how can we meet the Thunderbird pilots?"

"You want to meet some of the guys? OK, I'll try to arrange it," I said.

I took my bags up to my room and then went to the bar, as 15 or 20 of the women waited in the lobby.

The truth was, I'd only just met these pilots myself. If I were to say something right off the bat, I figured they would look at me and say, "Who is this guy?"

Luckily, someone else mentioned the flight attendants from United Airlines. So I piped up.

"How many of them would you like to meet?" I asked.

"What are you talking about?" one of Thunderbird pilots asked.

"How many of them would you like to meet?" I repeated. "I can arrange it."

Well, they responded with a few choice words. I was the new guy. What did I know?

"Just give me five or 10 minutes," I said.

I went back to the flight attendants, who were still milling around the lobby.

"How many women can you get together down here?" I asked.

"How many do you want?" they replied.

"How about a couple dozen?" I said.

"We'll see what we can do," they said.

Before long, about 20 women appeared in the lobby. I led them into the bar.

"OK, you Thunderbirds." I announced. "You thought I was pulling your leg. Here they are!"

It was pretty amusing. We all had a blast over the two or three days we were there. I got to be friends with one of the flight attendants. This was during the time when presidential candidates Richard Nixon and John F. Kennedy were having their first live television debate. I remember we sat and watched the whole thing together. It was quite an exciting thing in those days.

We attended Frontier Days, where I was amazed by the sight of so many old cowboys limping along or on crutches. Every cowboy in the West seemed to come in for the big round-up.

It was like the state fair with lots of amusement rides. Now, you'd think an Air Force pilot who was used to flying upside down and under all sorts of conditions in a jet fighter would have no problems riding carnival rides. Wrong.

Never in my life had I felt ill in an airplane, but it didn't take more than one or two go-a rounds on these whirly-gigs before I began to feel sick.

"Isn't this fun?" my date said. "Let's do it again!"

I didn't say anything. It was all I could do not to throw up! It was pretty embarrassing. Eventually I was able to tell her the rides weren't sitting too well with me.

"You've got to be kidding," she said, laughing. "A guy who flies a Thunderbird aircraft gets sick on a carnival ride?"

She never let me live that down the rest of the evening.

Finally, it was time to fly back to Las Vegas. I still had time before I had to report for my flight to Ramstein Air Base in Germany, so I jumped in my red and white, two-door, hardtop '56 Oldsmobile and headed home to Spencer, Ohio. There were three of us going to Ramstein, with a couple of others headed to Bitburg and Spangdahlem, but all had different travel arrangements than I did.

I spent the next three weeks hauling gravel for Mom and Dad's long driveway at the farm. It was the middle of August, but in the winter, the driveway was a sea of mud. Dad, who was still working at the foundry, had made arrangements to get gravel from a place down by the Black River, which crosses under the B&O Railroad at U.S. Route 224 in Lodi. It was open pasture then, but today it's all trees.

We had a Carter brand loader with one big hydraulic cylinder up front attached to a little four-foot bucket. It had no power steering and no live hydraulics, which meant every time you put in the clutch, the bucket would stop moving. It was a pretty primitive machine by modern standards.

Dad's 2 ½ ton International truck could haul about eight tons of gravel per load. It didn't have a hoist on it, which meant I was shoveling off every bit of the gravel by hand. I didn't keep track, but I must have shoveled off hundreds of tons.

Finally, I had an idea. I got out a slip scraper, threw it up into the truck and hooked it up to another tractor. I asked my sister Karen, who was probably 16 or 17 at the time, to help.

With the scraper in the back of the truck, I'd say, "OK, pull!" Karen drove the tractor, dragging the gravel out of the truck a little at a time. We probably unloaded 90 percent of the gravel that way.

I filled the driveway with a thick layer of stone from the road up to the barn. I said to myself, "That ought to last three years."

And I headed for Germany.

A Christmas Program

Months rolled into years and the years rolled into a new decade, the 1970s. I had been shot down on Father's day of 1965. Back home, my kids were growing up without me. I had missed five years of birthdays and five Christmases. I wasn't there to see my daughter Ali's first steps or my son Shawn's first day of school.

The world was moving on, too. The late-1960s was a volatile time in American life. Martin Luther King Jr. and Robert F. Kennedy had been assassinated. There were protests against the war. Changes in society, music and culture were sweeping the country. It was all happening very far away from the jungle prison camps of North Vietnam.

I was moved yet again. This time to a prison we called Camp Unity. It was only about a mile from Son Tay, where in November of 1970 U.S. Special Forces would attempt a daring helicopter rescue of American POWs. Eventually we were transported from Camp Unity back to Hoa Loa Prison in Hanoi.

For five years, my wife, children, parents, sisters, fellow service members and friends had no idea if I was dead or alive. I decided I would try to change that.

As I've mentioned, every Christmas, the North Vietnamese faithfully staged a dinner in which they filmed prisoners enjoying a "typical" meal of a turkey or chicken drumstick and half a bottle of beer. And, every year, I faithfully declined to participate in this ruse, knowing the movies would be shown as propaganda. Our captors wanted the world to believe they were treating us humanely, even generously, when the opposite was true.

When I learned I was classified by the U.S. as missing, not captured, I realized I owed it to my family to use the next propaganda film to let them know I was alive.

As usual, the North Vietnamese set the stage for a Christmas program. It was held in a building open on all sides. They took 30-40 of us from our cells to be lectured by a Communist "preacher," who told us we were criminals and not Christians. I volunteered to go the fifth year because I knew my country did not know I was alive. By going, I hoped the U.S. government would get a copy of the film and know I was not missing in action. There were about two dozen sets of large movie cameras. Every time it looked like one was panning toward me, I made sure my face looked directly into it.

The U.S. government invited families whose service members were listed as missing to come to a military base theater in Columbus to view the movies. My parents drove down from Spencer to see if they could recognize me in any of the footage.

Well, leave it to a mother to be able to pick her baby out of a crowd. As the camera panned the roomful of POWs, my face appeared in a corner of the film for less than half a second. I don't know how she did it, but Mom saw me. She asked the projectionist to replay the film and freeze it at that exact spot.

"That's Paul," she said.

Sitting with her in the middle of the base theater just in front of the projector, my dad was so excited he jumped up, ran down the aisle to the movie screen, and pointed to my face.

"That's my son!" he shouted. "That's my son!"

My mom, always the unemotional one, said, "Tony, get back here! You're embarrassing us!"

I have a copy of that frame from the movie, which one of my sisters, Carol, was able to locate in the archives at the Smithsonian.

Vivah Walters, who owned the store in Spencer when I was growing up and is now 104 years old, told me her family prayed for me at every meal. I know there were a lot of people like her who asked God to take care of me and bring me safely home. That was a blessing and I know it's why I'm here today.

By now, I began to be very sick. I'd had digestive problems from the beginning of my imprisonment, but this was the worst it had been. My stomach hurt terribly every time I ate. I would tell the camp commander I couldn't eat the cold food and greasy meat they were serving us. Occasionally, the guards would bring me a cup of warm milk. I guess they thought I had an ulcer. The milk didn't help, but I thought it was a humane gesture for them to offer it to me.

The number of POWs had increased dramatically. Here, there were about a dozen prisoners to a room. Our beds were mahogany boards, about an inch and a half thick, laid on the floor. My bed was in the back corner. I was so sick, most of the time, I couldn't even get up. I just lay there, day and night.

My first roommate from the Briar Patch, Robert Purcell, was our senior ranking officer at Hoa Loa. At one point, Percy thought I was on the edge of death. He began screaming for a medic. POWs weren't supposed to raise their voices.

The camp commander had instructed us to say words that sounded like "bow cow" when we needed something. I have no idea of the actual spelling or what the phrase meant in North Vietnamese. I can only assume it meant something like "help."

Percy began screaming, "Bow cow! Bow cow!" He probably didn't know if anyone even would hear him. Finally, the guards came and took him out for a "quiz." They slapped him around for being too noisy.

A North Vietnamese medic arrived and gave me an injection of adrenalin. It didn't help. I guess they thought I was about ready to check out and were trying to keep my heart beating. Thankfully, my condition eventually improved enough that I could be up and around again.

Don Spoon had been through the Air Force Academy had figured out how to weigh us. He fashioned a scale using a slat of wood from one of our beds as a lever and one of our toilet buckets as a counterweight. He calculated my weight at 103 pounds. Since being shot down five years earlier, I had lost 70 pounds.

This same POW weighed me again just prior to our release and I was back up to 133 pounds. When U.S. medical personnel gave me a physical shortly after we got out, they found he was only off by three pounds in his calculations. I thought that was impressive.

It was one day in late 1970 or maybe early 1971 when the North Vietnamese took a POW off to interrogation. As they brought him back, he began hollering at the top of his lungs.

"We landed a man on the moon!" he shouted. "We landed a man on the moon!"

The guard, who couldn't understand English, must have thought the POW was trying to start a riot. The guard marched him right back to the camp commander, where the POW was tortured—by being placed in irons and beaten with a broken fan belt.

He came back to his room the next day and told the other POWs he had received a care package with a packet of sugar in it. On the sugar packet was a picture of Neil Armstrong standing on the moon. So that's how we found out about Apollo 11's successful voyage to the lunar surface in the summer of 1969—from a pack of sugar! It's just one of the many events we missed as the world outside our prison walls marched on without us.

During our six months in this particular camp, another POW got a package from home. The U.S. government had placed a secret message inside one of the vitamin capsules. I don't know how they did it or how the POW knew to look for it. It was like microfiche, only smaller. The message basically said, "Keep on hanging on."

If it was intended to give us hope, it didn't work. It made me angry. At that point, I had been held prisoner almost six years. *Keep on hanging on? You S.O.B.s*, I said to myself. *That's all we've been doing is hanging on.*

Eventually, the North Vietnamese found one of those messages in another bottle of vitamins. From then on, they cut open every vitamin. And when air gets to vitamins like that, they lose their potency, so they weren't very effective. Fortunately, we were able to find our own ways to help keep our spirits up.

Since we now were being held as a group, the senior ranking officers decided we were going to begin holding church services. So, Sunday morning came, and we started singing hymns that we knew—loudly. We sang "Amazing Grace," "The Old Rugged Cross," and all the old favorites that POWs from different religious denominations knew by heart.

The camp commander said, "We can't have this!" To him, we were exercising too much freedom and he was afraid we would riot. He yanked the senior ranking officer out of the room and told him we weren't allowed to sing. But as soon as they took him outside, we started singing hymns again! The North Vietnamese came in and found the next senior ranking officer and took him out. As soon as he left, we resumed singing.

This happened again and again until they had pulled six or eight officers out of the room. Finally, the North Vietnamese came in and confronted those of us who remained.

"You can't do this," they said. "You can't have a church service. It's rebellious!"

We told them they could take every man out of the room and the last guy who remains is going to keep on singing. The North Vietnamese finally gave up and told us if we were going to sing, to keep it down.

The senior ranking officers came up with another morale booster. For evening entertainment, POWs took turns standing up and telling about our areas of expertise—whether it was talking about our college major or about an experience we had before we were shot down. We had very highly educated guys there who had graduated from the Air Force Academy and from West Point. There were electrical engineers and technicians of all kinds. And here I was with a degree in animal science from Ohio State!

A number of other POWs had given their talks when the senior ranking officer turned to me.

"Hey, Kari," he said, "what's your degree in?"

"Agriculture," I said. "Animal science."

"You think you have anything to tell them?"

"I don't know," I told him, "but I'll try."

Believe it or not, there was one other POW who was an animal science major—Alton Meyer, who'd studied at Texas A&M.

I decided the most useful thing I probably could tell my fellow POWs was what they or their wives should look for when they wanted to buy good meat at the grocery—which I had learned when I was on the meat-judging team at Ohio State. So that's what I did. I told them all about marbling and fat and protein and what characteristics they should look for. They must have found it interesting because they wanted me to come back the next night and talk about livestock judging!

Meanwhile, in Congress, the pressure mounted on the U.S. government to do something about American POWs. Just in case the United States attempted a rescue, the North Vietnamese decided they'd better not keep so many of their eggs in one basket at Hoa Loa Prison. So they took half of us to a camp near the Chinese border.

We took up our bedrolls and the guards loaded us into trucks. We traveled through the night, all day, and into the next night. We had no idea where we were going. It was far up in the mountains. We all worked together in memorizing the truck's every turn and trying to keep track of how far we had traveled by estimating our time and speed. One of the POWs—he was a navigator, I assume—was able to tell what direction we were traveling based on the stars.

He said we were five or 10 miles from the Chinese border. With God as my judge, we found out later that's exactly where we were. We were five kilometers or three miles from the border. To achieve that kind of accuracy under those conditions was absolutely incredible. I'm still in awe of the fact he was able to figure out our location so exactly.

In this camp—christened the Dog Patch—we spent the winter of '72-'73. There was no electricity. One of the POWs made a trip back there recently and said today it's all overgrown. Here, we enjoyed a little more freedom. Again, there were several buildings, each with multiple rooms. I believe seven of us shared the building I was in. Some of the guys would lay their pajama pants out on the roofs of the buildings, hoping a satellite might take a picture and the world would know we were there.

This is where I met up again with Spike Nasmyth—the avowed atheist whom the North Vietnamese had given a Bible. For entertainment one night, he asked us if we wanted to hear the story of the Bible.

"What do you know about it?" I asked. "You're an atheist."

He proceeded to lay out the entire Bible in chronological order, explaining how it all fit together. It made such perfect sense.

"Spike," I said, "God bless you. I've gone to Sunday school my whole life and I've never understood the Bible more clearly than you just explained it."

There was one guard at the Dog Patch we called "Hollywood" because he had a full head of hair, which he always combed up nice. He was one of the few guards who actually showed compassion for us. If the camp commander told him to tie one of us up and we winced as he pulled the rope tight, he would loosen it a little. And that was a great personal risk for him. If the camp commander told him to do something and he didn't do it, he could be tied up himself and punished.

My fellow prisoners always called me a pessimist. But I wasn't a pessimist. I was a realist. If a POW got an extra banana two days in a row, somebody would say, "Hey, we must be going home soon because they're trying to fatten us up!" I'd say, "No. We're not going home until U.S. forces really make the North Vietnamese hurt. And we haven't made them hurt bad enough yet."

That would soon change.

Years had passed since we last heard any U.S. bombings going on around us. In December of 1972, we began to hear explosions again in the distance. It went on day after day, night after night. Relentless bombing.

Later, when we finally were released, President Richard Nixon opened up an auditorium at the State Department and personally briefed POWs on the circumstances that led to our release.

He said, "I wanted to do what I did in December of '72 for seven years, but Congress wouldn't let me."

I believe that's true. President Nixon wanted to lay a one-mile-wide swath through downtown Hanoi with B-52 bombers. And that's exactly what he did. If it wasn't for that bombing, I might still be a POW. It was then the North Vietnamese finally said, "OK, we'll talk." Around the first of January in 1973, the guards loaded us up and took us from the Dog Patch to Hanoi, right back to Hoa Loa Prison.

For five years, Secretary of State Henry Kissinger had been engaging in shuttle diplomacy between the North and South Vietnamese in Paris, trying to negotiate an end to the war. They argued about the shape of the conference table for four years. The South wanted a rectangular table. The North wanted a round table. Finally, they settled on a layout using both kinds of tables!

Kissinger's strategy to end the war would require the North Vietnamese to stop fighting to reclaim South Vietnam, return all U.S. POWs, and give a full accounting of all missing American personnel. In return, the United States would pay for all the destruction that had taken place and help rebuild the country—at a cost of hundreds of billions of dollars. In these Paris Peace Accords, Kissinger also stipulated the North Vietnamese had to read to American POWs the agreement as to how they were to be released.

As soon as we returned to Hanoi, our treatment began to improve 100 percent. We were 60 men to a room. The Vietnamese brought us baskets of French bread. When the last loaf was gone, they brought us another basketful. Something serious was happening here, but we didn't know what.

Even a realist like me dared to think, *we might be going home.*

Sitting Nuclear Alert

CHAPTER 18

I drove from Mom and Dad's farm in Spencer to McGuire Air Force Base in New Jersey, where I boarded a C-118 for my flight to Ramstein Air Base in Germany. It would be my home for the next four years.

I had made arrangements to have my car shipped to Germany—which I didn't need to do, but it was a good car and it was paid for. I soon wished I could have driven it across the Atlantic. The C-118 was a four-engine, propeller-driven aircraft, the equivalent of a DC-6. The plane was filled with the wives and children of service members stationed overseas. All these poor kids did was scream and cry the whole trip! It was a long, long flight.

We stopped for refueling in Newfoundland, Iceland, and eventually in Shannon, Ireland, which was just beautiful. I immediately understood why Ireland was called the Emerald Isle. It was the greenest green I've ever seen.

Finally, we arrived at the airport in Frankfurt, Germany. There were two others from my graduating class on the plane—one was headed to Bitburg and another to Spangdahlem. Each had someone from their base there to meet them. There was nobody to meet me. After standing around a while, I went up to another service member and asked how to get to Ramstein. He told me there would be a bus leaving in three or four hours. So I waited for the bus.

I checked in at the Bachelor Officers Quarters at Ramstein. My room was on the first floor, right across from the South Side Officers Club, which made it kind of handy for breakfast and lunch.

The realization soon struck me that I was in a foreign country. The streets were much narrower. The farm fields were smaller. I found the German people to be very friendly, even though it was only 1960 and World War II had been over just 15 years. The Americans spoke English, of course, but the housekeeping staff at the BOQ all spoke German.

I didn't mind at all. In fact, I kind of liked it. My dad came from Hungary and spoke fluent German, so I had been around the language my entire life. It was all very exciting to me.

The next day, I went down to the squadron headquarters. Until the freight ship arrived with my car, I just caught a ride with whoever was headed that way. Here was where a second realization struck me—I had completed my initial training. This was the real thing. It wasn't until then that I learned what our primary mission would be, preparing for World War III, should it ever be declared. Our job was to sit at nuclear alert and to practice low-level flying to avoid enemy radar.

The squadron commander was Tom Stewart—a small, cocky guy with a mustache. The operations officer was Tom Arnold, who was brash and all business. I caught on to things pretty quickly. The old heads readily accepted me. We'd go up to the officers club for lunch or dinner and they'd ask me about my background and I'd ask them about theirs.

One particular pilot and fellow Ohioan, Bob Reickert, welcomed me and made me feel at home.

"What do you do over here all day?" I asked.

The weather in Germany seemed overcast and rainy. I was used to good weather and lots of flying time. It sure didn't look like I'd get that here.

Bob said the U.S. airport with the most instrument flight rule days—when it was too cloudy to fly strictly by sight—was Pittsburgh.

"Our best weather days over here are worse than Pittsburgh's worst weather days," Bob said. "So you'll be flying a lot on instruments."

That wasn't bad news to me. I liked flying by instruments. It was one of my strong points.

Even though being stationed at Ramstein was "the real thing," no one just handed a new pilot the keys to a jet fighter equipped with a nuclear bomb and told him to sit at alert. There was still a lot to learn about flying in Europe and, of course, about our potential targets.

Our little operations building was in a wooded area, which was kind of intriguing all on its own. Remember, this is Germany in 1960. There's a Cold War going on. Our ops building was completely fenced, with a guard at the gate who checked the I.D. cards of everyone who entered. Our aircraft—F-100 fighters—were parked on pads, hidden among the trees. Today, of course, a satellite could look right down and see them, but back then, it seemed like real cloak-and-dagger kind of stuff!

We were not allowed to sit at nuclear alert until we were cleared to fly on instruments. To do that, new pilots were scheduled to make several local flights. In Germany, you might take off in clear weather, but suddenly find yourself in overcast conditions, and have to divert to a different landing location. Often we had not one, but two alternate landing places, in case the first was socked-in, which it often was.

In Europe, unlike flying in the United States, you might encounter several different airspaces on a single flight. It's a relatively small area, where the skies can get congested. Things happen quickly. As soon as you took off in Germany, they'd almost immediately hand you off to an air route traffic control center in France, which would soon turn you over to one in Luxemburg.

We were supposed to fly at least 500 feet—but a lot of guys went lower, thinking it would be fun to buzz the countryside. Even though that's how we'd have to fly anyway on a real mission to stay under enemy radar, all that cocky low-level flying hurt U.S. relations with some countries.

I remember one training mission I flew with my operations officer, Tom Arnold. It may have been only my second time flying over there. He saw me kind of looking around. I was trying to spot a railroad crossing to use as a landmark.

"Paul," Tom said. "Don't ever look back. You'll just miss something that you should've seen."

It was good advice.

All of us new pilots were anxious to get checked out and cleared to fly so that we could sit on nuclear alert. Later on, we sort of looked at each other and wondered why we were ever so anxious to do it. Sitting on alert meant sitting! We spent one boring hour after the next sitting in the alert shack while others got to fly.

I had been at Ramstein maybe 10 days, with only a couple training missions under my belt. On this particular day, I was flying wing with another pilot and we were taking off in formation. For whatever reason, the pilot flying lead decided to abort his take off. I had enough speed, so I decided to go ahead and take off.

So there I was, solo, in a foreign country, with little experience. By the time I returned to Ramstein, it was socked in by the weather. I had to divert to an alternate landing site, which I had never done in my life. I found it on my chart and locked onto the radio beacon that guided me in. Somehow, I made it all by myself.

I got into the base of operations and called Tom back at Ramstein to tell him I was safely down.

He said, "You're on alert tomorrow! You just passed! If you can do that by yourself, you're qualified to sit at alert."

He was kind of joking, since it usually takes about a month for a new pilot to get qualified, but I knew I was ready. That was my introduction to flying with the big boys and sitting on nuclear alert. At Ramstein, I was fortunate to fly with the best of the best. I found flying in Europe to be very enjoyable.

There were four aircraft behind the guarded gate. Each plane was loaded with a 1.1 megaton atomic bomb, ready to fly at a moment's notice, 24 hours per day. We had our own maintenance officer who took a lot of pride in keeping our airplanes in top condition.

The pilots sat in an alert shack. It had a very small cafeteria, a pool table, a study area, and sleeping space for four people. There was also a guy who sat by a red telephone. If he got the call for us to go, he'd push a button that signaled us to run to our aircraft. A crew chief stood ready at the planes at all times. We had to be able to climb up the ladders, put our helmets on, strap in, close the canopy and have the engine running in less than two minutes. The crews pulled the ladders away and in another 90 seconds, we'd be at the end of the runway for take-off.

We never fired the engines in training, but we practiced sprinting to the aircraft. They timed us to make sure we could get there as quickly as we were supposed to. We drilled and drilled on it.

Four pilots sat on alert for 24 hours at a time. There were about 24 pilots, so you rotated in and out maybe every four or five days. The reason it didn't add up to every six days was because there might be a crew of four down at Wheelus Air Base in Libya North Africa for gunnery training, or maybe a couple of guys were out on leave.

After I'd been at Ramstein about six months, I began to ask some of the old heads there what they did on the weekends. Some would say they liked to go to London, others to Madrid—which was a favorite, because the weather there always seemed to be nice. Finally, I told them I'd like to go along some weekend.

"Well," they said. "You can't go unless you've already been."

Figure that one out! It was just their way of breaking in the new guy. Eventually, I weaseled my way onto one of the flights.

That's what our life consisted of. The Air Force tried to give us between 18 and 24 hours of flight time a month, which isn't a whole lot. It was a little less than we were used to. Fuel wasn't a problem back then. Fuel was cheap and the Air Force had the money to buy it. We had certain familiar training routes that we flew. Sometimes, if we had enough fuel on the way back to the base, we'd engage in simulated dogfights.

Zweibrucken Air Base was only about three miles away from Ramstein. The Royal Canadian Air Force flew out of there in their American-built F-86H fighters. That was a great aircraft, designed in the years between the 86s the U.S. used in the Korean War and the F-100s we were flying. The Canadians called it the Mark 6.

It was one aircraft I wish I could have flown. It was an excellent air-to-air combat plane. The Mark 6 was so powerful, that if you were making a low approach and went full-throttle, you'd exceed the speed limit for flying with your landing gear down before you could get your gear up. Unlike our F-100s, the Mark 6 could turn on a dime. We U.S. Air Force guys would be flying home to Ramstein and we could hear the Canadians in the Mark 6s, waiting for us. The F-100 wasn't a good turning aircraft. We'd get into practice dogfights with the Canadians and they'd always win.

The F-100 had two options when it came to fuel tanks: a 275-gallon size or 450-gallon size. The 275-gallon tanks were very streamlined. The 450-gallon tanks, on the other hand, looked like tubs and created a lot of drag. When we sat at nuclear alert, our aircraft were outfitted with two 450-gallon tanks. That, plus the internal fuel the plane could hold, gave us about two hours and 30 minutes of flying time at altitude. My alert target was about two hours and 20 minutes away.

You do the math. We had just enough fuel to get to the target and drop our nuclear weapon. We did not have enough fuel to get back home.

If I was called on to fly, I would take off from Ramstein. To save fuel, I'd climb up to about 20,000 feet. You burned less fuel at altitude. I'd head southeast toward Munich, then due east into Czechoslovakia, climbing to about 25,000. I'd head northeast over Czechoslovakia and due east into the Ukraine.

We knew the Soviets would be picking us up on their radar, but the flying distance was so great, we knew we wouldn't have enough fuel to make it if we flew low. So we would give ourselves away. We knew that was going to happen. U.S. Air Force squadrons based in Bitburg and Spangdahlem all would be flying similar missions to other targets.

As diligently as we drilled, and as well as we prepared ourselves using available intelligence, there were a couple of major variables outside our control. One was light conditions. If we were called on to fly at night, the enemy likely would turn off all lights and radio beacons so as not to give away their locations too easily. Today's aircraft have GPS. But back then, flying the F-100, we relied heavily on our radios and our ability to identify landmarks and use them to make time and distance calculations.

Even in Vietnam, when we flew F-4s with the inertial navigation system—which was normally off two to three miles—we chose an initial point to work from. It's a prominent landmark the pilot uses to orient himself and go from there toward his target.

Our initial point in Eastern Ukraine in calculating a nuclear delivery was a huge lake. Well, that seems helpful. It's big. It's blue. It's easy to see. Unless, of course, it's wintertime and the lake is covered in snow! Or if it's nighttime and everything on the ground is black.

My would-be course over a Russian Eastern Block country would take me southeast, then east, then northeast, as opposed to flying east on a straight light. It would help me avoid at least some of the enemy's defenses.

Cruising at altitude at about 400 knots, I'd begin to let down a bit and hopefully find my initial point. Flying at low level, I'd further reduce my speed to 360 knots. That translates to one mile every 10 seconds—easy to make course corrections that way. If all goes well, I'd see my next landmark or secondary point, and know I'm really on target.

Then I'd push my speed up to 500 knots—which would take a while carrying a heavy bomb load—and perform the LABS maneuver we endlessly practiced. After delivering the nuclear weapon, I'd fly as far as my waning fuel would take me—maybe enough to carry me another 80 miles or so, perhaps less if there was a headwind—and bail out, deep in enemy territory.

With World War III on, and so many missions like mine being flown by U.S. pilots all over Europe, chances were slim anyone would come looking for me any time soon. I would be on my own.

I sat alert on a target in the Ukraine for three years. In World War II, we shook our heads at the suicide missions of Japanese kamikazes. Our one-way missions wouldn't have been much different. In times of war, you do what you have to do. Not many Americans—including our own wives and families—were even aware what would happen if we had been called on to fly. Thank God we never had to go.

The other big variable in contemplating a one-way mission to deliver a nuclear weapon was the weather. As I have mentioned before, wind impacts the flight of the aircraft and of the bombs. There was no way of knowing exactly what the atmospheric conditions would be if we had to fly. I asked our weather officer one day why he never briefed us on the conditions at our target site, since that's where we'd be headed.

"I don't have to tell you," he replied. "You already know."

Because of weather patterns, the conditions in Germany today likely will be the conditions east of here tomorrow, he said.

I had never thought about it that way. At least it would give us a feel for what the clouds and wind might be like.

Sitting in our little alert shack through the winter, we'd all get creative. It would be awfully cold if we had to bail out over Russia, we reasoned. It may not be Siberia, but it's still likely to be frigid. What do you wear? We slept in our long underwear and opened the windows to let the cold air into our bunk room.

We had winter flight suits and winter flight jackets. In our G suits, we'd carry a few gold coins and a map. Into our pockets we might throw a little something to eat to last us a day, but we couldn't carry water. Survival would be difficult, to say the least.

We knew we were on the front lines of the Cold War and that we had an important job to do. Top Secret faxes arrived daily with information about what Russia was up to. Maybe one of their bases got updated fighter aircraft and we'd study them—learn their location, analyze their capabilities, study their tactics, and plan how we could get away from them to carry out our nuclear mission. But we were looking at information that was not always very reliable. There was a lot of guesswork, too.

If we had been called upon to deliver a nuclear weapon, we knew it was truly a one-way ticket. When we bailed out of the aircraft, the air would be so thick with radioactivity they probably wouldn't be able to send a team in for search and rescue. Besides, if it was the start of World War III, it would have been hard to say what else would have been going on or even who would have been available to fly in and pick us up. We were a write-off. Unfortunate, but that's just the way it was.

Now Paul Tibbets, the pilot who dropped the bomb on Hiroshima in World War II, had a Norden bomb sight. Of course he was flying up past 30,000 feet. That Norden bomb sight was so secret—it was in all of our bombers—they said if you go down with the airplane, blow up that bomb sight. Destroy it.

The bomb Tibbets dropped was only 10 kilotons. One kiloton is the equivalent of 1,000 tons of TNT. The bombs on Nagasaki and Hiroshima were 10 kilotons each. Tibbets said they could feel the blast at 34,000 to 36,000 feet. The ones we were sitting alert in Germany were 1.1 megaton, 110 times more powerful.

Around the year 2000, I was visiting my sister Carol in Colorado Springs. She is a piano teacher whose students included the children of a lot of military personnel and professional people from the area. Carol would invite them to dinner every once in a while and I happened to be there for one of these get-togethers. She had told me that among the guests would be some people from the Ukraine.

The area in the Ukraine I sat nuclear alert on was called…. Well, I got to talking to one of her guests and asked where in particular she came from.

You guessed it. They were from….

"Oh, my gosh!" I exclaimed in a loud voice.

The entire dinner party stopped. Everyone stared.

Well, it was an honest reaction of surprise and emotion in meeting someone who lived in the very town I had been prepared to annihilate with a nuclear weapon 110 times more powerful than the bombs dropped on Japan. I just couldn't contain myself.

Everyone in the room turned to look at us. Apparently they thought she had said something terrible to me to provoke that kind of a response!

Later on, Carol and my niece chided me for reacting that way, embarrassing my family and their guests. Finally, I was able to explain to them why the moment was so overwhelming for me. They had no idea that was my mission. No one did.

That poor lady from…. I'm sure she thought she had somehow said something wrong, but of course she hadn't. Thankfully, I think she and Carol are still friends!

Once, a fellow pilot in my squadron who was sitting on nuclear alert realized he had family members who lived in his target area! He was soon assigned a different target. But it all just goes to show how small this world can be.

They say in the Army, you command men. In the Air Force, you command airplanes. Still, the Air Force wanted its pilots to pick up some additional duty in order to get a little cross training. For example, one of us would take on the job of personal equipment officer. He'd be the one to make sure the airmen had all our helmets hanging up correctly for us and that the visors were clean. He'd make sure our parachutes went out for periodic repacking. Things like that.

Every day at 8 a.m., we had a pilots briefing. The squadron commander usually would make some announcements. He might tell us that a certain aircraft with mechanical problems was finally being sent down to Spain for a complete overhaul. The maintenance officer would get up and share a few items with us.

Well, our intelligence officer was Jack Chain. Each morning, he'd give us the latest news on our potential enemy's activities. Jack might tell us Russia had come up with a new and better bomber capable of striking Western Europe. He'd point out one of our targets and show us where heavier anti-aircraft artillery had been brought in. We took careful note of anything that might help us complete our mission, should this be the day we had to fly.

We had a book we called "The Big Pig." It was slang for The Basic Intelligence Planning Guide. It listed every location in the world targeted by a U.S. nuclear weapon. There were thousands of targets. It listed the size and type of the nuclear weapon involved, whether it was an air-burst, ground-burst or underground bomb burst.

As you can imagine, if World War III were to start, all those nuclear blasts had to be carefully orchestrated. Bombing routes had to be coordinated so if there's a bomb exploding 15 miles away, you weren't flying alongside of it.

Jack made a big impression on me. People really respected him. We enjoyed listening to him. Other than the maintenance officer who was responsible for making sure there were planes for us to fly, Jack probably had the most important job in the squadron.

I knew Jack would be rotating out to his next assignment in a year or two. I decided intelligence officer was an additional job I would like to have. Jack gave me the encouragement I needed.

"Paul," he said. "We can teach a monkey to fly an airplane. If you want to move up in the Air Force, you have to get a high-visibility job like this one."

The monkey line was a joke, but not too much of one. Those were the days when the U.S. was strapping monkeys into rockets and flying them into space!

Jack said he couldn't make me any promises, but when the time came for him to rotate out, he'd put in a good word for me. When the time came, I got the job.

Boy, Jack was sharp. He's the only guy—the only guy—who ever got on my butt in a dog fight and I mean it happened so fast.

There was an instructor in the Fighter Weapons School at Nellis Air Force Base named John Boyd. They called him "40-Second Boyd." One minute, you'd be trailing behind him nice and easy. Then, in the span of 40 seconds, he could flip his aircraft around and be on your tail. That's one maneuver they never showed us in training!

Falling victim to it was a rite of passage for the new guys coming into Ramstein fresh out of gunnery school. All the experienced pilots knew how to do it and passed the maneuver on to the incoming guys—after humbling them a bit in the process, of course. Jack is the one who showed it to me.

We went out together on a low-level training flight over France. On the way back to Ramstein, he positioned me in trail, about 500 feet behind him. He started down a bit then flew up a little. All of a sudden, he had some speed up, probably doing about 500 knots. I was hanging on to him OK, when before I knew what was happening, he was right behind me.

The F-100 used its rudder a lot to help it turn. John Boyd had discovered that if he pulled the stick back as hard as he could and kicked the left-to-right rudder, he could wheel around and get behind any aircraft that was following him. Not all airplanes could do this. There was just something about the F-100 that enabled it to perform that maneuver well.

Jack pulled the "40-Second Boyd" on me with perfection. In what seemed like an instant, I went from following him to being directly in his gun sights.

When we got on the ground, he debriefed me on it.

"What do you call that maneuver?" I asked.

"We call it, 'You're Dead,'" Jack replied.

I'm glad he taught it to me because that was the first and last time anybody every got on my tail. When it was my turn, I dutifully passed it along to the new pilots who came into Ramstein. Jack eventually was promoted to general and went on to become Wing Commander at Langley Air Force Base in Virginia, Strategic Air Commander, and United States Air Force Europe Commander.

Even now, as fully capable fighter pilots sitting on nuclear alert, the Air Force still kept a record of our bombing scores when we flew to Wheelus Air Base in Tripoli for ongoing training. We went down there three to four times per year, flying over the Mediterranean. The weather was always good.

The competition was constant. You had to get certain scores on all your bombing events. You took a tactical evaluation flight with someone at headquarters once or twice a year. We were graded on procedures. We had written evaluations.

We had to give briefings on the targets we were sitting in Russia or wherever else. You had to be able to relate the whole route, minute-by-minute, and explain what you would see to the left and to the right. For example, at two minutes and 36 seconds, you'd know you should be crossing a railroad track.

But then they'd ask you, "What if you hit the track at two minutes and 32 seconds? Which side of the route will you be on then? Left or right?" It would be the right side because you hit it early. "Now, how many degrees are you going to have to correct in order to hit your target on time?"

On and on and on and on. It was all about competition and how you scored on every classroom test and training exercise. And that's the way it should be, after all. Otherwise, there's little incentive to be exact and missions would become sloppy.

In 1963, after I had completed a low-level training flight, the squadron commander or operations officer came up to me and told me I'd been selected to represent the United States in the first NATO Gunnery Meet to be held at St. Dizier, France.

"Me?" I asked.

He said they'd looked at the record of every pilot at every U.S. base in England, France and Germany. The pilot with the highest gunnery scores was selected—and that was me.

My alternate was my good friend Hal Dortch, with whom I had trained at Luke and Nellis Air Force bases. Hal was based now in Lakenheath, England. Together, we comprised the U.S. team. My squadron commander, Woodrow Rauscher, was our team commander. There would be 12 to 15 pilots in the competition.

St. Dizier was home to a small French base, close to the gunnery range that would be used for the competition. We tried twice to land at St. Dizier, but the weather was so poor, we couldn't land. Finally, the next day, we got in.

Soon after we landed, we met a group of French and British pilots who had arrived the day before. We asked them how they were able to land with the weather so bad.

"It's a big sky!" was all they said.

"But you could have run into another plane," I replied.

"It's a big sky!" they repeated. I can still hear their accents!

Oh, Good Lord, I thought to myself.

They put us up in the Visiting Officers Quarters. The first day I was there, I went to the French Officers Club for breakfast. The server gave me a demitasse cup of coffee. She poured a little bit in the bottom. I looked at her.

"Fill 'er up!" I said.

She looked at me as if I'd just signed my own death warrant.

"What's wrong?" I asked. "Fill it up!"

"OK, monsieur," she said.

I took a sip. It was so strong you could walk on it! I found out that's what they called café au lait—coffee with milk. It's supposed to be half coffee, half milk, but I hadn't put in any milk! I learned. The food was excellent.

In the U.S. Air Force, we were not supposed to drink at all before a mission. And here were all these French pilots, Dutch pilots, and others, all drinking wine prior to flying.

"Your government doesn't prohibit pilots from drinking?" I asked in amazement.

"No, no!" they said in their heavily accented English. "We do it all the time! It's the way we live. You Americans don't drink?"

"No," I answered. "We're not allowed to have wine or beer within 24 hours of flying."

"Oh," they said. "It relaxes us!"

In the NATO competition, we were to fly two missions a day for four days. We had to make a different low-level flight every day, dropping a different kind of bomb on the range—a skip bomb, a toss, a dive bomb, an over-the-shoulder. We also had to fire our rockets and 20mm guns. They had all kinds of different events and you had to be proficient in each of them. There were spotters at every turning point to make sure you didn't cut corners and that you actually flew over the turning points.

As part of the challenge, we had to predict the exact second our bombs would impact on the range in each event we flew in. There was a large board, as big as a whole wall, listing our names and our scores. The weather was excellent for flying.

At the end of the third day, my score was high enough that if I hadn't flown on the last day, and all the other pilots got perfect scores, I still would have won the meet. It may sound like an exaggeration, but it's the truth. I'm so proud of that. My average time off a target was less than five seconds on eight missions. It was quite an honor to take part in the meet, let alone emerge as the winner. Again, I was very lucky.

The British had a two-man plane they called a Canberra. According to them, our F-100s couldn't hold a candle to it. They kept riding us at the officers club, saying, "You Yanks! We're going to whip your behinds!"

In addition to the pilot, the Canberra had a navigator who lay on his belly in the front of the plane to assist in dropping the bombs. They called the two-engine plane a fighter-bomber, but it was more of a bomber than a fighter. Anyway, the British promised to wax our butts—and of course, they didn't.

Well, a British company called Hawker Aircraft had sponsored all the trophies. They really thought they were going to win the competition because their planes had navigators while we American pilots had to fly and navigate at the same time. They were so mad the British didn't win that the representatives from Hawker Aircraft didn't even get up to present the trophy to my commander! They were really, really upset.

There was a great deal of competitive pressure. Every day, they'd put the scores up for each person—and there was only one pilot representing each country. I'd just look at the board and say boy, I lucked out. I got a good score.

I owed a lot to my training—all the tasks I performed in the competition were maneuvers we practiced and practiced. A lot of bombing is instinctive—you have to allow for the wind or make adjustments when your sights aren't quite right.

It came down to the pilot more than it did the airplane or anything else. The British, with four eyeballs in the plane instead of two, could see turning points, landmarks and all that a lot better than we could. I think that's what made them so terribly angry. All the other countries had single-seat fighters, except the British. They really thought they had the competition won, hands down. The British took immense national pride in their air force and they still do. They're wonderful, wonderful people and I'm glad they're on our side, but in that NATO Gunnery Meet, their strategy simply didn't prevail.

I came back to Ramstein and I was just another guy in the squadron. I'm not sure anyone even congratulated me. As I have mentioned, being an Air Force pilot is about competition at every level and about trying to maintain the highest possible scores. In that respect, the gunnery meet seemed like just another competition.

Now that I think about it, any one of my peers there could have traveled to France and done the same thing. It was no big deal that I was the one who earned Top Gun honors. I was simply the pilot who was chosen. Please see page 356 for a news clipping about the NATO Gunnery Meet from the July 6, 1962, edition of *The Stars and Stripes*.

It was a great honor to take part in the gunnery meet, but winning it wasn't something I dwelled on very much. That's just how I am. Another experience I had at Ramstein illustrates what I mean.

One day I took off for a training flight with the big 450-gallon fuel tanks on my F-100. And it was a low ceiling—visibility was poor. We took off from Ramstein and headed west toward Landstuhl Army Medical Hospital which was a huge complex.

The worst thing that can happen to a single-engine fighter is to lose oil pressure. It means your engine is likely to seize up. As soon as I took off and got my landing gear up, the engine warning light came on. It said low or no oil pressure. Holy mackerel!

My first problem was that I couldn't land with two full 450-gallon tanks on the plane. The tanks did not have baffles inside to stop the fuel from sloshing around.

Chances are, all that force moving inside the tanks would cause the plane to crash. I would have to release the tanks before I came in to land.

I called the tower, reported my zero oil pressure light and they cleared me to "punch" my tanks off.

Except, I couldn't just drop them anywhere. I was entirely in the soup—meaning, I couldn't see the ground due to the heavy weather. Somewhere down there was a hospital and villages filled with houses. I was flying strictly on instruments. I realized I had to figure something else out and fast.

I knew my aircraft pretty well. The tanks were on the outer pylons where you'd otherwise carry bombs. I decided I was going to set this up as if I'm dropping a bomb. I told the tower I planned to come in as if to land and drop the 450 gallon tanks as I came over the field.

We normally came down for a final approach at 160 knots with the F-100 holding about 1,500 pounds of fuel. Now I've got somewhere in the neighborhood of 10,000 pounds of fuel! I was so heavy, I had to come in at 195 or I'd stall the airplane.

I made the turn for the approach and I could see the field. I leveled off. "Piece of cake," I said to myself. Drop the tanks on airport property and I won't kill anybody. I didn't know if the tanks would explode or not, but that was another issue.

So I'm screaming in at 190 knots. I get right over the field boundary, hit the "pickle" button and nothing happens. The tanks wouldn't release!

Now what? I couldn't pull up and make another go-around. My only choice was to land and hope for the best.

I plunked it on the ground, got on my brakes, and popped the drag chute. It was about a 7,000-foot runway, with a barrier on the other end, designed to stop an out-of-control plane. I bet 95 out of 100 times, a pilot in that situation would have blown a tire or had to take the barrier, which is kind of humiliating. But I was able to slow it down in time.

So, I taxied the plane off the runway, went inside, wrote the aircraft up, and that was it. Nobody came out to say, "Good job, Kari! You didn't blow a tire! You didn't take a barrier!"

North American was the airplane's manufacturer and had a tech rep there with us all the time. I asked him what had gone wrong. After all, I could have easily crashed the airplane and killed myself. I was going so fast that if a tire had blown, I don't know what would have happened.

What they found out—and it was never listed in our emergency procedures—was that when your landing gear is down, your bomb-release button doesn't work. A safety feature! Now had I known that, there was another option. The F-100 had a big red button appropriately known as the panic button. When you hit that, a cartridge would blow everything off the wings, including the pylons that held the bombs, rockets or fuel tanks. Those pylons weren't cheap, but it's cheaper to lose a few of them than to lose an aircraft. Anyway, after my little experience, our emergency procedures were updated to let us know the bomb-release button wouldn't work in that situation.

I say all that to say this. A lot of other guys in the squadron would have come in from that experience and said, "Hey! Look at me! I did this. I did that. I didn't take the barrier." That wasn't me. I wrote up the incident and that was it. No one said anything about it, nor did I. It's just the way I was raised. You handle it and you move on.

Winning the Top Gun trophy at the first NATO Gunnery Meet was the same way. I was proud to do what I had been trained to do and honored to represent my country.

Then it was back to work.

As for the oil pressure light that led to the whole episode? It was the result of nothing more than a faulty gauge.

COMING HOME

About the first of February, 1973, the North Vietnamese guards ordered us all to sit down in our rooms at Hoa Loa Prison in Hanoi for an announcement. A deal for our release had been struck by Secretary of State Henry Kissinger. We were going home!

The camp commander would have preferred to keep us in the dark a while longer out of fear POWs would riot. However, one of Kissinger's conditions was that the exact terms of our release be read aloud to us. Our ranking officer, Robbie Risner, assured the North Vietnamese commander we would behave appropriately.

Robbie got word to every POW in every building at Hoa Loa Prison that we were to maintain our dignity and discipline. We marched into this hell on earth with our heads held high and we would walk out the same way.

"We have acted as officers and gentlemen," Robbie said, "some of us for more than eight years. If anyone so much as thumbs his nose at a North Vietnamese, gives them the finger, does anything like that, I will personally court martial you."

He didn't even have to say it. I don't think any POW would have turned violent or vengeful—and no one did.

The camp commander told us we'd be released in four groups, in the order we had been captured. Navy pilot Everett Alvarez, who had been shot down in August of 1964 was No. 1. I was No. 12, shot down June 20, 1965.

The North Vietnamese continued to fatten us up, with some success. I managed to gain almost 30 pounds in those final months of captivity. My goal was to regain enough strength so that when I stepped off that plane and finally saw my family again, I could pick up both my children in my arms at the same time. I had been gone from them for almost eight years. Shawn would now be 10 years old. Ali was 8 years old.

One POW, who had gotten terribly skinny, refused to eat. They gave him candy bars and he'd hide them in the bushes. I think he wanted people back home to see what we had been forced to become. Well, that wasn't me. I was the opposite. I ate everything they gave me!

The day before we were to be released, the North Vietnamese brought us light jackets, shirts, pants, dress shoes and socks. They also gave us a little satchel, like basketball players used to carry. In it, I had my cup, spoon and toothpaste, as well as cigarettes they had given us. Later, when we got to the Philippines, the people there had just experienced a terrible hurricane and were eager for any kind of donations. I felt sorry for them. Many had lost their homes and possessions in the storm. I gave them a lot of my stuff. I did bring home a pair of striped prison pajamas, along with a few other things, which I donated years later to the Smithsonian Institution.

The day came at last when they told us we were leaving for home. The North Vietnamese put us on buses with big red crosses on the sides—even though they never recognized the Red Cross and did not permit Red Cross packages to reach us for many years. They drove us out over the bridge to Gia Lam Airport. Finally, we were traveling without blindfolds and we could see the extent of the bombing that precipitated our release. We parked one bus after another. Off to the right, I could see a big tent with another red cross on it.

The North Vietnamese had told us, from the day I was shot down, that they were going to win the war. At that point, just like the French, they were going to give us a big banquet when they sent us home. We sat on the busses for about an hour and then went into the tent, which was open on the sides and filled with tables and chairs. At each place was a bottle of beer and a pork fat sandwich—which consisted of a piece of French bread cut in two with a piece of pure pork fat in the middle. That was our banquet! I traded my bottle of beer for another guy's pork fat sandwich. I ate two. The camp commander came around, smiling, saying, "Well, we promised you a banquet!" Then they put us back on the busses to wait.

From where I was sitting and with my damaged vision, I couldn't see the planes come in as well as some of the others could. But finally, one of the guys said, "There it is! Here comes an American airplane!" It was a C-141 with an American flag painted on it, along with a big red cross.

I said to myself, *these S.O.B.s have not seen me cry in almost eight years and I'm not about to let them see me cry now.* I bit my tongue down hard, because I could feel the tears and the emotion begin to well up inside me. I kept biting down hard and harder. So much so, that when I finally got on the plane, I could feel the indentations in my tongue. No one else can imagine the emotions we were feeling as the plane landed and taxied toward us.

Some time earlier, we had managed to send a critical message back to the United States. I was one of three among the more than 600 POWs who could communicate with the U.S. government when we had the opportunity to write a letter home. Any further explanation of the system would be beyond Top Secret. In about my second year as a POW, one of the other two code-writers chose me and taught me how to do it. Why he picked me, I'll never know—especially since the North Vietnamese prevented me from writing home for five years, likely because I was so "uncooperative" during my interrogations.

However, a pair of Americans had turned traitor. It was impossible not to notice the preferred treatment they received from our captors. The men were issued civilian suits and permitted to leave the prison camp for trips to the library in Hanoi.

LANDING AT CLARK AIR BASE IN THE PHILIPPINES, 1973.

We'd been able to communicate all this back to the United States. We told the government we wanted those two on the first airplane out of Vietnam, even though they had been captured much later than many of us. Kissinger asked for them by name and they were on that first flight. We didn't want them to have any further opportunity to divulge useful information to the enemy.

Many of the longest-held POWs were in bad shape and barely hanging on. They were put on that first flight, along with some of the B-52 pilots and crew who had carried out those relentless December bombing missions that lead to our release. Several of those who had been recently shot down and captured were badly beaten up.

I was on the first airplane, too. That C-141, tail No. 60177, today is in the United States Air Force Museum in Dayton, Ohio. There was quite a mix of men on that plane—long-held POWs in relatively good shape, recent POWs who were terribly battered, and two traitors.

They read our names off, in the order in which we had been captured. We walked, one by one, under an arbor toward the plane. In a final bit of irony, some of the very North Vietnamese guards who had tortured us were among those reading our names as we were released.

They called my name and I went through, all by myself, toward that C-141. About halfway to the plane, there was an Air Force colonel in a blue uniform walking toward me. By the time we met, I was in a sort of daze, but I remember the exact words he said.

He spun around, put his arm around me, and said, "Welcome home, you son of a bitch!"

That was just the way men talked, of course, and the tears started flowing. Where he met me was about 100 yards from the plane. And believe it or not, I remembered that aircraft from a picture I had seen in *Stars and Stripes*. It had gone into service just before I was shot down. It never looked better to me than it did in that moment.

As we got closer to the C-141, I could smell a sweet smell. It must have been the cologne some of the nurses were wearing, or the aftershave of some of the crew members. After not smelling anything like that for almost eight years, I noticed it immediately from 100 feet away. We entered the plane on a ramp that extended from the back.

I said aloud, "If heaven smells anything like this, I don't want to miss it!"

We all got in there and sat down. Everything was in a hurry. As soon as the last guy came in, the ramp came up and they started the engines. I said to myself, "I am not going to rejoice until we are 10 miles out and past the international boundary." But as soon as the wheels left the ground, everybody let out a loud holler.

Ten miles out, I went up to the cockpit and said, "Do you have a spare set of your orders? If so, I want you to sign them for my scrapbook."

It was an Air Force Reserve squadron out of Travis Air Force Base near San Francisco. The name of the pilot is written on the bulkhead of that C-141. The plane later was dubbed the Hanoi Taxi, because it made more trips to Vietnam to pick up POWs than any other plane. The pilot scratched around and found an extra copy of his orders and signed them for me.

I came back and shouted to the other POWs that we were 10 miles out and they let out another great, huge roar.

I don't know how long the flight took from Hanoi to the Philippines. It seemed to go by fast because we all were so giddy to be going home. Finally, the pilot told us to strap in as we prepared to land at Clark Air Base. A normal cargo plane would have nylon seats along the sides for passengers, but this plane had been outfitted with seats like a commercial aircraft. There were several rows, with three seats on either side and an aisle down the middle. There were 41 seats and behind those were 41 beds for POWs who were too weak or injured to sit.

What happened to the two traitors once we landed, I don't know. Perhaps they were hustled away to a different part of the base hospital. That's my guess. I don't remember talking to them, getting physicals with them, eating with them or anything like that at all.

It must have been around 11 a.m. on Feb. 12 when we left Hanoi and mid- to late-afternoon when we arrived in the Philippines. Oh my, the people that were lined up to greet us! We looked out the windows and saw crowds of well-wishers lined up behind ropes, waving and holding up signs that said, "Welcome Home." Most were Americans stationed at Clark Air Base and Philippinos who worked on the base. They must have been lined up five and six deep to see us. We disembarked, I believe, in the same order we got on the plane. We got on a bus and they took us right to the base hospital.

The Department of Defense had put out a list of returning POWs and asked for volunteers to serve as a personal aide to each one of us, like an aide to a general. They would stay with us for a couple of days or up to a week and handle paying our expenses and helping us settle back into the outside world.

There was a former duty officer at Ramstein named Dick Shrove who volunteered to be with me. He currently was stationed at Hickam Air Force Base in Honolulu. Dick met me at the hospital.

"Hey! I'm your aide de camp!" he said.

I gave him a big hug. It was so good to see him. Dick would make sure I got measured up for new uniforms and other basic necessities.

Although we POWs had been talking on the airplane, when we got to the hospital at Clark, it was the first time we really took a good look at each other. We hugged and shared our amazement that it had finally happened. We finally were free.

We immediately received a quick physical. I weighed 173 pounds when I was shot down, fell to 103 pounds at the lowest point, and was released weighing 133 pounds. My waist was 28 inches. On my thinnest day in captivity, I could flex my biceps and almost wrap my thumb and forefinger around it and touch them together. That's how skinny I was. During our final weeks in captivity, the North Vietnamese gave us all the French bread we could eat, so I was able to gain some of the weight back. I was 29 years old when I was shot down. Now I was 37.

That evening, the very first night after our release, they told POWs it was time to eat dinner. We went down to the hospital cafeteria, not really knowing what to expect. I remember they had a lot of flight surgeons on hand, expecting we might have difficulty readjusting to normal food.

Oh my, what a spread! They'd probably been preparing this meal for days. They had prime rib, steaks, pork, pork chops, pork roasts, chicken, fish, and all kinds of vegetables. There was so much food we didn't know what to eat! I know I filled my plate up.

I remember I had a hard time sleeping that first night, just dreaming how it would be to enjoy freedom once again. We had been told the next day would be a full one—with debriefings and numerous medical assessments.

The following morning, I was riding down the hospital elevator on my way to a meeting and overheard two flight surgeons talking. One said to the other, "Did you get called out last night because anyone ate too much and got sick?" The second flight surgeon said, "No." To their knowledge, not a single POW had any trouble with the food. I think most of us paced ourselves pretty well. We all probably ate a little more than we normally would, but not one made a glutton of himself.

We had breakfast and again they gave us the works; eggs any way we wanted them, bacon, sausage, everything. I had two eggs, over easy, and swabbed up the yolk with a piece of toast. Dick, who was there with me, started to chuckle.

"What are you laughing about?" I asked.

"The way you are getting every single calorie off that plate," he said. "I watched you last night and you did the same thing. You sopped up every drop of au juice from your prime rib. That plate was clean enough to eat off of the next morning!"

I hadn't realized it, but I guess that's what we POWs did to survive on the limited rations doled out to us in prison.

All our captors ever gave us to eat with were those big soup spoons, like the ones you often get at Chinese restaurants. I never liked those and still don't! I remember it was so nice just to have a regular spoon to stick in my mouth.

The Vietnamese never, ever, gave us enough water. They gave us that one-quart pitcher and only ever filled it half way. Whether it was calculated or they were just too lazy to boil water to make it safe for drinking, I don't know. Now, to be able to enjoy a drink of fresh water whenever I wanted it was a blessing.

Some POW habits took a while to change. In Vietnam, we were accustomed to using the tiniest square of toilet paper we could possibly use, because they gave us so little. For a while after our release, I still would take a little piece off the roll, just out of habit. Today, I'm wasteful! I pull off as much as I want, and then some. When I visit my daughter, she will say, "Dad! You went through a whole roll of toilet paper in four days!"

Dick had gotten me some Class A uniforms, which had to be modified to fit me. As soon as we got back into uniforms, they took us to a conference room, where they said they would show each of us our savings account and how much money we had in it.

Savings account? I didn't even know I had one.

About a year after I was shot down, someone in the Pentagon said the military needed to take a lesson from what happened to some World War II veterans who returned home with nothing in the bank to help them get back on their feet again.

The government had set up tax-free savings accounts for us that paid 10 percent interest. We had signed little yellow 5-by-7 cards that instructed the military what percentage of our money we wanted our spouse to have access to, for those of us who were married. But we certainly had no idea the terms of the account would be so favorable.

The last letter I received before I was shot down was from my wife Kathy, who had informed me she was no longer going to shop at the MacDill Air Force Base commissary in Tampa, Florida, near St. Petersburg where she lived. Instead, she planned to start shopping at Publix, the local supermarket, because it gave out S&H Green Stamps. It also happened to be the most expensive grocery in town! As I mentioned, to keep up hope, a POW spends a lot of time thinking of what it will be like to rejoin his family and begin a normal life again. For seven years and eight months, that letter came to my mind again and again. I worried we were going to have nothing in the bank when I got home.

At this meeting, the Air Force laid before us our financial records. There were probably a dozen of us in the room, seated around an oval table. They explained about the savings account and opened up our individual ledgers for us to see. I looked at mine and it said $13,000. I said to myself, that doesn't seem like very much, over so many years, at such a generous interest rate.

I looked to the guy on my left who was married, like me.

"How much do you have?" I asked.

"$49,000," he said.

I looked to the guy on my right, who was single.

"Skip, how much do you have?" I asked.

He said, "$90,000."

I said, "Oh, my."

I knew Kathy may not have been the thriftiest person in the world, but my first thought was that she must have taken the money out to invest somewhere else. That was my optimistic thought, but the truth was, I felt disappointed.

Still, I said to myself the important thing is I'm free. I'm not going to let that savings account get me down.

Later that morning of February 13, Robbie Risner said, "Paul, we've got to start debriefing."

He had tasked me with two important jobs while we were imprisoned. The first was to memorize each of the military orders he tapped through the wall so there would be a written record of them. He also had me memorize the comings and goings of the two traitors. In addition, several of us had memorized the names of all the POWs. I don't know how some of us were able to memorize and recall so much information, but we did.

One of the guys I was released with told me he wanted to go down to the library at Clark. The hospital got him a car. Another POW, Glenn Nix, used to recall information for us in prison—evening citing bibliographies four, five and six deep! This guy wanted to go to the library to see if Nix had been correct.

He came back and said, "You know, that S.O.B. was right, right down to the middle initials!" We all had a big hee-haw about that. Maybe when the body is held captive, the mind becomes more active. I don't know.

Between debriefing sessions, medical personnel were giving us physical assessments and treating any immediate needs we had. I had a lot of stomach problems, but they couldn't really determine why. A check of my eyes showed I had lost my center vision, but they didn't delve into it further than that.

They simply said they'd send me on to Wilford Hall Medical Center, the large Air Force hospital in Texas, for further evaluation and treatment. Basically, I was mobile, I could talk, and I wasn't in any terrible pain. All my immediate needs were covered. I told them about my back, but again, I was able to get around, so it was added to the list of things doctors would look into later. The patients they were really zeroing in on were the pilots and crew of those B-52s. They were the ones who needed the greatest medical attention.

That evening of our first day, the hospital told us they'd made arrangements for POWs finally to talk to their families. In preparation for our release, they'd rounded up all of our home phone numbers.

I remember I was so excited to talk to Kathy at last. I had even been thinking I would make a joke, just to break the ice.

In the Air Force, if we were flying a plane cross country and it broke down, or something unexpected happened that changed our plans, we would send what we called a "R.O.N." message. It stands for "Remain Overnight."

I dialed the number. Kathy picked up the phone.

"Hi, Sweetie," I said. "I'm really sorry I didn't get a chance to send you a R.O.N. message!"

There was not much of a laugh.

"How are you?" she asked.

I told her I was doing fine. I asked about Shawn and Ali. She said they were OK.

"What's going on there?" she asked.

I told her we were getting physicals, having uniforms fitted, and going over our financial records.

I said, "I saw you were able to save $13,000."

"How about that." she replied.

"Well," I told her, "the guy on my left had $49,000 and the guy on my right had $90,000."

"Oh," Kathy replied. "How is your health?"

I said, "Well, I have some eye problems. They don't know why—probably a vitamin deficiency. I don't have any center vision."

She was quiet for the rest of the conversation. I'd say something and there would be silence. I'd say, "Are you still there?" and she'd say, "Yeah."

Finally, I said, "Well, I'll be seeing you shortly."

"OK," she said.

When I got off the phone, I said to my friend Percy, "Something isn't right at home. Kathy asked me about my health and I told her I had a vision problem. From then on, it was a one-way conversation."

"Aw, PK," he said. "Don't worry about it. She's probably just overwhelmed that you're coming home. It'll be OK."

"I sure hope so," I said.

A Hurry-Up Wedding

I was a bachelor at Ramstein for about a year when I fell in love with a girl back home. Kathy and I became engaged when I was visiting on leave in late August of 1961. We planned to marry in another six months to a year. She was 20 and I was 25.

The escalation of the Cold War and the building of the Berlin Wall changed our plans. The Air Force announced any personnel who wished to bring their wives or children overseas had a 60-day window to do so. After that, security would tighten up.

I didn't want to put off our wedding for my entire three-year deployment at Ramstein. So, Kathy and I made our wedding plans over the phone on a Monday, I flew home on Wednesday, and we got married on Saturday! We had a nice wedding at Spencer Methodist Church and soon left together for Germany.

Our first months together followed that same kind of frenetic pace, which is the case for many military families. Almost the minute I landed at Ramstein with my new bride, I found out there were to be tryouts for the Skyblazers—the Air Force's aerial demonstration team in Europe. It was the equivalent of the Thunderbirds, but almost more prestigious because the Skyblazers performed for international audiences. I learned they had kept the tryout period open until my return, which made me feel quite honored. The Skyblazers were the crème de la crème of the Air Force.

However, if I were to be selected to join the team, it would mean I'd have to travel a great deal, not to mention the endless hours of practice. I was concerned for Kathy. Here she was, newly married, not only away from home, but in a foreign country where everything was different. Now there might be the added whammy of her husband having to be away a lot.

I told the Air Force I would have to talk it over with Kathy first.

Ramstein had no married housing available, so I had rented a house off base—what we called "on the economy." I drove over to the house and told her about the opportunity to try out for the Skyblazers and what it would mean.

"I wanted to ask you if it would be OK," I said.

"Of course!" Kathy said. She was totally supportive.

Well, after all that, I never did get to try out for the Skyblazers. Almost immediately, we got word the hierarchy back at the Pentagon canceled the whole program as a cost-saving measure. I was disappointed, to say the least.

But, as often happens in military life, one whammy is followed by another. Shortly after that, I was assigned to be a forward air controller with the Army for a major two-week exercise. A forward air controller is an Air Force pilot who moves in with an Army unit for the purpose of coordinating close air support.

So Kathy and I said goodbye as she dropped me off at an Army post outside Ramstein, where I was flown by helicopter to my temporary assignment. Here she was, all alone in a new country. She got going the wrong direction on the Autobahn and drove practically to the other side of Germany before she realized what she had done. It was a tough time for her those first few months.

Kathy also had to decipher Air Force lingo. When I went off to France to compete in the NATO Gunnery Meet, she followed the competition in the newspaper, *Stars & Stripes*. The reporter wrote something to the effect of, "Kari dropped another one down the pickle barrel!"

"Dropping one down the pickle barrel" was a colorful way of saying a pilot had dropped a bomb right on target, but it's easy to see how it would be confusing. Kathy had never heard that expression before. So she went up to a duty officer she knew named John Porter (we had bought a little schnauzer dog from him).

"What does this mean that he dropped another one down the pickle barrel?" she asked.

"That's what we call a bull's eye!" John explained.

"Oh good! Good!" Kathy exclaimed.

Our first child, Shawn, was born April 24, 1963, at Landstuhl Army Medical Center, adjacent to Ramstein. Decades later, that's where they brought all the wounded military personnel from the Iraq and Afghanistan wars for major surgery.

CHAPTER 20

The night before I drove Kathy to the hospital to give birth, we were lying in bed, talking.

"Oh, by the way, I have to brief Army Gen. Maxwell Taylor tomorrow," I said.

He was chairman of the U.S. Joint Chiefs of Staff and due to arrive at the base the next day. As intelligence officer following Jack Chain, it was my job to bring high-profile visitors up to date on our activities.

Our squadron was one of two tactical squadrons at Ramstein. There also was one from Bitburg sitting on nuclear alert at Ramstein. For some reason, dignitaries always came down to our squadron for a dog and pony show. The United States Air Force headquarters in Europe was in Wiesbaden, near Frankfort. However, the 4th Allied Tactical Air Force—comprised of Germans, Americans, Canadians and the French—was headquartered at Ramstein. So any dignitary of any position always ended up at Ramstein. They wanted to know what the Air Force was doing in Europe, what our targets were, and this and that. We had conventional as well as nuclear missions, and I briefed them on both.

At that time, we had four aircraft sitting on nuclear alert and four on conventional alert. We weren't far from Berlin and its newly constructed wall between East and West. If the Russians were to give U.S. aircraft any trouble, we'd get the call to go up to defend them.

After I briefed Gen. Taylor, I was instructed to hustle down to the alert area to sit as one of the conventional pilots on alert. They knew the general would want to head that way after the briefing and wanted to be sure everything was in good order.

Immediately after my presentation, as the general and the squadron commander were talking, I excused myself, ran down to the alert area, and got into my gear.

Gen. Taylor came in and began asking the duty officer, John Heinz, questions about our security procedures. In the event of an alert, the Pentagon would send code words, which were then verified by two officers. It was a sort of double-check to make sure it was a real alert.

"What's this red button?" the general asked.

"If you punch that button, we launch our aircraft," John told him.

"Oh, really," said the general. And he pressed the button!

I'm sitting with the other pilots in our lounge and suddenly we hear the alert siren go off. We just kind of looked at each other in disbelief.

"Is that what I think it is?" someone asked.

"Yes!" I said. "It's the real thing! Let's go!"

Those of us on conventional alert ran to our planes and took off. We actually were in the air, already 40 or 50 miles away from the base, before word came to us about what had happened. They had managed to hold back the pilots with the nuclear bombs! It was the first time any of us had ever gotten airborne on an alert.

We got back in, did our paperwork and I hung up my parachute and helmet. The general, squadron commander and other dignitaries were standing and talking as I walked by the front desk in the operations office. That's when someone called out my name.

"Hey, Kari!" they shouted. "The hospital just called. You've got a baby boy!"

I jumped with glee, right in front of Gen. Taylor.

"Oh my gosh! I've got a baby boy, General!" I shouted.

He looked at me.

"Aren't you the one who just gave us the briefing?" he asked.

"Yes sir!" I said.

"Well, you'd better get with it!" he replied.

I ran past him, got outside, and jumped in my Volkswagen. It was probably two miles to the hospital. I had taken Kathy there that morning, so I knew what part of the building she was in. I kind of slipped in the back way and ran through the halls toward her room. That's when I looked down and saw that I was still in my G-suit.

Holy mackerel, I said to myself. These people will think I'm crazy running through a hospital in a G-suit! So I pulled it off, ran back and tossed it in the car.

When I finally arrived in Kathy's room, she was holding Shawn.

"What took you so long?" she asked.

"You won't believe it!" I said and told her the story about the general sending us airborne by mistake.

"I'm proud of you," she said.

Later, we received a note that said, "Welcome, Baby Kari!" It was signed, "Gen. Maxwell Taylor." That was a really nice memento.

I put immense effort into my role as intelligence officer hoping as Jack suggested, that it would be a good way to get noticed by the higher-ups and help propel me to the next stage of my career.

I remember Jack gave me his briefing cards and each had "7-S" written in one corner. This puzzled me at first. Eventually I was able to ask Jack what it meant.

Our briefing room had a riser where the podium stood. It was about a foot higher than the floor where the audience sat. Now, Jack was at least 6-foot-2, probably taller.

"The '7' means I'm 7 feet tall when I'm up there," he said, "and the 'S' means I'm smarter than anyone sitting out there or else I shouldn't be up here briefing them!"

CHAPTER 20

SHAWN WAS BORN IN LANDSTUHL, GERMANY, IN APRIL OF 1963.

Serving as intelligence officer did take a degree of self-confidence. I took the job seriously and I gave it my best effort.

During my tenure, we got a brand-new intelligence room, much larger than the one Jack had. I devoted an entire year of my off-duty time creating a giant map on a back wall, about 10 feet high and 30 feet wide. If I wasn't flying or studying, I was working on this map.

On the left side, taking up almost half the wall, it showed the three routes into West Berlin. It listed every enemy airbase and every type of aircraft they had. I identified the location and capability of every anti-aircraft weapon.

Taking up the remainder of the wall to the right, I showed all of Western Europe, clear into the middle of Russia. I marked every location where one of our nuclear weapons would be dropped. I had it laid out to show how the attack would progress in 15-minute intervals. Again, I showed the locations of enemy artillery, anti-aircraft weapons, bombers and fighters.

To top it all off, I installed black lights overhead to shine down on the map. When I turned out the regular lights, the map glowed! It was cool. I asked our parachute people to make a floor-to-ceiling curtain for it. When they refused, I bought the material myself and Kathy sewed it up for me.

One day I was conducting a briefing. The audience included two three-star generals and two two-star generals from the Pentagon. After I gave them a basic briefing on our mission in Europe, one of them asked me a question. I don't recall exactly what it was, but I knew this was my big moment.

"When we're done here," I said, "I've got a map back in our intelligence room that will help you understand the big picture."

So we went back to the intelligence room and my wall with the giant map. I turned on the black lights and pulled open the curtain.

The generals were stunned.

"Holy sh--!" one of three-star generals said. "You've got to take all that down!"

"But general," I replied. "It took me more than a year to put that up! Isn't it beautiful?"

"It's beautiful, but you know too much," he said. "If you get shot down, or any of your people get shot down, they'll spill their guts! Your pilots know more than my men at the Pentagon!"

I wasn't going to give up without a fight. I said something I probably shouldn't have.

"General," I said, "If we ever get shot down carrying out these missions, it won't matter what our pilots know about the information on this map."

I think he was a bit taken aback. What I said was logical. Once World War III was underway, it wouldn't matter what was written on these walls. The whole plan would be in the process of being executed.

The general was silent and I was scared, struck by the reality of what I had just done. I was a lowly captain, he was a three-star general, and I had just corrected him.

"I don't care," he said. "I want you to take that down. That is an order."

"Yes, sir," I said.

As soon as the generals left, I took it up with my commander. He knew how much time I'd put into that map.

"I'll tell you what," he said. "Don't take it down. If they send a letter or make a phone call or something, we'll go from there."

Well, they never followed up.

The general wasn't entirely wrong. Many of us probably did know too much. I knew every unilateral war plan if America had to go it alone. I knew every multilateral plan if we had to go with the French, the Germans, the Canadians, the British, or what would happen if one of them backed out.

One thing the general may not have known is that during our training at Nellis Air Force Base, pilots were briefed in great detail on the atomic weapons our planes would carry. They showed us a mock-up of how it was constructed, even explaining to us the secret of how it worked. The trick was in getting an implosion from all sides of the device, so there were wedge-shaped detonators arrayed around the outside of the bomb. The technology is different today, so it doesn't really matter who knows that now, but back then, our enemies probably would have liked to have that information.

Even as our instructors were teaching us about the inner-workings of an atomic bomb, I wondered why we needed to understand it in that level of detail. Well, in those earliest nuclear devices we sat alert on, the plutonium was held separately from the rest of the bomb. As the fighter pilot approached his target, he actually had to hit a switch that would cause the plutonium to be inserted into the weapon. The instructors said they wanted us to know how it all worked in case a problem occurred and the plutonium didn't go in all the way or something.

What they expected us to do about a situation like that from inside the cockpit, I have no idea.

Looking back at those days at Ramstein on the front lines of the Cold War, I can't say we hung on every word that came from the Kennedy Administration or tried to read too much into whether World War III was inching closer or farther away. We were, however, very much in tune with the fact of how serious it all was. You don't sit alert on a nuclear weapon without considering what it would mean if someday we were called to carry out our mission. And there were times when we really thought we might have to do it.

I do recall clearly—as everyone who can remember 1963—the day Jack Kennedy was assassinated. Ironically, we were all at a "dining-in." That's the term for a formal military affair, everyone in their dress uniforms.

It was at the South Officers Club, right across from the Bachelor Officers Quarters. The wing commander came down from Hahn and we were just enjoying ourselves. About the time our food was served, the sergeant-at-arms came in and said something to the wing commander. He looked up, with a startled expression on his face. The colonel got up and gave us the news.

"We just got word the president has been shot and killed," he said. "We're going on a high state of alert."

The Germans and Canadians also went on high alert. No one was sure in those first few hours if the president's assassination was an isolated occurrence or part of a larger plot. The French, however, did not go on alert. They never went on alert. That's just how the French were.

I never got to see Kennedy, but I do remember when he came to Germany and made his famous "Ich Bin Ein Berliner" speech. In fact, I was flying a mission that day and listened to him on the Armed Forces Radio Network. I tried to spot his entourage from the air, but I couldn't see it.

Serving as intelligence officer over the course of my last two years at Ramstein, I had briefed everybody short of the president. I briefed Vice President Johnson, as well as the chiefs of staff of the Army, the Air Force and the Navy, and lots of politicians. They all wanted to come over there.

I had a beautiful tour of duty in Germany. I even extended it by a year, serving a total of four years. Looking back, I probably shouldn't have taken the extension because I likely missed out on other assignments. But I was thriving and having fun.

I eventually sold the '56 Oldsmobile I had shipped over when I first came to Ramstein. I put a notice on a bulletin board at the base and an Air Force sergeant bought it. What a hot car that was! Bigger than a Mercedes and it had those tear-drop fenders. I've wondered ever since what became of that car. I'd love to have it today.

My dream was to have a Porsche, but I could never afford it. Instead, I bought a '61 Volkswagen Beetle, a little red one. It was $1,300. For an extra $60, I got a sunroof. We used to love to go skiing in the winter when the weather turned cold. You'd stop at a stoplight in that Beetle and the windows would fog up. You had to keep a little can of alcohol on hand to spray on the window and keep the accelerator going so the hot air would come out of the vents.

One memorable story involving the '56 Oldsmobile occurred when I was still living in the Bachelor Officers Quarters at Ramstein, which were like two-man apartments. The entry way, which included a small refrigerator, led to a shared bathroom in the back. We had our own bedrooms, each with a door to the bathroom, which could be locked for privacy. So instead of "roommates," we called one another "john mates." I'm not going to use my former john mate's name, for reasons you will quickly understand.

One night, I came home and heard hollering and tussling in my john mate's room. It was a loud commotion. I went into the bathroom and I heard a woman's voice through the door.

"I want my money! I want my money!" she screamed.

Oh, no, I thought. He's brought a prostitute home or something. I cracked the door to his room—he hadn't locked it—and saw a middle-age German woman, dressed like a peasant woman of the time. He had a hold of one arm and she had hold of a post on the bed! He was pulling and trying to get her out the front door of his bedroom.

"No! I want my money!" she exclaimed.

"I gave my money!" my john mate replied.

The woman was bigger than he was. She'd momentarily lose her grip, then turn around and throw him around. She was really tussling with him.

I didn't know what to do. I went back into my room and lay in bed. I had no idea what had happened between them or who was right or wrong. Whatever it was, I thought *this is not going to turn out well.*

I heard the front door of his bedroom open. Evidently, he'd finally pushed her out and slammed the door shut. Oh, good, I thought. Hopefully this is all over.

Not by a long shot.

I heard the refrigerator door open, followed by the sound of shattering glass. My john mate kept wine in there.

"Oh my God!" the woman screamed.

I thought to myself, *she's slashed her wrists.* I opened the door to see her standing there, holding one of her arms. Blood was gushing all over.

Reacting more than thinking, I rushed to help her—walking across the broken glass, which embedded itself in my bare feet.

"What is going on?" I asked.

"He won't pay me! He won't pay me!" she said.

I instructed her to put pressure on the cut and went back into my bedroom to get a T-shirt to use as a tourniquet. I wrapped her arm up tight and finally got a couple of bandages on her wounds. She had cut herself badly.

"How much does he owe you?" I asked. "What do you want?"

I've forgotten the amount, but it was something like 40 marks. I went into my room and found 40 marks.

"Here," I said. "Please just take it."

"No!" she answered. "I want him to take me home!"

Well, as I was standing in that little cubbyhole of a hallway trying to get this poor woman doctored up, I heard my john mate's bedroom window go up as he crawled out and left. Our apartment was on the first floor.

"He's gone!" I said.

She wouldn't believe me until we opened his bedroom door and she saw for herself. The window was still wide open—I assumed so he could get back in.

"Where do you live?" I asked. "Let me take you."

She lived in a town outside Ramstein where there was a big Army post. We went outside and I put her in my '56 Oldsmobile. By now, it was midnight or 1 a.m. as we headed toward the main gate. All I was trying to do was resolve this situation, but I began to think of the trouble I'd be in if we were stopped by the guard. My mind began to race. What if there's blood all over the car seat? What if she dies? She had tried to kill herself, but would it look like I had done this to her?

"Get down!" I said, as we drew close to the gate. I pushed her head down to show her that she needed to duck out of sight.

The guard saw the officer's sticker on my car and gave me a salute. I saluted him back and rolled right on through.

"What are you doing?" the woman demanded, straightening back up.

"You had to put your head down or we would have been caught at the gate!" I said.

The story only gets better—or worse, depending on how you look at it.

We got on the Autobahn and she directed me to her home. She said she lived in a trailer. We pulled up to a sloping hay field outside of town. It was filled with circus trailers!

"Here?" I asked.

"Yes! I'm in the circus!" she said.

Naturally, her trailer was the last one, way in the back.

I was scared to death. I was sure somebody was going to identify my car—after all, how many '56 Oldsmobiles were there in Germany? I drove down past her trailer and started to loop around in kind of a 180-degree turn. The wheels began to slip in the grass. I just gunned it. The motor was racing. I was terrified I was going to get stuck.

That's when the door of the trailer opened and a goliath of a man stepped outside as if to say, "What's going on out here?" He was as tall as the door of the trailer.

"Who's that?" I asked.

"That's my husband!" she replied.

Oh, boy, I said to myself.

"You've got to jump out," I told her. "If I stop, I'll get stuck and I won't get out!"

I kept my foot on the accelerator and yet the car was just barely moving. I was afraid I was going to have to get out and run. The woman didn't want to do anything. So I reached over and opened the door and pushed her out. Her husband started toward the car. I just barely missed him.

Somehow, I made it out of the hay field and back onto the Autobahn. My heart was beating 100 mph.

I drove back into Ramstein through the same gate and found my john mate.

"I am going to kill you," I said to him. He hadn't even cleaned up the broken glass in the hallway. I had to do it myself.

"What happened?" he asked.

I told him the whole story of what had taken place after he crawled out of the window.

"I'm sorry," he said.

That's when I noticed his face was really scratched up. He had three or four gouges in his forehead, really deep.

The next day, his flight commander sent him to Wheelus Air Base in Tripoli for gunnery training—and healing.

There's one more Ramstein tale of intrigue and adventure—this time an Army training exercise called "Operation Devil's Spread," designed to prepare Special Forces to rescue a downed American pilot. Participants were more or less chosen at random and one year I was assigned to take part.

This was a really cool exercise because it actually took place in the German countryside. The authorities would announce the operation ahead of time in the local press so German citizens were aware of what we were up to.

The premise was that World War III had begun and Special Forces would be dropped behind enemy lines to rescue us. Those of us playing the downed pilots were allowed to steal cars, steal gasoline—do all the things we would do if we really were trying to survive and get back home. All this was announced in the news media complete with assurances from the U.S. government that the German people would be compensated for anything we took without asking. It was almost as big a game for them as it was for us.

Those of us on our normal training routine were instructed to wear the exact gear we'd wear if we were sitting on nuclear alert. The idea was that one day, without notice, we'd return from a training flight and be spirited away to Operation Devil's Spread, pretending we had been shot down instead of landing as usual. In fact, they'd take inventory of what we were wearing as well as everything on our person, just to make sure we weren't carrying anything more than we'd have if we were shot down.

So, shortly after touching down from a training flight, I was hustled to a base outside Munich, not far from the Alps. It had been the headquarters of the SS during World War II and was now the home of U.S. Special Forces in Germany.

Six or eight of us pilots were taken to a room and shown a very general map of Europe. It didn't contain much detail, so it was little help. We were instructed to memorize the map, along with some other pertinent information. After being dropped off in the countryside, we would have five or six days to make our way to a rendezvous point about 80 miles away. Our mission was to accomplish this while evading 1,000 American GIs who were out looking for us "downed" pilots. After all this was really their training exercise and we weren't supposed to make it easy on them.

They gave us 15 minutes to study the map and information sheet. It described the location of our rendezvous point, which was alongside a lake. There I would meet up with a "partisan"—a term for a guerilla working behind enemy lines. There was a path around the lake, with two trees on the east side of the water, planted six feet apart. As I walked along the path, I would be approached by someone who would utter a code phrase, to which I would give the appropriate response.

When our 15 minutes of prep time was up, they took away our maps and checked us over to make sure we didn't have any money on us. Unbeknownst to them, I had stowed a 20-mark piece—the equivalent of $5—in my boot. We were issued a canteen, one day's worth of C-Rations, and encouraged to steal whatever else we needed to survive. My flight suit was dark green, which was good for blending into the landscape.

They took us away in six-by-six trucks—blindfolding us and driving around to disorient us. We'd get a 30-minute head start before they loosed the 1,000 GIs to look for us. For them, the prize for locating one of us "downed" American pilots was a U.S. War Bond and a three-day pass. That was their incentive! If captured, we would be treated like prisoners and subjected to interrogation. That was our incentive not to get caught.

The planners running the exercise had said some of us would go in pairs, while others would travel alone. I piped right up and said I wanted to go single. Well, that must have ticked them off because I was teamed up with a pilot stationed in England who went by the name "Stump." It was easy to see why as he was about as wide as he was tall.

I wasn't too happy. I could immediately envision my slow-moving partner making this a very short-lived exercise.

"Stump," I told him, "the reason I wanted to go by myself is I'm pretty fast. You're going to have to keep up with me. I'm not waiting for you to get caught."

By now, it was nighttime. They drove us around, removed our blindfolds, and off we went into the darkness.

I was determined not to get captured—at least not right out of the gate. I picked a direction and told Stump we were heading that way. He gave me no argument and we started to run.

We could tell we were just outside a little village—which village it was, we had no idea. It was darker than dark that night. I thought I could hear someone approaching, so I ran like a bat out of Hades, with Stump trying to catch up to me.

Well, running in the pitch black, in unfamiliar territory, we never saw the deep ravine in front of us until it was too late. It was so steep it was almost like jumping off a cliff. I went ass over teakettle, saying a few choice words under my breath as I crashed to a stop at the bottom of the ravine. The next thing I knew, old Stump came rolling down the hill right behind me! Despite the rough descent, we had managed to elude whoever seemed to be after us.

CHAPTER 20

We walked all night, stopping and hiding during the day. On the second night, the sky was clearer and I could use the stars to get a sense of direction. Again, Stump and I walked until daylight. It was a cooperative effort and we felt confident we were headed in the right direction.

By now, I was out of water and thirsty. We had been given water-purification tablets, but didn't come across any place to fill our canteens that entire second night.

In this region of Germany, the ground in the woods was totally clear. Nearby residents collected every twig they could find for firewood. Stump and I found a small depression in the earth and piled leaves on top of ourselves to wait out the daylight hours.

That entire day, we heard nothing but voices all around us. It seemed like the entire U.S. Army was camped 100 yards away and here we were, like two pigs in a hog wallow. We heard one GI after another tramp out into the woods to relieve himself behind the trees. I worried all day long that we were on the verge of being caught.

When I wasn't thinking about getting caught, I was thinking about how thirsty I was. We had traveled miles through the night with nothing to drink and now here we were lying under a thick blanket of leaves. It was late October and still warm during the middle of the day. You could have struck a kitchen match on my tongue and it would have lit.

As soon as it got dark, I whispered to Stump, "We've got to get out of here!"

We skirted around the encampment and left. We walked and walked and walked. I was so thirsty. Finally, we came to a pond.

Now, you're supposed to fill your canteen and leave those water purification tablets in there to work for 30 to 60 minutes. But as soon as I saw the pond, I dipped my canteen into it and heard the beautiful gurgle-gurgle-gurgle of water pouring inside. I bet I didn't walk 100 feet before I said I've got to take a drink. I put the canteen to my lips and it tasted terrible! I was so dry, I didn't care.

We soon entered the mountainous terrain of the Alps and eventually came across a trail. In survival training, they tell you to stay off trails, which we had done until now. I don't know how many hundreds or thousands of feet up we had hiked, but it seemed to me we were so far from habitation that it was safe to take the easier route. It was densely forested with very beautiful views. By now, we were in our third day of travel and starved for food. Eventually, we came upon a cabin.

"Stump," I said, "stay here. I'm going to see if I can find anything to eat."

"Don't get us caught!" he said.

Well that's helpful advice. So what if someone does see us, I thought to myself. There's no one else around for miles. Whoever lives here probably doesn't even have a telephone.

So I went up and cased the joint, hiding for a while in the weeds. Finally, I thought I heard someone inside, so I walked up and knocked on the door. The cabin was like a beautiful Swiss chalet, way up in the mountains.

A woman came to the door. She looked at my American flight suit. She couldn't speak a word of English and I couldn't speak much German. I made motions to explain I was really hungry. She said, "Ah!"

Whether the woman realized we were part of a training exercise, I don't know, but she seemed to understand what we were up to. Again, using hand motions, I asked her please not to call the authorities. She made assurances she would not.

I said, "I've got some money!"

I went down into my boot and pulled out that 20-mark piece. I explained there were two of us and motioned for Stump to come out of the woods, the old weasel. She laid out a feast of sauerkraut and pork and baked bread. Oh, we ate like pigs!

"Here, take the whole 20 marks!" I said, between mouthfuls.

It was probably four times what the meal was worth, but I told her just to take it. She was happy and so were we. We filled our canteens with water and resumed our journey.

We walked another day or two, finally approaching the rendezvous point where we were to meet the partisan. We located a note left for us in a container next to a tree, so we knew we were on the right track.

Our instructions were to walk along this trail next to a lake, half an hour before dark. Someone would come up to us and ask us a question. As the sun was going down, I headed off down the path. Stump hid himself in the weeds and watched.

I had no idea what to expect. We had hiked some 80 miles in five days. Again, we were nearly starved. All I could think was *I hope someone shows up.* It was a long way to walk for nothing.

Sure enough, a man approached.

"Do you have a cigarette?" he asked.

That was the code phrase we were looking for. I gave the response.

"No, I don't have a cigarette," I said.

"Well, I do," the man replied. "Come with me."

It was a German civilian who had been contracted by the Army to play the part of a partisan. Stump joined us and the man took us to a barn.

We were cold, tired and hungry. I thought we had survived the challenge and were on our way home. But the intrigue had only begun.

The partisan instructed us to get out of our flight suits and handed us each some baggy, civilian clothes he had stolen—a shirt, pants, jacket and an old overcoat.

"Now we get to work," he said.

"What do you mean 'work?'" I asked. "I thought we were going home?"

"No," he said. "We've got a mission."

They sure seemed determined to make this training exercise authentic.

He took us to another barn where we found an Army sergeant in camouflage uniform and a second sergeant who was of higher seniority. They gave Stump and me something to eat and we slept for probably 12 hours.

The ranking sergeant had instructed the other sergeant to go out on reconnaissance. This junior sergeant was one of the toughest guys I have ever met. He walked all night at a fast pace and was back the next morning when we woke up. When he told me how far he walked, I couldn't believe it. He went 15 miles out and 15 miles back. I said to myself *man, oh man. I'm glad these guys are on our side!*

They told us what would happen next. Using a hand-cranked radio in the barn, they would call in the coordinates for a U.S. air drop. It would contain supplies we'd use to rig explosives on a series of high-tension wire towers to bring them down. The explosives would only be simulated, of course. We didn't want to actually blow up any German power lines!

The next night, we went to a clearing on top of a mountain and marked a drop zone, maybe 200 feet square, using eight C-Ration food cans filled with stolen gasoline. At the appropriate time, we'd light the gasoline and a C-130 would swoop in and drop our supplies.

I said to myself, "There is no way. I know the Air Force is good, but there's no way a pilot is going to be able to fly in here at exactly the right instant and find this drop zone." Remember, this was long before the days of GPS navigation.

But no sooner had we lit the markers, we heard an airplane approach. The pilot came in, cut his engines back, and flew over in a whisper. It was a perfect moonlit night and we could see a pallet on a parachute come out the back of the plane. I'll be darned if it didn't land more or less right in the middle of the drop zone. The pilot gunned the engines and flew off.

Whoa, I said to myself. *That's pretty good!*

Our "explosives" were blocks of wood that simulated dynamite. We gathered them up, put them in backpacks, and returned to our barn. The following night, we tied them around the bases of the towers as if we were planning to blow them up.

The mission complete, the sergeants stole an old Mercedes and told us they were going to try to sneak through the "enemy lines" to get us home. Again, these Army guys were good. Stump and I lay on the floor in the back seat as they talked their way past several Army checkpoints.

Finally, we were in the clear, headed back to the point where our adventure had begun a week earlier. In fact, we were retracing some of the route Stump and I had traveled. We recognized several landmarks—including the pond I had greedily gulped water from when I was so parched. I immediately saw why it had tasted so terrible.

"Stump!" I said. "Look at that pond. That's where we got the water!"

The stagnant pond was covered with ducks—and duck droppings.

I about threw up!

Looking back, Operation Devil's Spread was a wonderful experience; albeit one I never want to repeat. It was very educational to see how brave French partisans would have worked during World War II, rescuing pilots and carrying out missions. It was something we'd only read about in history books. I'm glad I got to learn about it the way I did.

I'm not sure how Stump and I did compared to the other "downed pilots" in the exercise, but I do know this. We heard later that one U.S. pilot who had been stationed in England was caught right away. He had on an orange flight suit which many American pilots wore because they flew so much over the ocean. If they went down in the water, the orange flight suit made them easier to find and rescue. However, in this training exercise, it made this particular pilot stick out like a sore thumb.

The Army caught him and ran him through the interrogation process, just like they promised. They stripped him and dripped water on his head until he broke down and spilled his guts. He told them all about the nuclear target he was sitting on.

In the end, they evacuated him out and took his commission away from him. It was a serious matter to know he had been brought to the point of confession during a training exercise.

I discovered my Air Force survival training prepared me well for what I would undergo as a POW in Vietnam. It was as close to the real thing as you could get. When I got shot down, I knew what to expect. I knew there was no end the next day, or the day after that, or the day after that. I knew that under interrogation, you had to toe a hard line, because once they found a patsy, they'd never let go.

My four-year tour at Ramstein came to a close in 1964. I enjoyed my time there, but I knew it was time to move on to a new assignment, and hopefully advance through the Air Force ranks.

Even though I had excelled in the high-profile job of intelligence officer and had briefed many dignitaries, I wasn't politically minded enough to lobby for choice assignments. I discovered most of those went to my peers who worked in the wing headquarters at Hahn.

But, I was fortunate enough to ask for and receive an assignment to further my training back at the Fighter Weapons School at Nellis Air Force Base in Las Vegas. For a fighter pilot, it was the next best thing to being a member of the Thunderbirds demonstration team. Only the top fighter pilots from squadrons around the world have the opportunity to go back to Nellis and participate in what's more or less like a graduate school program and learn the very latest in fighter weapons technology. Pilots there would serve as the weapons officer in their squadrons and be responsible for demonstrating the newest nuclear and conventional weapon delivery techniques to everyone else.

I was looking forward to it, and to returning home to America with my beautiful wife and our little boy. There was no way I could know that a message waiting for me on a bulletin board in New York Harbor would change the path of my career, and our lives, forever.

MEETING FAMILY

As our post-release tests and debriefing continued at Clark Air Base in the Philippines, I tried to push the awkward telephone conversation with Kathy to the back of my mind.

I had the opportunity to visit over the phone with my old flight commander, Caspar Sharpless Bierman, and his wife Mario. Cass was now the operations officer for the Alaskan Air Command. I even got to talk to my old back-seater, Curt Briggs. The last time we spoke had been in those terrifying seconds before we ejected over Vietnam. Having left the Air Force, Curt was now a commercial pilot with National Airlines, and later with Pan Am and Delta.

On Feb. 14, 1973, our second full day of freedom, Robbie and I continued our debriefing on his orders that I had memorized during our captivity. I spent as much time recalling the comings and goings of the two POWs who'd turned traitor than just about anything else. The government intended to use that information to prosecute them.

Let me be clear. I don't think any of us POWs were out for blood regarding these two fellow officers. We knew they had done the wrong thing and had to be prosecuted. The military needed to make an example of them so that in the future, some enemy interrogator couldn't point to them and tell a POW under torture, "See, these two gave out information and nothing happened to them when they were released. So you might as well save yourself a lot of trouble and cooperate with us."

That evening, Robbie and I were walking down a corridor at the hospital, probably just making small talk. He turned to me.

"Hey, what do you think about calling President Nixon?" Robbie asked.

"Yeah!" I said. "Let's do that!"

There was a phone right there in the hallway. He picked it up and said, "This is Robbie Risner. I want to talk to President Nixon."

Everybody knew Robbie Risner. Including the President of the United States. Robbie was our hero.

He looked at me, holding the telephone to his ear.

"I think they're going to patch us through!" Robbie said.

"That would be some kind of luck," I replied.

The next thing I knew, Robbie said, "Hello, Mr. President!"

By gosh, it was President Nixon. I listened in as they chatted a bit. Robbie told him we were grateful to the U.S. government for getting us out of Vietnam. Nixon said the country was really proud of us.

They probably were on the phone for two minutes. The president wanted to host all of us POWs in Washington once we were back in the States. The two said goodbye and Robbie hung up the phone.

"Wow! Wasn't that awesome?" I exclaimed.

"Yeah, it was!" Robbie said.

By the next day, Feb. 15, we had completed all our debriefings. Along with Dick Shrove, my old friend from Ramstein who had been assigned to help with my transition back to everyday life, I boarded a plane for the flight that would take me back to America at last.

We stopped to refuel at Hickam Air Force Base in Hawaii, where Dick was stationed. His wife, Lynn, whom I remembered from Ramstein and their three children, were there to greet us. In fact, there were hundreds of well-wishers lined up to welcome the returning POWs home. Lynn gave me a great big hug and members of the crowd stepped forward to place beautiful leis around our necks—real leis with real orchids, not the plastic kind!

We continued onward to Travis Air Force Base in California. I remember it was daylight when we approached the California coast. Over the intercom, the pilot told us we soon would be over San Francisco. He obtained special clearance from air traffic control to fly a circle right over the top of the Golden Gate Bridge.

It was a clear day, so we all got to take a good, close look at it. What an awesome sight it was to our weary eyes. I'm sure quite a few of us had to bite our tongues to keep from crying. During those many long days in our prison cells, the

Golden Gate Bridge was our vision of freedom, dreaming of that moment when we'd finally be home.

We landed at Travis, where I said goodbye to Dick. He flew back to Honolulu and they hustled about five of us to a small passenger jet bound for Maxwell Air Force Base in Montgomery, Alabama. Each POW was being flown to the regional military hospital closest to their home. It was a non-stop flight, but it's a long ride from California to Alabama in a smaller plane. By now it was dark.

Now I was really beginning to feel anxious to see my family again. I wondered what they would look like. I wondered how I would look to them. The plane had a dinky bathroom and I kept going back there and looking at myself in the mirror. Like many other POWs, my face was all broken out. We each had a perpetual case of skin irritation due to the filthy conditions we had been held captive in. I looked just like a teenager! When we finally began our descent to Maxwell, I fastened my safety belt and straightened my tie. I had no idea what my family was going to think of me.

It was maybe 9 or 10 p.m. when we got in and cold. There's nothing like the damp cold of the South. We landed and they opened the door of the plane. I was sitting in the back, so I was the last one out. I could look through the windows and see there were 20 or 30 people out there waiting, along with a few staff cars. As the four other POWs exited the plane ahead of me, I could hear their parents, wives and kids shouting, screaming and crying as they were reunited.

At last, it was my turn to walk down the steps of the plane. As I emerged into the chilly night air, I looked for Kathy, but she wasn't there.

The Air Force had made arrangements for POWs and their families to stay in the Visiting Officers Quarters at Maxwell. It was so cold that no one lingered very long outside. Everyone was pretty quickly getting into the staff cars and heading off together to the VOQ. Everyone but me. I was all alone.

As the last of the cars pulled away, I felt disheartened. This was not the homecoming I had pictured in my mind in the seven years and eight months I had been a prisoner. I could see the base of operations off in the distance—tall and lit up against the night sky. The building was about the length of a football field away. I pulled my jacket tight around me against the chilly air and began to walk.

It's hard to explain my emotions, but my heart had sunk into my shoes. My thoughts returned to the awkward telephone conversation I'd had with Kathy. She never did say, "Hi, Honey!" or "Welcome home!" or anything you might hope for your spouse to say after a long time apart.

As I drew closer to the base, I could see a blue Air Force staff car off to one side, just sitting there. As I got to within about 50 feet, a tall man emerged from the vehicle.

"Are you Maj. Kari?" he asked.

"Yes," I said.

"Get into the front passenger seat," he replied. "Your family is inside."

He introduced himself.

"I'm Col. Reed," he said. "I'm your escort."

Wow, I thought to myself. A full colonel.

I got in and shut the door. Kathy was in the back seat on the left and Shawn and Allison were back there on the right. I turned around to see them.

"Hi, Kath!" I said.

"Hi," she replied.

The kids were climbing up over the seat to get a look at Dad. They'd never seen Dad before. Not that they could remember, anyway.

Shawn was 10 and Ali was 8. The last time I saw my daughter, she was an infant. My son had been a toddler. Back in those days, of course, they didn't make you wear seatbelts, so I turned around and tried to give the children a hug over the seat. I remember Ali looked at me quizzically.

"You're Dad?" she asked.

"Yeah, I'm Dad," I answered.

Kathy didn't say anything.

Col. Reed spoke as the car pulled away.

"We've got rooms for you at the VOQ," he said. "Your dad and mom are here, and your older sister, Ruth, who's a nurse. The Air Force brought her in, too, because your dad has had a series of heart attacks and strokes."

It was no more than a five-minute ride, during which the kids and I talked and kept looking at each another, just trying to take one another in.

Col. Reed dropped us off. Kathy was standoffish when we got out of the car. I wanted to embrace her, but I thought to myself *I'm not going to push the issue.*

The Air Force had given us four rooms. Ruth was in Room 101, Mom and Dad in 102, Shawn and Allison in 103, Kathy and I in Room 104. After learning my dad had experienced so many health problems, and not knowing what kind of condition he was in, I wanted to see him right away.

I walked into the room and Dad could hardly contain his excitement. Mom smiled. For the first time in my life, she said the words I had always longed to hear from my parents.

"Well, Paul," Mom said. "We're proud of you."

Dad was choking back tears. I gave him a salute.

"I've seen a lot of generals and high-ranking officers, but you're the tops of all of them," I said. I went over and gave him a great big hug.

At age 68, Dad appeared worn out. Ruth told me he'd temporarily lost his ability to talk after his first strokes, but had gained it back. Dad seemed feeble, but he could still walk. Mom was now 59.

We talked for an hour. My parents told me they had moved to Colorado to have the cattle ranch Dad had always wanted. They told me all about their 800-acre spread—where it was and what it was like. The room at the VOQ was small—just a pair of double beds and a bunch of chairs. We all crowded in there together and talked and tried to catch up.

Soon it was getting on toward midnight. I knew I had to get up early the next morning, so we decided it was time for everyone to get to bed. We hugged each other and finally said good night.

I had brought little gifts for everyone. Kathy and I went to Shawn and Ali's room to let them open their presents.

Back at Clark in the Philippines, they had opened the base BX store to POWs. The staff had volunteered their time to let us shop. It was the first instance that I became frustrated with my vision problem. Everyone had congregated around the oval-shaped jewelry counter, talking and pointing to what they wanted to buy. I was standing behind them, trying to see what was there.

I'm not a pushy guy, so I wasn't going to weasel my way in. And no one was going to say, "Hey, PK. We know you can't see very well from back there. Why don't you come up front?" I couldn't see the prices or even what was in the jewelry case.

Inside, I became very angry at my eyes. I backed away and went to look at some of the less crowded areas of the store. I bought a big mahogany fork and spoon for my mom and dad, which I shipped home and they kept for a long time. What I bought for Kathy and the kids, I can't remember.

We went into the children's room at the VOQ and talked with them for a while, maybe another half an hour or so. I was exhausted and knew I had to get some rest. We said good night to the kids and Kathy and I went to our room next door.

There was a king-size bed and a couch. I was tired, but also happy to be with my wife again. I asked her to sit down next to me. She came over and sat down. The weather was cold enough that Kathy was wearing a fairly heavy topcoat. I put my arm around her and tried once more to make a joke to break the ice.

"Honey, I don't think you have to worry about me making any advances tonight," I said. "It's been eight years. I think I'd better take it easy!"

She pushed my arm off.

"Things are not the same anymore," she said.

I was so bewildered by what she said, I don't think I had a reply or even asked why. After pushing my hand away, Kathy immediately stood up.

"I guess I'm going to bed," she said.

Kathy walked around to the far side of the bed and lay down wearing her overcoat and all her clothes. She pulled the bedspread over her and remained that way the entire night.

I got into bed, but I couldn't sleep.

Oh, Good Lord, I thought to myself. What's happened?

The next morning, I got up and excused myself. I was due at the hospital, where they were to begin giving us a more thorough physical assessment. I had two aids, Col. Reed and a major. One of them picked me up and drove me to the hospital.

They photographed every square inch of our bodies and looked us over, inside and out. In between, they did a little more intelligence debriefing. The day was full.

Even though they kept us busy every moment, inside I was distraught. When at last it was time to go back to my family at the VOQ, I didn't know what to do. I asked if it would be possible for me to stay in the hospital. Kathy's words, "Things are not the same anymore," left me feeling mentally and emotionally overwhelmed.

That first day, each POW met with a psychiatrist. He asked me how my homecoming had been.

"Awful," I said, and shared what had happened between me and Kathy.

"Hold that thought," the psychiatrist said.

He left the room and returned with three or four more psychiatrists.

"You've got to hear this story," he told them.

After they had all trooped in, the psychiatrist asked me to repeat what I had said.

I got about half way through the story for the second time when they began whispering among themselves as I talked. The anger welled up inside me.

"You guys think this is funny? This isn't funny," I said. "I'm about to have a nervous breakdown. This is serious to me and you guys want to hear about it because it's entertaining to you. If you can't help me, I'm not going any further."

The psychiatrists kind of looked at each other. They didn't seem to know what to say.

I was torn up inside. I didn't know what to do. I didn't feel ready to go back to discuss things with Kathy, but I didn't want her to think I was rejecting her, either. I asked the doctors if they could tell her they needed to hold me in the hospital overnight for more tests. They agreed.

In just a few short hours, my emotions went from the top of the top at my release, to the bottom of the bottom with Kathy. I needed a little more time to process everything that was happening and to try to come to terms with myself before I could come to terms with anyone else.

I had been shot down, beaten, tortured, starved and imprisoned for almost eight years. Part of what made it bearable was the anticipation of being reunited with my wife and family. That was the moment when everything would be set right again. Everything seemed perfect when I left for Vietnam. I had a beautiful wife, a young family, a home and a career I loved. Instead of the joyous reunions so many of my POW friends were enjoying, my world seemed to have been turned upside down. I needed some time before I could face up to it.

That night, a nurse came into my hospital room.

"Would you like a rubdown?" she asked.

"I would love a rubdown," I said.

The nurse rubbed my back and my legs. It felt wonderful. No one had touched me in a caring, human way for so long.

The next day, it was back to more debriefing and intense physical exams. During the last four winters of my imprisonment, I had trouble drawing a deep breath. When I did, I felt a pain in my chest. It felt like a knife in my heart. I could only take short breaths. They suspected I had experienced an inflammation of the lining around my heart, a condition called pericarditis.

They examined my eyes and my teeth. I received a colonoscopy and an endoscopy because I had such trouble with my digestive system. The endoscopy showed the lining of my lower esophagus had been eaten away, right down to the nerves. That's why anything I ate caused me pain, no matter how good it tasted or how hungry I was.

Col. Reed came to see me at the hospital and asked how I was doing. I told him what had happened between me and Kathy. He wanted to help. Col. Reed suggested maybe things would go better if Kathy and I joined him and his wife for dinner at their home. They lived in a very nice house right on the base.

"Maybe if you came over, and it was in more of a family setting, it might help break the ice," he said.

"That sounded like a good idea," I said.

The colonel and his wife were very kind people. They served a nice dinner and the four of us sat and talked. Kathy remained stone cold. That night, we slept in the same room, in the same bed, and Kathy gave me the same cold shoulder. The efforts of the colonel and his wife to make things more comfortable between us didn't seem to work.

The next day brought more medical tests. The third night I was there, the major assigned to help me said Alabama Gov. George Wallace had invited all five of us POWs staying at Maxwell to the governor's mansion for a special banquet in our honor. Afterward, we were to go to the debutante ball held at a local country club.

I put on my Class A dress uniform. Kathy dressed up, too, and really looked wonderful. We posed for pictures together with Gov. Wallace, who was confined to a wheelchair after being shot in a 1972 assassination attempt. He was very pleasant and very talkative.

The five of us POWs were the governor's only guests. Some of us were alone, while others were with wives or girlfriends. Gov. Wallace's wife attended, too, and it was a lovely evening. She was a gracious lady. They served drinks, which Kathy took part of. I didn't have anything to drink because of the problems with my stomach. After an enjoyable couple of hours, the major told us it was time to go to the country club.

We got to the debutante ball and they introduced the five POWs to the crowd. A number of the young ladies came up and asked to dance with us. I asked Kathy—who was a good dancer—if she wanted to dance. She said no.

I obliged one or two women who invited me to the dance floor. One of them, a schoolteacher, surprised me by whispering something of a proposition in my ear! Let me tell you, when I left for Vietnam in 1965, it was like the Victorian Era. I quickly realized the 1970s were a different story.

Later, Kathy told me the kids had become excellent roller skaters. I learned they spent a large portion of their time at the rink while she was out doing other things. Kathy said Shawn and Allison were roller skating dance partners and had a regional competition coming up that Saturday in St. Petersburg. By this time, Mom, Dad, Ruth, and the kids had already left for home.

Kathy had arranged for an older woman named Mrs. Miller to look after Ali and Shawn. I told Kathy I would really like to fly to St. Pete this weekend to see the kids skate. However, I hadn't yet been officially released from the hospital.

Someone must have told the base commander my kids were competing in a big event back home. Col. Reed came to let me know that if Kathy and I wanted to go see Shawn and Allison compete, the base commander would see to it that Kathy and I were flown down to Florida in his personal plane. We accepted.

That Friday, we went down to base operations and got on board. I think it was a C-54, a big, four-engine prop aircraft. It probably seated 40-50 people, with rows of seats on either side and an aisle down the center. I picked a window seat to the right and Kathy sat across the aisle on the left. We flew like that all the way from Montgomery to Tampa. We were the only two passengers on the plane.

It seems unreal now that we would fly all that way and sit on separate sides of the airplane, but it's true. We had a couple of very short conversations about the kids, but didn't broach the subject of our relationship.

To this day, I don't know exactly what took place in Kathy's life in the almost eight years I was a POW. From the day I was shot down to the day I was released, it's like someone took an eraser and wiped out virtually everything that happened in her life and the lives of our kids. She wouldn't tell me a thing.

For example, I asked Kathy simple questions about the children's health. Did they ever have any broken bones? Did they have their tonsils removed? All she had to say was yes or no. Instead, Kathy would only reply, "We'll talk about it later."

I had no reason to be concerned about the kids and their well-being. I was just trying to get to know them and learn how they had spent the childhood years I had missed. Allison and Shawn seemed remarkably happy and healthy, but as far as their behavior, they were little hellions.

Financially, Kathy didn't have to work outside the home, but she had taken a management job with a radio company. In fact, I think she probably invested a portion of our money in the business, which I believe eventually went belly-up. I can only surmise maybe she was embarrassed about that and similar decisions she made that didn't work out.

Rather than hiring a baby sitter, Kathy would drop the children off at the local roller skating rink while she was at work. They were on their own. I was told later they even had their own credit cards. If they needed something when she wasn't around, they just bought it.

We landed at MacDill Air Force Base in Tampa, where we received a nice welcome. Kathy was wearing a polka dot pantsuit and looked really great. We drove across the Gandy Bridge over to St. Pete and the starter home we had bought when we returned to the States from Ramstein. The house seemed like it was out in the boonies when I left, but now the town had grown quite a bit in our direction. As we approached our street, there was a bank with a big sign that said, "Welcome Home, Maj. Kari." I thought that was really nice.

When we reached the house, it was Friday afternoon. A neighbor who lived catty-corner from us was a retired Army colonel. He came over to welcome me. We would soon become friends. A few of the other neighbors came up and we had a nice little homecoming.

The next day, Saturday morning, the kids and I got into Kathy's Grand Am and drove to the dance competition. By this time, the conflict inside me was ready to explode. In many ways, it felt good to be home. Yet, hanging over everything like one of those massive Vietnam storm clouds was my relationship with Kathy and our inability to discuss where our marriage stood.

We arrived at the skating rink and the kids ran off to get ready to perform. Kathy went to the opposite side of the room from where I was standing and began talking to her friends, seemingly oblivious to the fact I was even there. I was alone.

Finally, after a while, I just couldn't take it anymore. I went up to Kathy and told her I wanted to go home. She asked one of her friends to give me a ride back to the house.

I lay down in bed and began to sob. I felt as if I was about to have a nervous breakdown. Someone told me once that if you allow yourself to break down and lose control of your emotions, it will only happen faster the next time and the time after that. I could feel it coming, but I fought it and fought it.

Looking out the window, I noticed the retired Army colonel working in his yard. I went outside to see him and asked if he could come over for a few minutes. Back inside the house, I absolutely unloaded all my pent-up emotions.

"Colonel, I think I've just had the most awful homecoming of any of my fellow POWs," I said. "I don't know how to handle it."

After I told him everything that had happened with Kathy, I broke into tears and cried like a baby.

"What did she tell you?" he asked.

"She hasn't told me anything," I answered.

"Well," he said. "I can tell you a thing or two."

The colonel went on to describe a series of indiscretions involving Kathy that had occurred while I was gone. From where he lived, he had a pretty clear view of our house and could see when someone was there.

Ironically, about a year and half after I was shot down, my friend and cell mate J.B. McKamey had asked me, "What would you do if you got home and you found out your wife was running around on you?"

Years and years later after we were released, almost up until the time he passed away, J.B. teased me about what I said to him that day in our cell in Vietnam.

"Let me think about it and I'll get back to you in a week," I told him.

As if we were going anywhere! A week went by.

"Remember the question I asked you?" J.B. reminded me as we sat in our cell. "What's your answer?"

"Well," I said, "war is hell. If I came home and found out my wife had had affairs, but was very discrete about it, and the kids didn't know, I'd probably never bring it up to her. We all have needs. If she was very, very discrete and if she loved me when I got home and I could tell she still loved me, I'd never bring it up. However, if she was indiscrete and did it around the kids, which to me would be very wrong, I'd probably bring it up and ask her what happened and why she did it."

J.B. said. "You're a pretty forgiving guy!"

"Well, that's my answer," I replied.

As it happened, Shawn and Ali won their roller skating dance competition that day. They were very good. Shawn has always been very athletic and Ali was so slender she could just twist her body around like a noodle.

The next day was Sunday and I flew back to Maxwell to finish my medical tests. I was there for several days, but soon returned to MacDill on an Air Force plane. The wing commander there had offered the help of his administrative assistant in answering my mail. It was very kind of him. I had received hundreds of cards and letters from people everywhere welcoming me back. Many of the cards were from schoolchildren in the Tampa-St. Pete area and were handmade. It was one of the most uplifting experiences in my entire homecoming.

I soon discovered women's fashions had changed quite a bit in the years I had been away. The commander's attractive assistant, who was married and a very kind woman, wore miniskirts to work. Now, when I was growing up, I knew my mom and my sisters wore corsets and things to hold up their hose. The commander's assistant was always bending over to reach one thing or another. The miniskirt didn't hide much. I couldn't help but notice there was nothing like my mom and sisters wore holding up the hose on her legs.

"Ma'am, may I please ask you a silly question?" I said.

"Of course, sir," she said.

I explained that miniskirts were new to me and I didn't understand how a woman could wear one and keep her hose up.

"Oh!" she replied. "That's easy! Now we have panty hose!" And she lifted up her skirt to show me.

I thought to myself, *what have I missed?* I can't believe these women, but Lord, it sure is good to be home!

It took the better part of a week to answer all my mail. I was living at the house with Kathy and the kids, doing the best I could.

When I left for Vietnam, my 1956 Thunderbird was parked in the garage. Kathy said she had trouble starting it and traded it in on her Pontiac Grand Am—a pretty good trade for whoever took it! That Thunderbird was worth quite a bit of money.

Now the garage looked more like a dump. When I opened a side door to take a look inside, about six or eight remote control trucks belonging to Shawn spilled out. I asked him later why he had so many. Whenever a truck stopped working, Shawn explained, he would just get another one.

Clutter makes me uneasy. And I didn't need to feel any more uncomfortable than I already felt. I worked at trying to clean things up. I didn't throw anything away that was Kathy's. I just tried to organize the garage a bit.

I did one thing I regret. I only had two toys growing up—an army truck and team of horses pulling a little earth mover. The hitch was broken on the earth mover, which my dad had tried to fix with a piece of wire. It was there in the pile of stuff in the garage. I was so angry at the mess I threw my old toy away. It was made from cast iron and probably would be worth $1,000 today! They don't make toys like that anymore. However, I do still have the army truck.

Kathy had a huge swimming pool installed behind the house. It went all the way to the property line. She also had a big dog that would dig and tear the carpet all the way through to the concrete floor. There were spots all over the place.

"Kath, how come you let him do this?" I asked.

"Well, the dog's nervous because you're here," she said.

"I don't know," I said. "Maybe the dog has to go. We can't let him tear the house up."

"He's part of the family," she said.

A notice arrived in the mail saying the bank was foreclosing on the house. I couldn't believe it. Our house payment was only around $100 per month. I asked Kathy how it could have happened.

I learned she had taken out a second mortgage to buy the pool and hadn't been making the payments. Out of the $13,000 we had in the bank, I wrote a check for $8,000 to pay off the pool and stop the foreclosure.

It was a three-bedroom home. Kathy slept in the master bedroom, which had its own bath. The kids were in the second bedroom. I was in the third bedroom and used the bathroom down the hall. One morning, I was wearing boxer shorts when I walked the few steps from the bathroom to my bedroom to get dressed.

CHAPTER 21

"You can't walk around here like that!" Kathy said.

"I've got shorts on," I said. "It's my house! What's wrong with that?"

"It's not right," she said.

Kathy said that if I didn't move out, she would find a way to have me evicted. Ever since returning to live at home, I had been in the depths of despair. My soul had been stretched to the breaking point. At this point, fighting to stay in the house seemed like it would only make life even harder on the kids and on me, so I spent the rest of the summer living in the Bachelor Officer's Quarters at MacDill.

Our neighbors three houses down, Katie and Jim Turner, were good friends. It was a new development and we had moved in at the same time.

At one point, I confided to them that things were not going well at home.

"Let me tell you something," Katie said.

The evening I had first called Kathy from the Philippines, she went over to see Katie and Jim. They had been happy to hear my long ordeal was over. They asked her if it was true I would soon be on a plane back to the States.

"Yes," Kathy said.

"Did you get a chance to talk to him?" they asked. "How is he?"

"He said he's got problems with his eyes," Kathy told them. "And I'll be damned if I'm going to take care of him the rest of his life!"

That's exactly what Katie told me and it made sense, since I remembered that was the point in our conversation when Kathy entirely clammed up.

It wasn't long after she told me to leave the house I received notice she had filed for divorce. Word began to get around about what had happened. The military newspaper *Stars & Stripes* even ran a news brief on July 22, 1973, headlined,

"Former POW's wife seeks divorce."

According to Kathy, our marriage was "irretrievably broken," which was the only grounds required for divorce in Florida. A big law firm in St. Pete offered to handle my case for free, which I gratefully accepted.

TDY to UBON, THAILAND

About three months before Kathy, Shawn and I were to leave Ramstein for the United States, the Air Force asked me how I wanted to travel home. The choice was between a plane and an ocean liner. Immediately, I decided to travel by ship.

I wanted to sail for two reasons. First, I'd never traveled that way and it would be a new experience. Second, my father had traveled by ocean liner when he immigrated to America. It would give me a taste of what that must have been like for him.

Besides, it wasn't just any ship. It was the SS United States, America's premier ocean liner of the day, and we'd have first-class tickets. I couldn't imagine a more appropriate name for a ship to make a homecoming on, after several years abroad.

Kathy, who was now expecting our second child, wasn't as enthusiastic.

"I don't want to go that way," she said. "It'll take too long. I'd rather fly."

A neighbor in our apartment building, Col. Sam Green, talked her into it.

"Oh, Kathy, you've got to go home that way," Sam said. "It's a once-in-a-lifetime chance."

She finally agreed. I drove my Volkswagen up to Bremerhaven and put it on a cargo ship to New York Harbor. Shawn, Kathy and I, along with our schnauzer, Jock, would board the SS United States in Le Havre, which was in the northwest corner of France. We traveled there from Germany on a coal-fired steam locomotive—another new experience! And it was quite an experience.

It was in early September of 1964 and the weather still was quite warm. There was no air-conditioning in the train cars. The seats were hard and uncomfortable. And here was our traveling party—Kathy, who was pregnant, 18-month-old Shawn, and me.

It got so stuffy inside the train, passengers began opening the windows for ventilation. It wasn't long before the wind changed and blew clouds of soot from the smokestack right into the passenger compartment! I remember saying, "Man, this is what it was like in the Wild West!"

We finally made it to Le Havre after a long day on the train. We arrived at the shipyard and there was the SS United States. It was a huge ship. We walked up the gangplank and the ship's staff welcomed us aboard. They were all very courteous.

Although our room was far below deck and had no windows, we had a very enjoyable trip. One night, there was a captain's dinner where all the military personnel on board put on their mess dress and the ladies wore their formal gowns. It was a wonderful evening.

As I recall, it was about a four-and-a-half or five-day voyage. We had traveled about halfway across the Atlantic when the captain spoke over the intercom to tell passengers we'd be taking a detour around a large hurricane. Kathy gave me a look as if to say, "What have we gotten ourselves into?"

"No problem," I told her, confidently. "There aren't any icebergs around here. We've got nothing to worry about."

I'll tell you, the swells from this hurricane were as tall as the ship, and it was a big ship! The ship would ride up a giant wave, come down on its nose, and water would crash over the deck. Each time we rode over a massive wave, the whole ship would shake violently as the propellers rose out of the water.

Poor Shawn was sick. Kathy nearly was. I was fortunate that I felt OK. In fact, despite the crew urging caution, I wanted to go up on deck to see the storm. I made my way to the bow and braced myself in a doorway. The wind must have been 80 to 100 mph. It was something to feel.

We arrived in New York Harbor at last. They told us the Statue of Liberty would be on the right side of the ship as we sailed in. It was morning and everyone was up on deck to see it.

I hadn't been back to the States in three years. I'll tell you, when I saw the Statue of Liberty, I had to bite my tongue hard to keep the tears from flowing from my eyes. Kathy was there, holding Shawn and taking it all in. I didn't want her to see my tears, so I crossed to the other side of the ship for a few minutes until I was sure I had my emotions under control.

It's just such a wonderful sight to see that statue. I'll never understand how anyone could spit on the American flag or denigrate our nation's symbols. As I stood next to Kathy once again, my thoughts turned to my dad sailing into Ellis Island. It was a very meaningful moment for me.

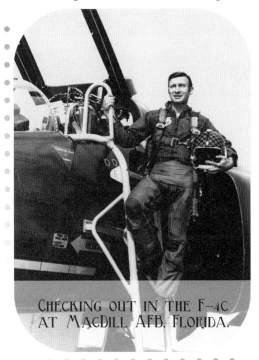

CHECKING OUT IN THE F-4C AT MACDILL AFB, FLORIDA.

It was customary to tip the ship's staff when you disembarked. The military had even suggested an appropriate amount to give them. There's a porter who makes your bed, another who waits on you at your table in the dining room, etc. There were at least four or five different staff members who did one thing or another for you and they were all standing and waiting as we left the ship. Well, we tipped them exactly what the military had recommended. The porters stared at us as if to say: Is that all? Boy, are you a cheapskate! The way they looked at us made us feel very small.

We left the SS United States and set foot again on United States soil. In this era before cell phones and e-mail, there was a bulletin board passengers were to check for messages as they disembarked. Posted there was a note for me that said simply: "Capt. Kari, call the Pentagon."

Uh-oh, I thought to myself. What's up?

I called and received news that would alter the course of my life.

Col. Levi Chase, who had been our operations officer in the 50th Wing in Hahn, Germany, was establishing a new wing at MacDill Air Force Base in Florida. He was recruiting pilots to fly the Air Force's latest aircraft—a new two-man fighter called the F-4C Phantom II. Col. Chase needed qualified pilots to learn this new airplane. He had asked for me by name.

Thanks, I thought. *Thanks a lot.*

I was livid. Yes, it was a compliment to my skills that he had asked for me to be added to his new wing. However, I had worked my tail off in Germany for four years so that I could have my choice of assignments in the next phase of my Air Force career. I was looking forward to going to Fighter Weapons School and furthering my abilities. The last thing I wanted—or any other pilot wanted—

was to fly a two-man craft. It wasn't that we weren't team players. We were. It's just that there is an immense amount of pride and freedom in piloting your own fighter. Splitting those duties with another pilot or navigator almost felt like an insult.

During the course of that phone call to the Pentagon, I expressed my desire to go to Fighter Weapons School at Nellis Air Force Base in Las Vegas as planned. My request immediately was denied. After having a little time to visit our families in Ohio, I was to report to MacDill. It was cut and dried.

I was so frustrated. It seemed all my efforts to maintain high test scores and to distinguish myself as an intelligence officer were for nothing. My old friend Jack Chain was right. You have to get visibility if you want to advance in the Air Force. However, I would add the caveat that you have to get visibility where visibility counts. Although I had the opportunity to brief a lot of dignitaries in my role as intelligence officer at Ramstein, I could see where my peers who had been stationed up at the wing headquarters at Hahn had been in a better position to make the right connections and move up into the positions they sought.

After collecting our bags and Jock the schnauzer, Kathy, Shawn, and I took a taxi to retrieve our car, which had arrived ahead of us from Germany.

It was terribly hot that fall in New York City. We stopped to get poor Jock a drink of water. He was walking on a leash and just panting, panting, panting. I stepped into a nearby restaurant to ask for a cup of water. That's when I got my first taste of the Big Apple.

"That'll be $2," said a woman inside the restaurant.

"For a plastic cup filled with water? It's for my dog!" I said.

"I don't care," she said. "It's $2."

I forked over the cash and Jock enjoyed his expensive drink of New York City water. We found our Volkswagen and made the drive home to Spencer. We were excited to introduce Shawn to his grandparents for the first time.

We arrived at the farm and were still standing outside visiting with Mom when Dad pulled into the driveway, coming home from his shift at the foundry.

"Hi, Dad," I said.

Dad looked at me.

"How are you doing?" he replied, and went on into the house.

That was all. He didn't even seem to notice Shawn, much less say, "Welcome back," or offer a hug.

"Dad!" I said. "This is your grandson! Your only grandson!"

Dad turned around.

"Oh," he said.

Dad bent over and gave him a kiss and a hug.

I was just shocked. It was almost as if my father was ticked off at me for leaving him with all the farm work. We visited three or four days in Spencer before driving down to MacDill Air Force base in Tampa.

We looked at off-base houses in Tampa and St. Petersburg, finding they were cheaper over in St. Pete. That's where we bought a three-bedroom starter home, about 1,200 square feet in size.

I checked in at the squadron and soon realized why Col. Chase had asked for me. He was putting a brand new wing together for the F-4, which was the newest aircraft in the Air Force inventory. In addition to me, he had two experienced pilots coming in from England. The rest were National Guard and Air Force personnel who had been through pilot training, but were relegated to "back-seater" status in the F-4. Initially, it was a terrible blow to their morale. I couldn't blame them. Any fighter pilot wants to do it all himself.

The Navy flew the F-4B, which had no pilot's stick in the back seat. The second man in that aircraft served as a radar operator. The Air Force made a mistake with the F-4 and put a stick and a pilot in the back seat, but gave him little opportunity to fly the plane. It could be frustrating for the back-seaters, many of whom had little flying experience and were anxious to learn.

I was assigned to Flight B with a back-seater who didn't seem to be up to my standards. Eventually I asked to make a switch and probably got the best back-seater from among that whole crop of new pilots, Curt Briggs.

Every pilot has an additional duty in a squadron and I was made assistant weapons officer. The job of the weapons officer was to post scores after pilots returned from the practice range.

At that time, we were firing a missile called the Bull Pup. It had a guidance control right next to the F-4's throttle. You'd come in at maybe 3,000 feet in sort of a glide, pull the throttle back, and hit your pickle button to release the missile. From there, you used the missile guidance control to fly the Bull Pup to its target.

These missiles sometimes had the unfortunate habit of going a little nuts. Our target down at the range was a tractor tire. That was the bull's eye. Every once in a while, the missile would whoosh off to the side by 500 or 600 feet. The Bull Pup's problems were well known. If one of them went haywire on you, you simply marked the missile as erratic.

Pilots achieved various designations based on their accuracy at the range. If you hit the bull's eye, you were awarded expert status. If you got it within maybe 75 feet, you were at the sharpshooter level. If you hit within a couple hundred feet, you were rated as marksman.

There was one pilot who was a particular blowhard. He was always puffing up his chest and bragging on himself at our squadron meetings. I saw by his test scores he was rated expert in everything. That was unusual because not too many people achieved expert status on every test. So I made a point of noticing his performance at the range. I watched many times when his shots with the Bull Pup missed the target by 75 feet or more. Any time he missed the bull's eye, instead of taking the lower score, he'd blame the missile and mark it down as erratic.

It concerned me enough to mention it to my flight commander, Caspar Sharpless Bierman.

"Cass," I said, "I think this guy is cheating. If he doesn't get an expert and a bull's eye, he's calling it erratic."

"Keep your eye on him," Cass said. And I did. It all came into play later, following our training on the F-4.

When I first saw the F-4, I was unimpressed. I said to myself: *Oh, boy. What an airplane.* That is the ugliest fighter God ever let man make. The nose sort of drooped down, the wings went out and then up. The tail looked different than what I was used to.

Of course, I found out later there was a reason for all those design elements. The F-4 was bigger and heavier than the F-100, but twice as powerful. It also turned out to be a very forgiving aircraft to fly. It was easy to bring in for those "grease-job" landings. You could touch down so smoothly on the runway, it was like the tires were kissing the ground. In fact, when the tires touched down, we pilots often would make a little "smooching" sound into the radio. The guy in the tower would always say: "Knock that off!" It was fun.

I attended a one-week ground school on the F-4, where my instructor was Charlie Hausenfleck. He was a nice guy; quiet and low-key, yet very thorough. The Air Force was in a hurry to get us up to speed on the F-4 and I was more than happy to comply.

I easily got checked out on the aircraft itself after flying just two missions. I did the same on conventional and nuclear delivery, which was supposed to take five or six missions to qualify. Again, I checked out in two flights.

One of the weapons we had to qualify in was the Bull Pup missile. Charlie happened to be the range officer the day I flew down for target practice. I fired the missile and knew from the puff of smoke I'd hit close to the bull's eye.

I caught up with Charlie the next morning.

"Do you know what you did?" he asked. "You put that thing right through the middle of the tire! I saw it through my binoculars."

"Well, that's just luck, Charlie," I said. "That's just luck."

It's true there's always an element of luck in hitting a target, but by the same token, I was proud of the flying abilities I had worked so long and hard to hone.

I soon discovered why the Air Force was so anxious to get the F-4 into service. Our wing had been placed on alert due to a growing conflict in Southeast Asia. Soon we would be headed there to fly combat. Immediately after we were checked out in the aircraft, the wing instructed us to "get all our affairs in order" in preparation for three months of TDY or "temporary duty."

In other words, we were to leave nothing undone—from making out our wills, to paying our tabs at the officers club. We were issued a checklist of the clothing and gear we would need for a 90-day deployment. It was to be packed in a footlocker and ready to go at a moment's notice.

They told us frankly the military had learned the hard way in World War II that it creates a mess at home when service members who failed to draw up their wills get killed or captured. The Air Force also gave us the opportunity to specify how our military pay and life insurance would be paid out, should we not return.

I laughed.

"I'm not going to get shot down and captured!" I said.

You could arrange to have any amount you wished either go to your spouse or be set aside in a savings account. The administrative assistant asked how much I wanted to be given to Kathy. At the time, it seemed like a ridiculous question.

"All of it, of course," I replied.

And I signed on the dotted line.

If the reality of being on-call for combat and making all these "just in case" arrangements had any effect on Kathy, she never seemed to show it.

Our lives had changed so much in a short span of time. We had returned to the United States in September of 1964, received the surprise assignment to MacDill in Florida and bought our little starter home. In January of 1965, our daughter Allison was born at the base hospital.

Before my deployment, I wanted to do a little landscaping around our house. In Ohio, the soil is acidic and plants require lime. So, being a good Ohio farm boy, what do I do? I wanted to sod the lawn, so I went out and bought 400-500 pounds of lime for our little front yard. I applied the lime to the soil and landscapers came in to lay the sod, which immediately began to die. I watered it and watered it, to no avail.

Exasperated, I called the county agricultural extension office and told the agent about my problem.

"Well, he said, "you know our soil here is basically very alkaline. Did you put any acid on it?"

"Oh my Lord," I exclaimed. "No, I put 400-500 pounds of lime on it!"

"Well, that's your problem, son!" he said.

When I left for Vietnam, I talked to the maintenance guy who worked for the builder in our development. I told him I was going to be gone for 90 days and gave him $100 to take care of the lawn during my deployment. He never did.

While I was in Germany, I had bought a '56 Ford Thunderbird. It had a hard top, the little port windows, and the spare tire mounted the back. I had it completely stripped down and painted. It was quite a car and I parked it in the garage when I left. There would be plenty of time to enjoy it. After all, I was only going to be gone for three months.

Finally, word came that we were to be deployed to Ubon Air Base in Thailand on April 3. The night before we left, all the pilots had to go up to the flight surgeon's office.

"OK," the surgeon said. "You're going to have some long flights. We're giving each of you a packet of pills and you're going to tape it up on the windscreen of your airplane. While you are here sitting in front of me, I want you to label the pills 'Go' and 'No-Go.'"

The "Go" pill seemed self-explanatory.

"What's the 'No-Go' pill?" I asked.

"That's for when you get to Honolulu so you can go to sleep, because the Go pill is going to keep you going," he said.

"Yes, sir," we replied, and followed the doctor's orders.

Kathy was very supportive of the Air Force and of my job as a fighter pilot. She brought Shawn and Ali to see me off. There were 16 planes, all lined up and parked at an angle right where the families could drive up close and see them. I was in the second airplane. Kathy looked beautiful. We were so much in love. We gave each other a great big hug.

"Sweetie, I'll be back in 90 days," I said.

I cranked up the engines and waved to them as I took off.

We always called Col. Levi Chase "Smiley" because none of us had ever seen him with a smile. My whole three years in Germany when he was the ops officer, I never saw him smile even though they said he had a wife and couple of daughters and was a great family man.

Before we took off, he gave us a stern lecture.

"OK, guys. I've had a lot of TDY deployments in my life," he said. "What I don't want is to have planes broken down and strung out all across the Pacific. We're taking off with 16 planes and I want to end up over there with 16 planes. Got that?"

We nodded our heads as he spoke, all probably thinking the same thought. *If someone's plane is going to break down, it ain't going to be mine.*

The flight from MacDill to Honolulu was nine hours and 35 minutes. The F-4 did not have what we called a "pee tube." The F-100 did. It had a small funnel on a tube the size of your little finger that went outside the aircraft. You did what you needed to do, opened up a little valve, and the suction would just take it right out of the plane. What did they give us in this new-fangled airplane? No pee tube, just a one-and-a-half quart jar with a lid. Believe you me, we filled them up.

The plan was to refuel the planes in the air all the way across the country. We got over into Texas and married up with some C-135 tankers. Once you joined up with the tankers, they did the navigating and you just kind of flew a loose formation off to the side. When we got low on fuel, we came up and got a drink, then flew back out. It was a piece of cake.

Col. Chase was flying the lead aircraft.

"All right, guys," he said. "Is everybody OK?"

Everybody was OK. We got over the coast of California and were heading to Honolulu, about a six-hour leg of the flight.

The F-4 had two engines, two throttles, and four stages of afterburner on each engine. When you went into afterburner, it dropped raw fuel into the exhaust area to give you 50 percent more thrust. The F-100 had just one afterburner stage.

Well, about three hours out from Honolulu, it was time to gas up again. I pulled up under the tanker.

"You're leaking fuel," the tanker's boom operator said to me over the radio.

We took on our fuel through a little pop-up door behind the back seat. The boom operator in the refueling plane was on his belly looking through a window.

When you were close enough to the tanker, he guided the nozzle at the end of the boom right into your plane's fuel door.

"It looks like the seal is not good," he said.

"What if I push up on the throttle?" I asked.

"That helps," he said. The O-ring seal was faulty and pressure on it lessoned the amount of leakage.

We landed at Hickam Air Force Base in Honolulu. As soon as the crew chief put the ladders to our planes, girls climbed right up and gave us leis made of orchids. Who the girls were or where they came from, I didn't know. But I thought that was pretty cool.

A friend who had been a secretary at Luke Air Force Base in Arizona was now stationed at Hickam. I had never been to Honolulu and I knew Kathy wouldn't mind if she drove me around the island to show me the sights.

The flight surgeon had instructed us to get to bed at a decent hour and get some rest for the next leg of our flight, which would be another long one. Well, I don't think I got to bed before 1 a.m. and had to get up at 4:30 or 5 a.m. I took a No-Go pill when I went to sleep, which seemed to have little effect. For that matter, the Go pill didn't do much for me, either.

The next morning, Col. Chase came over to see me.

"Hey, Kari. You were leaking a little fuel there on refueling. How serious is it?" he asked.

"Oh, I can make it, sir," I said without hesitation.

I look back now and I don't know what I was thinking. But I didn't want to be the first one to drop out. Of course, the leak wasn't my fault, it was the aircraft.

"You're OK?" Col. Chase asked.

"I'm OK, sir," I replied.

The next hop was to Anderson Air Force Base at Guam. If I'm not mistaken, that was an eight-hour trip. At the first refueling, again, the guy in the tanker said the plane was really leaking fuel. I said OK and pressed the throttle up a little more.

At the next couple of refuelings, the captains of the tankers came on the radio to tell me about the fuel leak. Every time, it was spewing more and more, and I pushed the throttles higher and higher. Before I got to Guam, I had both throttles full-forward and was on stage one of the afterburner. The tanker pilot said he could feel the thrust of my F-4 pushing against his huge craft.

As I look back on this, years later, I realize continuing to fly a plane in that condition was not a smart decision. We were out over the middle of the ocean! What if something happened that I could no longer take on fuel? I'd never make it. I'd have to bail out over the water. When you're young, you don't always consider the consequences. At least I didn't. All I could think about was that I didn't want to be the first one to "crump," as we called it.

Of course, Col. Chase could hear all this discussion of the fuel leak over the radio. We landed at Guam and again he came to talk to me.

"Kari, you're doing OK, right?" he asked.

"Yes, sir," I said. "I'm doing fine."

"You think you can make it the rest of the way? How bad is it?"

"Well, I was on full military and stage one on the afterburner," I told him.

"The next flight is only five-and-a-half or six hours. Can you make it?" he asked.

"I think I can make it," I said.

It was a brand new model of aircraft. I knew if I were to write it up and say it couldn't go, the Air Force would have to fly someone in from MacDill to fix it. Nobody in Guam knew anything about the F-4. That was part of my thought process in continuing on, but looking back, it probably wasn't too smart.

At my last refueling, I was on full military, plus one burner with all four stages going, and I was up to the second stage on the second burner. The leaking fuel was spraying all over the back of the aircraft.

"Boy, you're washing your tail off pretty good," the final boom operator said.

We were probably 400-500 miles out from the Indo-China coast. I had a .38 pistol and I pulled it out to look at it. This sounds silly now, but I said to myself, "I probably shouldn't load it just yet." As if a loaded weapon was going to be any help inside the plane. But, there was a war going on over there. The realization settled in for the first time: We were going into combat.

We searched the horizon for land and finally it came into view. We touched down at Ubon Air Base in Thailand on a short, narrow runway. It was 5,700 feet long and just 75 feet wide. That was one of the reasons the Air Force brought in the more powerful F-4s. We could take off and land on shorter runways than the F-105s, which had been in service in Vietnam only about four months at Takli and Korat air bases, maybe 120 miles away.

Col. Chase said, "Kari, you did a good job. We didn't lose any airplanes!"

I was glad I didn't have to drop out, but it was still pretty foolish for me to fly a damaged plane all that way across the ocean.

We shared the runway at Ubon with the Royal Australian Air Force, which flew the F-86H. It was Korean War vintage, but still a really hot airplane. This base was out in no man's land, so in our first briefing, Col. Chase instructed us to familiarize ourselves with the area and find landmarks that would help us navigate.

Evidently, the Air Force had sent a second lieutenant to Ubon just weeks ahead of us to construct our housing. They were military-style hooches about 10-by-18 feet in size. They consisted of little more than a tin roof and mosquito netting. There were about six of us who slept in there on cots.

There were lots of mosquitoes—and snakes. In my footlocker that had been shipped over on a cargo plane, I had packed an appropriately named .357 Python revolver. That was for use around our quarters in case a cobra came up.

The maintenance officer ordered the parts he needed to fix my plane, but it was going to take some time to fly them in.

"Hey, Kari," Col. Chase said. "You did such a good job bringing that limpy thing over here, you think you could fly a combat mission with it?"

All I could say was, "Yes, sir!"

I flew that leaky plane three times before the parts came in and only once did I have to refuel in the air. I was the only one who got scheduled with that fighter until it got fixed, since I was already acclimated to flying it.

Cass and I were the first in the squadron to escort two RF-101s from another base. They were photo reconnaissance aircraft taking photos north of the Demilitarized Zone. It's another occasion I look back on and realize what we did that day was not wise.

Cass, who was maybe five years older than I was, was a great pilot, an excellent bomber, and something of a cigar-smoking blowhard at the officers club. He took a lot of chances and did things he shouldn't have done.

"OK," he told me. "We're going to escort these 101's and we're going to let them know we're there to protect them."

These reconnaissance planes made high-speed passes with their cameras about 1,000 to 1,500 feet off the deck. Now, if it had been me leading, I would have been flying another 1,500 to 2,000 feet above the RF-101s. After all, we were there to guard against any enemy aircraft that might come in.

But it wasn't me leading. It was Cass.

"We're going right down at their level," he said. "You take one side, I'll take the other."

"Is it necessary to be that low?" I asked.

"Yes!" Cass insisted. "We're going to show them we're here to protect them!"

That was Cass for you. So that was our first mission.

Maybe a month into our deployment at Ubon, we were returning from a bombing mission and Cass said we were going to fly back at low-level.

"Why?" I asked.

"That's what we're going to do!" he replied.

Cass was right down on top of the sagebrush as we flew back over the jungle. I told him I was getting low on fuel.

"How much farther?" I asked.

Cass said he didn't know.

"We'd better pull up or I'm going to run out of fuel," I said. The plane consumed a lot more fuel at low-altitude than it does flying higher up.

Cass refused.

"Stay down!" he said.

Clearly, I had a choice. Follow Cass, run out of fuel and possibly crash, or pull up. I pulled up.

It turned out we were about 10 or 15 minutes out from Ubon. I was so low on fuel, one of my engines flamed out on the taxiway after I landed. I was furious.

"Cass, if you ever do that again, I guarantee you, I'm going to shoot you in the foot," I said. "That was absolutely stupid!"

He mumbled something that wasn't completely an apology or a promise not to do it again. Cass wrote it off as a joke.

I was flying with a great back-seater, Curt Briggs. Our squadron commander was Col. Bill Alden of the 45th Tactical Fighter Squadron from MacDill. Col. Alden said he didn't want any back-seaters flying planes until we got back to MacDill. He insisted their job was to run the radar and navigate. That was tough on those guys—three months of riding around in a back seat, not getting to fly. It would be a long dry spell for them. I felt bad for Curt and determined to see what I could do.

Our missions at Ubon included bombing selected targets sent up to us from Saigon, or escorting reconnaissance planes over the Tonkin Gulf as they listened in on the enemy. Sometimes we were sent up to guard F-105s from other bases against any MiGs that might come up.

Often during a mission, we flew in a spread formation. That would make it easier to clear enemy aircraft in case any of them did come up. I told Curt I would let him fly on the way out and the way back, but the instant he fell out of position—which could happen easily when you're trying to follow someone as adventurous as Cass—I'd have to take the stick back fast. I had become adept at anticipating his moves. You'd be flying along and Cass would suddenly go off in another direction, perhaps to avoid one of the giant storm clouds we frequently encountered. If I dropped out of position at all, he'd be suspicious.

"You can fly until I know Cass is going to get on my butt," I told Curt.

And he did a pretty good job. Only once or twice did I have to take the plane back from him in a hurry.

The living conditions at Ubon weren't very enjoyable. It was the rainy season and it lived up to its name. There were no sidewalks between our primitive buildings, only wooden pallets for walkways.

Then there were the snakes. The not-so-funny joke was there were two kinds: one-steppers and two-steppers. When a two-stepper bites you, you can make it two more steps before you die. If a one-stepper gets you, you were dead in a single step. We kidded one another about looking for cobras between the slats in the pallets whenever we walked outside. Thailand does have cobras, but thankfully, we never saw one on the base.

There was a mess hall, where our chef—whom we called "Cookie,"—served our meals. We only had two air conditioners on the whole base—one in the flight surgeon's office and another in what served as a library. One of the hooches had been converted into an officers club. It had a refrigerator, but obtaining ice was always a problem. The water they froze for use in drinks was not very pure. It's a wonder it didn't make us sick.

Some of our missions at Ubon were six or seven hours long. We'd go to the mess hall and say, "Hey, Cookie. We're going to be on a long mission today. How about making us some fried egg sandwiches?" He'd pack some up and we'd stick them in the pockets of our G-suits for our lunch. Our meals were pretty good. We might have grits, eggs, bacon, and potatoes for breakfast. Dinner was steak, fish or pork chops with mashed potatoes.

There was a town not far away. Local Thais came to the base to pick us up in "samlors"—a three-wheeled bicycle taxi with a seat in the back for two people. It was very inexpensive to ride, costing only about a quarter.

We'd go into town and look in the jewelry stores and other shops. I bought Kathy a pair of sapphire rings, which I sent home to her. We were able to exchange a few letters.

I went to a kick boxing fight in town, which was about the cruelest sport I'd ever seen. It was somewhat like the Ultimate Fighting Championships on TV today. I don't think they even used gloves. It was bloody.

One of the most memorable missions we flew during my time at Ubon was against a thermal power plant at Vihn. It was a critical facility and, we were told, as heavily defended as any target in World War II Germany. The Air Force sent up 16 aircraft—that's four flights of four—with instructions to take out both the transformers and the steam generators.

Well, only one of our 16 planes—all F-4s—hit the transformers that morning and it was mine. The amount of anti-aircraft fire the North Vietnamese threw at us was intense. Nonetheless, military commanders sent us back up that afternoon to try and knock out the steam generators.

Our flight of four was the second flight that went in. I remember as Cass and I came up to make our run, I could see the No. 4 plane in that first flight drop his bombs before he even rolled in. He was chicken. You look back in it now, and you just want to wring his neck.

I will say the anti-aircraft fire was coming up fast and furious. Bombing a hard target in North Vietnam was like flying through a shooting gallery. The sky was so filled with flak, it looked like you could walk on it. The air smelled like gunpowder.

I decided to skip the damaged transformers and go after the steam-generating plant. As we came screaming in, I did my best to concentrate on the target and tried not to think about the flak flying all around us.

As we pulled off after dropping our bombs, I looked down and I could see the steam billowing up hundreds of feet above the power plant. It was a direct hit.

"Curt! We got it!" I said.

Ours was the only craft out of 16 to hit the target. But our elation soon disappeared. The anti-aircraft fire ripped the radar nose cone right off the front of our plane. Now you can imagine what happens when a fighter jet traveling several hundred miles per hour loses its streamlined nose cone. The front of the plane suddenly becomes a flat surface rather than an aerodynamic one. It was like pushing a barn door through the air. The F-4 began to shudder violently.

"Hey, Cass!" I said into the radio. "My nose cone is blown off!"

"Holy cow!" he said.

As soon as we got out of range of the North Vietnamese weapons, I slowed down as much as I could. I thought I could nurse the plane home, but it was going to be a long, slow flight with all that air resistance. I wouldn't have enough fuel to make it.

"I'll call for a tanker," Cass said.

The problem was the big tanker planes that provided our air-to-air refueling were orbiting over Northern Thailand and weren't permitted to fly over unfriendly territory. In those days, Strategic Air Command was in charge of support services like refueling. Fighters were under the direction of Tactical Air Command. The Air Force has since been restructured, but back then, SAC and TAC were separate entities.

"Cass, I'll never make it back to Thailand," I said. I was almost at full throttle and only going about 350 knots.

That's all Cass needed to hear. He got back on the radio and switched over to the tanker frequency so that we could speak directly to the pilots.

"We've got a guy really hurting here," Cass said.

"How bad is it?" one asked.

"He won't make it," Cass said.

"We'll see what we can do," the tanker pilot said. And that was it.

It was all they could say over the radio, otherwise, SAC would have heard them and they would have been in a heap of trouble. It wasn't long before we saw those tankers up ahead, waiting for us. To this day, I get choked up when I recall this story. Those guys put their careers on the line to save Curt and me.

That is one of the greatest blessings of being part of the military family. SAC and TAC often seemed to be at the opposite ends of things—until one of us got into trouble. Then we were as close as can be. The Army, the Marines—every branch of the service is like that. When the chips are down, you can count on one another for help. It's a tremendous feeling to be part of a brotherhood like that.

We refueled and limped back to Ubon Air Base. That was the day I earned my first Silver Star—the highest military honor awarded by the United States government.

Another close scrape over Thailand had nothing to do with enemy fire, but with a pair of faulty bolts.

I made good on my promise to Curt to sneak him as much flying time as I could. The Air Force had thrown him straight into the back seat as soon as he finished pilot's training. He never had the opportunity to go through gunnery school, but hoped to do so when our deployment ended.

Curt was always excited when we made a successful bombing run. Sometimes I'd even give him the stick right after I dropped the bombs so he could practice what pilots call "jinking" or maneuvering away from danger.

"Man! That was fun!" he'd say, as we were pulling off the target. "We're kicking a-- and taking names!"

That was an Air Force expression.

Back-seaters didn't have gun sights like the pilots did. I told Curt that on a future mission, after I dropped the bombs, we'd pretend it's gunnery school and practice a bombing run on the way home.

The F-4 was built to take 7.3 Gs; or more than seven times the force of gravity. There are two needles on the G meter. They both go up, but when you ease back down to normal, one needle will stay as an indicator of your "high water mark," so to speak, showing the maximum number of Gs the plane pulled on that flight. The other needle goes back down. And in fact, all you had to do was press a little button and the marker needle would come back down, too. Every pilot always punched that off.

Well, one day we were bombing another target near Vihn. Again, the sky was thick with flak. Nothing but black puffs all around the plane.

I dropped the bombs and said, "OK, you've got it." Curt took over the controls.

Now, Curt's a big guy. He pulled back on that stick and we climbed so sharply that the G force almost made me black out. It's funny how different it is when you're flying the plane yourself, you kind of know when to suck in your gut and prepare for the forces that were hitting you. I was starting to get tunnel vision!

"Holy mackerel," I said. "Curt, ease off!"

"Oh, this is great!" he said.

We were screaming along and he hit the afterburner, bringing us up to about 500 knots. I told him not to go any faster. The pylons that held the bombs under the wings weren't rated for that kind of speed.

"That was fun!" Curt exclaimed. "Man, can we do that again on the way home? Will you show me how to set up for a bombing run?"

Sure, I said. When we were about 10 miles out from Ubon, I radioed Cass.

"Hey, Cass," I said. "I've got a little extra fuel here. Can we stay in the local area for a few minutes? I want to show Curt how we set up for a bombing run."

Cass said OK.

I took Curt through the basics. You want to start at about 10,000 feet and go in at a 45-degree angle—much sharper than the standard 30-degree angle, but it helped avoid getting hit by enemy fire. You want to release your bombs at 450 knots, but since you pick up speed on a dive, you can't start out that fast or you'll end up at 600 knots. You have to roll in at more like 250 to 275 knots. As I've said before, there are many different factors a pilot has to bring into alignment to hit a target.

Curt ate up every word. We practiced it about three times before our fuel started to get low and it was time to get back on the ground.

After we landed, Curt went off to handle the maintenance debriefing on our aircraft and I went into another of the hooches to debrief the intelligence part of our mission. It wasn't long before the maintenance officer came stomping in to find me. He was swearing a blue streak.

"Kari!" he shouted. "You wild a-- show-off! You broke my airplane!"

"What do you mean I broke your airplane?" I replied. "There's nothing wrong with it."

"Yes, there is," he retorted. "You pulled 8 to 10 Gs in that aircraft and you punched off the indicator so no one would know. Well, I know!"

It's true I had punched off the G meter after Curt took over the stick and put us into that sharp climb, but the meter had read only 7 Gs. I was well aware the F-4 was designed for a maximum of 7.3. Anything over that puts a dangerous level of stress on the plane's metal components.

The maintenance officer refused to believe me. He was so angry he went straight to the squadron commander and demanded that I be grounded. I wasn't about to tell him Curt was the one flying the aircraft.

Why was the maintenance officer so upset?

Inside each engine bay are rails that look like angle irons. The rails are used to slide the engine in and out when it's being replaced. The engine itself is fastened to the frame of the aircraft with two big bolts.

Well, both of those bolts had broken! The engine was more or less resting on tin. It was sitting loose inside the housing and there we were, practicing bombing runs.

I insisted we had pulled no more than 7 Gs, which was the gospel truth.

"Yeah," the maintenance officer sniffed. "All you pilots lie."

Later, Cass asked what happened and I told him every detail.

"I'll fight for you," Cass assured me.

Two days later, the maintenance officer came to see me and apologized for his harsh accusations.

"That's OK," I said. "But what happened?"

It turned out the Air Force had issued a maintenance bulletin warning the bolts were faulty and prone to breaking. They should have been replaced weeks ago, but we didn't receive a copy of the notice at Ubon—until it was almost too late.

Thank God it didn't do much damage. Both engines literally could have fallen out of the aircraft. Of course, Curt and I had our parachutes and could have bailed out, but who knows? It was one of several occasions I look back upon now and praise God for the fact I lived to tell the story.

CHAPTER 22

Even with the challenges and dangers of flying in combat, there were some more lighthearted moments at Ubon, too.

The runway at the base was so short the Air Force decided we needed a barrier in case an aircraft lost its brakes. About 500 feet from the end of the runway, they installed a pair of big B-52 brake drums, one on either side, mounted in concrete. A cable as thick as your thumb was attached to the drums and laid across the runway. Little rubber donuts held the cable about four or five inches off the surface.

The idea was that if you were landing a damaged aircraft, you could drop your tail hook to catch the cable and it would stop you. Like your parachute, it was something you were glad to have and hoped never to have to use. We were happy to see the barrier system go up.

Of course, someone had to test the barrier to make sure it worked. Charlie Hausenfleck, who had been my F-4 instructor at MacDill and was also stationed at Ubon, was chosen for the job. Again, there wasn't a nicer guy in the Air Force than Charlie. In addition to being an excellent pilot, he was just one of those people it was impossible not to like.

So one day, Cass and I and the other two pilots in our flight were returning to Ubon from a bombing mission. As we approached the base, we could hear over the radio that Charlie was just taking off. He'd have a quick go-around, then land again to test the barrier system.

I was on my final approach to the runway, when I got the idea to pull a dirty trick.

"Curt," I said. "Let's land and see if we can take that barrier on the back nine!"

Now, I had never dropped a tail hook or taken a barrier in my life. I kept up just enough speed to make sure we'd get in there ahead of Charlie. We landed, I slowed the aircraft with my brakes, and dropped the tail hook as we passed over the cables. It worked beautifully! The hook caught the cables and those big old B-52 brake drums eased us to a stop then gently pulled us back, like we were on a spring.

And here's poor Charlie. He had suited up, briefed, pre-flighted his aircraft, taken off, and I swooped in ahead of him to take the barrier.

Charlie was the kind of guy who never swore. But he did that day!

"Kari!" he exclaimed. "You dirty S.O.B.! That was something else you pulled!"

"I kind of enjoyed it!" I replied.

Charlie and I are good friends to this day. He never did get to test that barrier. They just wrote it up and said, "It works!"

Cass and I had our share of friendly rivalries, too. We used to wager on everything. One day, I bet him I could complete an aerial refueling faster than he could.

"No, you can't!" Cass replied with his usual bluster. And the bet was on.

We'd come up on the tanker together and I'd go off to the side, waiting with my watch.

"OK!" I told Cass. "Time's on!"

He'd swoop into position and the guy in the tanker would hook him up. I called out the time as it ticked by. Refueling usually took only three to four minutes. As soon as the boom operator said the tank was full, Cass zipped out. Then it was my turn. I could suck right up in there under that tanker in a flash and I'd always win our competition. It was fun.

Cass, however, could make it interesting. He was always smoking cigars, even in the airplane. As you might guess, this was against regulations. Period. Obviously, the combination of jet fuel and lit cigars is not a good one.

There would always be an airman or a sergeant operating the refueling boom, which was 20 to 25 feet long. The operator lay on his belly, looking down through a window, and moved the boom into place.

Cass would slide in there, pop off his air mask, light a cigar, and say to the boom operator, "All right, fill 'er up!"

It was impossible for the airman, positioned just above Cass and his plane, not to see him puffing away on his cigar and the cockpit filling with smoke. I just shook my head. It was one thing to ignore the rules. It was another thing for someone in a position of leadership like Cass to flout safety procedures in front of an enlisted man.

"Sir," the boom operator would say, "would you mind putting that out?"

"Bah!" replied Cass with his characteristic bravado. "You're up there, I'm in here. Don't worry about it. Fill me up!"

Cass was not acknowledging the fact that if his fighter blew up, he'd probably take the tanker and some of us with him.

On one particular occasion, the exchange between Cass and the boom operator must have gone back and forth three or four times, with the poor airman trying to convince Cass to put out his cigar. By now, the cockpit was full of smoke.

In the Air Force, when you're at a dining-in or banquet, you weren't allowed to smoke until the emcee said, "The smoking lamp is lit." When smoking was not permitted, he'd say, "The smoking lamp is out."

Well, the boom operator finally had enough. The next thing we knew, the captain of the KC-135 refueling tanker was on the radio to Cass.

"All right, Ziggy Lead," the captain said sharply. "The smoking lamp is OUT! Do you copy?"

"Yes, yes, yes," Cass said, and finally extinguished his cigar. Usually he'd spit into his hand and stamp it out there. I don't know how else you'd do it in a fighter cockpit.

When we eventually landed, I went up to Cass.

"That was a terrible, terrible example you set out there today," I told him.

"Aw," he said. "Don't worry about it. That's just how I am. You just keep your thoughts to yourself!"

That was Cass. He had a boat back at MacDill. One time before we deployed, I went down to see him. He was shucking a bunch of oysters and I watched as he accidentally jabbed an ice pick right through his hand. He just pulled it right back out. To put it mildly, not much fazed Caspar Sharpless Bierman.

There was still lingering resentment at Ubon over the fellow pilot and weapons officer who had in my opinion been cheating on his test scores back at MacDill—marking down any missile that missed the target as a faulty missile rather than accept a poor score. He behaved like a hotshot and everyone took him to be one of our best pilots. Cass and I knew different.

About three weeks after we went into combat, he and Cass got into a terrific argument inside the hooch that served as the officers club at Ubon. In fact, they got into it with one another more than once.

Booze was cheap over there. One particular night, like crazy fools, they were drinking too much.

Cass said to this pilot, "You're the biggest liar and cheater I've ever seen! Kari caught you cheating back there and never said anything. He told me, but I never told Col. Alden."

"Well," this guy retorted, "if Kari thinks he's so good then he can take over my job as weapons officer!"

As so often happened, I said to myself, "Thanks a lot, Cass."

Just like when I was an intelligence officer at Ramstein, I worked my butt off every spare moment during the next two months. We had a thick book called the Dash 1. It contained everything about our aircraft, including all the bombing charts. I took that information and condensed it into a bunch of briefing cards.

Despite its violent purpose, a bombing mission is a carefully choreographed dance. The timing and precision required to hit a target relied on factors including distance, the weight of all the different types of ordnance and the drag they put on the aircraft. You had to precisely calculate how much fuel all this would require to know if you had to arrange to meet a refueling tanker on the way home.

The F-4 still was a relatively new aircraft to most of us. I worked my fanny off to develop a set of charts to help pilots compute all those variables in just a glance. Remember, this was well before the day of on-board computers.

Years later, after I was finally released from Vietnam, I flew up to visit Cass in Alaska. He had become the operations officer for the Alaskan Air Command. Cass told me that all these years later, the Air Force was still using the charts I had developed at Ubon. I had spent a lot of time on it, so I was gratified to know my work had been appreciated—by all except the pilot I had replaced as weapons officer.

Flying combat was demanding, but I felt good about being able to test my skills and put all my years of training into practice. As I had discovered not long after that first airplane ride with my fraternity brother at Ohio State, flying came very naturally to me. My upbringing on my dad's farm had taught me self-reliance, hard work, and had fostered in me a desire to do the best job I could do, whether it was cutting hay or hitting a target with a missile.

In Vietnam, I was flying missions at a pace that might have exhausted some people, but I was truly thriving. I had read so much about my combat heroes like World War II Marine Corps fighter ace Gregory "Pappy" Boyington of "Baa Baa Black Sheep" fame. I wanted to be like him.

I also knew that to advance in my Air Force career, I needed as much combat time as I could get. I even dared hope I'd have the opportunity to go head-to-head with a MiG someday. They'd always appear tantalizingly in the distance then vanish, with no appetite for a dogfight.

Little did I know that what I hoped to be a long and productive Air Force career would soon disappear into the horizon, too, with my 69th and final mission on Father's Day of 1965. On that morning, I pointed the nose of my F-4 into the sky and began a journey that would exact a heavy toll on my health, my career and most importantly, my marriage and my family.

Eight years later, I would find myself not at the top of my life and profession as I had hoped, but at the depths of despair, starting over—not unlike that moment as a teenager lying on my back under the maple tree in Mom and Dad's front yard, contemplating my future. As an aspiring young farmer, I had watched hopelessly as cattle prices plummeted and everything I had worked for during the course of an entire year floated away, like dandelion seeds in the breeze.

My life seemed to be coming full circle. Now, as then, all I could do was look to the heavens and ask God, "What do I do now?"

THE DIVORCE

CHAPTER 23

Although my marriage to Kathy had ended, I was anxious to continue to build a relationship with Ali and Shawn. NASA had invited former Vietnam POWs and their families to attend the launch of one of its Apollo missions at Cape Canaveral. It's not every day you get invited to have a front-row seat for a rocket launch and I thought it was something the kids and I could enjoy together. There was only one small problem: I didn't have a car.

On those occasions when Kathy was unable to drop the kids off at the skating rink, she had hired a woman the children called "Grandma Miller" to baby sit them. When Mrs. Miller heard I was trying to find a way to take them down to Cape Canaveral, she said we could take her car and offered to come along.

I went to the same bureau of motor vehicles office where I'd gotten my driver's license after returning to the States from Germany eight years earlier. The news about my release and homecoming had been well-covered by the news media and the employees at the license bureau immediately recognized me from my pictures in the newspaper.

One of the clerks sent word back to the bureau manager that Maj. Kari was here. He came out and greeted me warmly.

"C'mon back!" the manager said, and motioned for me to follow him into his office. He told me it was good to see me.

"It's good to be home," I said. "I'm here to see if I can get a driver's license."

He asked me if I had a Florida license before being deployed to Vietnam. When I told him yes, he hollered up to one of the clerks.

"Hey! Pull Maj. Kari's record up and give him a new driver's license!" he said.

I thought to myself, *thank you, Lord! You're so good to me!*

Kathy was now working as a saleswoman in a Tampa department store. The day of the rocket launch arrived and Mrs. Miller and I headed to Cape Canaveral with the kids. On the way back, I offered to take a turn behind the wheel and I drove just fine.

Even if the "home" part of my homecoming was disappointing, I was touched by the way businesses and organizations continued to roll out the red carpet for returning POWs. After the trip to Cape Canaveral, a cruise line contacted us and offered a free cruise out of Miami. Since the Air Force had given POWs some time to recover and spend with their families, I was anxious to take Shawn and Ali on the cruise.

In the meantime, I stopped at the bank in our St. Pete neighborhood to say thank you for the nice welcome home sign they had put up for me. I met the bank manager, whose name was Earl Francis, and told him I'd like to open an account. I had resumed receiving my Air Force salary and needed a place to put it.

The $13,000 savings Kathy and I had on my release was now down to about $5,000. The government had approved legislation that would pay U.S. POWs $5 for each day of our captivity. The law actually had been passed on behalf of American diplomats in the event their embassy was overthrown and they would be held prisoner. However, the law was interpreted broadly enough to cover Vietnam POWs. With nearly 3,000 days in captivity, I was due to receive around $14,000, which would help rebuild my savings.

Years later, after I took a job at the Air Force Academy and eventually with the FAA, I'd always stop at the bank to see Earl when I came back to St. Pete to visit Shawn and Ali. Ironically, the bank is where I would meet my future wife—also named Kathi—who was the manager's administrative assistant. Bubbly and vivacious, she was so friendly you just couldn't help but like her. She was married at the time, so we were never anything more than acquaintances until after we both were single.

I also became friends with Jim Coil, who had recently gotten out of U.S. Special Operations and been hired by the bank to repossess cars. He in turn had a friend named Doug who had a nice sailboat. Jim had a small boat himself. I had jokingly told him that a Navy guy I'd met, whose name was Jim Bell, had taught me all the nautical terms any sailor needed to know. So one day Jim invited me to join him for a sail on the bay with Doug.

They also invited a friend of Jim's wife who had recently been divorced. Her name was Ginger. More than anyone in that summer of 1973, it was Ginger who helped me start to heal my broken heart, just by being there. She was educated, attractive, and a good listener. Just a sweetheart and to this day, we remain good friends.

I asked Ginger if she would like to go on this free cruise I had been invited to share with my family. I told her she and Ali could share a room, and Shawn and I would share a room. That's just what we did. We had a blast.

Ginger had this hot car, a Chevy Malibu, which we drove from St. Pete down to Miami. If you stepped on the gas on dry pavement, you'd squeal the tires. Ali was 8 and Shawn was 10. Of the two, Ali was always the daredevil, still is. When I took them waterskiing, she was the first to try it, even though she was younger than Shawn. He'd see his sister do it and then he'd give it a try.

Every once in a while, as we drove along on the Tamiami Trail, you could see alligators sunning themselves in the water along the road. I was behind the wheel and Ali said, "Dad, let me sit on your lap!" She climbed right up and sat with me as we drove along.

Of course, everything was different back then when it came to kids riding in cars. Even now, Ginger says, "I can't believe I let you drive my car through Alligator Alley with Ali sitting on your lap!" We got to the ship and we had a great time, cruising to Puerto Rico and all around.

Ford Motor Company generously offered each POW the use of a new car of his choice to drive free for one year, with the option to buy the car when the year was up.

I set my heart on a two-door hardtop, which had to be special-ordered. It was beige, with a pseudo-leather vinyl top. I went into the dealer and told them what I wanted.

"Give me all the options!" I said.

"That's the most expensive car I ever ordered!" the salesman replied.

I didn't care. That's what I wanted. I can't remember the model, but it was the top-of-the-line for 1973. The car cost about $6,400 new. At the end of the year, I was able to buy it for $3,200.

Later that summer, we also had a chance to go to Key West, just Shawn, Ali and me, all expenses paid. Shawn was only a toddler when I was shot down and Ali was just a baby. So it wasn't even a matter of renewing my relationship with them, since they had no real memories of me. It was a matter of getting to know one another and creating new relationships. They had been growing up with so little structure in their lives these extended trips together were occasions for me to talk to them about discipline, which was something ingrained in me, after so many years of military and POW life.

MY RETIREMENT CEREMONY.
USAF ACADEMY, 11/11/74.

While we were staying at the hotel in Key West, Shawn began picking on Ali and wouldn't stop. To get his attention, I took hold of him and put him against the wall. Not hard. I didn't hurt him. Just enough to get him to stop what he was doing and listen.

"You can't talk to her like that," I said. "Why are you behaving this way? You've got to act more human than that."

Well, it made an impression because to this day, they both remember that moment. Maybe it was the first time in their lives anyone had said anything like that to them. Later on, Ali returned the favor and said something that really put me in my place.

We were at a restaurant, eating oysters on the half shell. I never had eaten them before, but I wanted to try them and found out I liked them. Ali did, too. Shawn, always the more cautious one, didn't care to try them.

In the middle of dinner, Ali said she had a question for me.

"Dad, how come every time a woman walks into the room, you look at her all the way from her feet to the top of her head?" she asked.

Kids don't miss a thing, do they? I wasn't even aware I was doing that until my 8-year-old daughter pointed it out. I guess after all those years of imprisonment, many things still seemed novel to me, including the sight of the opposite sex.

There was a Navy base at Key West and the commander took us out sail fishing in his boat. We even caught a few! Ali and I tried parasailing together. Key West was such a beautiful place and we had a great time, just the three of us. After being on such an emotional roller coaster ride, I finally was beginning to feel renewed and ready to move on with my life.

The divorce would be finalized on Christmas Eve and Kathy would have custody of the children. A heck of a Christmas present, I thought to myself. At the courthouse, I remember my lawyer and I happened to be riding in the same elevator with Kathy's lawyer. The two attorneys joked and laughed with each other, which struck me as funny. I thought they were supposed to be enemies.

All Kathy requested was child support. She could have asked for half my military retirement—something that happened with a lot of my friends who had been divorced. Although the whole experience still was very painful, that was a blessing.

I knew, because of my vision, I had to leave the military. The Air Force had told me I wasn't fit for "Worldwide Duty." In a nutshell, it meant that because of my physical condition, I couldn't be assigned to some distant base that may not have facilities to meet my medical needs.

During the rounds of physicals when I returned home, doctors at Maxwell Air Force Base in Alabama had recognized my vision problems were beyond what could be treated there. They immediately sent me to Wilfred Hall Medical Center which was the Air Force's big hospital at Lackland Air Force Base in Texas.

There, they examined my eyes and diagnosed me with central scotoma. In layman's terms, it means a portion of the electrical circuitry between my eyes and my brain had been damaged during my imprisonment. Those nerves don't regenerate and can't be repaired. The doctors told me the level of vision I had now was likely what I'd have the rest of my life. It wouldn't get better, but now that I was getting the proper vitamins and nutrients in my diet again, it shouldn't get worse.

But, the doctors said, you'll never fly again. That was a crusher. After all, flying is what I was best at. It was the career I had chosen and what I loved to do. I told them I wanted a second opinion.

To the Air Force's credit, they made arrangements to send me to the No. 1 ophthalmologist in the country, if not the world—Dr. J. Lawton Smith of the Bascom Palmer Eye Institute at the University of Miami Medical School.

After giving me a thorough examination, Dr. Smith said, "I come to the same conclusion as the Air Force—that your eyes won't get any better and won't get any worse—with one exception."

Wow, did I really perk up. I was all ears! After all, Dr. Smith was the eye doctor sought out by Saudi princes and heads of state. He was the best of the best.

Dr. Smith looked at me and said, "This is how your eyes are going to be, unless God heals you."

I couldn't hold back the tears. I knew he was right.

After I wiped my eyes, I asked Dr. Smith where he attended church. In his home, he answered. Later, someone at the VA told me Dr. Smith was an author on religion. So I knew he was a man of great faith, as well as great medical skill, and I took him at his word.

I am grateful for the level of vision I have, even if it was no longer good enough to fly a fighter jet. If I look at, say, a Christmas tree, on the other side of a room, I can see the shape of the tree. I can see that it's green. I can tell there are ornaments on it, but I can't make out the shapes of the ornaments. I don't have a blind spot, exactly. I have a blurry spot, right in the center of what I'm trying to see. If I look off to the right of the Christmas tree, then I can pick up more of the ornaments in my peripheral vision. For some reason, I can see a little better when I look off to my right than when I look off to the left.

Even a person with normal eyesight has some blurring in his or her peripheral vision, which they don't recognize because their center vision comes in to help them see details. I don't have that. Everything looks slightly blurry to me. It doesn't matter if it's close or far away. As far as reading, I am able to do that fairly well when I use a magnifying glass or enlarge the print on a computer screen.

In that summer of 1973, I had the opportunity to fly to Honolulu and visit with Dick Shrove and his family. Dick had been my aid when I first was released. When word got around that I was coming, people there organized a party to welcome me. There were a couple of Marine helicopter pilots who asked if I ever had a tour of the islands. I said no, but I'd like to. They said they'd see if they could get authority to take me up in one of their helicopters.

According to Marine regulations, a helicopter could go up alone if it had twin engines. If it only had a single engine, it had to go up with another single-engine helicopter for safety. The pilots were able to get permission to take me up in a single-engine helicopter, so a second one followed along.

I had never ridden in a helicopter in my life. It's totally different from an airplane. We took off from Honolulu and landed on one of the islands.

"Sir," I said to the pilot, "I've never flown a helicopter. Do you think I could give it a try?"

No one with us that day knew about my eyes.

"Sure," he said. "I'm an instructor pilot. Let me give you a rundown on all the controls."

The pilot explained how everything worked. As I've said before, I'm pretty mechanically inclined, but I asked him to make sure he was right there on the other set of controls in case I got into trouble. He assured me he would keep close watch.

It probably wasn't the smoothest take off, but I got us off the ground and off we flew to the next island, where he took over the landing.

After we were airborne again, I said, "Do you think I could try landing?" I had watched him do it now a couple of times.

"OK," he said.

He was at the ready, but I landed it all by myself. I flew the helicopter the whole rest of the day.

"Are you sure you've never flown a helicopter before?" the pilot asked.

I had never even been *inside* a helicopter before!

By the time we finished the tour and headed back to Hickam Air Force Base, it was getting dark. I knew I had been pretty lucky and I didn't want to push it with a nighttime landing. My lack of center vision meant my depth perception was not what it used to be. I could see the bright lights of the base as we approached.

"Sir, I think you'd better take the landing," I said.

"Why?" he asked. "You've been doing so well all day!"

When I told him I had no center vision, he couldn't believe it. He gave me some good-natured ribbing about it.

"Why didn't you tell me?" the Marine pilot asked. "You could have gotten us into a lot of trouble!" He laughed about it the whole rest of the time.

In my heart, I think I could have continued to fly in the Air Force. Flying in formation wouldn't be a problem. I would have difficulty reading the writing on the cockpit gauges, but I could see the hands. I'd simply have to memorize which gauge was which. That wouldn't be hard for me to do. I may not have been able to see instrument landing lights as quickly as the average guy, but I could have done it safely.

I wish I'd had the chance to show the Air Force I could still fly, but nothing I could do was going to overcome the results of my eye tests. My days as a pilot were over.

When first I hit the Philippines after my release, Dick had told me I had been promoted to major during my imprisonment. Later, while I was at Wilford Hall, getting the Air Force's opinion on my eyes, I found out one of my best friends, Mike Kirby—we flew together as captains at Ramstein—had become a full colonel after 14 ½ years in the Air Force. Mike is from New York City and a very sharp guy. In fact, I learned that a number of my friends also had achieved the same rank, becoming "full-bull" colonels.

I thought to myself, *my efficiency reports and bombing scores were at least as good as my peers, if not better. They're all colonels and here I am, a major*. It made me really angry at the Air Force, and to some degree, I still am. When I asked about it, I was told, well, we just promoted you to major, along with all the other average guys. But I wasn't average!

When I argued my case, I was told, "That's just the way it is."

I went to my friend and POW ranking officer Robbie Risner, who had been promoted to one-star general, and told him the story.

"This isn't right," I said. "These guys are all very sharp. I don't begrudge them. They had their chance to shine and they did. I never got that chance."

I argued I should at least be at their same rank.

Robbie told me he would see what he could do. But not even he could get the powers-that-be to award me the rank I'd been on track to achieve before being shot down and losing eight years of my Air Force career as a POW.

They were going to retire me as a major. After all I'd been through, that wasn't very much of a pension.

I called Mike, who was an assistant to Gen. Roberts, a four-star who was head of Air Force personnel. I told him I felt I had been wrongly deprived of at least one or two promotions in rank. Mike agreed and said he would speak to the general.

"The Air Force wants me to get out right now," I said. "I want to stay in at least until I get one more grade."

Mike called me back. The general said I would have to take my case all the way up to the Secretary of the Air Force. As it happened, Gen. Roberts would be at the Pentagon the following week. If I wanted to fly there to meet him, Gen. Roberts would go in with me to meet with the Secretary of the Air Force.

So that's just what I did.

I remember Gen. Roberts knocked on the Secretary's door. A voice said, brusquely, "Come in!"

The Secretary's head was bent down over his desk, where he was busily writing something. He never looked up. The general and I walked in and stood before him, waiting as he finished what he was doing.

The Secretary finally looked up.

"What can I do for you?" he asked.

Gen. Roberts looked at me.

"Go ahead and speak your piece," he said.

I introduced myself, said I was a returning POW, and explained the medical problems that had resulted from my captivity. I was currently a major, but asked to remain in the Air Force until I made at least one more grade.

"I'll have to think about it," replied the Secretary.

That was it. Gen. Roberts asked me to step outside.

Less than a minute later, he emerged.

"You can stay until you make lieutenant colonel," Gen. Roberts said. "I'll take care of it."

During these weeks of reconnecting with friends and family, I flew out to Colorado to visit my sister and to see Dad's ranch. I found out that Eddie LaVelle, with whom I flew at Ramstein, was now a full colonel and the Assistant Commandant of Cadets at the Air Force Academy.

While staying with my sister in Colorado Springs, I went to visit Eddie, who introduced me to the Commandant of Cadets, Gen. Sandy Vandenberg. He was a one-star general whose father was the first Air Force Chief of Staff when the Air Force became a separate entity from the Army.

During the course of the conversation, I told Gen. Vandenberg about my desire to stay in the Air Force. He invited me to come work for him.

"We've had a couple of recent suicides among the cadets," he said. "We're trying to understand why it's happening and what we can do to prevent it, but we haven't been successful. I want you to do a staff study and see what kind of changes we might make. Maybe you'll have some new insights."

I accepted the job. As I was getting ready to move to Colorado Springs, I asked my friend Ginger if she'd like to ride out there with me in my new Ford car. I told her if she wanted to come along, I'd pay for her plane ticket back to St. Pete. Ginger said she'd love to go.

When you're breaking in a new car, you aren't supposed to drive it at a constant speed. In varying the miles per hour, I decided to nudge it up a little faster, and then a little faster. All the way from Florida to Texas, we didn't see a single highway patrol officer.

"Watch it," Ginger said. "You don't want to lose that driver's license!"

The country two-lane highways in Texas were just beautiful. The freeways were three lanes and wide open.

"I'll be careful," I told Ginger. "I'm just going to speed up for maybe five minutes."

I think the speed limit was 70 mph. I pushed it up to 80 and hit the cruise control. The next thing I knew, we were going down a hill. The speedometer read 92 mph.

"I told you, Paul. Watch it!" Ginger said.

"Oh, it's all right," I told her.

We rolled over two more hills. And right there, just over the second hill, was a highway patrol trooper. I switched off the cruise control and passed him doing about 85 mph. I looked into the rearview mirror and sure enough, he followed me and turned on his lights to pull me over.

Now, the funny thing is, I had been gaining weight since my release. I was wearing a pair of Bermuda shorts that had gotten to be so tight, they were uncomfortable. Since it was such a long drive, I had them unbuttoned. The whole time he was following me, I was madly sucking my gut in, trying to fasten my shorts again.

In my imagination, I knew that because I was going so far over the speed limit, he was going to yank me out of my car, throw me up against his cruiser to arrest me, and my shorts were going to fall right to the ground!

"I told you! I told you this was going to happen!" Ginger exclaimed.

"Steer the thing while I get my pants buttoned!" I told her.

Finally, I got them fastened.

I pulled over and the trooper walked up to the window. Someone had placed a "Welcome Home POWs" bumper sticker on the back of my car.

"What's your hurry?" barked the Texas trooper. "Do you know how fast you were going?"

"Yes," I confessed.

I told him the story about how I had gotten the car and that I was trying to break it in by speeding up and slowing down. I had no excuse, I said. I was going too fast.

"Were you one of those POWs?" he asked.

"Yes, sir," I said.

"Well, take it easy, will you?" the trooper ordered. "It's good to have you home."

I drove a whole lot slower the rest of the trip.

Once at the Air Force Academy, I conducted the staff study and suggested a few ways the academy might change its approach to training cadets. For example, at the academy, it was traditional for upperclassmen to stop freshman cadets and pepper them with questions. This often happened during meals, so it was difficult for the new cadets to get enough nourishment. And the questions would be about the most inconsequential things.

First of all, I suggested letting the freshmen eat. I knew what it was like to go without food and what that did to your body and your spirit. Second, if the upperclassmen were going to badger them with questions, the questions should at least pertain to what the cadets were studying—like Air Force history or something useful. The academy adopted that idea and it's still in use today. That summer I also assisted in the rebuilding of the survival training camp.

While at the academy, I taught a course on leadership—where I learned I was not a teacher. I had to teach the same material to six different classes. During the first 40-minute class, I was very enthusiastic about what I had to tell them. The next class, I felt like I was repeating myself. By the time the third class rolled around, it was very difficult for me to repeat it again. I knew I was not going to have a career in education! I never even made a very good Sunday school teacher, even though I always enjoy attending. I served at the academy from September of 1973 to November of 1974.

When they gave out medals, they normally waited until there were at least a couple of officers due for awards and did them all at the same time. The ceremony is usually held just before lunch. The 1,000 cadets stand at attention to honor the officer receiving the medal as his entire citation is read aloud.

One day in the fall of 1974, I was at the barber shop when I got a call from the commandant's office. It was Gen. Vandenberg, who told me all my medals had come in and I would be promoted to lieutenant colonel on Nov. 14. The barber immediately stopped cutting as soon as he heard it was the general on the phone!

We hung up and as the barber started cutting again, I thought to myself, *the Armistice was signed at the 11th hour of the 11th day of the 11th month. Wouldn't it be cool if I retired at that exact same time?*

"Hand me that phone again," I said to the barber. I called Gen. Vandenberg.

"What do you want?" he asked, gruffly.

I said, "Sir, I have a request."

I told him my idea.

"Hell!" he said. "I can't let the whole cadet corp out in the middle of a class for that!"

"Oh, well," I said. "I just thought I'd try."

I hung up the phone.

Gen. Vandenberg called me back in two minutes.

"We're going to do it!" he said.

I'd become friends with a civilian who worked in the public affairs office. As soon as I'd arrived at the academy, they put me on the speaker's bureau. I traveled to prisons to talk to parolees who were about to be released. They sent me around the country to talk to potential cadets. Basically, I told them the Air Force was looking for leaders. There are kids out there who are good athletes and lots of students who get straight A's. But you've got to be a good leader if you want to be selected to attend one of the military academies. I advised them to take part in activities that gave them leadership experience, like becoming president of their class.

We can train a monkey how to fly, I told them, repeating the old line I had heard long ago. We need leaders. That was my speech in a nutshell.

Once, I spoke to the convicts at the prison in Cañon City. The penitentiary there had three sections—one for maximum security, one for regular prisoners, and another for inmates who were just about to be released. I spoke to the prisoners who were due to get out about what they might expect and what they needed to do to get their lives back in order.

Afterward, I asked the warden if I could see the solitary confinement cells in maximum security. He readily agreed. The only stipulation, he said, was that I had to remove my rank from my uniform. I said I couldn't do that, but I would take off my jacket. Even so, the prisoners could tell I was in the Air Force because I was wearing dress blues.

In the solitary confinement section of the prison, there was a hallway and about four rooms with bars. The cells were maybe 8- by 10-feet, each with a bed, toilet and a place to wash hands.

As we walked along, I could see half-pint milk cartons and other things strewn throughout the hallway.

"What's all that?" I asked.

"The prisoners get mad and throw things out," the warden said. "In fact, you have to be careful. They're liable to throw anything at you."

As we made our way through, one of the inmates said, "Hey, Air Force puke. What are you doing here? You come to see how we live?"

I stopped to talk with him. "How is solitary confinement?" I asked.

"It's terrible," the prisoner said.

"You don't know what terrible is," I replied. "I could stand on my head for a month doing what you're doing."

At that, he began throwing things at me from his cell. The warden pulled me back.

Solitary confinement wasn't what I had expected at all. It really didn't look much different from the cells where the regular prisoners were housed.

My whole career, I had been shy about having my picture taken. I told the public affairs office at the academy I didn't have a single photograph of me in front of an F-4 before I got shot down. I asked if they could take a few pictures of my promotion and retirement ceremony. That's all they needed to hear. They had cameras everywhere, even on tops of the buildings. Later, they handed me a whole portfolio of photographs. I've got more good pictures of that day than of almost any other event in my life. I'm grateful to them for that.

I told my mom and dad—God love them—that this was going to be one of the biggest days of my life and I'd like them to please be there. Even though the ranch was only 40 miles away from the academy, it turned out they were back in Ohio. I don't recall why they were there, but they said they wouldn't be able to make it. My sister, Carol, however, was able to be in attendance.

It was a wonderful ceremony, although it was a cold day. All the cadets were standing there as Gen. Vandenberg read my citations in full, one after the other. It took a long time.

After a while, I whispered to Gen. Vandenberg out of the corner of my mouth, "How many more do you have to go? Just say 'Silver Star.' You don't have to read the whole thing."

"I can't do that," he replied. "I've got to read the whole thing."

By then, I was thinking, "We've been standing out here 20 minutes. These cadets are going to hate me!"

But, the general read them all. It was a nice way to leave the Air Force, even though it meant the end of a career in which I didn't have the chance to achieve everything I had hoped for. Surprisingly, I didn't feel as emotional about it as I thought I would. I still loved the Air Force, even though I didn't like the way it treated me in regard to my rank.

It may sound funny, but the moment that prompted the strongest emotion came later when I was required to turn in all my gear. That's customary, of course, for anyone leaving military service. Because I had been a POW for so long, I didn't have much left—no helmet or anything like that. Mainly just a few personal items I had been issued on my return.

As I was literally signing out of the Air Force, the clerk to whom I handed my gear noticed my wristwatch.

"That's a government watch," he said. "You'll have to turn that in."

It was just an inexpensive Bulova watch, but taking it off and handing it over got to me more than anything else. It was then that I realized I really did have to leave the Air Force. It was only a cheap watch, but without it, I felt naked. I knew that my career was over.

When I left Mom and Dad's Spencer farm for the Air Force, my mother gave me a watch. As I prepared to return home—wherever that might be—I had to give up the watch the Air Force had given me.

Life has the amazing ability to march onward and in full circles at the same time. I didn't know exactly what lay ahead; only that it was time for me to begin a new life.

CHAPTER 24

My Cattle Venture

In the spring of '74, while I was still at the academy, Dad had another series of strokes and heart attacks. He had been forced to completely give up his Hereford cattle operation.

Knowing I'd be retiring with not much money and would need a source of income, I went to Dad's small-town bank. I told them I wanted to take out a loan to buy a couple hundred head of cattle to put on Dad's pasture. He wasn't going to charge me to keep them there. I borrowed enough to buy 130 head of stockers, about 600 pounds each. I went to a local auction with a neighbor who helped me get them.

I spent the summer tending cattle. The fat in grass-fed beef appears yellow due to all the carotenes the animals eat, which some consumers find unappetizing. So I invested in supplements to make it white, like the fat in grain-fed beef. I put a lot of money into that herd—and a lot of sweat. One day, my mom called me at the academy to tell me the cattle had broken through the fence.

"They're gone with the wind!" she said.

I raced home, got on a horse, and began rounding them up, one by one. By then, they had wandered miles from the ranch. It was very frustrating.

I paid 62 cents per pound to buy the cattle. That fall, they sold for 32 cents per pound. You don't have to be Albert Einstein to figure out I just lost a pile of money that I couldn't afford to lose.

All those years ago, lying under the maple tree on Dad's farm in Spencer, Ohio, I had made the decision to enter college because I lost money in cattle that first summer after I graduated from high school. Even though I now had a degree in animal science, I told myself, *this is it. No more raising cattle.* I came home from Vietnam and lost my family. Now I lost my shirt on cattle. This is never going to happen again.

To try to lessen the financial hurt, I went around the academy asking, "Who wants beef?" I started selling it on the half and had it cut to order. I probably sold 12 or 15 head that way. Most people liked it, but a couple of people still complained the fat was yellow.

Since my return from Vietnam, my relationship with my parents was warmer than it had been before. Mom and Dad both seemed to treat me a bit more kindly because of what I had been through as a POW.

Even though Dad had wanted to be a rancher ever since he came to this country, he told me he had bought the ranch for me shortly after they learned I was still alive and being held prisoner. He said if I wanted it, he would sell it to me for what they had paid; $60,000. It was worth probably around $80,000.

After I lost my tail on cattle for the second time in my life, I told Dad this farming business was for the birds. I just didn't know what to do.

"Well, you don't have to buy the farm," he said.

It wasn't a heated argument or anything, but I think we both were deeply frustrated with one another. It was a difficult time for each of us. To him, I was refusing his generous offer on the farm. As for myself, I couldn't understand why he'd moved out here in the first place. The soil was relatively poor and the corrals and the cattle loading facilities were not very good, either.

"Why did you have to go and buy this broken-down ranch and try to fix it up?" I asked. "You lost your health in the bargain and cattle prices have done nothing but go down. Why did you sell that beautiful farm in Ohio?"

What I said really hurt his feelings and I regret it very much. He was pretty upset at me. I don't think he ever forgave me for that.

Even so, I did go ahead and buy the farm in the summer of 1974. There were 400 acres adjacent to it I bought for $32,000. It seems cheap now, but it was the going price. So I had $92,000 invested in the two farms. Dad retired from farming and he and Mom remained in the farmhouse, rent-free. He had his pension from the foundry, as well as Social Security. They had always lived modestly. Mom and Dad never needed much by way of money or possessions to be content.

I had heard the government was partnering with landowners and paying almost three-fourths of the cost of building terraces in dry land areas like ours. I applied through the county and lined up a man to do the work. That summer, we did more than 150,000 linear feet of terraces, which is almost 30 miles. We terraced the whole ranch. The excavator said, "Nobody's ever done that before!"

My only problem was I needed a tractor and a tillage tool to work the terraces and seed them. That was the year after a big Russian wheat import, when prices and equipment all went sky high. I couldn't afford a good tractor. But, there was a guy who went to Dad's church who had two John Deere D tractors, built in 1948. I asked him if he'd sell me one and he said yes.

As a side note, I should have kept that tractor. I eventually sold it for about $500. Today it would be worth $15,000 to $20,000. They're highly sought out by collectors.

Because I was commuting a lot between the Academy and the ranch, I decided to buy myself a motorcycle. It would be cheaper than a car or truck. When I was young, my mom never would let me have one. I never had a chance to talk about it with Kathy, but she probably would have not wanted me to have a motorcycle, either.

I bought a BMW 700 with opposing cylinders. It was really a nice bike and I added a few things to it, like a new windshield.

There were two ways to get to the farm. There's Route 94, which goes straight east out of Colorado Springs, and another way that was a little more roundabout. One day, I took 94.

These motorcycles are so well balanced. They still are. That's why the California Highway Patrol uses them. They've got a nice, low center of gravity. I know this sounds crazy, but I got so I could lock the throttle, fold my arms across my chest, and just sail along, smooth as glass. The road seemed deserted. I might see one car every 10 miles or so. If I wanted to pass a car, all I had to do was lean a little bit to one side, then lean back. The bike was that well balanced. I really enjoyed riding it.

I did this for a couple of months. One day, I was heading back to Colorado Springs the other way on the back roads. Out there, what they call a gravel road is really mostly sand. I came riding up over a hill, and there right in front of me was an old farmer poking along in a pick-up truck, probably looking at his cattle. I swerved to miss him and laid the bike down in the ditch. I was only going about 35 mph, so thankfully I didn't get hurt.

Another time, I had stopped at a bank where I was a customer. The road was macadam and the wind had filled it with sand. I went to make a 180-degree turn on the slippery surface and the motorcycle went right out from under me. As I struggled to pick it up, I looked back at the bank and a couple of women were standing there, pointing and laughing at me. I finally got the bike upright again, put the kickstand down, and went back into the bank.

"Hey!" I told the women. "That wasn't very nice!"

"We couldn't help it!" they said.

We all had a good laugh at my expense. Eventually, I decided I had better sell the bike before I hurt something other than my pride.

For a time, I was dating a woman who worked at the bank at the academy—why I seem to be attracted to bankers, I don't know! That's just where I seem to run into women. She lived down at Cañon City, a little more than an hour from Colorado Springs. She'd come out to the ranch and help me fix fences, which we enjoyed doing together. But, her children and my children didn't get along very well, so it never developed into a long-term relationship.

The summer of 1974, I flew Ali and Shawn out to Colorado for a couple of months, where they stayed either with me or with Mom and Dad at the ranch. We had a good time. On the Fourth of July, there was a big fireworks display at one of the parks in Colorado Springs. The kids and I went down there and lay on a blanket as we waited for it to start.

Ali, who was 9, said, "Dad, throw me up in the air with your legs!" She's the athletic and adventurous one, as I said.

I told her no, but she kept asking. Finally, I consented. Ali sat on my legs and I launched her. I probably shouldn't have done it, but she was persistent and it was more or less the kind of playful roughhousing dads and kids like to do.

Well, Ali was a skinny little thing. She fell when she landed and broke her arm. I could hear it snap.

I carried her to the car, which was about a quarter mile away, and rushed her to the Air Force hospital at the academy. I should have listened to my instincts and not given in. I felt terrible.

So that's what I did that summer of '74—chased cattle, lost money, built terraces, and rode a motorcycle.

Back in Germany I had sketched farm layouts on scraps of paper. While a prisoner, I dreamed of the freedom of working in wide-open fields and the joy of watching things grow. But losing that money and the frustration of chasing runaway cattle really took the wind out of my sails.

During my time at the Air Force Academy and while I was working on the ranch, I sometimes would drive around Colorado to look at all of the farmland. Despite my earlier frustrations, if there's dirt in your blood, it's hard to get it out. I still had an itch to farm. Dad's ranch just wasn't the best set-up. I decided that if you were going to buy a dry land farm in Colorado, the best thing to grow is wheat. And the best soil for that is in the northeast corner, which had the highest production. I thought, *if I ever have any money, that's where I'm going to buy ground.*

I decided to sell the ranch, hoping someday to buy a farm more suitable for what I had in mind. It was on the market for a year and a half before I finally sold it to a dentist from California. Mom and Dad moved into a brand new house in Calhan, about 25 miles northeast of Colorado Springs.

During one of the POW debriefings following our release, the Department of Defense had offered to assist those of us who wanted to retire from the military, or had to retire for medical reasons. The government would connect each of us with a vice president of a major American corporation who would help us with our transition to careers in the private sector. These executives would work with us in setting up job interviews and making sure we weren't taken advantage of.

Following World War II, the DOD had learned some companies will hire a veteran or former POW just for the splash of good publicity in the media, then quietly lay them off six months later. Our assigned helpers were supposed to make sure we were treated fairly. My "assistant" turned out to be a vice president at General Electric! He lined up four two-week trips for me, during which I interviewed for jobs around the country.

I had spent my professional life learning to fly some of the world's most powerful fighting machines, and I was good at it. I don't mean to sound immodest. By that, I simply mean that each of us is born with a gift. For some, it may be playing a French horn, shooting a basketball, fixing cars, or designing buildings. As a boy working on my father's farm, I discovered my gift was the ability to operate machines instinctively and accurately. A fighter jet fit me like a glove. It was an extension of myself. And now that part of me was gone.

I loved the Air Force and its way of life. But, nearly eight years of torture and depravation had taken its toll on my body and brought that life to an early, unwilling end.

It's hard to find the right words to describe my feelings as I faced the future. I wouldn't say I was devastated. If being a POW teaches you anything, it's to be grateful for every day of freedom. I guess I felt a bit rudderless. I had driven myself for so long to be the best I could be at one thing—flying fighters. No other job could compare with that. Knowing my options were limited due to my damaged vision, I wasn't exactly excited to begin my next career, whatever that may be.

One the places I visited in hopes of landing a job was the Federal Aviation Administration. The head of public relations was a recently retired full colonel from the Air Force. He and I got along well. I told him I'd had a lot of interviews, all of them offering good pay, but I worried I wouldn't be able to do the jobs justice because of my vision. I can speak better than I can read.

"I think we've got a job here for you," he said.

He told me to come back after I was able to retire from the Air Force and he'd start me within a month.

I called to follow-up every one to two weeks and received assurances the civil service hiring process was moving forward, albeit very slowly.

Somehow, I got it into my head—wrongly—that if I went to D.C., things might move a little faster. I was anxious to begin earning a paycheck again. I had an old Ford pick-up truck. I bought a cap for it, threw all my belongings in back, and headed for Washington. I made arrangements to stay in the home of some friends, Sam and Margaret Green. Sam and I had lived in the same apartment complex during our Air Force days in Germany.

Well, I quickly discovered there was nothing I could do to make the government's hiring procedures go any faster. So I stored my stuff in the crawl space under Sam's house and drove back to Colorado Springs, Colorado to work on the ranch.

Finally, in the spring of 1975, I was hired on with the FAA. I came in as a GS-13 which was the equivalent of a major. Now I just had to find a place to live.

Things are very expensive in Washington, D.C. I decided I was going to live in Arlington, Virginia, which is across the Potomac River. I got an apartment in a relatively new high-rise complex that overlooked what's now known as Ronald Reagan Washington National Airport.

My only hesitation was in signing a year-long lease. If it turned out that I really liked it in D.C.—which, frankly, I didn't think I would—perhaps I'd want to buy a house. I didn't want to get slapped with a bunch of financial penalties if I wanted out of the contract.

The management company suggested I rent a penthouse on the top floor. It was an extra couple hundred dollars per month, but they told me if I got trans-

A Colorado Rancher.

ferred or decided to move, the penthouses rented very quickly and they wouldn't charge me a penalty.

So that's what I did. My window overlooked both the airport and the Potomac. It was a pretty easy commute to work. I took a bus across the river and caught another bus to the FAA building.

Still, this old country boy was not used to the crowded city. People seemed to be squeezed in like sardines. I began to not like Washington D.C. very much. Plus, I got stuck working in the department within public affairs that handled complaints against the FAA. Most of my work was writing, and writing is my worst endeavor in life!

My boss would give me various complaints to answer—mostly by quoting regulations that explained what the FAA could and couldn't do for them. I'd write the replies and then he'd call me into his office to go over them. He'd pick up a pen and begin scribbling all over the letters, criticizing what I had written.

I soon found out the general public had a low opinion of the FAA. They seemed to think we were always trying to hide things which we weren't.

For example, later on as a public affairs officer, my job was to answer media inquiries. If a Turkish DC-10 went down, the *New York Times* or *Los Angeles Times* would call and ask what happened. Often, I'd have to say, "I don't know yet, but as soon as I find out, I'll give you a call." That was the truth and they understood that. The big papers all had full-time aviation editors who were very knowledgeable and very fair.

It was the smaller papers that would call up right after a plane went down, demand to know what happened and complain if I didn't have all the details yet. They'd accuse me of trying to hide something. About 80 percent of the job involved confrontations like that, which I did not enjoy. It was very frustrating for me, but I stayed with it about a year and a half.

I had bought a new Volkswagen Scirocco—which was kind of a little sports car—when I left Colorado Springs. I drove home to Spencer about every other week, where my middle sister Karen lived. She was recently divorced and had a little boy named Eric, whom I adored. I spent many weekends with them.

I used to see how fast I could cruise down the Pennsylvania Turnpike without getting caught. I can't recall exactly what my record time was, but it seems to me I could make it from D.C. to Spencer in just under six hours, without even taking a break to go to the bathroom. That VW was a fun car to drive. I just flew. When it was time to go home, I'd stop at a gas pump in River Corners near Spencer, squeeze 15 gallons into the Scirocco's 14-gallon tank, and cruise back to Washington.

Well, they say it takes about a year to a year-and-a-half to get "Potomac Fever." Originally, I had resented the whole town. I didn't like the news media I often had to deal with and just generally felt like an out-of-place country boy. But sure enough, I actually grew to enjoy life in the U.S. capital and all it had to offer. I made sure to see all the sights while I was there.

There was a woman who lived in my apartment building named Beryl Cohen. We met at the bus stop. Beryl worked in the Commerce Department, where one of her responsibilities was managing the U.S. exhibits at the LeBourget Air Show in France and the Farnborough Air Show in England. They're major air and aerospace trade shows. She was the kind of person who could type up a letter to a foreign minister or head of state and the first draft would be perfect. And these were the days before computerized spell-check. She was very smart. Her father owned a big security company in Philadelphia.

Beryl, who was in her late 20s, also had the curliest hair I've ever seen. All she had to do was run a comb through it and it looked gorgeous. She was very knowledgeable about wines and cheeses. On Saturday mornings, we'd go to the Georgetown markets together and she'd buy little portions of about 15 different types of cheeses, along with just the right wines. I enjoyed spending time with Beryl, who was one of the people who helped make my time in Washington enjoyable.

Once we went shopping in some big department store. Beryl would pick up a piece of clothing, look at it, and drop it back on the shelf in kind of a pile. After watching her do this half a dozen times, I said, "Beryl! What are you doing?"

"I'm just checking them out," she said.

"Well who do you think has to fold all those things back up?" I asked.

"I never thought of that," she said.

It was just my personality coming out again, I guess. From the earliest days of mowing fence rows on Dad's farm back in Ohio, I've always liked things neat.

I had the opportunity to buy a house—and this was a time when the housing market in the D.C. area was just booming. Homes in Arlington were going up in value as much as $10,000 per month. I'd saved enough money to put a down payment on a house there, knowing I wouldn't have any trouble selling it.

It was a two-story and it needed a little work—including a new patio. I moved all the dirt with a wheelbarrow, and boy, did I mess up my back. I've had back problems throughout my life from ejecting when I got shot down, but this time, I really aggravated it. I could hardly get out of bed. Finally, I had to get up to go to the bathroom and I crawled on my knees all the way back to my bed.

Fortunately, I had a phone at my bedside and called an emergency squad to take me to the hospital at Andrews Air Force Base. The front door was open, so the two EMTs came right up to my bedroom. Amazingly, they didn't have a stretcher. They said they would just carry me down, which, if anything, made my back problem worse. I was in the hospital three or four days.

To add insult to injury, the night I went into the hospital, someone robbed my house. They stole my car, as well as a Zenith Trans-Oceanic Radio. I don't know for certain, but I have always had an inkling that at least one of those EMTs had something to do with it. They would have known I was a bachelor and that I was going to be in the hospital for a while. The police later found my wrecked Volkswagen with members of a motorcycle gang. That was one of the downsides of my tour there.

I met another young woman at the bus stop—Laurie. She'd grown up an Iowa farm girl and was working in D.C. as a secretary. After we had been dating a while, I made the observation to her that among all my old pilot friends, the only couples who were still happily married seemed to be the Mormons. I asked her if she'd like to learn more about the Mormon faith. Laurie said she would.

I invited some Mormon missionaries over and we listened to what they had to say. We both decided we would stay with the faith we were raised with.

The year of America's Bicentennial in 1976 was a wonderful time to be in Washington. I remember Laurie and I sat on the steps of the Lincoln Memorial and watched the most incredible fireworks celebration I have ever seen. After that, any fireworks display is almost a letdown. It went on and on for what seemed like an hour.

At the FAA, I had become friends with a colleague named George Brewer. He had a son at the Air Force Academy and George worked in the Flight Standards department, which writes the regulations for pilots. George later became the FAA's representative to Denver when the international airport was built there.

We had a lot in common and often ate lunch together in the cafeteria. I enjoyed talking to him as it helped the day go a little faster in a job I didn't like very much.

George introduced me to the head of the FAA's Aviation Education program, Dr. Mervin K. Strickler. He really took a shine to me even though I immediately told him I wasn't cut out for teaching. Nevertheless, he told me Congress had approved legislation requiring each of the FAA's nine regions in the U.S. to have an aviation education officer.

The education officer's job was to go out and tell teachers about studies that had been done in Los Angeles and Washington D.C. in which aviation had been woven into virtually every part of the school curriculum. The results were clear that when English, math and even public speaking were flavored with illustrations from aviation, it held the kids' attention and the students were more successful in their studies.

For example, for kids who struggled with their speech, if you showed them how in aviation you had to speak very clearly through the radio—being distinct and to-the-point—it really did help them learn to speak that way, too.

In math, a student might complain, "Why do I have to take algebra?" So, you give them a story problem a pilot might have to solve regarding things like distance, wind speed and fuel consumption. It got the students interested. It was very effective. Suddenly they'd say, "Oh, that's how you would use algebra."

Dr. Strickler knew my parents and sisters were in Colorado and that I didn't particularly like my job in D.C. He said there was an opening for an aviation education officer in Denver that was mine if I wanted it. I jumped at it and I am forever grateful to him. I was to spend six enjoyable years there.

One of my colleagues put me in touch with a Denver real estate agent named Gary Gray. I called him up and he asked me what I was looking for.

"Well," I began, "I'm a farm boy and …"

"I know, I know," he said, interrupting. "You probably want a mountain view and a babbling brook in your back yard!"

"You got it, baby!" I replied. Gary and I became very good friends.

He took me to an older home in Littleton, Colorado. It had about two acres and a view of the mountains. I was looking for someplace that would accrue in value a little faster than this house likely would. I asked him to show me a few more options.

Finally, I settled on a brand new house, also in Littleton, in a development called Green Oaks. It had four bedrooms and a second-story deck with a beautiful view of the mountains. I paid $115,000 for it 1976. In those days, real estate here, too, was going up as much as $10,000 per month.

The neighbors accepted me and I enjoyed living there. There was an irrigation canal that ran right through and I liked to jog around the neighborhood. It was about 70 miles from where my parents lived and I went to visit them often.

Even though I'm a country boy at heart, I loved Denver. It felt like a very youthful city. The air was wonderful and there were always opportunities for hiking and snow skiing which I soon learned to enjoy.

My job with the FAA was to go out and talk with teachers in the six-state Rocky Mountain region about flavoring their courses with aviation. I traveled a lot with the regional FAA administrator and we'd visit all different places in Wyoming, Montana, the Dakotas, Utah, and all over Colorado. It was a very successful program. I was able to persuade probably 20 to 30 percent of the teachers in the region to integrate aviation into their lessons in some way.

I liked my new boss in Denver, but I wasn't received as well by my coworkers in the public affairs office. Many of my colleagues were tenured government workers with 20 or 30 years experience. They seemed to resent me coming on board. I always felt a certain tension among them. Nevertheless, my time in Denver was my best tour of duty in the civil service. I was mostly on my own and I had a mission, so to speak. It was a lot of talking and observing, not too much writing, so it suited me pretty well.

I continued to date, and met several very nice women, but none of the relationships became long-term. I enjoyed indulging in my love of cars. I had a new navy-blue Volkswagen Scirocco with studded snow tires. That car could almost climb a tree. It was great for the snowy mountains. I also had a Chevy diesel pick-up truck, a '68 Camaro muscle car, and a Pontiac convertible.

One winter I was skiing up in the mountains. Being a former fighter pilot, I guess I was still a bit of a daredevil. I was on one of the slopes rated black for its high degree of difficulty. Well, I probably shouldn't have been on it, because I fell and hit my back in such a way that I was temporarily paralyzed from the waist down. I pinched something badly and lay there for the longest time, unable to move my legs. Finally, I was able to recover enough to get up and make my way back. It scared me enough that it was the last time I ever skied.

Several times throughout the year, I returned to Florida to visit Ali and Shawn. Always when I came to St. Pete, I'd stop to say hello to Earl Francis, the president of the bank in my old neighborhood.

In '78, on a trip to spend time with the kids, I stopped at the bank and Earl asked, "Are you ever going to get married again?"

"Never!" I said. I had my heart broken once and wasn't interested in taking that risk again.

"Well, my former secretary, Kathi, recently got a divorce," Earl said. "I think she'd make someone a good wife."

Her ex-husband, whom she had married as soon as she graduated from high school, was a professional gambler. She was now working at a different bank across town, but I remembered her because she had such a bubbly personality. Earl gave me her phone number and I called.

"Who's this?" she asked.

"It's Paul," I said.

"Paul who?"

"Maj. Paul!"

"Oh! OK!"

I asked her if she'd like to go out the next time I came to St. Pete to visit the kids, which would be Easter. She agreed and put it on her calendar.

She was 28 and I was 43. She was so bubbly and vivacious that I was just smitten with her. She had a 2-year-old daughter named Jaime. I loved her instantly. She was a little girl who needed a daddy and after having missed so much of Ali and Shawn's early childhoods during my time as a POW, I enjoyed spending time with her.

We talked routinely on the phone for about a year and we saw one another whenever I visited Florida. We each were spending probably $100 per month on our phone bills!

Kathi said she'd like to move out to Denver, which I tried to discourage. I was the only soul she knew in Colorado. As much as I liked her, I worried that if things didn't work out between us, she would be stuck and I would feel responsible.

The next thing I knew, she called and told me she had sold her house in St. Pete and had three days to move out. Putting my concerns aside, I offered to fly out and drive her to Colorado. She had a little MGB sports car, which barely had enough room in the back for Jaime and a pair of suitcases.

Kathi wanted to make a stop in Hernando, just north of Tampa, so I could meet her parents, Ralph and Margaret. We drove pretty far off the beaten path into rural Florida and eventually pulled up to a four-acre lot with two or three old house trailers on it. There were some vehicles in the yard in various states of repair, including a pick-up truck with its engine hanging from a chain in a nearby tree.

I thought *what have I gotten myself into?* My internal radar told me right then and there that we should turn around, go back to Tampa, and I would fly home.

I was in a state of surprise to think Kathi's mom and dad lived in a place like this. I learned her father had been an alcoholic. But I checked my doubts and we got out of the car. Everyone deserves a chance, I reasoned. In truth, her parents were kind to me. Margaret always liked me, though Ralph would become a different story.

However, her brother George, a meat cutter, said, "If you do anything to my sister, I'm coming after you!"

During the drive to Denver, we found ourselves in the middle of nowhere in Texas and poor Jaime had to use the bathroom. There was absolutely no rest room in sight. Eventually, we came to an abandoned building. We drove around back, pulled out Jaime's little potty seat, and sat her down. Just then, a sheriff's deputy pulled up and asked what we were doing back there. We told him and he let us go about our "business." He had children, too, the deputy said.

Even though we had been dating some time and I had a big beautiful house—albeit with no furniture—I didn't feel right living together. I had told Kathi this before she moved to Colorado and arranged for an apartment where she and Jaime could live.

Kathi found a job as a bank teller, though it did not pay very much. She was barely skimming by on her expenses. She enrolled Jaime in preschool, so she had that payment on top of her rent, groceries and everything else. It was a real struggle for her. I repeatedly offered to help, but she always declined.

Since arriving in Denver, I had been able to invest in some rental properties and one of the houses became available. I insisted Kathi live there rent-free, just to give her some breathing room until she could get on her feet.

I was at a point in life where I was ready to settle down and I asked Kathi to marry me. She was anxious to get married, too, and had said so many times.

I asked her if she would consider a prenuptial agreement. I had just begun to rebuild my finances and I was concerned about losing what I had worked so hard for.

Kathi didn't like that idea at all.

"If you loved me, you wouldn't ask me for that," she said.

Whenever I hesitated about getting married, Kathi became angry.

"Either you marry me," she said, "or I'll find someone who will."

About a year before Kathi and I were married, I moved the kids from Tampa to Denver. I realized they were getting no church upbringing whatsoever and had very little structure in their lives. Of course, to bring them closer to me, their mother came along.

I talked to my pastor, who advised against it. I talked to my mother, who said, "Paul, don't be stupid!" But I prayed about it and decided it was for the best. I didn't want to move back to Tampa, because I finally had a good job with the FAA in Colorado. I did what I felt I had to do and my ex-wife agreed to the plan. I arranged for an apartment not very far away from where I lived, rented a moving truck, and Shawn and I drove it out together. He was 16 and Ali was 14.

My children needed to develop a sense of responsibility. That was part of the reason I wanted to be a stronger presence in their lives.

The kids got along well in school and Shawn became a great soccer player. In his first game, he scored a hat trick—three goals—which immediately made him into a bit of a hero! Their mom soon found a job as a secretary.

I enrolled the kids in the youth programs at the Nazarene church we attended and both gave their hearts to the Lord. Shawn joined a church singing group and spent two summers touring the country with them. He had a blast. I think those experiences helped make him into the strong Christian person he is today.

At last, Kathi and I made arrangements to be married in a small ceremony at the Nazarene church on Oct. 4, 1979. One of our neighbors, Day Younker, whose husband Mel was the chief pilot for Western Airlines, stood up for Kathi.

Kathi—who was always very witty and funny—picked our wedding date. When I asked her why she chose Oct. 4, she quipped, "That way, whenever anyone asks me if I'm married, I can say, 'That's a big 10-4!'"

After the wedding, Day drove us to the airport in her Mercedes and watched Jaime for us while we went on a honeymoon to San Francisco.

That night, I took a shower and walked out into the room to find Kathi already in bed, reading a book. She had the book spread in front of her so I couldn't even see her face. She hadn't spoken to me since the wedding ceremony.

Her mother was very domineering and never treated her father very kindly. I said, "Kathi, I don't know what's going on, but I don't want you to treat me like your mom has treated your dad his whole life."

She dropped the book just below her eyes and stared at me. Then she raised the book again and resumed reading.

That was how our marriage got started.

Later on during our honeymoon, Kathi came down with strep throat. I ended up taking her to the military hospital there to get some medicine. Soup was the only thing that sounded soothing to her poor throat, so I went out one night at 11 p.m. and walked Fisherman's Wharf up and down until I found her some, which she appreciated. Eventually, she recovered enough that we were able to enjoy touring some of the California wine country before returning home.

After we were married, she announced she had to return the MGB she was driving to her ex-husband, Larry. I was surprised to learn she didn't own the car. He had simply let her borrow it and we had to return it to him in Florida. In fact, Kathi told me she had never owned a car in her name.

So, for her next birthday, July 16, I bought her a brand-new, red, four-door, 1980 Honda Accord. She was working at a bank and I told her Jaime and I would come by and pick her up on her break because I had a surprise for her. We drove to the Honda dealer where her new car was sitting and gave her the key. Even though I had arranged to pay for the car, I put it in her name.

Kathi was the kind of person who gave few accolades to others. When anyone gave her a gift, she would say one word, one time, "Thanks!" It had almost a flippant tone to it.

Jaime hopped into the new car and we excitedly showed Kathi all its features.

Kathi never showed any enthusiasm, never hugged me, never said anything like, "Oh, Sweetie, this is really nice." She simply got in, started it up, and got ready to drive off.

A little disappointed by her muted reaction, I said, "Don't I at least get a kiss or a thank you or something?"

Kathi stuck her head out the window, said, "Thanks!" and sped away.

I have to confess, I was crushed. It made me feel like I never wanted to buy her anything again.

At this time, the Denver real estate market was booming. If ever I felt depressed, I would call Gary Gray up and ask, "How much is my house worth today?" and its rapid increase in value would cheer me up. I had bought the house two years earlier for $115,000. We sold it for $250,000. In this market, you just couldn't miss. We moved into a cute little house on the Arapahoe Lakes, which I began to fix up.

Now, I recognize God, family, health, freedom and a great many other things are more important than money. But when you're wasting away in a squalid prison cell in Vietnam, you dream of the future—of all the things you'll build and do when you regain your freedom. Achieving some kind of financial success was a measurable way of proving to myself that I was making the most of the new life God had given me—and making up for lost time.

Through my real estate agent, Gary, I had bought and sold a couple of houses as investments. In fact, I'd be traveling for the FAA and Gary would call to say, "Paul, there are two townhouses coming onto the market. They're in an excellent location and I think you ought to buy them."

I'd say go ahead and do it, without even seeing them. That's the kind of rapport I had with Gary. At any one time, I probably owned four rental houses. I was doing very well in the local real estate market.

I bought a 640-acre wheat ranch in the Northeast corner of Colorado near Sterling and turned that old girl around. I remember Kathi painted a little picket fence in front of the house.

There was barbed wire around every field. The problem was the tumbleweeds would roll through and catch on the fences. Then the soil, which was very sandy, would blow around and collect on the tumbleweed. Pretty soon you'd have a mound. I did a lot of work cleaning all that up.

"Why are you working so hard on that God-forsaken place?" Kathi would ask.

It was hard work, and sometimes I think I paid for it later on in the toll it took on my body but it was sweat equity, which is a major part of farming.

There were a lot of pheasants running around this farm and the wheat that year was a lush, dark green. It was exciting for me because it was the first farm I had bought all on my own. The former owners were still living in the house and I asked if I might rent a room from them when I drove up from Denver to spend the weekends working on the farm. They were cool to that idea, so for most of that summer, I slept in a tent in the back yard whenever I went up there to work.

It was pheasant season when the former owners finally moved out. I suggested to Kathi we go up there and stay so I could do a little hunting.

While we were there, some pheasants walked right out of the fields, almost into the yard. I took a shot and the pheasants simply flew off. Next time, I got even closer. I took a shot and again, the pheasants flew away. All I could figure was there was no shot in those shells. All the blasts did were make poofs of smoke. Kathi never let me live that down! She made fun of my marksmanship every chance she got.

However, I did get my pheasant that day.

On our way back to Denver, I was following another car when the driver accidentally hit a pheasant. I slowed to a stop where the dead bird lay. I know this technically is "road kill," but it happened right in front of us. So at least it was fresh road kill!

I hopped out and grabbed the pheasant. Kathi couldn't wait to tell all her friends about the only way I could manage to get a pheasant dinner. It was pretty funny, I must admit.

Two of my FAA colleagues worked in the Airway Facilities division. They were members of a Baptist church and asked me if I'd speak at a stewardship banquet, where church members make pledges for their giving in the upcoming year. I agreed.

They told me I might be interested to meet a man in their church who was in the commercial real estate business.

"He makes money a lot faster than you do," they said, teasing.

I was getting a little tired of buying houses to fix-up and re-sell, so the opportunity to learn about investing in commercial real estate piqued my interest.

I spoke at the church about how my experiences as a POW related to everyday life, tying it in to the topic of stewardship. I never take any money to speak to a religious organization or to a civic group, but they did give me a big Bible as a thank-you gift.

I met the real estate investor and we talked several times after that. I told him about the promise I had made to God while I was a POW that if he got me out of captivity, I would give half my income to the Lord. He thought that was very nice. I'm not going to mention his name for reasons that will soon be apparent.

I told him I was thinking of investing in an office building. The agent told me there was a new one under construction in Colorado Springs. In fact, it was right across the street from a planned shopping center. He took Kathi and me to see it and we both fell in love with it. It was about a $500,000 investment, but I thought I could swing it. I sold the wheat farm in Sterling as well as other properties to generate some cash.

About this time in 1981, the nation's air traffic controllers went on strike. All of us in management positions at the FAA were on call 24 hours per day, trying to keep U.S. air travel moving. In the midst of this, my real estate agent called with the news we had gotten the building. He wanted to stop by for me to sign the papers.

"That's great news," I said, "but we're practically in lock down here. There's no way I can meet you right now."

He persisted.

"Is there any way you could just come out the front door of the FAA building and sign the purchase agreement?" he asked. "It'll only take a minute."

"OK," I said. "I'll try to sneak out." Which I did.

I take full blame for what happened next.

The agent had the agreement folded in such a way that all I could see was the place I had to sign. He was in a real rush.

"We have to get this done so I can get to the bank by 4 p.m.," he said. And I signed it.

Sometime later, when the strike was over, I phoned my agent, anxious to follow-up on my big investment.

"Let's go down and see it," I said.

"Go down and see what?" he asked.

"The office building in Colorado Springs," I replied. "The one I signed the purchase agreement on."

"No," he said. "The building you bought is in Westlake."

"What?" I asked, incredulous. "What about that building you showed me? That's the one I signed for!"

"No, it isn't," he said.

I was so angry I could have killed him. I went to see what I had bought. It was a run-down building and half its offices were empty. I was its sole owner. And I was devastated.

I don't know how a person can do something so completely without conscience. His secretary later told me, "Paul, every time you walked into the office, I wanted to tell you to run away as fast as you can."

"Why didn't you?" I asked, a little angry.

"I was afraid," she said.

I was now deeply in debt on this building. It took both my FAA income and my Air Force retirement income just to make the payments on it and keep my head above water. This is where Kathi really helped me. She had a job as secretary with Diners Club. For six months, her salary was all we had to live on.

I got hold of a lawyer who had once brought a successful case against this same real estate agent. I sued to try to get out of this agreement and to get some kind of compensation for what he had done to me.

Well, this real estate agent wasn't done yet.

I had the building up for sale. I was prepared to take almost any offer just to get out from under it. He placed a *lis pendens* on the property, which is Latin for "suit pending." It has the effect of putting the title to a property in question, making it much less attractive to prospective buyers. He was smart enough to know that in order to sell the property, I'd have to drop my lawsuit against him. In the end, I did manage to sell the building, but I lost $476,000 of my $500,000 investment.

If being dropped by my first wife was the most discouraging point in my life, this rotten commercial real estate deal was a close second. I was in shock. How could someone do this to another person? Especially after I told him my goal in life was to give half of all I had to God's work? The whole episode left me deeply depressed and put a strain on our marriage. I was consumed by anger toward this man.

Then one day, I happened to be making the bed, and I thought to myself, *what if he were to ask God's forgiveness for what he did, but didn't have the guts to come to me to ask my forgiveness?* I hated him so much, I wasn't sure God would accept me into heaven with so much hatred in my heart.

"Lord," I prayed, "this picture doesn't look very good. I'm going to do something about it."

So I called up the man who had wronged me so badly and suggested we have dinner. But, I told him, we're going Dutch! After all the money he cost me, I wasn't about to buy his meal. I let him know I simply had something I wanted to share with him.

We met and I said, "I still don't know how you could do what you did to me, but I want you to know I forgive you."

He looked at me, puzzled. I could tell my words went in one ear and out the other. When you have no conscience, I suppose nothing pricks it.

My best friend in Denver was Paul Eckel, whom I knew from our days together at Ramstein Air Base. He became the chief pilot for Continental Airlines at a very young age—in only his late 30s or early 40s—and was stationed in Denver when I moved there.

As I mentioned, when I first came to Ramstein, there was almost no support network for new pilots. I fended my own way to the base from Frankfurt. I didn't like that and worked to set up a system in which each new pilot would have a sponsor to help with the transition to Ramstein. As it happened, I became Paul's sponsor and showed him the ropes.

Paul finished his Air Force career during the time I was shot down and moved up quickly through the ranks at Continental. He was an excellent pilot and eventually left Continental to start his own airline.

When I arrived in Denver, Paul returned the favor and helped me get acquainted with life there. It made the transition so much easier to have a friend like him who could show me the ropes.

Airline pilots make a lot of money, so one day I asked him about his investments. Paul told me that he, along with many other pilots, had hitched their stars to an auto leasing company.

Once again, I'm not going to mention any names. Consider it an indication of the outcome of this story and what kind of investment it turned out to be.

The more Paul told me about it, the more red flags it raised in my mind. But, I told myself, I knew Paul well and he would never get involved in something that wasn't above board. He assured me if I ever lost a dollar, he would make it up for me.

I couldn't afford to pour as much money into the company as Paul and his fellow commercial pilots, but I did invest thousands of dollars from about 1978 to 1981.

My worst fears were realized when the Internal Revenue Service raided this auto leasing company's offices. They took every file, including one with little, old Paul Kari's name on it, and issued charges against the investors, which amounted to thousands of individuals.

I wanted out of this mess as quickly as possible and offered to pay whatever it would take to settle the charges. I was told the case had to proceed to court before any possible settlement could be reached.

The case dragged on for years. I had myself completely convinced I was about to lose virtually everything I owned—again—because another investment had blown up in my face. I was in a near constant state of worry. Whenever I found myself working hard at something, I thought, *what's the point? I'm going to lose it all soon, anyway.*

By the late 1980s, the attorneys working for the investment group discovered the IRS had done something illegal in its work on this case. Now the IRS was eager to settle the matter out of court. My share of the penalty amounted to $50,000, which I managed to scrape together and pay.

The story doesn't end there.

Just a couple of years ago, I received a letter saying the investment group had continued to appeal the case until finally a Seattle appeals court ruled against the IRS. We were all now owed a refund of our investment and penalty—with interest! It added up to $90,000.

This may sound funny, but at this point, I had no desire to receive a dime. I didn't trust the IRS and I just wanted to be done with the whole thing. However, my attorney told me I had little choice in the matter. When the government owes you money, it's going to send you a check, whether you want it or not.

It was in 1980 that my dad, Tony Kari, passed away. On top of all the troubles with his heart, he came down with pancreatic cancer. He was in the hospital and Mom called to tell me to come right away. I sped to see him, but he died just before I arrived. He's buried in a beautiful little Colorado cemetery covered in buffalo grass. It's a place that seems to suit the love my dad always had for the great American West and for what it represented to immigrants like him.

CHAPTER 25

The FARM at SPENCER

In late 1980, the FAA decided to merge its Rocky Mountain Region and Northwest Mountain Region. I was being transferred to Seattle, where I would take over the Public Affairs Office—a GS-14 position. Kathi remained in Denver while I flew up to get settled in a new city.

I stayed with a couple who worked at the FAA and opened up their home to me. We were good friends and I rented a bedroom from them for a couple of months until I bought a house of my own.

I was assigned to a new regional director and things did not go well. I found myself back in a position similar to when I first joined the FAA in Washington, D.C. and spent most of my time in confrontational situations with the news media.

It was a very busy office. If a plane anywhere in the world was seeking FAA certification, it was our director's responsibility to go there to make sure it met FAA specs. Obviously, that required constant travel. He made it abundantly clear whose responsibility it was to field calls from reporters back at the regional office.

"Kari, the only reason we have a public affairs officer is because I don't like the media," the director informed me. "When they call, you answer them, not me. You have 24 hours to get information to them."

As before, the bigger newspapers had aviation editors who understood how things worked. It was the smaller papers who smelled a conspiracy every time I told them it would take me a few hours to track down the details of a plane crash in, say, Saudi Arabia. They would always accuse me and the FAA of covering up the facts. It seemed like 90 percent of the conversations I had with the media were like that. I hated it.

Complicating matters, there were some personal problems in the office, which were very difficult to resolve. Because of these kinds of problems, the FAA required all managers to take an accelerated training course on how to help employees work better together.

I GAVE THE CORN CRIB TO AN AMISH NEIGHBOR.

A consultant came in and pulled half the managers out of the office at a time for a four-day, off-site training session. From my earliest days of pilot's training, I saw the benefit of good instruction, so I actually was looking forward to the opportunity to improve my management skills.

We broke into groups of about six and were handed a paper that described a problem to be solved. We were to read it to ourselves, then put our heads together to find a solution.

With my limited vision, reading is a real challenge for me. The papers they handed us were a full page of text, single-spaced. By the time my peers had finished reading the problem and were ready to begin discussing it, I was still making my way through the first paragraph.

Perhaps only a person with a similar physical condition can understand how stressful it is to be in a group of people with normal eyesight who can leave you in the dust. After struggling through about the third problem, I could feel the frustration welling up in me so strongly I thought I was on the verge of a nervous breakdown.

"Guys," I said, "this isn't for me. My eyes just won't let me do it." And I left.

I told the administrator if this is what would be expected of me in the future, I couldn't hack it. I suspect he wanted me to quit, anyway, which would allow him to promote another employee to my job.

"Why are you even in the FAA?" he asked. "You already retired once from the Air Force."

"I'm here because I want to lead a productive life," I replied. "I don't have to go to these seminars to do my job. And I didn't move all the way up here just to retire on disability. If you want to get rid of me, you'll have to find some other way."

So, it was not a good environment for me at the FAA, although I fell in love with the city of Seattle, which is one of the best-kept secrets in the United States.

It's so scenic and it's green, all year round. There's always great seafood to be found, too. People complain about the rain, but it's really only a mist. You put on a windbreaker and you soon get so you hardly notice it.

I had found a beautiful home in the hills east of Seattle. When I first saw it, the yard was overgrown. I learned it had been foreclosed. Kathi and I already had sold our home in Colorado, earning about $100,000 in equity.

Checkbook in hand, I paid a visit to the bank that owned the Seattle house. It was priced at $130,000.

"I've got $100,000 in my pocket," I told the bank real estate manager. "Give it to me for that and I'll write you a check."

I assumed he'd balk at such a low offer—and he did.

"Well, thank you very much," I said and got up to leave.

This was part of my ploy. I had picked up some new negotiating techniques by watching J.R. Ewing on the TV show "Dallas!"

"Wait," the manager said. "Let me talk to the bank president."

In the end, I got the house for $105,000. Before Kathi and Jaime moved in, I recruited a friend, Ken Thomasson, from the FAA to help me fix it up. I poured $14,000 into the landscaping alone. A contractor brought in big boulders and timbers that suited the Northwest. However, I wasn't interested in mowing grass.

"I only want a yard big enough for three beach towels," I told the landscaper.

And that's what he built. It took me longer to get out the mower than it took to cut the grass. The landscaping really made that house. The only downside was it was an hour-long commute—each way, in stop-and-go traffic—to the FAA offices. That wasn't something I relished.

In the midst of the gas crisis of the late '70s, before we left Colorado, I had converted my pick-up truck to run on propane. I went to a farm auction far in Southeast Colorado in hopes of buying a propane tank. It sold for more than I wanted to spend, so I thought I was out of luck. However, a farmer came up to me after the auction. His name was Linly Stum and we became good friends. He said he had propane tanks at his farm that he'd be willing to sell at a good price.

We had the same philosophies regarding agriculture, so we hit it off right away. In fact, my son Shawn went to work for Linly his senior year of high school and lived with him at his farm, which was almost on the Kansas state line.

Shawn graduated from high school there in a class of just six students. He grew to love the area and hoped I'd buy another farm in Colorado, which I eventually did.

Linly's two boys graduated from Fort Hays State University in Kansas. Shawn went on to his first three years of college there and it's where he met his future wife, Christi. Her father owned a stockyard in Russell, Kansas. Ali remained in Denver, living with her mother.

Once, when Shawn and Christi came out to Seattle for a visit, their car broke down. He phoned and told me where he was. As it happened, the FAA had an airway facility nearby. I had met the chief stationed there, so I called him and asked if he could help Shawn and Christi. My hope was he could pick them up, find them a motel and get their car to a mechanic. And he did all that as a favor to me.

Later, we were all shopping together on the wharf—Shawn, Christi, Jaime, Kathi, and I—and I saw a pack of smoked salmon for maybe $35. I decided I would buy it and send it as a gift to the FAA colleague who had helped my son and his wife get squared away. Shawn thought I was crazy to spend that much money on a thank-you.

"Shawn, you've got to take care of the people who take care of you," I said.

He didn't understand it at the time, but years later, he did.

"Dad, I can see why you do what you do," Shawn would say. "That's why you have friends all over."

Kathi—who was a superior worker and had an outgoing personality—was always able to get a job anywhere she went. Shortly after moving to Seattle, she found a secretarial position in a different department at the FAA. It was a good job and she enjoyed it.

Eventually, I was forced to take medical retirement from my job at the FAA. The combination of the issues with my eyesight and the director's challenging demands were too much.

But, when one door closes, God opens another. It was about this time that Dave Reisinger, a good friend from high school, called and told me he was ready to sell his farm back in Spencer, Ohio.

"You always wanted to buy a farm in your hometown," Dave reminded me.

That was true, but I knew Dave's brother owned the farm next door. Why not sell it to him? After all, it was where both of them were raised. Didn't they want to keep it in the family? Dave would never quite answer my question.

I wasn't sure it felt right. But, after the FAA, my career options were limited. I couldn't fly and my eyes couldn't handle a job that required heavy-duty reading. I talked it over with Kathi and we decided I'd fly out to see the farm.

When I arrived, I couldn't believe the sight that greeted my poor eyes. The farm and the house were in rough shape. But, I had to earn a living and this 213-acre farm was the only opportunity I had in front of me. I bought it for $200,000.

In addition to the major investment disasters I've already mentioned, I had tried putting my money into a variety of other things—from gold and precious stones to penny stocks. In each case, I either lost my shirt or made very little. The only thing that consistently worked out for me investment-wise was residential real estate.

So, I decided I'd better stick with what worked. Besides, the opportunity to buy a farm in your hometown doesn't come along every day.

I saw the farm in January and made arrangements to close on the sale with Dave in March. When I returned, I discovered he had made a deal with a company from Cleveland in the meantime to dispose of sludge on the farm. The company drove heavy equipment all over the fields, badly compacting the wet soil and creating deep ruts. There were also piles of scrap equipment everywhere you looked.

The sight was so discouraging, I thought about not going through with the deal. But, you have to honor your commitments and I had told Dave I'd take the farm. On the way to the closing, I had stopped to visit Dave's brother, Francis. I still felt he deserved the first chance to buy it. I asked him if he had any interest. Based on the condition of the farm, he clearly didn't. I suspect some other family dynamics were at work there, too.

Our home in Seattle sold quickly and we made a little money on it, though not as much as on our homes in Colorado. One thing I'll say for Kathi is she was always game for an adventure. Whenever we contemplated a move, her attitude was, "Let's go do it!" Of course, she liked some places better than others, but she was always willing to try. And as I mentioned, she always had the ability to land on her feet and find a job anyplace we went.

In Seattle, we had made a spot for a little garden. Kathi put in a tomato plant and it thrived under her care. But one day, we came out to find a slug had eaten it to pieces. Kathi couldn't believe it.

"After all that hard work," she said.

"Well, that's agriculture," I told her.

"And that's the line of work you want to go into?" she asked.

I had rented out the Spencer house and farm for about a year before we were ready to move in February of 1983. We finally headed east for Spencer in the biggest moving van I could rent, towing our Toyota Corolla. Kathi followed along behind, driving our Honda.

We were traveling along State Route 162 when the farm at long last came into view. Seven-year-old Jaime was riding with me in the truck.

"Look, Jaime!" I said. "There it is!"

She didn't seem enthused.

"Dad," Jaime said, as if to scold me. "Why are you bringing us to a haunted house?"

When we were packing back in Seattle, I saw Kathi loading big containers with all the canned goods from our kitchen cupboards.

"Kath," I said. "That's a lot of extra weight. Why are you packing all that food? You should just donate it to a local church or something. We can stock up when we get there."

"Oh, no," she replied. "I'm taking it."

Well, thank God she did.

For starters, the boiler that supplied the hot water heat for the farmhouse was shot, which I didn't know. Otherwise, I would've had it fixed. All there was for heat was a wood burner in the kitchen. However, the chimney was so clogged with soot, I was afraid to start a fire in the stove.

Somehow, we managed to huddle up and survive the first night. We knew there was a bad winter storm headed our way the next day. We drove into nearby Wellington, where we bought a hot plate and a kerosene heater.

We were snowed in for three days. The driveway was drifted so badly, we couldn't get out. Thank goodness the electrical service stayed on, because all we had to eat was the food Kathi brought from Seattle, cooked on that little hot plate.

That was our initiation to our new life in Spencer.

After we dug out from the storm, I turned to my good friend Dave Aikman, who had bought my mom and dad's farm where I grew up. Dave became a mentor to me—helping me solve problems and teaching me about modern farming.

Dave assisted me in lining up a local Amish man named Sam Shetler who did home remodeling. His crew started to work on the house almost immediately. They tore down the chimney and broke up the old concrete floor in the basement. After laying drainage tile, Sam poured a new cement floor and we installed a new hot water boiler—all within about two weeks. The house at least felt warm and somewhat livable.

In the Air Force, I received training every step of the way so that I was ready and comfortable with every job I had to do. Suddenly, I found myself on a farm again but with no training in today's methods and equipment. The industry had changed dramatically in the 25 years since I had left my dad's Spencer Township farm. When I was growing up, farmers cultivated for weed control using equipment to dig up the weeds between the rows. Now, they used herbicide. And the tractors and implements were much, much bigger.

I had a lot to do and learn in the short couple of months before spring planting. There were many times I felt overwhelmed and days when I wondered if my damaged back would stand up to the backbreaking physical work of farming.

Finances also were a part of the challenge. After all the unproductive investments I made, my net worth probably was around $100,000. I had bought the farm for $200,000 and now I was faced with buying the tractor, tillage equipment, seed and fertilizer necessary to start a farm operation. My military pension, loans and eventually income from crops provided the money. I was fortunate to get loans from the Spencer Farmers Bank, in particular, Howard West, the President, who I knew as a kid.

Another lucky break for me was to be introduced to Roger Shopbell, who produced liquid fertilizer. We have become lifelong friends.

Once again, I turned to Dave, who provided invaluable counsel on which farm dealers I should trust and where I could find the best prices on what I needed. When I had to have an electric motor repaired or needed welding done, Dave told me where to go. That was so helpful.

The spring of '83 was a really, really wet spring. The farm, which had been a nice dairy farm when I was growing up, had nine fields, located on both sides of a state highway. There was a railroad track to the north and a pretty good-sized creek running to the south. With today's bigger equipment, I knew one of the first tasks I faced would be to take out fence rows and turn those nine small fields into four larger fields.

Dave pointed me to a guy by the name of Freddie Martin in LaGrange who had a Caterpillar D5 bulldozer. He came out and spent days and days helping me clean up the farm. He tore down the dilapidated buildings and shoved all the abandoned equipment into a huge pile just east of the main barn. The pile was 12 feet high, 40 feet wide and nearly 150 feet long. I wish I had a picture of it! What I wasn't able to burn, we dug a hole and buried.

The farm had a drive-through corn crib that was in good shape, but was in the way of a driveway I had planned. I talked to an Amish man named Jake Shetler who lived not too far away on Camp Road. It was his brother Sam who had done a lot of the work on our house. The corn crib had wooden runners on it, so I offered to give it to Jake if he'd haul it away.

Jake talked to one of his neighbors, Joe Wills, who came up with the biggest tractor he had. They hooked onto it and after a couple of tries, got it moving. It took up the entire road. They dragged that corn crib west on State Route 162, a mile south on Firestone Road, then east for another mile. I remember the sparks were just flying from underneath that thing as they towed it down the highway!

Once they got it going, they didn't want to stop. I had no idea how they were going to make it around the turns. I hopped in my pick-up to follow along. Joe was moving at about 12-15 mph and I was sure at least once it was going to topple over. It made me so nervous, I finally turned around and went back home. But, they made it and as far as I know, that corn crib is still in use today on Jake's farm.

We worked out another mutually beneficial deal later that spring. I was so busy pulling out fence posts and rolling up old barbed wire that I had no time at all to devote to my lawn—which I wanted to tear out and replant, anyway. The grass had grown to almost four-feet tall. Everyone around us must have wondered what kind of nut had moved into the neighborhood who never cuts his grass. I told Jake if he'd bring his horses and sickle-bar mower over, he could cut the grass and have it for hay, which is just what he did!

My efforts to clean up the farm were complicated by the fact there were tile blowouts all over the fields. Farmers often install underground tile two-and-a-half to three feet deep to drain wet areas of land. If something happens and one of the clay tiles breaks, the water comes down from the surface and pretty soon you have a big hole there. In other cases, groundhogs will get into the tiles, get stuck and plug them up.

There were areas north of the railroad tracks that were eroded so badly, I could have buried a Holstein cow in the hole. Instead of fixing the blowouts, previous farmers had just planted around the holes.

The way to fix a tile blowout is to hire a backhoe operator to come in and dig out the bad section. I didn't have the financial wherewithal to do that. So, I began digging out the problem tiles with a shovel. I put in many 16-hour-plus days digging.

John McCourt, the pastor of the Baptist church we attended, had a son named Shawn who occasionally helped me with jobs on the farm the first year. As we cleared fence rows and fixed tile blowouts by hand, he'd rib me, saying I really needed to get a backhoe.

"A backhoe would be just great, but I can't afford one! And if you don't be quiet about it, you're fired!" I replied in jest.

Shawn was a great kid and he worked his butt off. Today, he manages a fertilizer company near Polk. Years later, his father told me Shawn's love for agriculture stemmed from those days he spent helping me. That means a lot to me.

Dave took me down to a new John Deere dealer in Ashland. That day, we each bought a new 135-horsepower John Deere 4440 tractor, one serial number apart. This, to me, was a really big tractor. It had a nice cab on it. I needed a second, smaller tractor to pull a planter. At the same dealership, they had a 105-horsepower John Deere 4050 without a cab. I bought them both on John Deere credit.

As spring drew closer, I attended farm auctions and bought a plow, disk, harrow, and cultipacker. The weather was wet and Dave helped me know when the soil was dry enough to plow. When it finally came time to put seeds in the ground, I rented a six-row planter from the tractor dealership.

I had an Amish construction crew come out to build a new corn crib. I had it laid out in an L-shape and put it behind the barn where it also would serve as a wind break. It was made from solid oak and it'll last 100 years. However, what I should've done was build a new house and used the old house for a corn crib because it was so drafty!

As our home remodeling continued, Kathi suggested we buy or rent a mobile home to live in while the work was being done. I regret not doing that. I checked into it and was told the local zoning code wouldn't permit a house trailer. I found out too late that we could have gotten a variance to have a mobile home temporarily.

We had read in a women's magazine a list of the top-10 most stressful things in life. No. 1 was the death of a spouse. I don't recall No. 2, but No. 3 was living in a house at the same time you're trying to remodel it. I found that to be very true. It was a stressful time for Kathi. After working on the house all day, the Amish construction crew would leave tools and sawdust all over the kitchen. By the time I came into the house for our evening meal, she'd have it cleaned up. I didn't even know about it.

After a week of this, Kathi finally told me she was tired of cleaning up after the workers. I felt badly that she hadn't told me. I met with the contractor the next morning and told him I didn't care what time they had to knock off work in the afternoon, they needed to leave themselves time to clean-up their mess so my wife didn't have to. And they did.

Kathi wanted to help with the remodeling and stripped all the old wallpaper. It was a big house, so it was hard work. I offered to hire someone or at least get a steamer to make the job easier, but she was determined to scrape it all off. One of the Amish boys had really taken a shine to Kathi, so I told him I'd pay him if he helped her. Kathi repapered all the rooms except for a tall staircase, which was too hard to reach.

I hired a paper hanger to come and do that part of the house. Now, you've heard all the jokes about a one-armed paper hanger? Well, I came in from the fields one day to discover I'd hired a one-armed paper hanger! He truly had only a single arm. But he and his wife worked together and they did a really nice job.

I asked him what it would have cost if I'd hired him to do the work Kathi had done in stripping off all the old wallpaper and hanging the new. He priced the labor alone at $2,000 per wall. So that was $4,000 Kathi saved us. She wanted to contribute to the effort and she worked very hard at it.

Jaime attended a private Christian school near Elyria, about half an hour away. That meant Kathi spent a lot of time each day driving her to school and picking her up. Kathi also was the best cook I have ever known in my life—always making everything from scratch.

Finally, we were ready to put corn and soybeans into the ground. As a boy, I had done every kind of farm labor, except for planting. It was the one job Dad always did. I was very unsure of myself. You've got to make sure you don't plant seeds too deep or too shallow, or in soil conditions that are too wet or too dry.

Adding to my anxiety was the fact I was renting the planter from the John Deere dealer in Ashland. The ground was ready to plant and I'd call there every day asking when I could get the planter. They kept putting me off. Obviously, there was a lot of demand for it that time of year. Finally, my turn came up and I went to pick it up at a farm between Spencer and Ashland. The farmer remembered my name because years ago he had bought my dad's Farmall M—the tractor I was raised on. It's a small world.

I finally got the corn and soybeans in, albeit a little late. We were coming home one Sunday from church and I was so proud to see for the first time the tiny corn plants poking up through the soil every seven-and-a-half to eight inches, just the way they should. I felt like a little kid on Christmas morning.

"I did it!" I said. "Dad would be so proud!"

Since it had been a dairy farm, the fields got a fair amount of manure and the soil wasn't in as poor condition as it could've been. I had it tested and we steadily improved the farm's productivity over the years by adding lime and fertilizer.

Because the farm was our source of income, getting it up to full production took precedence over some of the other projects around the house. Once planting was done, I could devote more time to remodeling. It took about three years to complete the house—in part because I was the new guy in town and it often took a while before a contractor worked his way down to me on his job list.

And it was an extensive project. We knocked a wall down between the kitchen and what was initially the dining room. We completely redid the kitchen, installed bay windows on the east side of the house, and put in two new bathrooms. We removed a wall between two smaller rooms to create a big master bedroom. The plumbing and electrical systems were re-done. A mud room was added on the back—which on a farm, really helps keep the house clean. Before we put on new siding and shutters, a contractor injected foam insulation into the walls. It cut the drafts by at least 90 percent.

Charlie Siman from Chatham Township did most of the carpentry. He was just a jewel. Charlie never got upset when he had to re-do something because we changed our minds about it. When we were all done, it was a gorgeous home. In fact, it was touted in the local daily newspaper, The *Medina Gazette*, as one of the prettiest farmhouses in Medina County.

My sixth-grade teacher, Bertha Rowe, was raised on that farm. She was my first teacher when my family moved to Spencer in 1946. Bertha saw all the renovations we were doing and told me when she was growing up, the house had a wraparound porch. She asked if we would consider adding one.

"Bertha, for you, I'll do it," I told her. We rebuilt the porch and it really set off the whole house.

I had saved the bricks from the old chimney and decided to build a sidewalk along the east and south sides of the house, connecting with the old milk house. I dug it all out, put in a base of sand, and laid every brick myself.

About the time we were done with the renovations, I decided I wanted to get into selling real estate—no houses, just farms. I contacted Bob King, who owned a real estate company in Wellington, and asked if I could be his farm specialist. He said sure, so I got my Ohio sales license. I converted the old milk house into a beautiful office and put out a big sign that read, "King Realty Farm Sales Office."

Before I bought the farm, Dave Reisinger had built an 80- by 100-foot building free stall barn for his dairy. Having lost my shirt twice on cattle, I was determined to stick with crop farming. I hired a contractor to come in, remove the stalls, make the doors bigger, and convert it to a machine shed. The problem was when it was originally built they didn't use roofing materials that would stand up to all the acid in cow manure. So the roof leaked like a sieve. I had to cover the machinery in plastic to keep it dry!

Dave Aikman told me the first thing a farmer should buy is a loader tractor. He was right except I couldn't afford one. The second thing he said I needed was a heated workshop. As soon as I was able, we converted what was an old heifer barn into a shop. We put in a door, poured a nice cement floor, insulated, and installed a wood burner. We also made a three-car garage between the shop and the renovated milk house.

There was a 20- by 60-foot silo I converted into use for shelled corn storage and built two grain bins with a dryer. I had built the corn crib when we first came to the farm and bought a two-row New Idea picker from my neighbor, Floyd Hirschman. We picked corn and dried it on the ear when I was young and I figured it still would be the least expensive way to do it. Farmers like Dave Aikman had already moved to a system that shelled the corn as it was harvested and stored it in grain form.

Well, I used my beautiful new corn crib exactly one season. I was working by myself picking corn—I couldn't afford a hired man—and it was terribly time-consuming. I kept telling myself, "This is a dumb way to harvest corn."

Finally, I asked Dale Ziegler, a friend from church who was already done with his harvest, if he'd come and just help drive wagons back and forth to the fields while I was running the picker. He said yes.

The weather forecast called for a terrible snowstorm that was predicted to be the blizzard of the decade. I realized I had to get that corn out of the field in the next day or two, or else it was going to be there until March or April.

It was way below freezing and the wind began to howl. The temperature was about 15 degrees—probably zero with the wind chill factor. I was pulling this two-row corn picker around the field on the John Deere 4050 without a cab. I was wearing two sets of Carhartt work clothes and thermal underwear.

Now Dale was an outdoorsman who took hunting trips to Colorado. He was accustomed to all kinds of weather. The crib was full and he began hauling wagons of corn to the grain elevator in town. By 4 p.m. he just couldn't take the cold anymore. I told him I understood and thanked him for his help.

Somehow, I was able to get it done. I remember when I finally dragged myself into the house that night, after suffering all day in the cold to get the crop in, I felt hurt that Kathi had never come out to bring me something to eat or a cup of hot coffee. I was within sight of the house all day, sometimes less than 100 yards away, and she never came out to see how I was doing.

"When I was growing up, our whole family worked as a team," I said. "It's cold out there. I can't believe you didn't at least bring me something warm to drink."

All she said was, "Well, it's cold in here, too."

She didn't seem to understand why I just couldn't let the harvest go until the weather was better. That corn represented our income and I just couldn't risk leaving it in the field any longer. I was upset by what felt like a lack of sensitivity to a person who was really struggling.

Earlier in the harvest season, my classmates from high school were planning a party. I was still hustling to get the corn in, so a classmate's husband named Kent came over to help me load corn into the crib from the wagons. While I went to the field to pick more, he'd use a wheelbarrow to collect ears that had fallen to the ground.

Finally, it was close to the time for our get-together. I told Kent he'd better head home to pick up his wife and I'd see them at the party. By now, it was dark and I didn't yet have any lights on the machine shed. Knowing I was running late,

I put the picker away and sprinted up the pathway to the house in the pitch black. Well, Kent had left the wheelbarrow standing up on end right in the middle of the path and I crashed into it at full speed.

Fortunately, I was OK, but I still gave Kent a hard time about it at the party. We had a good laugh about it.

"You owe me!" I said. "I almost knocked my teeth out!"

That's the kind of season it was that first—and last—year I harvested corn by the ear. What doesn't kill you makes you smarter, I guess. It was all part of the education in my return to farming. That first year, the farm broke even. There were several times that without my military pension, I'm not sure we would've made it. During many months, that retirement check is what bought our groceries and paid our bills.

In some respects, it felt good to be home. My old Spencer High School classmates always treated me very, very well. In fact, not long after my release after nearly eight years as a prisoner of war, the community had thrown a big parade for me.

The people who knew me as a kid, like Floyd Hirschman, knew my roots, knew where I came from and were always helpful. However, the people who had moved into the community after I left home didn't always treat me as well.

When I first began farming and bought those two new John Deere tractors, some of my neighbors seemed to think I was too big for my britches. Maybe if I had started with a team of horses, worked my way up, and paid my dues in their sight, they would have accepted me. As it was, they weren't so friendly.

I installed new stainless steel tanks to store liquid fertilizer. Shortly after, I saw my neighbor to the east, Francis Reisinger, out working and stopped to say hello. Francis was about 10 years older than I was.

"Mighty fancy equipment you've got there, boy," he said.

That was how it went with many of my neighbors.

At farm auctions, I'd try to say hello to someone and they would ignore me completely. When I got home, I'd relay the story to Kathi. I usually could let it roll right off my back, but it always bothered her to feel like we were not accepted. In fact, later on, Kathi grew so upset by it, she wanted to move.

I did my best to be a good neighbor. A nearby farmer stopped one day to tell me he and his wife were divorcing and had to sell their 40-acre farm. He offered it to me, but asked if I would promise to sell it back to him if he was able to get back on his feet financially. I agreed to sell it back to him at the purchase price, plus any improvements I made. I systematically tiled the fields and improved the soil with lime and fertilizer.

Sure enough, a couple of years later, he returned and asked to buy back his farm. It was now worth twice what I had paid for it. But, my word is my bond. I could have doubled my money on the open market, but I sold the farm back to him per our agreement. Friends in Spencer bring this story up to me even today.

I recall another occasion when the telephone rang at about 2 a.m. It was someone calling to tell me my cows were out on the highway. Well, I didn't have any cows! I figured they must belong to my neighbor, Francis.

I pulled on my clothes and went to see if there was anything I could do to help. I woke Francis and told him his cows were loose and out on the road.

His farm had what's called a manure lagoon. It's a pit dairy farmers use to store animal waste. The solids sink to the bottom and the liquids rise to the top. It wasn't fenced in and we found several cows had wandered into the lagoon and couldn't get out.

After rounding up the other animals with Francis and his two sons, we turned our attention to the ones that were stuck. Francis didn't know what to do.

Looking back, it's one of those times in my life when I took a risk that easily could have been fatal. I suggested to Francis that he take his backhoe and extend the boom as far as it would go out over the lagoon. I would crawl out to the end with a rope and try to lasso the cows.

In retrospect, it was a stupid thing for me to do. But, I was eager to win over my neighbors and be accepted in the community as one of them. I always felt Francis should have been the one to buy their childhood farm from his brother, not me. Even though I had talked with Francis about it and he declined to take the farm, our relationship had been frosty ever since.

I was in my mid- to late-50s and easily could have fallen off the backhoe and drowned in the slurry of manure. Somehow, the plan worked. I managed to rope three cows and we pulled each to safety with the backhoe. No one ever thanked me.

That first year, I had a 1-ton Ford pick-up truck and a gooseneck trailer, which I used to haul just about everything. When I bought the second John Deere tractor, the dealer told me his delivery truck had broken down and he'd accept my pick-up as a trade-in toward the tractor. I agreed.

However, it left me in need of a pick-up truck. My brother-in-law, Don Hendricks, who was a rancher in Colorado, had 13 of them including a green one I always liked. I arranged to buy a Ford F-100 from him and Kathi offered to fly to Colorado and drive it back to Ohio. It became a family joke that this was a big mistake because in preparation for the trip, I taught Kathi how to read a map. And after that, she never stayed home!

Evidently, Don failed to look over the truck to make sure it was in good shape for a cross-country drive. He used his trucks fairly hard to haul hay to his pastures.

Its radiator fins were clogged with bits of hay. Kathi called me from somewhere in Kansas to say the truck kept overheating. She took the drive slowly, which ended up adding a couple of days to her journey.

Finally, she made it. It was a two-wheel-drive truck with a rusty bed, and that's what I farmed with for the next five years. I'd drive to farm auctions where guys had parked their shiny, new, four-wheel-drive pick-ups and here would come old Kari in his rust bucket! You do what you have to do. I ended up selling it to Dave Reisinger's son, Tommy, who drove it a few more years.

After the learning experience of that first year, I went to a farm auction near Nova and bought a John Deere four-row combine. That's what I used for harvest until I graduated to a six-row combine a few years later. I had a pretty good fleet of gravity wagons for hauling shelled corn.

We must have been doing something right that first year, because a man by the name of Glenn Cross stopped in to say he liked what we'd done with the farm. He was looking for someone to rent his 600-acre farm near Wellington and offered me the opportunity.

I went out to look at his land and it had nice, big fields—a couple of them 100 acres or more each. I agreed to farm it, which expanded my operation to 800 acres. It was a challenge, since my workforce consisted of only me and two tractors. I worked many 16-hour days up there the next spring, tilling and planting. I bought a six-row corn planter, which was a welcome addition to my roster of equipment.

Kathi's parents came up from Florida to visit us before our house renovations were complete. I think they were surprised by what they saw. After all, our homes in Denver and Seattle had been nice, fairly new houses. And here we were living in an old, broken-down farmhouse in Spencer, Ohio. The farm buildings were not in the greatest shape, either. It soon would be a showplace, but in the beginning, everywhere you looked, there was a lot of work to do. It was a temporary hardship and not as hard as the life I knew when I was a kid.

One night, I planned to work until midnight plowing at the rented farm. So I asked Kathi if she would bring me dinner and some water. Then I'd get up at 5 a.m. and do the same the next day.

The one thing about Kathi was when her family was visiting they were her No. 1 priority. As I mentioned earlier, when I was growing up, we all helped Dad with the work of the farm. Whatever job was to be done that day—especially when the timing was critical—it became the focus of our whole family's efforts.

Well, during one of those long days of plowing, my drinking water ran out at about 4 p.m. I knew Kathi would be there between 5 p.m. and 6 p.m., so I wasn't worried. The rented farm was about three or four miles away from our house and I had drawn a map to make sure she knew how to get there.

Soon it was going on 7 p.m. and no sign of Kathi. It grew dark. Every time I saw headlights coming down the road, I expected it to be her car, but it wasn't. I was starting to get a little hot under the collar.

I wrapped up at about 11 p.m. and came home to find everyone in bed. I took a shower and turned in myself, after a long day of work.

Kathi's parents, Ralph and Margaret, were planning to leave the next day, so I waited around to be sure I had the chance to say goodbye to them.

I also took the opportunity to ask Kathi about the day before.

"Kath," I said, "why didn't you bring me any food or water? You knew I was up there working all day long without anything to eat or drink."

"Well, I was spending time with Mom and Dad," was all she said.

At that, I became a little heated. I didn't use bad language, but I told her I couldn't understand how she could do something like that.

This exchange made her dad angry. I went to work and when I returned home at about 3 p.m., I knew something was wrong. The house was empty and there was no note. I knew that Kathi's mom and dad had taken her and Jaime with them.

I was in disbelief. Here was a man who drank much of his paycheck, forcing his wife to work to provide for their family. He had not been a good husband or father. And yet, he would take Kathi and Jaime away from me while I was out working hard to make a living on our farm.

I made a few calls and found out Kathi was at the home of one of her friends from church. The friend had tipped off our pastor as to what was going on. Pastor McCourt visited Kathi and urged her to return to her home and to me.

However, her father told her, "If you go back to him, I will never talk to you again."

Ralph was true to his word. Kathi returned home and he never spoke with her the rest of his life. He died in 1985. Kathi didn't talk a lot about it, but I'm sure it hurt her deeply. She loved her dad, despite his problems.

Apparently, the day I was plowing and ran out of water, Ralph told her, "I don't want you ever to help him. If you do, he'll eventually have you pulling the plow."

Although Kathi wasn't one to do very much outside, he didn't know how hard she had worked stripping wallpaper and helping with our interior renovations. She was always eager any time we moved to a new home. Still, it would have meant so much to me if she had been able to recognize those times when I was struggling with the farm work and offered to help.

I recall one day when I was hitching a gravity wagon full of corn to my battered old pick-up truck to take it to market. It seemed like I had to move the truck eight or 10 times before I got the two lined up. The tongue on the wagon would only move about half an inch. It wasn't a very good set-up, but it was all I could afford at the time.

As I was getting more and more aggravated, I looked up to see Kathi sitting in one of the bay windows, sipping a cup of tea, watching me trying to accomplish this frustrating task. I was continually moving the truck a fraction of an inch, hopping out, going back to see if I had it lined up with the wagon, then going back to the truck to move it some more.

When I finally got it, I walked into the house.

"Have you been sitting there the whole time I've been trying to hook this wagon up?" I asked.

"Yes."

"Why in the world don't you ever, ever volunteer to help me? Or see when I'm struggling?"

Kathi's retort was, "You're the one who wanted to play in the dirt, not me."

Again, her words cut me deeply. To me, farming was the one way I could still make a living for my family. To her, it was playing in the dirt.

The house was beautiful, the farm was turning around, we had a nice car, there was food on the table, and Kathi had made some good friends through church. Yet, she was unhappy and our relationship often was filled with tension. Somehow, she just never seemed pleased with me.

When she made that comment about not wanting to play in the dirt, I think it perhaps had something to do with her friends back home, and what they must think of her now that she was a "farm wife." She enjoyed the jobs she had as an administrative assistant in high-powered business offices. She was good at that work and I think it made her feel good about herself.

One day I came up to the house for lunch. Instead of driving, I walked in from where I was working behind the barn. Kathi didn't hear me as I came into the mudroom and took off my boots, but I could hear her laughing and carrying on with someone on the telephone. It was one of those times when we weren't talking very much, so it caught my attention to hear her having such an animated conversation. As soon as I entered the room, she hung up.

"I noticed you were having a lot of fun on the phone," I said. "Who were you talking to?"

"Oh, it was just Larry," she said. He was her ex-husband.

I had the feeling she always kept the lines of communication open with him, just in case our marriage didn't work out, despite the fact that to my knowledge he never paid her child support to help in raising Jaime. More than once, I told Kathi that wasn't fair to her, to Jaime, or to me. The court had ordered it and he should do his part.

Finally, after many attempts to persuade Kathi to hold him to account, she said, "If I do that, then he will want to be involved in Jaime's life. And I don't want that."

"That's not fair to Jaime," I replied. "She needs him to be involved in her life."

"Well, that's just the way it is," Kathi answered.

And for the most part, that's the way it stayed. Although, Larry did come to visit Jaime once and took her to the amusement park at Cedar Point. He flew in to Cleveland and we gave him the use of the Honda for his stay. I always tried to be good to him, which led me into quite an adventure.

During a period around 1984 when our relationship had taken a turn for the better, Kathi told me she needed a favor.

"I've got a job for you," she said one day when I came in for lunch. "A big one."

Kathi told me she sensed Larry was in some kind of trouble, but he would never be clear about it. Finally, he called to tell her he was in the Nevada State Penitentiary on a four- to five-year sentence for dealing drugs. I have to say I was not surprised.

Larry had been living in Las Vegas, where he owned four rental houses. His girlfriend, who occupied one of the houses and also had been dealing drugs, had not collected rent in four or five months. Larry's lawyer told him to find someone he trusted, give that person full power of attorney, and ask them to clean up his financial affairs.

The problem was, Larry didn't have any friends he could trust. He had phoned Kathi as a last resort.

"Well," Kathi said, "I know someone you can trust. Paul."

"Do you really think he'd help me?" Larry wondered.

"I'll ask him," she said.

I agreed to try, for Kathi's sake and with the hope that if he got things straightened around, he might honor his obligations to her and to Jaime. Larry said he'd pay for my airfare and hotel, so I set off for Las Vegas.

Only then did it begin to sink in what I had gotten myself into. For what I knew, all of Larry's tenants could be drug dealers. What's to stop one of them from shooting me when I knock on their door and ask them for their rent?

My first stop was the prison to meet with Larry and obtain his power of attorney. He was very appreciative of my willingness to help him. Before I went out there, I was told to be sure to wear a pair of dress slacks to the prison. Visitors were not permitted to wear blue jeans because that was what the prisoners wore.

CHAPTER 25

Before going to Larry's rental properties, I opened up the Yellow Pages and hired a security guard. We met at the home of Larry's girlfriend. I watched as this skinny little guy got out of his car. I could see he wasn't carrying a gun.

"Don't you have a weapon?" I asked.

"I don't need one," he replied, casually. He was a martial arts expert.

As we talked, we saw the garage door open. A woman I assumed to be Larry's girlfriend pulled out. The door shut and she drove away. The body guard and I knocked down the door and went inside.

In three or four days, I managed to change the locks and security codes in all four houses. I hired a rental agency that would take over running the properties for Larry. It was hectic, but things went pretty well, all in all.

I went back out to the penitentiary to see Larry. When I got to the front gate, I realized there was a small problem. I was wearing jeans and wouldn't be allowed inside. The prison was way out in the boonies, some 70 miles north of Las Vegas.

I didn't know what to do. I didn't have time to drive all the way to the city and back for a pair of pants or I'd miss my flight. So I headed to the nearest town, which was Indian Springs. There was a bombing range there when I was stationed at Nellis Air Force Base. I stopped in the BX, which was the store on base but all they had were jeans.

Pulling into a gas station, I saw a guy get out of a car. He was about my age and about my size. A lot of the people who live in that area are retired military personnel. I walked up to him and introduced myself.

"Sir, this is going to be the strangest request you've ever received in your life," I said, and explained my predicament.

"Oh," he said, matter-of-factly. "Just follow me."

We drove 10 or 15 minutes to his home in the mountains, where he handed me a pair of blue slacks and a belt. I don't even remember his name.

I returned to the prison, met with Larry, then drove back to the man's house to return the pants I had borrowed. I was sure he thought he'd never see them again, and that's exactly what he said!

Larry begged me to help get him released from prison, afraid of what the other prisoners might do to him. I wrote a letter to the Nevada department of corrections and stuck my neck out for him. I told them my own story in hopes of convincing them I was not just some crank. Larry made a mistake, I wrote, but if they saw fit to give him early release, I would take responsibility for him and make sure he stayed on the right path.

I don't know if they even got the letter, but perhaps they did, because a few months later, Larry was released. He never did pay Kathi one cent of child support that I'm aware of.

I farmed the rented 600 acres for two seasons and enjoyed pretty good crop yields both years. The agreement was that I paid for all the inputs and the landowner received one-third of the harvest. So, every third wagon of corn or beans went into the grain bins on site and the other two wagons came back to my farm. The weather those years was rainy, which made things all the more challenging. It was a lot of physical wear and tear on me hauling wagons up and down the road in an open-cab tractor.

I finally was able to re-do our lawn, tilling and reseeding it. Once again, I felt a bit frustrated to be doing it all myself. Normally, I don't work on the Sabbath, but one Sunday, I announced we were going to stay home, finish the job on the lawn and spread straw over the seeded ground. Kathi was a bit surprised, since she enjoyed going to church, but she and Jaime came out and helped get it done.

We welcomed an addition to our family on Aug. 30, 1985, when our daughter Jackie was born. Kathi had a smooth pregnancy and Jackie was a beautiful baby girl.

My son Shawn had become a veterinarian, so I knew he likely would not be going into farming. While we were expecting, I mused to Kathi that if it was a boy, maybe he would want to follow in my footsteps.

Years later, Kathi must have told this to Jackie, but made it sound like I had been hoping for a boy and was disappointed we had a girl. Nothing could be further from the truth. When I first saw Jackie, I thought she was the most beautiful baby I had ever seen and I loved her from that moment forward.

Jackie was home from the hospital only a couple days when I noticed her breathing seemed abnormal. Often, there was a long pause between breaths, followed by a sharp intake of air. We took her to the doctor and she was diagnosed with apnea. We were fortunate that one of the country's leading physicians specializing in apnea was based in Cleveland.

Jackie was fitted with a heart/breathing monitor she had to wear at all times. It would alert us if her heartbeat/breathing went below a preset range for her age. There were suction cups that had to be placed on her chest. We had to keep an eye on them because if they moved out of place, they wouldn't pick up her heartbeat. The suction cups made her skin beet red and must have been uncomfortable for her. It certainly was a frightening experience for her parents.

If Kathi drove Jaime to school and took the baby along, the monitor had to go, too. There were a couple of times when Jackie's heart/breathing stopped for up to 28 seconds. Once, Kathi had to give her mouth-to-mouth resuscitation on the hood of the car.

The doctor estimated Jackie would outgrow this condition in about nine months. Well, 18 months later she still was wearing the monitor and had another episode in which her heart stopped again for almost 30 seconds. We were worried and discouraged.

Finally one night, I told Kathi to hold Jackie and we were going to pray over her. To this day, I get goose bumps when I think back on this. I can't tell the story without becoming emotional.

I prayed. "God, you have given us this beautiful baby girl. Now, tonight we are going to unhook this monitor. If you want us to raise her, please heal her."

From that day forward, Jackie never had another occurrence of apnea.

She was a gifted little girl and a joy to raise. Music emerged as one of her greatest talents. Not once did we have to tell her to study or to practice piano. Jackie always had the motivation and maturity to do those things on her own. Never once did she sass back. She was the perfect child. Kathi said if she'd known it would be so much fun, she would have had five more. Jackie was a delight.

About the time Jackie was 2-3 years old, the landowner I'd been renting the 600-acre farm from let me know he was going to rent it to someone else. He was straightforward about it, which I appreciated, but still it made me angry. I'd put a lot of effort into farming that land and had a pretty good system in place. As fast as my operation went up to 800 acres, it plummeted back to 200.

One of my dad's good friends operated a large nursery in Akron. Both were Hungarian and enjoyed talking together in their native language. When we were finishing the renovations on the house, I brought him in to do the landscaping and plant trees for a windbreak. He would always say, "Landscaping a house is like putting lipstick on a beautiful woman. It's the final touch!"

Later, Dad's friend got me involved in growing burning bushes. It's a variety of shrub used in landscaping that gets its name from its bright red fall foliage. He told me I could buy them small for less than 50 cents each, grow them four or five years, then sell them for up to $5 apiece. That sounded like a winner to me.

I started small and the bushes did well enough to inspire me to increase my investment. I planted 30,000 of them in the field right across the road from the house. I rented a machine that dropped them into the ground and spent a lot of time cultivating them to keep down the weeds. Everything seemed to be going fine until one day I noticed some of the bushes no longer looked healthy. I was afraid they were dying.

I left messages for Dad's friend who had encouraged me to get into this business, but I didn't hear back from him. I begged him to come out to take a look and tell me what to do. Finally, someone from Ohio State University was able to identify the pest or disease that was attacking the plants and told me how to treat it. In the meantime, I lost about 10 percent of the bushes.

When I eventually sold the farm, we had an auction on New Year's Day. It was well-advertised, but a terrible snowstorm came up that day. People got stuck all over the place. The sale did not go well and I ended up losing my shirt on the burning bushes. I invested $10,000 to $15,000 and several years of labor, only to receive about $3,000 for them. Somebody got a good deal, but it wasn't me.

I have different ideas about education today, but back then, Kathi and I wanted both girls to go to a Christian school. Every day, Kathi drove Jaime to Elyria and Jackie almost to Lorain to attend school. It amounted to almost a two-hour round trip, twice a day. So Kathi devoted a lot of time to running the girls back and forth.

Kathi rarely, if ever, got sick. But one day, she was not feeling well and asked me to drive Jackie to preschool. When it was time to go, little Jackie refused to get in the car. I pleaded and pleaded with her, but all she would do was cry. Finally, I picked her up and swatted her one time on the hind end. It was the only time I ever spanked her. Still, she refused to go. In the end, Kathi managed to drive Jackie to school.

When Kathi got home, she told me what had happened. Jackie told her a boy at school had bitten the teacher the day before and Jackie was afraid the boy was going to bite her. Kathi knew about it, but hadn't told me. I felt terrible! I never would have gotten after her and tried to make her go if I had known Jackie was afraid. I just loved that little girl.

Jackie was smart as a whip. One day I had the combine in the farm's shop, greasing it up and changing the oil. I wanted to start it to check the oil pressure. Jackie, who was about 3 years old at the time, was with me. She watched as I went through the procedures to start the combine's engine. There were several safety steps you had to follow before it would fire up.

When I was done, I shut it off and went to work on something else. In no time at all, I heard the combine start up again. After watching me run through the procedures, Jackie had hopped into the seat, did everything I had done, and started it right up! I bolted into the cab of that combine and shut it off, afraid she might drive away. It scared me to death. I couldn't believe that kid. She's brilliant.

Jaime turned out to be a good basketball player. She was a real scrapper. Jaime also joined 4-H and raised a couple of sheep as projects. They were the only livestock we had on the farm, besides Rosie the dachshund. Jaime liked to help on the farm and worked with me to water the trees we planted as a windbreak. I'd give her the water hose and tell her to let it run at each tree for one minute. She'd get out her watch and have it down to the exact second! When I visit Spencer, I still enjoy taking pictures of the trees and sending them to her to show her how big they've grown. Jaime spent more hours as a young girl helping me on the farm than everyone else put together. She was always such a delightful, obedient kid.

Before we left Seattle, Jaime had asked for a puppy. So, one Saturday, we went to the pet shop at the mall and she fell in love with a little red Dachshund named Rosie. I always thought they were kind of ugly dogs, but Rosie was the sweetest thing you'd ever want to meet and we all adored her.

That first night, we told Jaime that Rosie would need to be housebroken.

"That's OK," Jaime said. "We can keep her in the bathroom and I'll sleep in there with her!"

So we peeked in later that night and there was Jaime, God love her, curled up in her little sleeping bag with Rosie.

I recall one Christmas when we couldn't find Rosie anywhere. We searched and searched the hills all around our house in Seattle. Shawn had come to visit with his wife Christi and they joined in the search, too.

Finally, we gave up and came inside, where we found little Rosie in a closet. She'd been there the whole time.

At the Spencer farm, one of her favorite hiding tricks was to bury herself in a pile of leaves when I raked in the fall. Once I came into the house in panic when I couldn't find her. Kathi laughed and pointed to the leaf pile. She was right under my nose, hiding in the leaves, but I didn't see her due to my eyesight. Everybody liked to play tricks on poor Paul's eyes, including Rosie.

One of the saddest moments of our time in Spencer happened when Rosie was killed by a car on the highway in front of our house. We'd grown so attached to her. It was hard on all of us, especially Kathi.

When I was a POW, I had promised God half of my income. After we had finished renovating the house, this promise started to weigh heavily on my conscience. I had made a vow to God and I really hadn't done very much for him besides paying my tithes at church. I wanted to do something more.

The ministry of evangelist Jimmy Swaggart was at its height in those days and we watched his TV program regularly. I heard on one of his shows about a ministry called Child Care International. The previous year, it had donated 60,000 tons of wheat to South Africa to help feed hungry children. A light bulb went off in my head.

"Kath," I said, "I'll bet they're paying full price for that wheat. I'm going to get involved in that. I know I can help them."

I called numerous times and—rather naively—asked to talk to Jimmy. Of course, I didn't get very far with that.

Finally, I connected with Dave Ohlerking, the head of Child Care International. He agreed to meet with me and I paid for my own flight to see him at Jimmy Swaggart's headquarters in Baton Rouge, Louisiana.

I explained who I was and what I was up to. Dave said my idea was very admirable.

"I want to take you to meet Jimmy," he said.

Whoa, I thought. That's pretty cool. His show goes out to millions and millions of people each week and here I was a farmer from Spencer, Ohio, about to meet Jimmy Swaggart.

He knocked on the door to Jimmy's office and he called for us to come in. There he was, sitting behind his desk and wearing a pair of cowboy boots.

Dave explained why I was there.

"Great!" said Jimmy. "I want you to stay on until Sunday and give your testimony on our TV program!"

So there I was, on Jimmy Swaggart's television show, giving my testimony. It was fairly short, about five or six minutes long. I thanked the Lord for the stamina to survive my nearly eight years as a POW in Vietnam.

Dave showed me all around and I was very impressed with the entire operation, especially the school. I came home and told Kathi I had found the school I wanted the girls to attend. We made plans to rent an apartment in Baton Rouge the next year. Kathi, who as I always say, had the ability to find a job anywhere, became secretary to the dean of Jimmy Swaggart Bible College. She thrived there. I stayed home to work the farm, but frequently flew down on weekends.

Well, Jimmy's fall from grace in the late 1980s is well-known. Dave left Swaggart's ministry and started his own called Children's Cup. Years later, Dave and I would take a trip together to Vietnam to revisit some of the places I had been held during the war.

I told Kathi I thought it would be best if she parted ways with Jimmy Swaggart, too, and came back to Spencer. She disagreed, really feeling as if she had found her calling working at the college. We had a pretty good argument about it, but eventually she saw the handwriting on the wall, and Kathi and the girls returned home.

As I mentioned, I'd obtained my Ohio real estate license and put my shingle out on my milk-house-turned office. A Cleveland businessman pulled in the driveway

THE FINISHED HOUSE.

one day and pointed to the King Realty sign.

"I see your farm's for sale," he said.

"No," I replied, and explained it was a real estate business sign.

"That's too bad," he said. "I've been driving by this farm for five years and watching you turn it around. I always tell my wife, 'Someday, I'm going to own this farm.'"

Until then, selling hadn't really entered my mind. Kathi brought it up from time to time, whenever she felt someone in the community was unfriendly or treated me unfairly. I remembered helping rescue my neighbor's cows from the lagoon and how not even risking my life seemed to put a dent in the way I was treated. And to tell the truth, I had accomplished most everything I had set out to do. I was ready for a new challenge.

The house and farm looked beautiful as I showed him around. He made me an offer, but there was one problem—he didn't want the whole property. I said I would sell him the house and 135 acres, but keep the frontage along Firestone Road to will to my kids to help pay for their education. I wanted to have some resources available, since I wasn't sure what the future held for me. He agreed and we made the deal. I banked the money from the sale, thinking I would use it to buy another farm.

Kathi's oldest sister, Marlene, and her husband, Buddy, were in the tomato business in Florida. In fact, they had recently completed construction of the largest packing house in the entire state. Buddy bought tomatoes from farmers by the semi-truck load, graded them by size and color, and shipped them to stores, including Publix, which was one of the biggest grocery chains in Florida.

Sometimes during the winter, when work on the farm slowed down, I went down to help Buddy. And when I sold the farm in 1991, he offered me a full-time job.

There were only two things Kathi asked me never to do. One, was buy an ultralight aircraft. They were just becoming popular at the time we were both working for the FAA and they seemed to lead to a lot of tragic accidents.

Second, Kathi told me never go into business with Buddy.

Well, I followed her advice on the first, but not on the second.

I told Buddy I may be a farmer, but I didn't know the first thing about the tomato business. That didn't matter to him. In the produce market, there's always the temptation to make under-the-table deals. His last manager succumbed and it had cost Buddy a lot of money. He wanted someone he could trust.

"I'll teach you everything you need to know," he said.

Buddy had designs on not only being the tomato king of the Southeast, but the banana king, too. He was at work on a deal with DelMonte. Publix was expanding into Georgia and he was expanding with them. Buddy wanted me on board to run his new operation in Atlanta. I told him I'd do it for $1,000 per week—which back then was a very good salary. He agreed. Of course, I realized too late I should have told him $1,000 net after I saw all the deductions that got taken out of my pay.

I headed for Georgia and found a 6,000-square-foot house on a 600-acre lake for about $300,000. It was huge and needed work, but it had lots of possibilities. Kathi—always open for an adventure—soon followed with Jackie. I had planted the Spencer farm in wheat and flew back several times to finish that last harvest. Jaime, who had turned 16, announced she had enough of moving and wanted to live with her father, Larry, who was now in Phoenix. It was an amicable decision on all sides.

Buddy had rented a warehouse in what was called the Farmers Market. At 200 acres, it was one of the largest complexes in the country. I told Buddy I could manage his facility, but I was not a natural-born salesman. Buddy was. I could sell my own real estate, but I was not going to sell produce. No problem, he said. Someone else would handle that part of the operation.

After helping Buddy completely renovate the warehouse and tool up for business, the produce started arriving by the truckload. I soon learned that ripening bananas involved tricky timing. Picked green, they are gassed with ethylene during shipping to make them ripen. Once that process started, there was nothing you could do to stop it. Tomatoes were a bit more forgiving. If some got ripe too quickly, those tomatoes could be sorted out and sold to hog farmers for feed.

There's only a short window of opportunity to move produce through a warehouse before it becomes worthless, which can be very stressful. We were constantly inundated with shipments. Once, when things weren't moving fast enough, Buddy chided me, saying, "You need to sell more!"

THE FARMSTEAD WITH A NEW WIND BREAK.

I reminded him I was not there to hawk bananas and tomatoes. If they weren't moving as quickly as he liked, then he needed to hire more sales people. Buddy said he couldn't afford it, but continued to expand.

To simplify things, Publix asked Buddy if he could distribute other produce coming through the Farmers Market. Say another company was in the garlic business. We'd buy the garlic from them, ship it on to the grocery, and bill Publix a handling charge in addition to the cost of the garlic. Since it was a new venture, we agreed on a charge of something like 30 cents per flat, with the mutual understanding we would negotiate a higher price if there was more to the process than we expected. Publix agreed.

And as it turned out, 30 cents per flat wasn't nearly enough to pay for the labor and logistics of handling a whole new array of produce. When I told Buddy, he instructed me to jump our fee to $6 per flat.

"You can't do that," I protested. "That's not what we agreed on. All we have to do is talk to them and they'll be fair with us."

"Just do it," he said.

"No," I insisted. I'm not going to do something that's unethical."

A short time later, Buddy fired me. And he didn't even confront me himself. He sent a young salesman to do it for him.

So, here we were in a 6,000-square-foot house and me without a job. Nevertheless, it was one of the happiest days of my life. I told Kathi I was sick of looking at tomatoes all day and my back hurt from moving case after case from one truck to another. And if I had to get fired, I was glad it was for standing up and doing the right thing.

I didn't talk to Buddy for years after that. At one point, Kathi found out her sister Marlene needed a car. We had a 1989 Honda Accord with 313,000 miles on it. Even though it was mechanically perfect, right down to brand-new tires, I couldn't find anyone to buy it with that kind of mileage.

"Let's give it to Marlene," I said.

So, we met them and gave them the car. I don't think I'll be going into business with Buddy again anytime soon, but we've managed to be friends.

High Plains Farming

An opportunity arose to sell the remaining land in Spencer to a developer for $250,000. It has never been my desire to see prime farmland sold for houses, but considering my current circumstances, I reluctantly accepted. I regret not offering it to Glenn, who had bought the rest of the farm. I still need to apologize for not extending the courtesy of talking with him about it first.

It took about six or eight months to sell our big albatross of a house in Georgia. In the meantime, I called Darris Cumming, a Colorado real estate broker who specialized in farms and ranches. Darris was based in Julesburg, on the old Pony Express route, in the extreme northeast corner of the state.

When I was with the Air Force Academy, I fell in love with Colorado and longed to own ground there. I wanted to buy a wheat farm. Even when I didn't have any money, I traveled all over the state, scouting out possible locations. My dream was to work the farm in the summer, then travel to South America to help build churches in the winter. I learned the best wheat-producing areas were the counties in the northeast corner of the state.

I first met Darris in 1973 and brought Dad along as Darris showed me properties. I knew Dad would enjoy seeing that flat wheat country. I remember my father said to Darris, "Now, Mr. Cumming, you treat this boy fairly!" It was one of the few times I ever heard Dad stick up for me.

I called Darris and asked if he had any land for sale. He told me he'd sold more in the last six months than he had in the last six years. It seemed to be one of those stretches where older land owners were passing away and families were looking to sell.

"Well, I'm ready to start buying," I told him.

I went out there to meet with Darris in 1992. In the span of about 18 months, I put 16 quarters together. That's almost 2,500 acres—which is just about unheard of. You can't simply go out and buy a big chunk of land like that. It just doesn't come available because farmers are established in their operations. You have to buy a piece here and a piece there. I just happened to be buying in the right place at the right time.

I told Darris I needed a good bank for my western enterprise and he recommended Adams Bank & Trust of Ogallola, NE. They have been so good to me over the years and I still deal with them decades later.

Kathi and I flew out together to look at houses, but couldn't find anything we liked. One day, Darris sent us a picture of a house in Julesburg that had just come on the market.

"Let's just buy it and step out on faith," Kathi said.

"OK, I'm sport," I said.

Although it was small, it turned out to be one of the best houses we ever owned. It was right across from the local public school, where Jackie would attend.

I had been having problems with my back. During one of my physical rehabilitation sessions, I met Richard Rhoades. He was recovering from surgery for prostate cancer and we became the best of friends. We still are.

What Dave Aikman did for me in Ohio—helping me and teaching me about modern farming— Richard did for me in Colorado and Nebraska.

Out on the plains, dry land farming, as it's called, is totally different from farming in Ohio. Every part of the operation is geared toward disturbing the soil as little as possible to conserve moisture. You treat the ground as if it's never going to rain again. There, you may get 12 to 14 inches of rain per year. In Ohio, rainfall may be 33 to 35 inches. That's why the Great Plains are best suited for growing small grains. You may only plant sections every other year to conserve enough moisture to produce a crop, so you had to have a lot of land to make it work.

Jackie, who had a very quiet personality, told us about a child at school who was bullying her. One day I saw Jackie walking home with her head hung down, I knew she'd had a bad day and it just broke my heart.

Several of our new friends recommended a school in Big Springs, Nebraska, which was a few miles up the road, just across the state line. We visited the school and Kathi liked it. Rather than put Kathi in the position of doing a lot of driving again,

HIGH PLAINS WHEAT PLANTING

we decided to find a house there. The one we found was in need of major remodeling, on top of the fact it had been filled with cats and smelled to high heaven. Learning a new way of farming was going to take a lot of my time, so Kathi offered to coordinate the plumbers, roofers, cement contractors, carpenters and electricians involved in re-doing the house.

I was afraid she didn't quite know what she was in for. And sure enough, she fired the first contractor on his first day on the job.

"I didn't like the way he worked!" she exclaimed.

As I said when we lived in Spencer, when you're new in town, it's difficult to find good contractors and even harder to get on their job list, because they are highly sought after. But, Kathi and I worked together and managed to get the renovation project moving forward.

However, even after the work was complete, we just couldn't get comfortable there. So, we bought a ranch-style house at auction. It had a fantastic design; although we learned too late it had mold issues, which we eventually corrected.

It felt like a new life and a new start for all of us. To a boy from Ohio, where farms are measured in the hundreds of acres, learning to farm on the Plains where operations are measured in the thousands of acres, was very exciting to me. My dad always was in love with the West and I guess I was, too, from the days when Brother Steinberg visited our Lafayette farm and told stories about his native Kansas and fields so big you could only make two rounds on them per day.

When I was in geography class at Spencer High School, my teacher Sid Sooy would talk about the Ukraine as "The Breadbasket of Europe." He showed us pictures of the seemingly endless plateaus of wheat. My schoolmate Dave Reisinger and I talked about farming like that some day. Now was my chance to finally do it in the breadbasket of America.

At about 8 years old, Jackie was really coming into her own as a musician. We bought her a nice piano and she won all sorts of awards for her playing abilities. Recognizing her potential, the school band director told her he was in need of a French horn player. Knowing Jackie had a gift for music, he asked her if she would give it a try. We learned there were two types of French horns, a single and a double. The band teacher told her she could learn to play the double French horn, even though it was more difficult. The problem was the school didn't have an instrument to loan her. We'd have to find one for Jackie to play. So we began to look.

Wheat-planting time was mid-September. I'd bought a 60-foot-wide wheat drill and was on the tractor in the midst of planting when my cell phone rang. It was the owner of a music store in a town about 15 miles east.

"Are you sitting down?" the music store owner asked.

"Yes, sir, I am," I replied. "I'm planting wheat!"

"A new double French horn is going to be $2,500," he said.

I stopped the tractor which is not good to do because it generally leaves a gap in the seeding when you start it up again. I was expecting it to cost $400 to $500, so this took a few moments to digest. But in the end, I told him to go ahead and order it. Jackie was a talented musician and I wanted her to have every opportunity we could provide. We still have that double French horn.

Jackie later began attending a Mennonite school in Grant, about 40 miles south of Big Springs. It was a private school Kathi had heard about. Again, it put her in the position of spending almost four hours of her day driving Jackie back and forth. Finally, Kathi decided it would be simpler for her just to stay at the school and work there as a volunteer. And that's what she did the next two years or so. It was a small school and Kathi's willingness to help was appreciated.

Some 640 acres of the land I farmed was in two equal pieces on either side of a major north-south highway that ran through Julesberg. Truckers would travel that highway all the way from Houston to Canada. The land, which was gently rolling, included an abandoned Sears and Roebuck mail order house. I had hoped to restore it, but learned it was too far gone to save.

It wasn't the best land, but I decided these two parcels were good candidates for terracing to help conserve the soil's moisture. It would allow the land to grow a lot more wheat, but the trade-off was terraces made it more challenging to plant and harvest.

Things were moving along well until about 1995 when I began to have frequent nosebleeds. A sinus doctor told me it was due to the dry climate which was ironic, he said. Many people find a drier environment clears up their sinus problems. I turned out to be the opposite. The doctor suggested I would function better in a climate that had more moisture in the air.

Great, I said. Just when we were all feeling settled into our new life.

I phoned a friend back in Ohio, Roger Shopbell, who was owner of a liquid fertilizer company in Ashland, and asked him to keep an eye open for an 800- to 1,000-acre farm in Marion or Van Wert or another of the state's good agricultural counties.

I didn't hear anything back from Roger for a year. The fall of 1996 turned out to be a very wet fall in Nebraska and Colorado, pushing wheat-planting time into late-September. It was rain, rain, rain. Roger called to say one of his salesmen had seen a farm for sale near Wilmington, Ohio, in the southwest corner of the state. It was 628 acres, all in one piece.

Kathi and I were having coffee on a Saturday morning and she encouraged me to go have a look at the farm.

Of course, there was still plenty of Ohio in my blood. Despite my travels, it was where I was born and raised. My roots were there and it would always feel like home. Yet, it was an agonizing decision. I had gotten the hang of dry land farming. Overall, the 2,500 acres I put together had turned out to be very productive ground. If the good Lord saw fit to give us a decent crop this season, we would be out of debt. The prospect of starting all over again was difficult for me to swallow.

"I don't know. I don't know," I told Kathi.

"Yes, but your health comes first," she said. "You should at least check it out."

"You really think I should go?" I asked.

"Yes," Kathi said. "Besides, the ground is so wet here you know you aren't going to be able to get into the fields for a week."

It was still about 9 a.m. when I decided to go. Within an hour, I was packed and on the road to Ohio in my 1989 Honda. Kathi gave me a whole list of things to investigate in Wilmington—the library, the churches and the schools.

"I'll be back in a week," I said.

I found Wilmington on the map and drove straight through, arriving Sunday morning. I pulled into the driveway of the farm and immediately disliked everything I saw. The fields looked terrible. It had been a bad year and the tenant who had rented the land was a poor farmer on top of it.

I took a bunch of pictures, turned around, and drove back home.

"What in the world are you doing back here so soon?" Kathi asked.

I proceeded to list everything that was wrong with the farm in Wilmington. It had small fields—which I didn't think I could ever get used to again after farming out West. It was run down and I was tired of fixing places up.

Eventually, the weather in Colorado dried up enough for me to get the wheat in. Later that season, while cleaning up some old barbed wire in one of the fields, I fell and tore my rotator cuff. Kathi came and picked me up and I ended up at a surgeon's office in Colorado Springs recommended to me by the Air Force Academy. The doctor sewed me up, but my arm was in a sling for some time, which made planting that fall an adventure.

WILMINGTON, OHIO, FARM

I hired a kid to help me load the seed into the grain drill and I planted 1,600 acres of wheat driving the tractor with one hand.

The place in Wilmington remained on my mind and Kathi encouraged me not to give up on the idea of buying it. Even if the land and the set-up wasn't what I wanted, its location was perfect. The city of Wilmington, which was the county seat, was nearby. The medical center at Wright-Patterson Air Force Base and the Cincinnati International Airport both were just a short drive away.

I had told my real estate broker Darris I was thinking about moving, but I couldn't buy the place in Wilmington unless I could sell the one in Julesburg.

He said, "I have 12 of your 16 quarters sold right now!"

One of my neighbors had placed a standing order with Darris. He wanted to own 100 quarters in his lifetime. My 12 would put him at 101. God has blessed me to have been able to get top market value for every farm I have ever sold and this land was no exception. I paid some $400 per acre and sold it for about $600 per acre. I also received one-third of the income from the wheat crop that was in the ground when I sold it.

CHAPTER 26

The Wilmington farm was due to go on the auction block Oct. 16, 1996. I finished planting wheat and decided to drive to Ohio to attend the auction. I made sure I got there a couple of days early to check out the house and the community. I did not want a repeat of our experience of discovering mold after we'd bought our current house. Unfortunately, the Wilmington house still was occupied by renters and the auctioneer said I couldn't go inside.

The auction took place underneath a tree outside the house. It was between me and another prospective buyer in open bidding. He was on his telephone the whole time. The auctioneer kept halting the bidding to give the man time to consult with whoever he was talking to, which I found irritating.

I got the farm for $1.7 million. It took a long time for that price tag to sink in. I couldn't believe an old farm boy from Spencer, Ohio, had just spent that much money. My dad would have been flabbergasted!

I hired a local pilot to fly me over the farm so that I could get a good feel for it. The renter still had corn in the fields and aircraft rules forbade the pilot to fly below 1,000 feet, so I didn't get as good a look at it as I wanted. Only when I shipped one of my big tractors to Ohio to do fall tillage did I discover how badly the land had been neglected. Once again, I had bought a farm with multiple tile blowouts and terrible erosion. I was so angry. I couldn't believe I was selling 2,500 acres of really good ground in Nebraska and Colorado to buy 628 acres of neglected land in southern Ohio.

And the fields were only the beginning.

SETTLING in SOUTHWEST OHIO

The renters living in the Wilmington farmhouse had come outside for the auction. When it was over, I asked them if I could take a look inside the ranch-style home. They agreed. The house smelled musty and there was mold a quarter-of-an-inch thick growing in the bathroom. I was furious with the auctioneer for refusing to let me see the house before I bought it. I wouldn't speak to him when Kathi and I flew back later to close on the property. As it happened, there was a second home on the property, a converted one-room schoolhouse. It was in better shape than the farmhouse, so we decided to remodel it first while we worked to rid the other house of mold and make it livable again.

My local John Deere dealer in Colorado connected me with the company that shipped equipment for him and I arranged to have my year-old tractor, an antique Farmall H and a truck hauled to Ohio.

That winter, I set to work repairing the more than 60 tile blowouts throughout the farm. I heard about an excavator named Roger King and hired him to bring in a backhoe and do the digging.

Before we even got into the fields, the first thing we did was install drainage tile around the foundation of the house. There was no basement under the home, only a crawl space. Due to poor construction and a lack of drainage, the water had been pouring into that crawl space for 20 or 30 years.

We trenched all the way around the house below the footer, installed perforated tile, tied in the downspouts with solid tile, filled the trench with gravel, and drained the whole thing to a nearby creek. Just before we poured in the gravel, I told Roger to poke a hole through the foundation wall. The water poured out.

When I first came to Wilmington, I was befriended by an AGCO farm equipment dealer named John Mayer. He traveled extensively to Europe and South America where he sold used equipment that was too small for American agriculture, but perfect for farming operations in other countries.

John knew the ranch house and old brick schoolhouse on my farm needed a lot of work. Because he was recently divorced and spent so much time traveling, his own home was often empty. Kathi and Jackie had not yet made the move to Ohio, so John invited me to stay at his house while I worked on the farm. I accepted, but only on the condition I paid my way. He agreed and I stayed there for a couple of months while the work on the schoolhouse moved along.

It was a former one-room schoolhouse with sagging floors and a crawl space underneath. It had been remodeled into a two-bedroom home with a kitchen and a small living room. A local plumber named Steve Brown came in and installed all new plumbing and heating systems. We jacked up the floors and remodeled the bathroom. I discovered the water wasn't very good, so I had a new well drilled.

In March of 1997, I received a call from the 560th Tactical Fighter Training Wing at Randolph Air Force Base near San Antonio, Texas. I had never received what was called my Final Flight after my retirement from the Air Force. They had called to schedule it two years earlier, but it was during my return trip to Vietnam, so I had asked to reschedule.

Just like its name suggests, the Final Flight program gave retiring Air Force personnel one last opportunity to fly. However, when I first came home after my time as a POW and learned I wouldn't be allowed to be a fighter pilot again, I was so disappointed I was in no mood to take the Air Force up on its offer. Apparently, in checking their records, they realized I had never had my Final Flight and got in contact with me. Enough time had passed that I welcomed the opportunity to fly again.

I flew down to Randolph and was met there by Kathi and Jackie who flew down from Nebraska. I hadn't seen them in what seemed like forever. While recovering from my rotator cuff surgery, I had gained a lot of weight. Living by myself in Wilmington, working like a dog and not eating much, I had lost almost 30 pounds. Jackie, now about 11 years old, gave me a big hug and said, "I can get my arms around Daddy!"

I also invited my son Shawn and his family, as well as John Mayer and his girlfriend Carol, whom he later would marry. The Air Force intended to put me and my family in the VIP suites, and John in the Visiting Officers Quarters. I said no way. If John couldn't be in the VIP, I wouldn't stay there, either. They relented and let him stay with us. We all had a wonderful time together.

Jackie's teacher had suggested she keep a journal about her trip to San Antonio and my Final Flight. She was cute running around with her notebook writing everything down. Jackie was so busy with her head bent down taking careful notes I think she missed half of what was going on! John was enthralled with the whole thing and took lots of pictures.

There was a preflight briefing, just like the old days, and I was taken through a refresher course on how to use the oxygen system and the ejection seat. The plane was a T-38, which is a tandem trainer. I got into a flight suit and strapped in with a major, who was an Air Force Academy graduate.

I had not had my hands on the stick of an airplane since the day I was shot down in 1965. I asked the major if I could place my hands on the stick just to feel the movement of it as he took off. He said that would be fine.

As we were rolling down the runway, almost ready to take off, I said, "Hey, how about letting me try to take off?"

"OK," he said, "but I'm keeping my hand on the stick!"

FINAL FLIGHT

The T-38 was quite a bit lighter than the F-4 I had flown in Vietnam, so it bobbled around a little on me, but I soon had the feel for it and we lifted off.

"That was pretty good!" the major said and let me have the controls almost 98 percent of the flight.

We were in a flight of four aircraft and our airplane was flying position No. 2 – just like I did in Vietnam with my old larger-than-life flight commander, Caspar Sharpless Bierman.

If the weather was good, the plan was to make a fly-by over the base where family and friends could see us. We were to fly in what's called the Missing Man Formation. As the aircraft fly in together, one pulls up to create a hole in the formation, symbolizing a pilot who had been shot down or killed. Unfortunately, the only thing that wasn't good about the whole day was the weather and we were not able to perform the fly-by.

We were in the air for about 45 minutes. I felt the same sense of exhilaration I felt the first time I ever flew in an airplane all those years ago at Ohio State. Yet, I also felt a twinge of sadness that my flying career had been cut short when I was shot down.

Finally, it was time to land. We were instructed to come down in pairs.

"Is this a formation landing?" I asked the major.

"I don't know," he said. "They didn't brief us on this."

The weather was awfully thick.

"Do you think I can land it?" I asked.

"Why don't you try," the major said. "You're doing pretty well so far. I'll keep my hand on the stick and throttle."

Now in the F-4, as soon as your wheels touched down, you lowered the nose of the plane, popped the drag chute, and got on the brakes. That gave you the most amount of drag to slow the plane.

Well, the T-38 had aerodynamic braking. The plane was designed to slow down with the nose held up. We hadn't briefed on any of this.

So we came down with the lead aircraft and as soon as I dropped the nose of the T-38, we surged ahead of the lead plane. A big no-no when it comes to flight protocol! The No. 2 plane is never supposed to go ahead of No. 1. There must have been hundreds of people watching us.

"Oh, no!" the major said. He pulled back on the stick to bring the nose up, slowing the plane enough to let the lead aircraft go by us. "We're going to get chewed out for sure!"

Everyone would definitely know it was me landing the plane, not the major. But no one said a word.

Ironically, Shawn and Kathi both had cameras—and both missed my landing.

"It's OK," Kathi told him. "I'll just take a picture of the No. 3 and 4 planes coming in and tell Paul it's him landing."

"Oh, no," Shawn said. "Dad will know by the tail numbers that it wasn't him!"

That night we had a "dining-in" which was a big, formal dinner in full uniform. It was only supposed to be for military people, but the major found a suit for Shawn and sneaked him in.

"I can't believe your dad," the major told my son. "I'll take his word for it that he hasn't had his hands on a stick in all this time, but he flies like it was only a couple of years ago."

Other than the fact the plane felt so much lighter, it was like riding a bike—once you learn how, you never forget. Flying was as instinctive for me as ever.

CHAPTER 27

It was back to reality. Kathi and Jackie flew back to Nebraska and I continued to work on the Ohio farm. Our plan was to complete the schoolhouse renovation by the time Jackie finished the school year, and she and Kathi would join me in Wilmington. Roger, the excavator, continued to help me fix the blowouts and gullies.

Now, I always had good fortune with John Deere equipment, but the problem was I was living with a guy who was always trying to sell me on AGCO tractors and planters. It's a wholly U.S-owned company, like John Deere, and its lines included Allis Chalmers, Massey-Harris, White and Oliver. They bought out a lot of short-line equipment companies like Sunflower Tillage and Hesston Balers.

Somewhat reluctantly, I bought a brand-new White six-row planter and it gave me no end of problems. I must have had half a dozen service calls on it.

However, John gave me another recommendation that turned out to be one of the best I ever received. I told him I was in need of a young hired man. John suggested I get in touch with Monte Anderson, who was dean of agriculture at Wilmington College. Monte would put out a notice to students that I was looking for help.

The next day, I received a call from a student named Chris Maxwell, who would become the best hired man I ever had. He was a farm boy and was eager to learn. We met at Burger King and I hired him on the spot. Chris already had excellent mechanical skills. He could weld and do just about any job on the farm.

Years later, he told me he learned more when he was working for me than he learned in college. To me, that's the highest compliment any farmer could receive.

I hired Chris to do the tillage while I ran the planter, the planter that gave me fits. He'd see me make a couple of rounds, then stop. Chris would stop what he was doing and come over to help.

"What's wrong, Mr. Paul?" he'd ask.

It was always this or that and Chris would help figure it out. He must have done that a dozen times in the course of the planting season. In the end, I think John found another buyer for that planter and I went back to the green equipment that's always done me well.

Within a couple of years, we put all new grass waterways on that farm. It's one of the most difficult jobs to do and do correctly. They are important components for good farm drainage and help check erosion.

Generally you install waterways in July or August when the weather is dry. You sculpt the ground, plant grass seed, cover it in straw, and hope for a gentle rain to sprout the seeds. Sometimes you get a gully-washer that wipes out all your work. Then you have to re-shape it, re-seed it, re-straw it.

Waterways have to be nicely sculpted so when you come to one during planting, you just lift the planter over the grass, drop the tractor down a gear, then lower the planter on the other side and resume planting, all in one smooth motion. The waterways on that farm turned out to be as beautiful as any lawn.

Headquarters

There was a mile-and-a-half-long creek that meandered through the farm. It was all grown up with trees. We cleaned out the trees and straightened the creek. We had piles of brush that were as big as a house, which we burned and buried.

The farm came with a grain dryer similar to one I had in Spencer, which always gave me trouble. I did away with that and we built a brand-new 50,000-bushel grain bin, coupled with a new dryer. It was a first-class operation.

I soon was able to buy bigger equipment and owned everything I needed, except for a combine. That ended up being a blessing, because Jeff Miller from Valley City in Medina County would bring his combine down and do my harvest. I was enough farther south that he could get into my fields a couple of weeks earlier than he could get into his own. He'd finish my harvest and I'd write him a check as he pulled out of the driveway. The check was enough to make his annual payment on his combine. Jeff and I did that for about three years and it worked out very well for both of us.

Kathi, Jackie, and I moved into the remodeled ranch house and we enjoyed pretty good yields on that farm. I got a John Deere diesel lawn mower that Jackie used to mow the grass.

Now as I look back, I recognize it must have been hard on her to move as often as we did and change schools over and over. Yet, she never, ever complained. It's bothered me over the years and later when Jackie was grown, I apologized to her for any hardship it caused her.

Kathi and I moved 10 times in a span of about 30 years. That's probably about the average for a military family during the course of a career. It all stems back to the devastating investment loss I suffered in the Denver office building fiasco years ago. Since I couldn't work at an office job, buying and selling farms was the only way I knew I could rebuild my finances and provide for my family.

I was able to buy another 130 acres on the other side of Wilmington. It was in need of work, so we installed a drainage system and fixed it all up. It had a nice woods right in the middle of it and I planned to build Kathi a house there. We'd lived in nice homes back in Colorado, but after a string of fixer-uppers, she deserved a brand-new house. I trimmed up the woods and built a nice big pond.

Then one Sunday in the winter of 2000, I was relaxing at home, watching a NASCAR race on TV. The ranch house at the farm had a long driveway and I noticed someone pull in, driving a beat-up Dodge pick-up truck. The truck turned around and drove off, so I didn't think anything of it.

A short time later, as I became engrossed in watching the race, there was a knock at the door. I opened it and almost before the man introduced himself, I knew what he did for a living. He was a hog farmer. Let's just say there's a certain smell that gets into the clothes of farmers who spend their days working with pigs.

His name was Dave Wurzelbacher and he was interested in buying the farm.

I started laughing.

As with the farm in Spencer, there was no for sale sign in the yard. I had just spent four years in Wilmington working my tail off to restore the fields, refurbish the houses, and get to full production. I had been able to gradually upgrade my equipment to the point I had a whole line of new John Deere tractors and implements in my machine sheds.

I had casually told a real estate agent in Washington Courthouse, Paul McClish, that if he ever had a big, out-of-state buyer come along and inquire about land, to let me know. But otherwise, I wasn't interested in selling and politely said so to Dave. I was 65 years old and looking forward to settling down.

He said, "Would you mind showing me around anyway?"

I agreed.

There was a driveway that ran the whole length of the farm. It was kind of a wet, misty day, and we got in my pick-up and drove back to look at the farm. It seemed so beautiful to me. The land "laid nice," as farmers say, with its gently rolling hills. It looked good to Dave, too.

"Tell me," he said. "What do you want for it?"

"I don't do business on Sundays," I replied. "Let me think about it and I'll get back to you on Monday."

I called him the next day and told him I'd take $2,050,000 for the farm. I added the $50,000 just on the off chance the Washington Courthouse agent had given Dave my name and I would need to pay him a commission.

"I'll call you Thursday and let you know," Dave said.

As promised, on Thursday, my phone rang.

"When do you want to move?" asked Dave.

Truthfully, I didn't want to move! I told Dave I was not going to sell unless I could reinvest in another farm. And since I hadn't been looking, I had no idea what was out there that would interest me.

Dave's attorney drew up an agreement that was contingent on me finding another property. I'd paid $1,670,000 for the Wilmington farm and invested $300,000 to $400,000 in it over the past four years, so I really wasn't making any money on the deal. But, I guess I still had that drive inside to want to trade up to a bigger and better operation.

The only place I loved as much as Ohio was Colorado. So I phoned my old friend Darris Cumming back in Julesburg and told him what I'd gotten myself into. I was interested in farming in Colorado again, but I wanted an irrigated operation this time. I wasn't anxious to get back into dry land farming.

"I wondered when you were going to get smart!" Darris said with a laugh.

He told me a landowner could make more money renting out an irrigated farm than he could by operating a dry land farm himself. Darris said he would start looking.

In late January, I decided to drive to Colorado and see some prospective farms for myself. Obviously, access to water is the whole key to irrigated farming, and I had learned there were wide variations in water quantity and quality in the high plains.

My mom was living about 30 miles east of Colorado Springs and I stopped to visit her.

"What in the world are you doing back in Colorado?" she asked.

"Looking for land," I told her.

"You're never happy, are you?" she asked, though it was more of a statement than a question. "Why don't you keep what you have? It's time for you to settle down. Do you know how old you are?"

There was no arguing with Mom, especially when I was asking myself the same questions.

I called up my old friend Linly Stum, whom my son Shawn lived with and worked for during his senior year of high school, and told him what I was looking for.

Linly and his family are wonderful people and always welcomed me with open arms. I went to visit them and Linly began calling around to real estate agent friends in southern Colorado and Kansas. We looked at a lot of farms, but no luck.

"If I can't buy something that's really choice land, I'm not buying," I said. I wasn't about to invest in a marginal operation.

I also got in touch with Richard Rhodes who had taught me how to dry land farm when we lived in Big Springs. On Feb. 11, on my way to see Richard, I ran into a brutal snowstorm. It was so bad the state patrol closed the roads. I holed up in a motel and called Kathi, who reminded me the next day was the anniversary of my release as a POW. I was so focused on my search for a farm, I'd forgotten all about it. Kathi told me I should treat myself to a big breakfast in the morning to celebrate, which I did.

When I was able to get back on the road, I decided to stop at a John Deere dealership in Holyoke, south of Julesburg, to visit Perry Dutton—a friend there I had witnessed to about the Lord. As we talked over lunch, he asked me what I was doing back in Colorado. It was a popular question!

"I'm glad you asked," I said.

Holyoke was choice farm country. I told Perry I was looking to buy eight or ten quarters. One quarter equals about 160 acres.

Perry just laughed.

"You're lucky if one or two per year go on the market in this county," he said. "And they're usually marginal at best."

Well, all I can do is try, I told him.

Throughout this entire trip, I prayed, "Lord, if this is to be, I want you to open the door wide so that I can walk right through it and know what I'm supposed to do. If the door doesn't open for me, then I will be at peace with that, too."

I drove on up toward our old home of Big Springs, Nebraska, just across the Colorado border. It was getting late, so I called Richard and told him I'd book into a motel for the night and see him the next day.

As I unlocked the door to my room, I heard the telephone ringing inside. I dropped my bags and hurried to answer. It was Kathi.

"How did you know I was here?" I asked. "I had planned to stay with Richard."

"Ah," she said, teasing. "You can't keep any secrets from me!"

As it turned out, Perry had called my home number in Wilmington and told Kathi he needed to speak to me immediately. She called Richard, who told her where I was.

I called Perry right away.

"You are the luckiest guy I've ever known in my life!" he said.

Half an hour after I left, a real estate agent walked into the dealership and told Perry he'd just listed eight of the best quarters in the entire county. In fact, it was land Perry used to own.

I'd planned to head home to Ohio the next day, but I asked Perry if he could show me the irrigated farms if I turned around and came back to Holyoke. He was running a multi-state used equipment auction the next day and his time was limited, but he graciously agreed to give me a quick tour of the property.

It was perfect—flat, beautiful, with excellent water. I knew I had to buy it.

I returned home, worked out a contract with the seller, and put the dominos in motion. Dave was selling 320 acres north of Cincinnati to a developer to buy my 628 acres, which I was selling to buy 1,280 acres in Colorado.

A problem with one of the property surveys on Dave's end delayed closing on the sale of my farm for weeks. When the landowner I was buying from in Colorado threatened to void our contract, I begged him to reconsider. He agreed—for another $50,000. I told him I'd ante up a non-refundable payment of $50,000, but only if it was applied to the purchase price. I didn't like taking that risk on circumstances outside my control, but it bought us enough time to get the deal done.

COLORADO HIGH PLAINS—
2,500 ACRES OF IRRIGATED LAND.

Now I had all this practically brand new John Deere farm equipment to do something with. I didn't want to have an auction, so I made an offer to Dave. I'd sell the farm to him, if he agreed to lease everything back to me for five years. We settled on a price and he accepted.

I was farming the 760 or so acres in Wilmington and flying out to Colorado every month for a week at a time to farm out there. So much for slowing down.

A neighbor of mine owned a diesel Volkswagen Beetle that got 50 mpg. That sounded pretty good to me, knowing I'd likely be doing some long-distance driving between the two farms. Additionally, I thought a Beetle would make a good car for Jackie to drive to school when she turned 16 in about a year. I decided it would be a surprise for her.

CHAPTER 27

Kathi and I picked up Jackie at school. Instead of following our customary route home, we headed toward the VW dealership in Dayton. She's a smart kid, so she knew right away something was up.

"All right, guys," she said. "What's going on here?"

"We're just taking a little trip," I said.

Jackie tried to guess where we were going, but never would've had a reason to think we were going to buy her a car.

Once on a trip to Colorado Springs, Jackie had spotted a light-green car that she really liked, so that was the color we picked out. I made arrangements with the salesman to have the Beetle sitting in the middle of the showroom with a big sign that read, "Hello, Jackie!"

When she saw it, her mouth dropped open.

"This is your car, baby!" said the salesman.

She just couldn't believe it. It was a lot of fun.

One of the next times I was due to head back out to Colorado, I decided to take the Bug. Now, there's a reason I've owned 15 Hondas in my lifetime. There's just something about the design of the seat that fits my injured back.

I got as far as the Indiana border in the Volkswagen before my back really started to hurt. There was no way I could drive another thousand miles that way.

So, I turned around and drove all the way back to Wilmington. I pulled in the driveway, hopped out of the VW and put my bags into the Honda.

Kathi came outside.

"I knew you'd be back!" she said.

I gave her a kiss, started the Honda, and headed off again.

Looking back over my life, I have always thrived on learning new things whether it was working my way up through pilot training or learning new ways of farming. I looked forward to the challenge of learning the ins and outs of irrigated farming.

The new farm started at the Colorado-Nebraska state line. It went west two miles and north two miles. When its wells were first drilled, the records showed they produced 3,000 gallons of water per minute. Needless to say, they were terrific wells. Some of them had pumps with electric motors as big as 150-horsepower. We rebuilt the pumps and motors as needed. The shafts had to be perfectly aligned for them to function correctly. Over the years, people had thrown trash around the bases where the long sprinkler arms pivoted. It looked like a junk yard.

At each pivot point, there was an oil reservoir that dripped oil down on the bushings to keep them lubricated. Oftentimes, when I went out to look at them, the reservoir would be dry, which is hard on the machinery. I ended up installing five-gallon oil systems on some of the pivots to make sure they stayed in good condition.

My deal with the seller was that he would farm the land the coming season. I decided I was going to find a tenant the next year who would do his part to help maintain the equipment. I did some asking around and worked out a deal with a good farmer named Larry Weber.

"Larry," I told him, "you don't know much about me, but I'll tell you this. We're going to clean this pigpen up."

I told Larry I'd pay to have all the junk hauled away. Then, around the base of each pivot, we would lay down a nice bed of gravel so that it looked neat and orderly.

The giant sprinkler arms roll on tires, just like automobiles. One of the pivots kept getting stuck. When I went to investigate, I discovered the brand new tires I had installed on the irrigation system had been switched out with old, bald tires. In fact, I noticed some things were missing from the farm's grain storage system, too.

I had reason to believe the farm's former owner was the culprit. I contacted my attorney. It so happened he worked as a visiting judge in that county and couldn't take the case. Instead, he advised me to represent myself in small claims court.

Never having done anything like that before, I was hesitant.

"All you've got to do is tell the truth," he told me.

I decided to give it a try, but I wanted at least one friendly face in the audience behind me. I called up my old friend Richard.

"I need some moral support," I told him. "Would you come down and just sit in the gallery, please?"

And he did. Richard was the only spectator in the room.

Naturally, the former property owner hired the best lawyer in a 100-mile radius to defend him. This attorney had once won a major water-rights case before the United States Supreme Court. And I'm up against him!

Well, that high-priced lawyer went right to work, laying out his very carefully prepared case. It didn't take long for him to begin to say things that weren't right.

"That's a bunch of B.S.!" I shouted, interrupting the proceedings.

"You can't have an outburst like that," the judge told me sternly.

"I'm sorry, sir," I said.

The lawyer went right back at it. Again, I couldn't contain myself.

"That's not true!" I yelled. "You can't say that! That's a lie!"

"I'm telling you, Mr. Kari, you can't do that," the judge repeated.

Finally, it was my turn. I did what my attorney advised and told the truth.

"I'll be back with my decision in five minutes," said the judge, and he left the courtroom.

True to his word, he came right back.

"Mr. Kari, you won the case," he said.

I said to myself, *Whoa, baby.* It was about a $4,800 judgment.

These eight quarters I bought used to be what was called "flood irrigated," which is just like it sounds. They let the water in at the top of the grade and it flows down to the other end of the field. It wasn't very efficient. Leftover water collected in a pool at the lower end of the field and got pumped back. These pits made beautiful places for pheasants to hide, but they were no longer necessary and we filled them in.

The next generation of irrigation systems sprayed water up into the air, which wasn't very efficient, either, since some of the water would be lost to evaporation.

Our sprinkler system had drip lines that hung almost down to the ground. The arms pulled the lines through the crops, giving the plants a good drink of water. We rebuilt virtually every component in the system.

I had the opportunity to buy another 640 acres of good irrigated land. The soil was sandy, but had a lot of organic matter in it. We fixed up the watering system on that land, as well.

My old broker friend Darris called to tell me about 540 acres next to the Julesburg Airport. It lay right in the Platte River Valley between the Union Pacific Railroad line and Interstate 76. The soil was what was known as sugar sand, which tended to blow around. It didn't sound promising.

"You can buy it for the right price," Darris said.

So, after some contemplation, I bought that, too. The irrigation system needed a lot of work because all that grit was awfully hard on the plumbing. We also installed an electronic monitoring system so that my renter, Gill Anderson, who planted it all to alfalfa, could look on his computer at home and tell where each pivot was and how much water the crops were receiving.

The irrigation system had what's called an end gun on the end of the arms. It literally shoots water 100 feet to 150 feet from the end of the arms to reach crops outside the pivot circle.

Well, there was a train going by every couple of minutes on the Union Pacific line. It was a busy track. One day, we turned the irrigation system on and the end gun wasn't adjusted right. It was shooting water right at the railroad track and it nailed the train operator through the open windows of the locomotive! As you might imagine, the engineer was some kind of P.O.'d.

Now, I was a brand-new landowner in the area. My renter was brand-new. You wouldn't think anyone would have any idea who we were. Still, within 15 minutes of the engineer getting wet, my phone rang. It was Union Pacific. I'm telling you, they must be just below God, because they know everything.

"If you don't shut that thing off, we're shutting it down *permanently*," they said.

Believe me, we got that thing adjusted correctly and set it up so that it wouldn't happen again.

I split my time between Colorado and Ohio, where we continued to rent the Wilmington farm from the fellow I'd sold it to. We really loved the area. We attended a great church and had a lot of friends in the community. We decided to look for a house and the real estate agent we were working with showed Kathi what seemed like about every home in the county.

Eventually, she found a house she liked in a new development called Sycamore Glen. Houses were still going up there and I offered to look into building one. Kathi thought a new one would be too expensive. I insisted and we bought a lot. But then we both had second thoughts.

Kathi pointed out that I had always lived an active life. She didn't think I'd be happy in a development and worried about my health if I retired and didn't have some kind of farm work to do every day. Kathi was right.

Ironically, I ended up throwing in a little extra cash and trading that lot to a farmer I knew named Bobby Lucas for a slightly used John Deere tractor. I was looking for something to pull a 12-row planter, but this tractor ended up not quite fitting the bill. I went to the John Deere dealer a week later and traded it in on one just a little bigger—an 8100 with low hours to go with the John Deere 8400 tractor I already had.

By the way, we had met a couple who was building a house in the Sycamore Glen development, Don and Caroline Blythe. Both were retired GS-15 government employees from the U.S. Department of Agriculture. They picked Wilmington because it was the midpoint between their son's home and their daughter's home. They invited me in to see the house. It was a beautiful home and we became friends.

Even though we had wavered on buying a house there, I guess it was still somehow in the back of my mind. Kathi's too.

One day, Kathi told me she had noticed the house the Blythes had just built was for sale. I stopped in to visit and Don told me Caroline had developed cancer and passed away. He was asking $410,000 for the house, which was on the high end of its market value. It didn't sell and the price gradually got lower and lower.

I stayed in touch with Don and in November of 2002, I called to wish him a Happy Thanksgiving. He didn't pick up the phone, so I left him a message. A few days later, his daughter called with startling news.

Her father had moved into a double wide trailer on her farm. Don had been there only two weeks when he had a heart attack and died. She had driven to Wilmington to check on the house and listened to my message. She told me she had a sales contract on the house for $300,000.

"You know," she said, "my dad always wanted you to buy this house."

"Why?" I asked.

"Because on his way to visit me, he always drove past your farm," she said. "He saw how beautifully you had cleaned it up and how well you take care of it. That's the kind of person he wanted to have his house."

"Please don't do a thing until you hear from me!" I said.

I ran to find Kathi.

"I've got to buy this house for you!" I said.

"That's too much money," she replied.

I told her there was an offer on the house for $300,000. I wanted to offer up to $325,000.

"That's still too much money," Kathi said.

WILMINGTON, OHIO, HOME

I went to our real estate agent and told him I wished to make an offer on the house. He found out there was not just one other offer on it, but two. He called the agent representing the two would-be buyers and told her my offer, which you never do in real estate. You never spill the beans right away on what you're willing to spend. You start the negotiations lower and work your way up.

Well, I was on pins and needles the rest of the day. Finally, I called the owner's daughter to find out what happened.

"The other two offers were higher," she told me, "but I accepted yours."

Tears welled up in my eyes.

"I told you Dad wanted you to have it," she continued. "I know you'll take good care of it."

I was so moved by what she did, that when we closed on the house, I paid her the cash difference between the top offer and my offer. We moved in during February of 2003.

Jackie graduated from Xenia Christian School with straight A's. Like Jaime, she was a joy to be around. I always told Jackie I had one request when she finished high school and that was for her to attend a Christian college for at least one year. If she didn't like it after her freshman year, we'd talk about it.

One of her good friends was going to Cedarville University which was a Christian college not too far away from Wilmington. Bless her heart, I think Jackie was a little burned out on Christian schools, having attended so many while she was growing up. After her first year at Cedarville, she told me she wanted to attend Miami University of Ohio. It made old Dad a little uncomfortable—I still wished she would stick with a Christian school—but she headed to Miami, where she was a double major in English and French.

Kathi told me I needed to think about slowing down a bit and again, she was right. I was 68 years old and it was time for me to give up some of the rigors of day-to-day farming. However, I still had two years left on my rental of the Wilmington farm. I began talking with some of the larger operations in our area. If they would buy my equipment at its market value, I would let them take over the lease. Well, these were all farmers with big, 24-row planters. Mine was 12-row equipment, which was too small for their needs. They weren't interested.

In the end, I was able to make that deal with a young farmer named Mike MacFadden. I told him it was going to turn out to be the smartest move he ever made. And it was. If things didn't work out for him, he could sell the equipment and move on. If things went well, my bet was he could work out a much longer lease with the buyer of my farm. And that's exactly what happened. Some of those bigger farmers that turned me down were no doubt kicking themselves.

That year, the state of Colorado announced it was going to shut down as many as 135 wells along the South Platte River. Nebraska and Kansas had sued Colorado years ago, saying landowners there were taking too much water. The courts ruled in favor of Nebraska and Kansas, but Colorado officials had been dragging their feet. The pressure was beginning to mount for Colorado to comply with the ruling.

CHAPTER 27

I began to get nervous. All this ground I'd bought and fixed up would be worthless without wells to irrigate crops. It wouldn't even make good rangeland without water. So, I did a little research. I learned there was one way a Colorado landowner could improve the odds of keeping his wells. If you owned land on the river, you were allowed to drill a well and pump the water up to a mile-and-a-half away, as long as you built ponds to recapture the water and allowed it to sink back into the aquifer.

The problem was none of my property adjoined the Platte River. There was one guy who could help me change that. Darris. I told him I was up a creek and needed to find a way to connect my land to the Platte. Sure enough, Darris told me he probably could call in a chip or two and help me out.

He set up a meeting with a landowner in Julesburg who had property on both sides of the river. She was a spirited 90-year-old and we worked out a partnership. She would supply the land for the ponds. I would rent them for 20 years and pay to drill a well on the river.

I installed a line of 15-inch pipe connected to a 150-horsepower submersible pump. Since her land was along the river and vulnerable to floods, it seemed a better bet than an above-ground pump. The whole system cost me almost $60,000, but it was touted as a model for other landowners, which I was proud of.

Even so, in my studies of Colorado water use policy, I had discovered something that still made me uneasy. On almost the last page of the document, amidst all the government gobbledygook and legalese, Colorado listed its business priorities for the state water supply. No. 1 was to support residential housing development. No. 2 was to support industry. No. 3 was to support agriculture.

Farmers seemed to be at the bottom of the totem pole. My land was my life's investment. I couldn't afford to risk it. I told another real estate agent in Holyoke that if he had a buyer, I might be interested in selling. It turned out he had an acquaintance who had been raised in Holyoke, went off to Texas and made his millions there, and was looking to come back home. I sold nine quarters to him, leaving me with the land near the airport.

Any time I talked with Paul McClish, the Washington Courthouse, Ohio, real estate agent I knew, he would ask me all kinds of questions about my irrigated farms in Colorado. Finally, one day I asked him if he had someone who was interested in the property.

"Yes! Me!" he said.

Like another Paul I know, he always dreamed of having a farm out west. So he bought it, added more land to it, and just loves it out there. My remaining land, I sold to one of Gill Anderson's hired men.

So, it was back to Ohio once more.

THE BOMBSHELL

With the proceeds from the Colorado farms, I bought 700 acres in Fayette County, where Washington Courthouse is the county seat. That farm had one field that was 400 acres, a size almost unheard of in Ohio. As on so many farms before, I tiled the fields and cleared out a wooded area for maximum productivity.

I bought another 200-acre farm about six miles away that was a former hog farm. It was broken up into six small fields. We cleared out all the fence rows and buried the remnants of the old concrete hog houses and pads, then tiled it, as well.

Out of the blue, I got a call from a company called Westchester. Based in Champaign-Urbana, Illinois, it's one of the largest farm management real estate businesses in the country. They had a cash buyer from Ireland who was interested in my land. Actually I was looking for about another 300 acres to add to my operation, not to sell it. But, additional land was hard to come by there. I just wasn't sure.

By this time, it was 2005. I started looking at ground in west-central Ohio, near Lima and Celeryville, mostly in the $3,000-per-acre range. A real estate agent told me about a 966-acre farm he just listed in West Liberty, which is in Logan County. It was on the market at an incredible $5,000 per acre. I started laughing.

"For development?" I asked

"No, for farming," he said.

"What makes a farm worth that kind of money?" I asked. "I can't afford it, but I'd like to see a $5,000-per-acre farm."

So, he showed it to me. It was good ground in a beautiful valley. It made a real impression on me, but it still was an awful lot of money.

I went back to fixing up the 700-acre Fayette County farm. About two years later, I got a call from a West Liberty area farmer named Brian Watkins. I'd attended school with his dad at Ohio State. They had a contract to purchase the 966-acre farm I'd looked at in Logan County and wanted to know if I would be interested in buying it and renting it back to them.

I called up Westchester and they were still interested in the Fayette County land. So, I made the sale and bought the farm in West Liberty. Just like all the others, I went to work upgrading the grain storage system, installing drain tile, putting in driveways for better access to the fields, and cleaning up some of the overgrown places.

Jackie graduated from Miami University as a double major in English and French. Miami offered her a full-ride scholarship to go on to get her master's degree there, but she really wanted to go to France to teach English for a year. Jackie asked the college to hold the offer open for her which it did, and she went on to earn her first master's degree in English.

From there, she went into the English MFA program at George Mason University in Fairfax, Virginia. After a year, Jackie wasn't happy with George Mason, so she applied and was accepted at four other schools, including Louisiana State University, which she is attending. Her goal is to go on to receive her Ph.D.

She's a poet, teaches classes while working on her MFA, and has done prize-winning work translating French poetry into English. Because it's poetry, you can't simply translate it word for word. You have to capture the deeper meaning of it, too. It's challenging. Jackie has grown into a stunningly beautiful young woman and I'm very proud of her. She is a bit of a workaholic—a trait she admits she comes by honestly from her dad.

I confess I am driven. I was driven to become the best fighter pilot I could be; driven to survive almost eight years of torture and deprivation as a POW; driven to rebuild my life after my career was taken away from me; driven to achieve a measure of financial stability after some disastrous investments.

But I say with all honesty, I loved Kathi and always wanted to provide the best for her. I would have given her anything she asked of me.

CHAPTER 28

In all our years of marriage, I rarely heard the words "I love you" from Kathi. She never said, "I'm glad you're my husband," or "I'm happy to be married to you." Even "thank you" was difficult for her to say to me.

I know she had love and caring inside her because she was devoted to her family and to her friends. If you were Kathi's friend, and you needed something, she would bend over backwards to help you. It just always seemed like there was something holding her back from truly loving me. And it was painful for me to bear.

I longed for her companionship. There were many times I invited her to come with me when I was working around the farm. I told her she didn't have to do a thing. I just wanted her to be there with me.

While most others couldn't see it, that sort of friendship and enjoyment of one another's company was always missing from our marriage. It was a source of constant tension in our relationship. Finally, in October of 2007, it came to the surface.

"What are we going to do?" Kathi asked.

"All I have ever wanted is to be No. 1 in your life," I told her. "But I guess I'm a zero."

Kathi has always been quick-witted. Nothing ever takes her aback.

"Well, I guess I should go look for an apartment," she said, then paused for a second. "And maybe I should talk to a lawyer."

It was a painful irony that I had so deeply wished for Kathi to be a partner in the farming enterprises that gave us our income. She rarely ever helped me on the farm. Yet, Ohio law doesn't take that into account. In a divorce, a spouse is entitled to 50 percent of the assets. In marriage, we were never true partners, but in divorce, in the eyes of the law, we would be.

Kathi moved out of the house and into a second-floor apartment in Wilmington. It was a horrible place. The carpets hadn't been cleaned in 20 years. It smelled like smoke. There were holes in the walls you could stick your fingers through to the outside. A friend brought her a twin bed to sleep in.

That first night, all I could think about was Kathi in that terrible place. The next day, I went out and bought her a full-size bed and a microwave. The following morning, she called. For only about the second time in our marriage, she said "thank you" from her heart.

Before she moved out, Kathi showed me a budget she had worked out. It was the first time in 27 years she had ever created one. I thought it was very realistic, but Kathi felt she might be $100 or $200 short. She was working at ABX-Air, but I assured her I would help her if she needed it.

We attended counseling, but I knew from the beginning it held out little hope. My understanding is that in ordinary circumstances, a counselor would interview us separately one or two times, reflect on our differences, then bring us together to talk them out. This counselor brought us in at the same time from the beginning and it was no help.

Months went by as I anxiously waited to see what would happen. Finally, I received a registered letter from the court. It was devastating to me. My attorney, John Smith, arranged a meeting at the courthouse with Kathi's attorney.

We sat in a big rotunda together—Kathi on one side of the courthouse, me on the other, as our lawyers conferred. When my attorney came over to talk with me, it was about a whole lot more than helping Kathi with a couple hundred dollars to meet her monthly expenses.

"Her lawyer wants $3,500 per month for spousal support," he said.

My heart almost stopped beating.

"You're lucky they're not asking for $4,500," added my attorney.

He went back to confer with the other lawyer and I soon found out what was going on.

"They'll drop it to $2,500 if you'll write a check to her attorney for $20,000 to cover his fee," my lawyer said. Clearly, this wasn't just about helping Kathi. It was making sure her attorney got his money. I had little choice but to take the deal.

A year later, we agreed to pursue what's called a Collaborative Divorce. It's when both spouses and their lawyers work collectively to negotiate a settlement. My attorney recommended another lawyer from the Cincinnati area, John McElwee, who taught Collaborative Divorce law.

As we were sitting at a big table with our attorneys, Kathi said, "You want to give half your estate to missions, right?"

Yes, I told her. I had said that many times over the years.

"That's what I promised the Lord when I was a POW and that's what I intend to do," I said.

"Guess what?" she said. "I never made that promise!"

It really hurt me to hear her say that.

"And he wants his own nurse when he gets older!" she continued.

"That's right," I said. "My intention was to be able to have someone to take care of me so that you and the kids didn't have to and I wouldn't have to go into a nursing home."

The third thing she did during these many meetings that was very hurtful was to point to my attorney and say, "If it wasn't for me, he wouldn't have what he has!"

"I beg your pardon …" I began to reply, but John, my lawyer, clamped his hand down on my leg under the table.

He knew she had no call to say something like that and knew how upset it made me. However, John had given me one important piece of counsel before we started these negotiations, "Be hard on the issues, be easy on the person." And that's what I endeavored to do. I did my best to control my emotions.

"Any other client I've had would have leaped across the table," John said to me later.

I became very good friends with John and his wife, Mary, who is a judge in Wilmington. They have since made it a point to invite me to their home each year for Thanksgiving dinner. I enjoy spending that time with them.

Things began to drag out over the next few weeks and months. Kathi moved to Westerville, near Columbus, where she became an office manager for the Ohio Poultry Association.

I don't like things to go unresolved, so I called her and suggested we meet over dinner to see what we needed to do to bring our divorce to a conclusion. She agreed.

I learned her attorney had instructed her to have the West Liberty farm appraised.

During this collaborative negotiation process, I had told Kathi's lawyer I would sign over 423 acres to her debt-free, and put 543 acres, along with the $700,000 debt still owed on the farm, in my name. Her attorney came back and said she wanted to know where the land was.

I laughed and said to him, "Of course she doesn't know!"

He left to confer with Kathi once more. When he returned, he told me Kathi's exact words were, "What do I want with land?"

If she would let me keep the farm, I would be able to give half its worth to my children when I died and half to support missions and honor my promise to God. If she did not agree to my offer, I would be compelled to sell everything and give her half the proceeds.

Her lawyer said, "Forget the missions. We're divvying it all up."

In the end, to keep the farm, which is the culmination of 73 years of my life's work, I decided to offer her a cash settlement. Part of the benefit for her was that it would be tax-free. She accepted the cash offer.

For me, however, to service that divorce debt will take the farm income, supplemented by my Air Force retirement, for the next 15 years.

My good friend Lawrence Kuznia's father, Tommy, was a big wheat and sugar beet farmer in the Red River Valley of Minnesota. As Tommy once said, "More good, honest farmers have been ruined by divorce than by drought or pestilence." What a profound statement and one I can certainly relate to.

Later, Kathi left her job in Westerville to go to Phoenix and work for her first ex-husband, Larry, who was now in the sporting-goods business.

There was a period during the divorce when I lost connection with Jackie. I knew she was still driving that old Volkswagen Beetle which now had upwards of 170,000 miles on it. For years, I'd wanted to buy her a new Honda Civic. Kathi helped me get in touch with her and I was able to get her a safe, reliable car.

When Kathi headed West, I drove up to Westerville to help her pack and to make sure all her moving arrangements were in order. Despite everything, I still cared about her. More than anything, I think the fact I was still willing to reach out to Kathi helped renew my relationship with Jackie.

In addition to its emotional impact, the divorce was disappointing because we were on target to have the farm paid off. I had planned to put funds aside just in case any child or grandchild had need of health insurance or college tuition. Now that money is going to pay interest, when I'd rather see it go to them or to the Lord's work in missions. That, too, is part of the difficult cost of the divorce.

My Sunday school teacher Tom Isaacs asked me what has been harder on me mentally—my divorce or my time as a prisoner of war in Vietnam. That's a tough one. I told him I had to think about it.

When you're a POW, you've been trained how to survive. And you have faith that someday your country will come and get you. A divorce, by contrast, never ends. The pain is always there—the pain it causes your children, the pain of having someone you love leave you, the pain of the financial burden, and lastly, the pain it inflicts on one's health. I lost 25 pounds and the stress caused me to develop ulcerative colitis.

In prison, you tell yourself, "I'm going to give it my all. If I die, I die." I think most American POWs feel that way. But in divorce, Satan tempts you to want to get even. You know that's wrong and so you don't do it, but the temptation is always there.

The Scriptures teach that God forgives us to the extent we are willing to forgive. Some people carry animosity toward others around in their hearts their entire lives. What they don't realize is that refusing to forgive someone does not punish the other person. It punishes you. Lord knows, I've made enough mistakes in my life that I have asked him and others to forgive me for.

I told Tom I think the divorce has been harder on me than my imprisonment because the divorce actually began 30 years ago when Kathi and I were first married. And its impact will continue for a long time to come.

Yet, I am thankful to the Lord that despite what we've been through, Kathi and I are on speaking terms and we both are there for our children when they need us.

In the meantime, here I was at age 78, starting over as I have done so many times before.

Shawn at his veterinary clinic in California.

Jackie and Jaime

Ali, 2014.

Jaime and her family.

REFLECTIONS

In the 40 years since my release from Vietnam, I've been invited to speak about my experiences as a prisoner of war many times. I frame my message—especially when I have the opportunity to talk with young people—by saying most of us make three decisions that will chart the course of our lives.

In order of importance, they are:

1.) The kind of relationship we choose to have with Jehovah God
2.) Our choice of a spouse
3.) Our choice of vocation

Listeners often are surprised to hear that, especially when I say that vocation ranks last. It's all too easy to get our priorities out of order, putting our career ahead of God and ahead of our families. I know because I have sometimes faced that same struggle in my life.

After speaking to a group, invariably I would be asked the same question, "When are you going to write a book?"

I often thought if I did write a book, it would be for two reasons. First, to tell my kids more about their dad—where he came from and why he does what he does. My hope is this book will give them insight they might have missed when we were separated by distance and by circumstance.

The second reason for this book is to give honor to God for giving me the strength to endure, the wisdom to cope with the enemy, and the blessings of health and welfare.

I'd like to bring you up to speed on some of the people you have met over the course of reading this book specifically my children, grandchildren, and sisters. I hold them all very close to my heart and I am proud of who they are and what they have accomplished.

My son Shawn is a graduate of Colorado State University and is a veterinarian in the Los Angeles area, specializing in ultrasound technology. He married a wonderful woman from Kansas named Christi, who is a Christian fiction writer. They have two children, Jessie Paul and Alexis.

My oldest daughter Allison—we call her Ali—is now an RN and is working on her Master's Degree in nursing. She has three children and a grandson. Her son Spike is very athletic. He loves baseball and wants to be a Major League Baseball player. Her daughter Katie is attending Marquette University. Ali's daughter Randi, who earned an Associate Degree in dental assisting, has a son named Logan.

My middle daughter Jaime is married to Dan Long, who has a business in Scottsdale, Arizona. Jaime is an astute young woman who currently is working on the thesis for her master's degree in English from Arizona State University. They have a 5-year-old son named Easton. Although I never formally adopted Jaime, I have never thought of her as anything other than my own daughter.

My youngest daughter, Jacqueline, graduated from Miami University in Ohio with a double major in English and French. She speaks fluent French and has spent time in France teaching English. She holds two Master's Degrees and is now in a PhD program in creative writing at the University of Georgia.

My sister Ruth, who is a year-and-a-half older than I am, married a rancher and they have a sizeable cattle ranch about 35 miles east of Colorado Springs. My middle sister Karen, a retired schoolteacher, also lives just east of Colorado Springs.

Carol, the youngest, is a highly sought piano teacher. She has four pianos in a beautiful studio at her Colorado Springs home. She and her husband Peter have two daughters. Tonya is a music major and harpist who is always in great demand as a performer. Monica is working on her master's degree in music management in the Washington D.C. area. When Peter was a child, his family fled Communism in Europe following World War II. It was my father, Tony, who sponsored Peter's family and helped them come to America.

When I was a POW sitting in solitary confinement, I tried to keep my mind active and my hopes alive by designing home plans and farm operations in my head. After decades of remodeling the houses we lived in during our many moves, I finally had the opportunity to build a home from the ground up at my farm in

West Liberty. Architecture has changed in the past 40 years, so some things are different, but overall, it is the house I visualized in my cell so long ago.

I wanted a design that was energy efficient, yet felt roomy. After you've been confined in small spaces, you like to be able to stretch out your arms and to be able to see the world around you. The interior of the house has only one small hallway. The rest is open. There are plenty of windows with views of the farm and the beautiful surrounding valley. Construction was completed in February of 2016.

I made a promise to God that if he would get me out of that hellhole in North Vietnam I would give him 50 percent of my time and 50 percent of my finances to help further the Gospel. I've done well on my tithing and I plan to leave a sizeable amount from my estate. However, I am way, way behind on that promise when it comes to the giving of my time.

Now that I am almost finished cleaning up and improving my 26th farm property, I plan to spend more time working with my local church to visit the sick, the elderly, and those who may be at a point of discouragement in their lives. I'd like to visit service members in Veterans Administration facilities. There are so many amputees and others who suffer from post-traumatic stress disorder who could use a word of appreciation and support. I've been through some of the emotions they are experiencing. I want to spend more time working with missions from various churches locally, as well as with national Christian organizations, such as The Moody Church and John Hagee Ministries.

As many times as I moved around the United States, there's a lot of America I have missed. After being imprisoned in North Vietnam for eight years, then putting my nose to the grindstone for the next 40 years trying catch up with my peers, there are parts of this great country I would still like to see.

I had four wonderful years at Ramstein Air Base, yet I have not been back there since 1964. It's totally changed, but I would like to see it again. As I write this, I am also planning a trip to my father's native country, Hungary, to visit his birthplace.

When you live a long and eventful life, it's natural to look back and wonder if there is anything you'd do differently, if given the chance.

Despite what I suffered in the Vietnam War, I don't think I'd change my decision to become a fighter pilot in the U.S. Air Force. Once I was bitten by the flying bug in college, I was determined to become the best fighter pilot I could be. I tried to do that, but unfortunately in war, things happen and the outcome isn't always what you hoped it would be. My years as a POW and dealing with the damage to my center vision have been a difficult test, but hopefully I have emerged from that struggle a better person.

However, there are a couple of things I would do differently in my life. While I was imprisoned, my dad suffered a series of heart attacks and strokes. The physical vigor that made him the hardest-working man I have ever known was now severely limited. He lost his ability to speak, but regained it over time.

After my release, I was eager to move forward with my life and I was not as patient with my father as I should have been. I deeply regret that. It has haunted me to the point that I have told God I would happily relinquish everything I own just to spend one more day with my dad.

My advice to others is simple; take time for the ones you love, especially your parents and your children.

Farming puts great demands on one's time and health. When I was working so hard to catch up on the years I had missed, I sent my children to Christian schools to make sure they would learn the Bible and became strong in their faith.

I realize now that was my responsibility. It was my responsibility to be a godly father and a godly husband. I delegated that to some degree, which was not right. That, too, I would change, if I could. Still, I am proud to say my children are good, kind, well-educated people and much of the credit for that is owed to their mothers. But there's one thing I don't regret and that is the fact I gave my heart to the Lord at age twelve and was saved. And thanks to that, over the years, he has given me the strength to endure. After I came home from captivity, I joined a big church in Denver and rededicated my life to God, which gave me a new second wind in my desire to serve him.

My favorite Bible character is my namesake, the Apostle Paul. My dad read the Bible incessantly—usually a German-language Bible—and even though we never talked about it, I know that's where my name came from.

As dedicated and zealous as Paul was in his mission to persecute Christians before his conversion, he became just as dedicated and zealous for the cause of Christ after his conversion. His life made a 180-degree turn on the road to Damascus when God confronted him and asked, "Why do you persecute me?" He went on to write 13 of the 66 books of the Bible.

I think my life and the life of the Apostle Paul traveled a little bit on the same path. The Apostle Paul was shipwrecked. He was persecuted. He was tortured. He was bitten by a snake. He was imprisoned. He was put in chains.

I was shipwrecked, in a manner of speaking, when I was shot down. I was beaten, tortured, shackled and imprisoned. I wasn't bitten by a snake, but I did have to eat one!

Paul spoke of having "a thorn in the flesh" and three times asked God to take it away. Each time, God said, "My grace is sufficient for you," and the thorn remained. We don't know what it was that gave Paul such difficulty—some speculate it was a vision problem, which I also suffer from.

Paul is a character I look up to because he never gave up. He fought the good fight. As I look back, I think that's what a lot of us did in Vietnam. We persevered, we conducted ourselves with honor, and we supported one another through difficult circumstances.

There are two passages of Scripture found in the Old Testament that I try to live by.

Though the fig tree does not bud
And there are no grapes on the vines,
Though the olive crop fails
And the fields produce no food,
Though there are no sheep in the pen
And no cattle in the stalls,
Yet I will rejoice in the Lord,
I will be joyful in God my Savior.
Habakkuk 3:17-18

And call upon me in the day of trouble: I will deliver thee, and thou shalt glorify me.
Psalm 50:15

Those lines almost seem to be written for a farmer, but you don't have to make your living from the land or be a former POW to understand what they mean. You just have to be a human being. At times in life we all will be battered by events around us—by war, by hardship, by loss—but we are not controlled by them. What's important is what's inside us, where God is our hope and strength.

No matter what challenges we are called to endure, God's grace is sufficient. For that, I will rejoice in the Lord. Because He has delivered me from hardships, from events, from heartaches, I want to exalt His name.

From the July 6, 1962, edition of "The Stars and Stripes" (pictured above):

"ST. DIZIER, FRANCE (Special)—Pilots of the 4th Allied Tactical Air Force clinched victory in the first annual NATO tactical weapons meet here Wednesday afternoon, building up an insurmountable lead over the 2nd ATAF.

"With only four sorties remaining, the 4th ATAF had a 2,158–1,436 edge over the 2nd ATAF, thus winning the Broadhurst Trophy, scheduled to be presented in Friday ceremonies at this French Air Force Base ...

"Big gun, in the truest sense of the word, for the 4th ATAF squad was USAFE 1st Lt. Paul Kari of the 417th Tactical Fighter Sq. In four low-altitude bombing system (LABS) flights, Kari scored an impressive 696 out of a possible 800."

About the Author

PAUL KARI

Paul A. Kari was born in Akron in 1935. He graduated from Spencer High School in 1953 and earned a Bachelor of Science degree in Animal Science from The Ohio State University in 1958. Upon his graduation, Kari entered active duty in the United States Air Force, where he served with distinction as a fighter pilot until being shot down in North Vietnam in 1965. He was held as a Prisoner of War until 1973.

Upon his release, Kari served at the United States Air Force Academy until his retirement from the USAF as a Lieutenant Colonel in 1974. He worked as a Public Affairs Officer for the Federal Aviation Administration, retiring from the FAA in 1983.

Since then, Kari has made his living buying and restoring farms in Colorado and Ohio. He currently splits his time between his 907-acre farm in West Liberty, Ohio, and his home in Wilmington. Kari's military honors include:

Silver Star with One Oak Leaf Cluster
Legion of Merit
Distinguished Flying Cross
Bronze Star with One Oak Leaf Cluster and with V Device
Purple Heart with One Oak Leaf Cluster
Air Medal with One Oak Leaf Cluster
Air Force Commendation Medal with Two Oak Leaf Clusters
Air Force Outstanding Unit Award
Prisoner of War Medal
Combat Readiness Medal
National Defense Service Medal
Armed Forces Expeditionary Medal with One Oak Leaf Cluster
Vietnam Service Medal with Three Silver Stars and One Bronze Star
Armed Forces Longevity Service Award Ribbon with Three Oak Leaf Clusters
Republic of Vietnam Campaign Medal
Small Arms Expert Marksmanship Ribbon

In 1962, Kari won Top Gun honors in the Inaugural NATO Gunnery Meet. He was inducted into the Ohio Military Hall of Fame for Valor in 2010.

INDEX

A
ABX-Air, 346
Adams Bank & Trust, 318
Advanced Gunnery School, 158
AGCO, 326, 329
AIDs orphans, 353
Aikman, Dave, 294, 296-297, 299-300, 318
Air America, 39
Air Force Academy, 137, 165-166, 254, 261-262, 271, 317, 322, 327
Alaskan Air Command, 215, 250
Alden, Bill, 241
Allison, Jack, 51
Alpha Gamma Sigma, 94-95
Alvarez, Everett, 82, 187
America's Bicentennial, 275
Amish, 72-73, 294-295, 297
Anderson Air Force Base, 238
Anderson, Gill, 337, 341
Anderson, Monte, 329
Andrews Air Force Base, 275
Angus Air Force Base, 64
Apollo 11, 166
Apostle Paul, 81, 354-355
Arapahoe Lakes, 281-282
Arizona State University, 352
Armstrong, Neil, 166
Arnold, Tom, 172-174
Assembly of God Church, 53
Autobahn, 206
Autz, Fred, 69, 76

B
B-52 bombers, 168, 189, 195, 247
Bachelor Officers Quarters, 128, 171-172, 203-204, 227
Bainbridge Air Base, 128-129, 131
Bascom Palmer Eye Institute, 257
Basic Intelligence Planning Guide, 179
Berlin Wall, 197
Bierman, Caspar Sharpless, 4-8, 21, 39, 59-60, 157, 215, 234, 240-250, 327
Bird & Son, 39
Bitburg fighter base, 158, 160, 171, 199
Black River, 118, 161
Blythe, Caroline, 338
Blythe, Don, 338-339

B&O Railroad, 161
Bowen, Kathleen Suzann, 73
Bowen, Walter, 73
Bowers Dairy, 16
Boyd, John, 179-180
Boyington, Gregory "Pappy", 250
Boy Scouts, 72
Brewer, George, 276
Bradley, Jack, iii
Briar Patch, 102-104, 106, 121, 123, 141, 145-146, 148, 165
Bricker, John, 94
Briggs, Curt, 4-5, 7-8, 21, 23-24, 37, 61-63, 215, 233, 241-246
Brigham Young University, v
Broadhurst Trophy, 356
Brothers, Bill, 153
Brother Steinberg, 18, 55, 319
Brouse, Roy, 51-52
Brown, Steve, 326
Buckingham, Carol, 53, 94
Bull Pup missile, 233-235
Burger King, 329
Burton, Chris, 352

C
C-54, 223
C-118, 171
C-130, 211
C-135 tankers, 237
C-141, 188, 190
California Highway Patrol, 269
Camp Unity, 163
Canberra, 182
Cape Canaveral, 253-254
Caterpillar D5 bulldozer, 295
Cedarville University, 340
Cessna 140, 114
Cessna 172, 116
Cessna T-34, 130
Cessna T-37, 130
Chain, Jack, 179-180, 199-201, 232
Chain, Jr., John T., iv
Chase, Levi, 231, 233, 237-240
Cheyenne Airport, 159
Child Care International, 312
Children's Cup, iii, 312
C.I.A., 134

Cincinnati Eye Institute, iii
Cincinnati International Airport, 322
Clark Air Base, 189, 191, 194, 215, 219
Cleveland Hopkins International Airport, 113
Cohen, Beryl, 274-275
Coil, Jim, 254
Cold War, 172, 177, 197, 203
Collaborative Divorce, 346
Colorado State University, 352
Commerce Department, 274
Continental Air Lines, v, 285
Cooper, Roy, 132-135, 138-139
Creek, Pawnee, 71
Creston Auction, 70
Cross, Glenn, 303
Cumming, Darris, 317-318, 332, 337, 341

D
Daily Ninh Zanh, North Vietnamese propaganda newspaper and, 89
Davis, Don, 113-114
Dawes, Charles, 131, 137
DC-6, 171
DelMonte, 314
Demilitarized Zone, 240
Denton, Jeremiah, 104
Department of Defense, 191, 271
Diners Club, 284
Dog Patch, 167-168
Don Scott Field, 114, 116
Dortch, Harold, 128, 153, 181
Drotloff, John, 15, 47
Dutton, Perry, 333-334

E
Eckel, Paul, v, 285-286
Einstein, Albert, 267
Elm Farm Dairy, 13, 47
The Evangel, church monthly magazine and, 18

F
F-4B Phantom, 233
F-4C Phantom, 3, 21-22, 86, 176, 231, 233-235, 237-239, 243, 245-247, 250, 264, 327-328
F-4C Phantom II, 231
F-86H fighters, 175, 239
F-100 F model, 153
F-100s, 158-159, 173, 175, 180, 182-183, 234, 237
F-105s, 3, 5-6, 104, 109, 239, 241
F-105 Thunderchiefs, 3

Farmall H, 15, 27-28, 31, 34, 51, 56, 325
Farmers Market, 314-315
Farnborough Air Show, 274
Federal Aviation Administration, 116, 272-273, 276-277, 280, 282-284, 289-292, 314
Federal Land Bank, 13
Field & Stream magazine, 30
Fiftieth Wing, v, 231
Fifty-Seventh Fighter Weapons Wing, ii
Fighter Weapons School, 179, 212, 231-232
Fisherman's Wharf, 281
Five hundred sixtieth Tactical Fighter Training Wing, 326
Flags of Our Fathers (Bradley), iii
Flint River, 131
Florence, Dwight, 92
Florence, John, 92
Flying Farmers, 113
Ford Motor Company, 255
Fort Campbell, 40
Fort Hays State University, 292
Fort Knox, 40
Forty-fifth Tactical Fighter Squadron, 3, 241
Four hundred seventeenth TAC Fighter Squadron, iv-v
Fourth Allied Tactical Air Force, 199, 356
Franchester Farms, 77
Francis, Earl, 254, 278
French Field House, 119
French Officers Club, 181
Frontier Days, 159-160

G
Gandy Bridge, 223
Geneva Conventions, 124
George Mason University, 344
Gia Lam Airport, 188
Giar, Joe, 49
G.I. Bill, 98, 118
Global Leadership Academy, 353
Golden Gate Bridge, 216-217
Gott, Lloyd, 49
Gray, Gary, 276-277, 281
Greeley, Horace, 11
Green, Margaret, 272
Green, Sam, 229, 272
Grime's Field, 115

H
Hahn Fighter Base, 158
Harrington's Grocery, 32
Harvey, Paul, 74

Hausenfleck, Charlie, 234-235, 247
Hawker Aircraft, 182
Heartbreak Hotel, 81, 88, 101, 103, 146
Hendricks, Don, 302
Hereford Air Force Base, 64
Hickam Air Force Base, 191, 216, 238
Hirschman, Floyd, 299, 301
Hoa Loa Prison, 65, 81, 149, 163, 167-168, 187
Holdridge, Harold, 29, 34
Horseshoe, 119

I
Internal Revenue Service, 286
international war crimes tribunal, 141-152
interrogations
   as incentive not to get caught and, 208
   camp commander's office and, 108-109, 123-124, 148, 150-151
   Cubans in the camp and, 148-149
   "downed pilots" exercise and, 212
   drawing a hard line early on, 89
   four interrogations per day and, 84
   Hanoi March and, 141
   length of, 86, 88, 101
   Lyndon B. Johnson and, 89
   MiGs and, 87-88
   moon landing and, 165
   not allowing letters home and, 189
   objective of, 86
   Paul's prayer and, 111
   tap code and, 85, 88
   techniques of, 81, 83, 105
   thinking of Shawn and, 145
   walking back to cells and, 106
Isaacs, Tom, 348-349

J
Jimmy Swaggart Bible College, 312
John Deere, 27, 34, 46, 64, 115, 269, 296-298, 300-303, 325, 329-331, 333-334, 338
Johnson, Lyndon B., 89, 203
Johnson, Milton, 56-57
Julesburg Airport, 337
Junior-Senior Banquet, 71

K
Kari, Allison, *350*
   asking good questions and, 256
   becoming an RN and, 352
   breaking her arm and, 270
   building a relationship with, 253-254
   going on a cruise and, 255
   living in Florida and, 278, 292
   meeting Paul after return home and, 218
   Paul's thoughts of while a POW and, 25, 145, 163, 188, 223
   roller skating and, 222, 225
   trip to Colorado and, 270
Kari, Carol, 12, *48*, 49, 178, 265
Kari, Jackie, 92, 308-310, 318, 320, 326, 329-330, 334-335, 340, 344, 348, *350*
Kari, Karen, 12, *48*, 75, 161, 352
Kari, Kathi
   birth of Jackie and, 308-309
   Blythe house and, 338-339
   buying a home in Seattle and, 291, 293-294, 297-298
   buying Jackie a car and, 335
   choosing schools and, 318
   Diners Club job and, 284
   divorce and, 344-349
   driving Jackie to school and, 310
   ex-husband Larry and, 306-307
   FAA job and, 292
   farm auctions and, 301
   Jimmy Swaggart and, 312
   map reading and, 302
   marriage to Paul and, 280-281
   meeting Paul and, 254
   Mennonite school and, 320
   Missing Man Formation and, 328
   move to Denver and, 278, 289
   on being a "farm wife" and, 305
   parents visit and, 303-304
   Paul's love for, 344
   Paul's meeting her parents and, 279
   pheasant hunting and, 282-283
   renovation project and, 319
   Rosie and, 311
   snowstorm and, 333
   telling Paul to slow down and, 340
   tomato business and, 313-315
   Wilmington farm and, 321-322, 325-326, 329, *330*, 331
Kari, Kathleen
   awkward telephone conversation and, 215, 217
   bank balance and, 194
   birth of Shawn and, 200
   divorce and, 253, 256-257
   Germany and, 77
   "just in case" arrangements and, 235

    Paul's return home and, 195, 218-224, 226-227
    Paul's thoughts of while POW and, 145
    sapphire rings and, 242
    Skyblazers and, 198
    SS United States and trip back, 229-232
    supportive of the Air Force and, 236-237
    Tampa department store and, 254
    wedding plans and, 197
Kari, Paul
    4-H Show steer and, *52*
    Air Force training and, 127-139
    Briar Patch and, 102-104, 106, 121, 123, 141, 145-146, 148, 165
    capture of, *36*, 38-43, *65*
    checking out the F4C and, *20, 162, 228, 231*
    Christmas program and, 163-169
    Colorado rancher and, *266, 273, 334*
    coming home and, 187-195
    early life on the farm and, 11-19
    eating snake and, 63-64
    Father's Day Mission and, 3-9, 21-25, 250
    Final Flight and, *327*
    graduation from high school and, *78*
    gunnery training and, 153-161
    Hanoi March and, *120*, 121-125, 141
    high plains wheat planting and, *319*
    initial outfitting and, *128*
    landing at Clark Air Base and, *186, 189*
    learning to fly and, 114-115
    livestock and meat-judging teams and, *90, 97*, 98
    mowing hay and, *66, 74*
    new colt and, *55*
    Ohio State University graduation and, *98*
    Operation Devil's Spread and, 207-212
    photograph with sisters and, *48*
    pony and, *14*
    promotion to lieutenant colonel and, 263
    Reserve Officers Training Corps (ROTC) and, 98, 118, 129, 137
    retirement ceremony and, *256*
    Spencer High School and, 78, 92, 301, 319, 357
    T-33 Trainer and, *126, 133*
    T-37 Trainer and, *112, 131*
    tap code and, 82
    Top Gun honors and, 183, 185
    torture and, v, 64, 86-88, 110-111, 221, 271, 344
    visiting Hanoi Hilton and, *84*
    Wilmington home and, *322, 339, 342*
    Zoo and, 101-102, 121, 146, 149

Kari, Ruth, *12*, 13, 17, 28-29, 32-33, *48*, 70, 219, 352
Kari, Shawn, *111, 201*
    birth of, 198, 200-201
    Cape Canaveral and, 253-254
    Colorado State University and, 352
    cruise and, 254-256
    fathers Final Flight and, 327-328
    Fort Hays State University and, 292
    meeting his father and, 218-219, 223, 226
    move to Florida and, 278
    roller skating and, 222, 225
    search for Rosie and, 311
    soccer and, 280
    SS United States and, 229-230
    T-33 Trainer and, *2*
    thoughts of while POW and, 25, 111, 145, 163, 188
    veterinarian and, 308, *350,* 352
    visit to Colorado and, 270, 280
    working for Linly and, 291, 333
Kari, Tony and Mary
    Assembly of God church and, 53
    cattle business and, 55, 68, 78, 267-268
    Christmas program and, 164
    dairy business and, 97
    early years of, 11-19
    Farmall H and, 56, 115
    hauling hay and, 73-74
    International stake truck and, 72, 75, 161
    Kasper Foundry and, 68, 117-118, 160, 232
    knowing of Paul's capture and, 25
    Lehman Farm and, 31
    love of ice cream and, 76-77
    parenting style of, 33-35, 70-71, 92, 94-95
    Paul's decision to attend Ohio State and, 91, 93
    Paul's return home and, 218-219, 232-233
    photographs of, *12, 55*
    religious faith and, 96, 119
    sheep business and, 54
    Spencer Township farm and, 45-48, 171, 265, 267
    Tony's death and, 287
    Wallace Implement and, 28
    work ethic of, 11, 67, 69
Kasper Foundry, 68, 117
KC-135 refueling tanker, 249
Kennedy, John F., 160, 203
Kennedy, Robert F., 163
Kerby, Michael C., ii
King, Bob, 299

King, Jr., Martin Luther, 163
King Realty, 313
King, Roger, 325-326
Kirby, Mike, 259
Kissinger, Henry, 168-169, 187
Korat Air Base, 239
Korean War, 65, 83, 145, 175, 239
Kostecki, Frank, 71
Kuznia, Lawrence, 347
Kuznia, Tommy, 347

L
LABS maneuver, 176
Lackland Air Force Base, 127-129, 257
Lafayette School, 14, 17, 35
Lake Erie, 15
Landstuhl Army Medical Center, 198
Langley Air Force Base, 180
Laredo Air Force Base, 132
LaVelle, Eddie, 261
Lawson's Dairy, 76
LeBourget Air Show, 274
Lehman Farm, 31
Life magazine, 30
Lincoln Memorial, 275
Lockhart, Hayden, 82
Lodi Equity, 73-74
Long, Dan, *350*, 352
Long, Jaime, 278-281, 291-294, 298, 304, 306, 308, 310-311, 314, 340, *350*, 352
Lons, Jr., Charles, 92
Lons, Nancy, 92
Look magazine, 30
Los Angeles Times, Federal Aviation Administration and, 273
Louisiana State University, 344, 352
Low-Angle Bombing System, 155
Low, Jim, 65, 89
Lucas, Bobby, 338
Lujack, Johnny, 49
Luke Air Force Base, 137, 153, 158, 238

M
MacDill Air Force Base, 223, 225, 227, 231-233, 235, 237, 239, 241, 247, 249
MacFadden, Mike, 340
Mann, Ellet, 29
Marine Corps, 85, 153, 244, 250, 259
Mark 6, 175
Marquette University, 352
Martin, Freddie, 295
Maxwell Air Force Base, 217, 225, 257

Maxwell, Chris, 329
Mayer, John, 326-327
McClish, Paul, 331, 341
McCourt, John, 296
McCourt, Shawn, 296
McElwee, John, 346
McGuire Air Force Base, 171
McKamey, J.B., 105, 107, 121-123, 125, 224-225
Medina County Fair, 51
Medina Gazette, prettiest farmhouses in Medina County and, 299
Mershon Auditorium, 96
Meyer, Alton, 167
Miami University of Ohio, 340, 344, 352
MiGs, 3, 87-88, 241
Miller, Jeff, 330
Minh, Ho Chi, 109, 124
Missing Man Formation, 327
Montrose Drive-In, 129
Morgan, Scotty, 85, 102
Morgenthau, Hans, 18
Mormons, 275
Morse Code, 146
Mushay, Larry, 27

N
NASA, 253
NASCAR, 331
Nasmyth, Spike, 101-102, 168
NATO Gunnery Meet, 128, 181, 182, 183, 185, 198, 356
Nazarene church, 280
Nellis Air Force Base, ii, 156, 158, 159, 179, 181, 212, 213, 232, 307
Nevada State Penitentiary, 306
New York Harbor, 213, 230
New York Times (I)
  Federal Aviation Administration and, 273
Nix, Glenn, 194
Nixon, Richard, 160, 168, 216
Norden bomb sight, 177
North Vietnamese, 3, 24, 37-40, 42, 59-63, 81, 83-85, 87-89, 101-109, 121-125, 141-145, 147, 149-151, 163-169, 187-190, 192, 243, 369, 61
North Vietnamese Air Force, 88
Northwest Mountain Region, 289

O
Oberlin Inn, 71
O Club, 59

Ohio Poultry Association, 347
Ohio State University
  agriculture department and, 52
  animal science program and, 103, 137, 167, 357
  barley cooker and, 52
  Don Davis and, 113
  Dr. William J. Tyznik and, 94
  dying plants and, 310
  Horseshoe and, 119
  meat-judging team and, 97-98
  Mershon Auditorium and, 96
  pilot training and, 115, 250, 328
  ROTC instructors and, 129
  telling father of his decision to enroll at, 91-92
  tuition and, 93
Ohlerking, Dave, iii, 312, 353
Olentangy River, 114
Ondes, Clarence, 132
Ondo, Kanichi, 130
Operation Devil's Spread, 207-212
Outdoor Life magazine, 30

P
Pamer, Bob, 45-47
Pamer, Jack, 15
Pamer, Jacob, 12
Pamer, Mary, 12
Pamer, Mary Julia, 33
Paris Peace Accords, 169
Pentagon, ii, 193, 198-199, 201-202, 231-232, 260
Pig Sty, 146
Pine Tree Inn, 71
Platte River, 341
Platte River Valley, 337
Port Columbus International Airport, 116
Porter, John, 198
POWs
  Briar Patch and, 102-104, 106, 121, 123, 141, 145-146, 148, 165
  coming home and, 187-195
  Hanoi March and, 121-125, 141
  Hoa Loa Prison and, 65, 81, 149, 163, 167-168, 187
  international war crimes tribunal and, 141-152
  interrogations, 81, 83-89, 101, 105-109, 111, 123-124, 141, 145, 148-151, 165, 189, 208, 212
  tap code and, 82, 85, 88, 101, 122, 141, 146-147, 149-150

  torture and, iii, v, 64, 82, 85-89, 105-106, 109-111, 122, 144-146, 149-150, 165, 190, 215, 221, 271, 344, 355
Prack, Donnie, 69, 76
Producers Livestock, 94
Public Affairs Office, 289
Purcell, Robert, 104, 165, 195
Python revolver, 240

Q
Quality Control, 136

R
Ramstein Air Base, ii, 38, 65, 89, 129, 158, 160, 171, 173-175, 180, 183, 191, 197-199, 203-207, 216, 223, 229, 232, 259, 261, 285
Randolph Air Force Base, 326
Rauscher, Woodrow, 181
Red Cross, 188
Red River, 6, 347
Red River Valley, 347
Reickert, Bob, 172
Reisinger, David, 49-50, 96, 292, 299, 303, 319
Reisinger, Tommy, 303
Reserve Officers Training Corps (ROTC), 98, 118, 129, 137
RF-101 Voodoos, 5, 61, 240
Rhodes, Richard, 318, 333, 336
Riemann, Christopher D., iii
Risner, James Robinson "Robbie", 62-63, 101, 145, 150, 187, 194, 216, 260
Rocky Mountain Region, 289
Ronald Reagan Washington National Airport, 272
Rowe, Bertha, 49-50, 299
Royal Australian Air Force, 239
Royal Canadian Air Force, 175
Russell, Bertrand, 89, 141
Russian prison camps, tap code and, 85

S
Search and Rescue and Homing Beacon (SARAH), 5, 37-38, 60
Shetler, Jake, 295-296
Shetler, Sam, 294
S&H Green Stamps, 193
Shiflit, Don, 132-133
Shopbell, Roger, 295, 321
Shorthorn Air Force Base, 64
Shrove, Dick, 191-193, 216-217, 258-259
Shrove, Lynn, 216

Shumaker, Bob, 82
Sihanouk, Norodom, 109
Siman, Charlie, 299
Skyblazers, 197-198
Smith, J. Lawton, 257
Smith, John, 346-347
Smith, Mary, 347
Smithsonian Institution, 188
Sooy, Sid, 319
South Officers Club, 203
South Platte River, 340
South Side Officers Club, 171
Spangdahlem fighter base, 158, 160, 171
Special Forces, "Operation Devil's Spread" and, 207-212
Spencer farm, *44, 46, 288*
  Bertha Rowe and, 299
  boy's basketball team and, 71
  corn crib and, *290*
  Dave Reisinger's farm and, 292-294
  drive to McGuire Air Force Base and, 171
  driving home to help with farm and, 96, 119
  finished house and, *313, 315*
  grain dryer and, 330
  Kathi's parents and, 303
  manure lagoon and, 302
  moving to, 45-56
  returning home to visit and, 110, 232-233
  Rosie's hiding tricks and, 311
  travel to Lackland Air Force Base and, 127-128
  wheat planting and, 314
Spencer Farmers Bank, 295
Spencer High School, 78, 92, 301, 319, 357
Spencer Methodist Church, 197
Spoon, Don, 165
SS United States, 229-231
Stars & Stripes, 356
  C-141 and, 190
  "Former POW's wife seeks divorce" and, 227
  NATO Gunnery Meet and, 198
Statue of Liberty, 230
Stewart, Tom, 172
Storz, Ron, 150
Strategic Air Command, 244
St. Dizier, France, 356
Strickler, Mervin K., 276
Stum, Linly, 291-292, 333
Swaggart, Jimmy, 312

T
T-33 Trainer, 133, 138
T-38, 327-328

Tactical Air Command, 244
Takhli Royal Thai Air Force, 3
Takli Air Base, 239
tap code, 82, 85, 88, 101, 122, 141, 146-147, 149-150
Taylor, Maxwell, 199-200
Texas A&M University, 167
Thomasson, Ken, 291
The Thunderbirds, 159-160, 212
Tibbets, Paul, 177
Time magazine, Vietcong and, 25
Tonkin Gulf, 241
torture
  Apostle Paul and, 355
  Bertrand Russell and, 89
  confessions and, 144
  Cubans in the camp and, 149
  Dave Ohlerking and, iii
  eating and, 146
  Paul Kari and, v, 64, 86-88, 110-111, 221, 271, 344
  reading the daily newspaper and, 109
  release of POWs and, 190
  Ron Storz and, 150
  shaving and, 106
  strategy and, 87, 110, 144-145, 215
  tap code and, 82, 85, 149
  wrist irons and, 122, 165
Travis Air Force Base, 190, 216-217
Turner, Jim, 227
Turner, Katie, 227
Tyznik, William J., 94

U
Ubon Air Base, 3, 7, 236, 239, 241-247, 249-250
Ubon Royal Thai Air Base, 59
Ultimate Fighting Championships, 242
Union Pacific Railroad, 337-338
United Airlines, 159
United States Air Force Museum, 189
United States Supreme Court, 336
University of Buffalo, New York, 352
University of Miami Medical School, 257
U.S. Department of Agriculture, 338
U.S. Joint Chiefs of Staff, 199
U.S. War Bonds, 208

V
Vandenberg, Sandy, 261, 263, 265
Varney, Frank, 51
Veterans Administration, 353

Vietnam War
   Briar Patch and, 102-104, 106, 121, 123,
      141, 145-146, 148, 165
   international war crimes tribunal and,
      141-152
   interrogations, 81, 83-89, 101, 105-109,
      111, 123-124, 141, 145, 148-151, 165,
      189, 208, 212
   roster of U.S. POWs and, 82
   torture and, iii, v, 64, 82, 85-89, 105-106,
      109-111, 122, 144-146, 149-150, 165,
      190, 215, 221, 271, 344, 355
Visiting Officers Quarters, 181, 217-220, 327
Volkswagen Beetle, 204, 348

W
Walker, David, 27
Walker, Russell, 27
Wallace, George, 222
Wallace Implement, 28
Walters, Vivah, 164
Washington Courthouse, 331-332, 341, 343
Watkins, Brian, 344
Weber, Larry, 336
Western Vietnam Military Training Area, 5, 40
West, Howard, 295
West Point, 166
Wheelus Air Base, 174, 180, 206
Wilford Hall, 259
Wilford Hall Medical Center, 194, 257
Williams Air Force Base, 137
Wills, Joe, 295-296
Wilmington College, 329
Wilson, Bob, 130
World War III, 154, 172, 176-177, 179, 202-
   203, 207
World War II, iii, 17, 114, 119, 130, 155, 172,
   176-177, 193, 207, 212, 235, 243, 250,
   271, 352
Wright-Patterson Air Force Base, 322
Wurzelbacher, Dave, 331-332

X
Xenia Christian School, 340

Y
Younker, Day, 280
Younker, Mel, 280

Z
Zenith Trans-Oceanic Radio, 275
Ziegler, Dale, 300

The Zoo, 101-102, 121, 146, 149
Zweibrucken Air Base, 175